D1784126

People of Consequence

People of Consequence

Key Personalities of the Modern World

Roger East

Assistant editor: Catherine Jagger

London: The Stationery Office

A CIP catalogue record for this book is available from the British Library
A Library of Congress CIP catalogue record has been applied for

First published 1999

ISBN 0 11 702657 3

Published by The Stationery Office and available from:

The Publications Centre
(mail, telephone and fax orders only)
PO Box 276, London SW8 5DT
Telephone orders/General enquiries 0870 600 5522
Fax orders 0870 600 5533

www.tso-online.co.uk

The Stationery Office Bookshops
123 Kingsway, London WC2B 6PQ
020 7242 6393 Fax 020 7242 6394
68–69 Bull Street, Birmingham B4 6AD
0121 236 9696 Fax 0121 236 9699
33 Wine Street, Bristol BS1 2BQ
0117 9264306 Fax 0117 9294515
9–21 Princess Street, Manchester M60 8AS
0161 834 7201 Fax 0161 833 0634
16 Arthur Street, Belfast BT1 4GD
028 9023 8451 Fax 028 9023 5401
The Stationery Office Oriel Bookshop
18–19 High Street, Cardiff CF1 2BZ
029 2039 5548 Fax 029 2038 4347
71 Lothian Road, Edinburgh EH3 9AZ
0131 228 4181 Fax 0131 622 7017

The Stationery Office's Accredited Agents
(see Yellow Pages)

and through good booksellers

Typeset by Spire Origination, Norwich
Printed in the United Kingdom by The Stationery Office
J95664   11/99   456867

Preface

The lives and careers of the famous and powerful, besides being fascinating in themselves, often provide the sharpest of contrasts when compared one with another. Such contrasts certainly stand out among the 111 *People of Consequence* selected from around the world for inclusion in this volume. Hereditary monarchs are on the list alongside people born in rural third world poverty or in small-town obscurity in the industrialised West. Some of those featured here spend their time in the air conditioned offices of top corporations, or travel from one international summit meeting to the next, while others are held under house arrest, or have spent long decades in prison before achieving their current pre-eminence.

People of Consequence brings together in one volume a succinct portrait of each of 111 people whose careers, seen from the vantage point of the end of the 1990s, have had the greatest impact in shaping the world in the last decade. Religious figures, established politicians and opposition leaders, dictators, despots, democrats and diplomats, top business executives, global entertainment industry and sports megastars are among those included.

The individual portraits cover the current situation as of June 1999. They combine factual biographical information with a description of each individual's career to date, written with the aim of bringing out for the reader the key events with which they have been associated, and the extent of their impact upon them. Each portrait begins with a short summary, set in italic script, followed by a photograph.

In many cases, official biographies and information sheets have provided essential details not available from any other source. At the same time, an enormous range of other material has been collected, quarried and sifted, by the staff at Cambridge International Reference on Current Affairs (CIRCA), by assistant editor Catherine Jagger, and by contributors who worked on initial drafts of many of the entries, thereby easing the author's task.

The resulting portraits are designed to inform their readers, rather than to praise, condone or criticise their subjects. They do not pretend, however, that the careers they describe are without controversy. The intention has always been to reach judgements carefully, and to convey them in a manner which is clear and free from polemical intent. Responsibility for this, for the selection of what is deemed significant, and for any errors which have crept in despite our best efforts to be meticulous, rests with the author.

Roger East, Cambridge, June 1999

Acknowledgements

Thanks are due to the many people who have assisted in a range of different ways in the preparation of this book. Among those who have much improved the final portraits by their work on them at various stages, Catherine Jagger is especially to be thanked for giving the broadest possible interpretation of her role as assistant editor, encompassing research, the management of the project as a whole, and the initial drafting of several of the entries as well as the final checking of the text.

For the drafting of entries, acknowledgement and thanks are due also to a number of contributors:

Lawrence Joffe for entries on Naomi Campbell, Madonna, Steven Spielberg, Quentin Tarantino, Desmond Tutu and Gianni Versace;

Frances Nicholson for entries on Silvio Berlusconi, Gro Harlem Brundtland, Michel Camdessus, Tansu Çiller, Jacques Delors, Wim Duisenberg, Felipe González, Mikhail Gorbachev, Radovan Karadzic, Jean-Marie Le Pen, Aleksander Lebed, Winnie Mandela, François Mitterrand, Andreas Papandreou, Mary Robinson, Gerhard Schröder, Margaret Thatcher, Hans Tietmeyer, Lech Walesa and James Wolfensohn;

Rosemary Payne for entries on Bob Hawke and Paul Keating;

Farzana Shaikh for entries on Koffi Annan, Cory Aquino, Hanan Ashrawi, Aung San Suu Kyi, Benazir Bhutto, Boutros Boutros Ghali, Rajiv Gandhi, Kim Il Sung, Shimon Peres, Javier Pérez de Cuéllar, Pol Pot, Yitzhak Rabin, Ali Akbar Rafsanjani, Salman Rushdie and Mother Teresa;

Michael Wilson for entries on Richard Branson, Warren Buffett, Michael Eisner, Bill Gates, Alan Greenspan, Lee Iacocca, Rupert Murdoch, George Soros, Donald Trump and Ted Turner.

Grateful acknowledgement is due to Associated Press and the many other organisations and individuals who provided photographs – a full list of photo credits is given at the back of the volume – and to the staff of organisations, companies, embassies and governments throughout the world for providing information which has been invaluable as source material.

Gerry **Adams**

The main public face of the Irish republican movement for almost two decades, Gerry Adams came to the fore with the new generation of militants emerging in the Northern Irish "troubles" from the 1960s onwards. A "graduate" of the internment camps, it was he who led the movement towards accepting the view that political engagement was ultimately more fruitful than the armed struggle. If the dual strategy of "the Armalite and the ballot box" was the rallying call of the early 1980s, Adams's identification with the political aspect of that strategy, through his leadership of Sinn Féin, *has become more pronounced through the 1990s. He remains a hate figure among Unionists and large sections of the British public, who see any distinction between* Sinn Féin *and the Irish Republican Army (IRA) as specious, and who decry Adams for condoning terrorism when he stops short of unequivocally condemning the use of violence.*

Gerard Adams was born on 6 October 1948 in the Falls Road area of west Belfast. He was the eldest son of Gerard Adams, a building labourer, and Annie Hannaway, a linen mill worker, both from active Irish republican and trade union backgrounds. The family, expanding to ten children, left the slum housing conditions of the almost entirely Catholic Falls Road area and moved to a small house on the Divismore Park housing estate in Ballymurphy. Despite showing promise as a pupil at St Mary's Christian Brothers School, the young Gerry Adams left school as a teenager after his O-levels, taking a job as a barman.

He was soon drawn into politics by the civil rights campaigns, which were launched in the mid-1960s to contest the unfair treatment of Catholics vis-à-vis the Protestant majority, especially in terms of housing and employment where Protestants had an effective monopoly of opportunities in many areas. In 1966 Adams joined *Sinn Féin*, the Irish republican party whose section in the six counties of Northern Ireland was banned there between 1956 and 1973. He was also a member of one of the "self-defence teams" formed in Belfast to protect Catholic demonstrators against the growing numbers of loyalist paramilitaries. Whether or not he had also joined the IRA (the military wing of the republican movement), he was arrested in March 1972 for subversive activity as a Provisional IRA battalion commander, and interned without trial. Although he was still only in his early twenties, Adams's political views and arguments had considerable influence among his fellow inmates. Reflecting his credibility within the republican movement, his skill in argument and his strategic astuteness, he was released in July to head a five-member delegation for secret but ultimately fruitless

talks with the British government. On his return to Belfast he was briefly reunited with Colette McCardle, whom he had married the previous year, but was soon on the run from the police and was arrested again in 1973, shortly before the birth of his son Gearoid.

Interned in the Maze prison along with numerous other prominent republicans, Adams used his time to learn and discuss aspects of revolution, socialism and colonial occupation, both current and historic. Within a year of his release in 1977, he had become a vice-president of the now unbanned *Sinn Féin* and a natural leader of its militant and mainly Northern-based younger generation. (The party, like the IRA, had split in the late 1960s into Official and Provisional wings, the former evolving to become the Workers' Party while the latter – to which Adams belonged – became known simply as *Sinn Féin*.) Popular support for the party reached an emotional high in 1981 with the election of hunger-striking prisoner Bobby Sands to the UK House of Commons a month before he starved to death. Adams was a key advocate of campaigning in elections to get the party's views across, under the dual strategy of fighting for a united Ireland through both "the Armalite [rifle] and the ballot box". This did not mean, however, actually participating in those political structures which it regarded as products of the division of Ireland and therefore illegitimate. Adams, one of the party's members elected to the Northern Ireland Assembly in 1982, accordingly boycotted that body. Similarly, when he became the only successful *Sinn Féin* candidate in the UK-wide general election the following year, winning the West Belfast constituency, Adams refused to take his seat in Westminster as this would have entailed swearing allegiance to the British crown. The British government more than once placed him under exclusion orders banning him from visiting mainland Britain on the grounds that he condoned the use of terrorism, and he was also unable until 1994 to obtain a visa to visit the USA. From 1988 until 1994 the UK media were not allowed to broadcast his voice, under a ban designed to "deny terrorists the oxygen of publicity", with the farcical result that he was frequently shown making a speech while an actor did a voice-over of the words.

Elected president of *Sinn Féin* in November 1983 – the first time a Northerner had held this post – Adams survived an assassination attempt in March 1984, when he was shot five times by three Unionist gunmen belonging to the paramilitary Ulster Freedom Fighters. Subsequently his life has been dominated by security precautions and he has tried to keep his wife and children out of the media spotlight; on one occasion they narrowly escaped death when a bomb exploded outside their home.

The West Belfast constituency re-elected Adams in the 1987 UK general election, but in 1992 he was narrowly defeated, due to tactical voting by Unionists for the (mainly Catholic-backed) Social Democratic and Labour Party (SDLP). Victorious once again in the 1997 general election, Adams still refused to take his seat; he did, however, attempt to invoke the status of MP to attend a meeting at the House of Commons, but was prevented when the Speaker refused permission.

Through the latter part of the 1980s, in the absence of any real signs of movement towards resolving the situation in Northern Ireland, *Sinn Féin*'s political role was unclear, while Adams's opponents denounced him as little more than an apologist for the IRA because of his refusal to condemn their continuing armed struggle. His political philosophy was nevertheless being refined in this period, and coming out in his writing. As was subsequently revealed, he was also engaged in secret talks with SDLP leader John Hume in 1988, working out how *Sinn Féin* might become a participant in a comprehensive peace process, having reached the conclusion that the British and the Unionists were not going to give way under the threat of violence. The eventual outcome was a joint peace strategy declaration with Hume in September 1993, an initiative which became a major factor in breaking the apparent deadlock. When the IRA declared a ceasefire in August 1994, *Sinn Féin* was still excluded from multiparty talks, however, with the British government insisting that the decommissioning of IRA weapons must begin before this situation could change. On the other hand Adams gained permission to travel to the USA, where interviews and a meeting with **Bill Clinton** greatly raised his public profile, and his most recent exclusion from mainland Britain was revoked in October 1994.

When the IRA ceasefire was broken in February 1996, a settlement looked unreachable, and Adams's balancing act – encouraging a ceasefire, insisting that he could not speak for the IRA, and refusing to be drawn into any direct condemnation of IRA violence – appeared untenable. He was physically barred from entering talks at Stormont on a new Northern Ireland forum. When elections were held for this new body, *Sinn Féin* did take part, with considerable success, but then boycotted the institution. Further terms for a ceasefire were published by Adams and Hume in September 1996, but Adams rejected in disgust the conditions upon which UK Prime Minister John Major insisted before *Sinn Féin* could join all-party talks.

The Labour government elected in the UK May 1997 general election brought a fresh opportunity to reinvigorate the Northern Ireland peace process. In September 1997, six weeks after a renewed IRA ceasefire declaration, Adams was finally allowed to join the talks at Stormont. This historic development, accompanied by an unprecedented meeting with UK Prime Minister **Tony Blair** on 10 September, was followed up by Adams holding talks with Blair at 10 Downing Street on 11 December 1997. The pace of negotiations quickened dramatically in the run-up to the historic Good Friday agreement in April 1998. Signing that agreement, and leading his supporters in a "yes" vote in the referendum held on it the following month, left Adams committed to trying to make it work. To do so, he needed to convince die-hard republicans that the Good Friday agreement was not a sell-out. Not surprisingly, the decommissioning of IRA weapons became a litmus test. Were republicans to give up their weapons before they could see the fruits of participation in the peace process? Well into 1999, Adams continued to repeat that while he was in favour of making progress on decommissioning, it was not a precondition; under the agreement, he insisted, *Sinn Féin* now had the right to posts in the new Northern Ireland executive.

In addition to his political writing (notably *A Pathway to Peace* and *The Politics of Irish Freedom*), Gerry Adams has published a memoir entitled *Falls Memories*, an autobiography, *Before the Dawn*, two collections of short stories, and numerous articles. He is a member of PEN, the international guild of writers. He is a fluent speaker of Irish, keen to foster the renaissance of its culture, and also an enthusiast for Gaelic sports.

Bertie **Ahern**

Bertie Ahern became Ireland's youngest-ever Taoiseach *(prime minister) in June 1997, at the age of 45. A member of parliament since the age of 25 and a prominent figure in Dublin city politics, Ahern was once seen as heir apparent to Charles Haughey as head of the conservative, nationalist* Fianna Fáil *party. His elevation to the leadership, although delayed in the early 1990s in the interests of party unity, came in 1994 and marked a decisive change of the generations in Irish politics. The most striking achievement of his premiership has been his role in the signature of the Good Friday agreement on Northern Ireland in April 1998, and he has shown both patience and determination through the subsequent difficulties in implementing that historic accord.*

Bartholomew Patrick (Bertie) Ahern was born on 12 September 1951, in a working-class Dublin family. Educated at the local national school and by the Christian Brothers, he became an accountant after graduating from Rathmines College of Commerce and University College, Dublin. Bertie Ahern married Miriam Kelly in 1975 and they have two daughters. Ahern is now separated from his wife and lives with his partner Celia Larkin, a *Fianna Fáil* party worker.

He was first elected to the *Dáil Éireann* (the lower house of the Irish parliament) as a *Fianna Fáil* deputy at the age of only 25, in 1977. Since 1979 he has combined his career in parliament, where he represents Dublin Central, with membership of Dublin City Council. He was lord mayor of Dublin from 1986 to 1987.

Ahern first held government office as an assistant whip from 1980 to 1981. In 1981 he was appointed party spokesperson on youth, and in 1982 became minister of state in the office of the *Taoiseach* and the department of defence, and government chief whip. After the defeat of *Fianna Fáil* in the November 1982 general election he became opposition chief whip and *Fianna Fáil*'s leader of the house. Party vice-president from 1983 to 1994, Ahern was also director of by-elections for *Fianna Fáil* in the 1980s and chaired the party's constituency and organisation committee from 1987 to 1992.

With *Fianna Fáil* back in government after the 1987 general election, Ahern began a seven-year spell as a cabinet minister. His first portfolio was as minister for labour, making his name as architect of a social consensus, which was embodied in a programme for national recovery and a programme for economic and social progress. At the European level, Ireland's turn in the rotating presidency of the European Union (EU) Council of Ministers meant that in the first half of 1990 he was president of the EU Council of Ministers for Social Affairs.

In November 1991 Ahern moved to the finance ministry, filling a gap caused by the departure of

Albert Reynolds, who left the government after challenging the leadership of the then *Taoiseach*, Charles Haughey. The resignation the following February of the discredited Haughey gave rise to a leadership contest from which Ahern, hitherto seen as Haughey's heir apparent, withdrew his own candidacy so that the party could unite behind Reynolds. Ahern retained the post of finance minister in the Reynolds government. He was also a member of the board of governors at the European Investment Bank (which he chaired in 1991/92), the International Monetary Fund (IMF), the World Bank, and the European Bank for Reconstruction and Development (EBRD).

In the November 1992 general election, a poor result made *Fianna Fáil*'s coalition with the Progressive Democrats (PD) unviable. Ahern, adept at bridge-building, eventually succeeded in negotiating a new coalition agreement with the greatly strengthened Labour Party. In the resulting government, which took office in January 1993, he once again took up the finance portfolio under Reynolds.

This coalition collapsed in November 1994 when Reynolds ignored Labour objections and pushed through his favoured appointee for the post of president of the high court (the country's second highest judicial post). Reynolds was forced to resign in the uproar which followed. Ahern, now free to seek what was widely regarded as his rightful place as party leader, was elected to that post by *Fianna Fáil* on 19 November, but found himself on the opposition benches rather than in power, because *Fianna Fáil* was excluded from a new three-party coalition government headed by John Bruton of *Fine Gael*.

During the ensuing period the Northern Ireland question loomed large in Irish politics. Bruton, as prime minister, was noted for his conciliatory approach. He pursued a joint initiative with the UK government which was intended to bring the representatives of the province's rival political traditions into an inclusive peace process. *Fianna Fáil* was traditionally more nationalist. Under Haughey in the mid-1980s, its pro-republican stance on Northern Ireland had been a major factor in driving out a group of party dissidents, who had split away to form the Progressive Democrats. Ten years on, Ahern was aware that maintaining such a stance could mean missing an opportunity for a lasting settlement. Thus, although he was frequently critical of Bruton for bending too far towards the British line, he nevertheless led his party into the June 1997 general election declaring that he would seek to form a coalition with the Progressive Democrats.

Ahern's high personal popularity rating helped boost the otherwise lacklustre performance of *Fianna Fáil*, which emerged from the 1997 election with 77 seats. This was eight more seats than in 1994, although the party won only a fractionally increased share (39.3 per cent) of the vote. After two weeks of negotiations on the formation of a government, Ahern was sworn in on 26 June at the head of a *Fianna Fáil*–PD coalition, which nevertheless lacked a parliamentary majority.

Declaring it to be his primary objective to work to achieve a settlement in the talks on Northern Ireland, Ahern formed an effective working relationship with the new UK prime minister **Tony Blair**, both of them being representatives of a younger generation of political leaders. The momentum which they sustained in driving the Northern Ireland peace process forward had its moment of apparent triumph with the Good Friday agreement concluded in April 1998. Throughout the subsequent protracted difficulties involved in moving that agreement forward from signature to implementation, Ahern has remained committed to making it work and has sought to resolve the particularly thorny issue of the decommissioning of weapons held by paramilitary groups.

Kofi **Annan**

Lengthy experience within the UN system over some 35 years was one of Kofi Annan's main credentials for the post of UN secretary-general. In the political nature of such appointments, however, it was more critical that he was Ghanaian, in view of the strength of the lobby to choose a black African for the first time, and that he spoke French well enough to overcome the initial hostility of France to a non-francophone. Approachable and candid, Annan has won high esteem among his colleagues and has tackled the overdue reform of the UN administration with both energy and tact. On the global stage, however, he has struggled to reassert a pre-eminent role for the UN in peacekeeping and crisis management. Both in Iraq and over Kosovo, he has worked assiduously to rebuild a consensus position acceptable to the UN Security Council as a whole in the wake of more assertive US-led action.

Kofi Annan was born on 8 April 1938 in Kumasi, Ghana, the son of a prominent hereditary chief of the Fante tribe. He received his early education in Ghana where he studied at the University of Science and Technology in Kumasi before going on to complete an undergraduate degree in economics at Macalester College in Minnesota, USA, in 1961. From 1961 to 1962 he was a graduate student in economics at the

Institut Universitaire des Hautes Etudes Internationales in Geneva, Switzerland. Kofi Annan is married to Nane Lagergren, a Swedish artist and lawyer, and they have three children.

In 1962 he embarked on a career as an international civil servant, assigned to his first UN post as administrative and budget officer at the World Health Organization in Geneva, where he remained until 1971. In 1971/72 Annan was elected a Sloan Fellow at the Massachusetts Institute of Technology where he received a master's degree in management. He returned to UN service in 1972, holding posts in Geneva and Cairo, and spending two years (1974–76) in Ghana on secondment to the Ghana Tourist Development Board.

During the 1980s, Annan pursued a varied career at the UN which sharpened his talents as an administrator handling complex financial procedures and an elaborate bureaucracy. Among the posts which were to prepare him for international leadership were deputy director of administration at the office of the UN High Commissioner for Refugees in Geneva (1980–83); director of budget in the Office of Financial Services (1984–87) and assistant secretary-general in the Office of Human Resources Management (1987–90).

Annan's skills as a diplomat were first seen on the international stage in 1990 following the Iraqi invasion of Kuwait, when he took charge of negotiations to secure the repatriation of over 900 international staff and the release of Western hostages held in Iraq. Later he led negotiations on UN-supervised sales of Iraqi oil, which resulted in the 1996 "oil for food" agreement between Iraq and the

UN. In March 1993 Annan was appointed under-secretary-general for peacekeeping operations which put him in charge of 17 military operations and as many as 80,000 multinational troops worldwide. He also undertook a number of special assignments from November 1995 to March 1996 as the special representative of the UN secretary-general to the former Yugoslavia, during which he oversaw the signing of the 1995 Dayton peace agreement which ensured the smooth transfer of power in Bosnia-Herzegovina.

Annan's managerial experience and his outstanding performance as a negotiator and peacemaker gave him advantages over the several other candidates vying to succeed **Boutros Boutros Ghali** as UN secretary-general from January 1997. As a Ghanaian he was also favoured by the growing number of countries pressing for the election of a black secretary-general. A fluent speaker of both English and French, Annan won the support not only of the USA, his strongest backer, but of France, which had originally vetoed his nomination by the Security Council. In the context of the UN's growing emphasis on the merits of transparency and openness in administration, Annan's personal accessibility and candid manner proved to be additional virtues in favour of his candidacy.

On 17 December 1996 Annan was elected UN secretary-general for a five-year term, running until 31 December 2001. Saddled though he was by constraints, not least a shortfall in UN reserves arising from an estimated US$1.5 billion still owed by the USA, Annan moved decisively to further his objectives on administrative reform. In 1997 he secured a pledge of US$1 billion for UN operations from the US media tycoon **Ted Turner**, and introduced a "collegial" system allowing the UN's main departmental heads to implement policy co-operatively. Annan also showed his commitment to

greater administrative decentralisation by appointing the UN's first deputy secretary-general, Louise Fréchette, in early 1998. However, the success of these reforms will depend upon Annan's skill in balancing the domination of the USA, upon which the UN still depends for its financial survival, with pressure from other member states for increased influence within the UN's main decision-making body, the Security Council.

Difficult obstacles also confront Annan on the diplomatic front. The UN's authority has been challenged repeatedly by Iraq, which has on several occasions suspended the work of arms inspectors or threatened to obstruct their investigations unless UN sanctions are lifted. Annan has claimed some notable negotiating successes by securing eleventh-hour agreements, enabling **Saddam Hussein** to avert further US-led military action by agreeing to restore compliance with UN resolutions. The risk for Annan is that, by accepting such promises, he can be made to appear too credulous when the Iraqis indulge in further brinkmanship. In the USA in particular, his tireless efforts for peace are portrayed by the more "hawkish" commentators as obstructing the implementation of more resolute measures against Saddam Hussein's regime.

The first two years of Annan's term were also clouded by setbacks for UN peacekeeping in the Congo (former Zaïre), where UN monitors have been forced to abandon their mission, and Angola, where a hard-won peace agreement has crumbled. In early 1999, the status of the UN appeared to reach a low ebb when Western countries launched their own military action against Yugoslavia, over its brutal treatment of the ethnic Albanian majority population in Kosovo. As the risk of a protracted conflict became more apparent, however, Annan was once again involved, working to put together the elements of a wider international initiative.

Cory **Aquino**

*Propelled into the limelight by the 1986 "people power" revolution in the Philippines, Cory Aquino made the leap from privileged housewife to popular leader through her involvement in the struggle against political authoritarianism. Inheritor of her assassinated husband's mantle, her transformation made her an inspiration for women across the world. She stands in what has become a tradition of Asian women reaching top positions as widows or daughters from leading political families – a line running from Sirimavo Bandaranaike and Indira Gandhi via Cory Aquino, **Benazir Bhutto**, Bangladesh's Khaleda Zia and Mrs Bandaranaike's daughter **Chandrika Kumaratunga** in Sri Lanka, to those leading opposition figures of the closing years of the century, **Aung San Suu Kyi** in Burma and Megawati Sukarnoputri in Indonesia. Cory Aquino's presidential term in the Philippines, however, lasting until 1992, was marred by the volatile insubordination of right-wing military cliques, and the intractable economic problems bequeathed by the "crony capitalism" of the Marcos dictatorship.*

Maria Corazon Cojuangco was born on 25 January 1933 into a wealthy Roman Catholic family in Tarlac province on the island of Luzon, in the northern part of the Philippines. Her father, José Cojuangco, was a Filipino–Chinese businessman who, after building up the family fortunes as sugar plantation owners in Tarlac, followed his own father's example by entering politics and becoming a member of congress. Her mother, a pharmacist, belonged to a prominent political family from Rizal. Aquino was educated at the exclusive Assumption Convent in Manila and then in the USA, where she attended the Ravenhill Academy in Philadelphia and the Notre-Dame Convent School in New York before graduating from the College of Mount St Vincent in New York. In the early 1950s she returned to the Philippines to study law at the Far Eastern University in Manila but abandoned it in 1954 to marry Benigno Simeon Aquino, known as Ninoy, a journalist and scion of another prominent family in Tarlac.

Aquino spent much of her married life in relative obscurity. As a wife and mother of five children, she supported her husband's political involvement as he rose to be Liberal Party leader and the main figure in the opposition against President Ferdinand Marcos – for which, in the 1970s, he was imprisoned and at one time sentenced to death. This sentence was commuted thanks to international pressure, and in 1980 Cory followed her husband into exile in the USA. Three years later he decided to return to the Philippines to resume his political activity, but he was assassinated upon his arrival at Manila airport by a military guard on 21 August 1983.

The campaign to pin the responsibility for the killing squarely on Marcos, and more broadly to expose the rampant corruption of his regime, coaxed Cory into an increasingly prominent political role on her own account. Although initially reluctant to assume her husband's political mantle, she was quickly adopted by the Filipino liberal establishment, to become the symbol of what eventually grew into the "people power" revolt against the Marcos regime. At the same time, she could only fulfil this role because she was

Benigno's widow – confirming that the main stronghold of power in Asia remained the political dynasty, and that women could not yet aspire to establish themselves politically in their own right.

When a presidential election was eventually scheduled for 7 February 1986, Cory Aquino agreed to stand as the presidential candidate of the opposition alliance, *Lakas Ng Byan*, and claimed victory at the polls, rejecting the efforts of President Marcos to rig the results and claim a majority for himself. Marcos's subsequent attempts to stay in power were thwarted by the tide of growing popular anger against his government and by the desertion of key sections of the armed forces, which lent their support to Aquino. On 25 February Marcos was forced from office, leaving Aquino to take over as the Philippines' first woman president.

Aquino began her term in office with immense popular support both at home and abroad. The euphoria over the "people power" revolution put paid to the original idea that she should merely be an interim president, standing down as soon as fresh elections could be held under less repressive circumstances. In February 1987 a landslide majority approved a new constitution drawn up by her government and in May of that year her candidates won a decisive majority in the legislative elections.

However, huge problems confronted Aquino on the economic front. Her failure to introduce far-reaching reforms, necessary to overcome the effects of years of mismanagement and "crony capitalist" corruption under Marcos, drove many to seek alternative solutions being offered by communists and the Muslim separatist movement in the north. Her inability to quell dissent among right-wing military leaders, and her distaste for the politics of patronage also eroded her authority. Having once been feted by American liberals – who voted her *Time* magazine's Woman of the Year in 1986 – she lost popularity in the USA when she began negotiations in 1990 to dismantle US military bases in the Philippines.

Overwhelmed by the scale of the Philippines' economic and political crisis, she refused to seek a second term as president. However, her influence on national politics was clearly underlined by the election to the presidency in May 1992 of her chosen successor, Fidel Ramos. He had been her defence minister for four years, and previously the armed forces chief of staff, having swung key elements of the military behind her "people power" revolution in the heady days of February 1986. Aquino continues to play an important role in political affairs, especially through her involvement in campaigns aimed at preventing the political reinstatement of close members of the Marcos family or any of its associates.

Yassir **Arafat**

Instantly recognisable as one of the most controversial figures of the last three decades, although latterly much diminished by ill health, the Palestinian guerrilla leader turned elder statesman, Yassir Arafat, has experienced a marked change in his international profile. Condemned by many as a terrorist leader in the 1970s, and still the object of hatred among large sections of the Israeli public, he was nevertheless being applauded in the West by the 1990s as a pragmatic moderate, and shared the Nobel Peace Prize in 1994 with Israeli government leaders for their contribution to the Israel–Palestine peace process. Conversely, the halting of progress in the transfer of territory to Palestinian control since the mid-1990s leaves him more vulnerable to the accusation from radical critics that his dealings with Israel have compromised the Palestinian cause.

Mohammed Abdel-Raouf Arafat al-Qudwa al-Hussein was born on 24 August 1929 in Cairo, Egypt. He was nicknamed Yassir, meaning "easy", and spent most of his childhood in Jerusalem, living with his uncle after the death of his mother when he was four. In 1944 he joined the League of Palestinian Students. Aged only 17, he began procuring weapons for an anticipated battle for Palestinian territory.

During the Arab–Israeli conflict which surrounded the creation of the state of Israel, Arafat fought with forces backing the grand mufti of Jerusalem, and in 1948 he fled to Cairo, one of some three-quarters of a million Palestinian Arabs left stateless. He began studies in engineering at Cairo University.

In 1952 he joined the Muslim Brotherhood and Union of Palestinian Students, of which he became president. At the outbreak of the Suez crisis in 1956, he participated in the Egyptian army. Moving to Kuwait that year, he worked as an engineer before founding his own company.

In 1957 Arafat co-founded *Al Fatah*, the Palestine National Liberation Movement and underground organisation which mounted several attacks on Israel. In 1968, Arafat and *Al Fatah* received international publicity when they fought off Israeli troops who had entered Jordan. *Al Fatah* soon became linked with the umbrella Palestine Liberation Organization (PLO), becoming its dominant faction. Arafat was himself elected as PLO chairman in 1969 and has retained this post ever since. From this time the PLO moved from a stand of pan-Arabism to an increasing preoccupation with the cause of a specifically Palestinian nationhood. Arafat and the PLO won wide international recognition as "the sole legitimate representative of the Palestinian people", the UN voting in 1974 (after Arafat addressed the General Assembly) to give the PLO observer status and to recognise the Palestinians' claim to self-determination.

Forced out of Jordan in 1970, the PLO switched its main activities to bases in Lebanon, from where it continued to carry out raids against Israel until it was again driven out, this time to Tunisia, by the Israeli forces which invaded Lebanon in 1982.

On 15 November 1988, an independent state of Palestine was proclaimed, at a meeting of the PLO's "parliament", the Palestine National Council, in Algiers. The territory of Palestine was defined as comprising the West Bank and the Gaza Strip, at that time in the throes of a popular uprising or *intifada* against Israeli occupation. Arafat went on to declare before the UN that the PLO renounced terrorism, and that it supported the right of all parties to live in peace. This declaration, going much of the way to meeting the Israeli complaint that the PLO opposed its right to existence as a state, led to an expansion in the international recognition of the PLO, and was a diplomatic success for Arafat. The following year, he was elected president of Palestine by the central council of the Palestine National Council, although a period of diplomatic setbacks followed, with the PLO's standing in the West in particular suffering from Arafat's backing for the Iraqi side in the 1991 Gulf war. The outlook for Arafat appeared particularly bleak at this time – although on a personal level 1991 was the year in which he was married, to Suha Tawil. The impetus within Palestinian nationalism appeared to be passing from his essentially secular vision to the radical Islamic groups and younger activists in the *intifada*, where stone-throwing youths repeatedly confronted Israeli security forces in a sustained bid to make the territory ungovernable. The following year, on 7 April 1992, Arafat was involved in a plane crash in Libya, and later had a blood clot removed from his brain. A deterioration in his health became more pronounced in the ensuing years, to the extent that there were rumours in 1998 of his impending retirement and speculation that he had Parkinson's disease.

US-led negotiations launched in Madrid in 1991, aiming to set in motion a comprehensive Middle East peace process, bore little positive fruit in respect of the Palestinian issue. Matters did progress, however, after secret negotiations, when in 1993 the Oslo agreement laid down a "land for peace" formula. Arafat's own international standing increased significantly when, in recognition of the importance of the Oslo agreement, he, **Shimon Peres** and **Yitzhak Rabin** won the 1994 Nobel Peace Prize. Israeli forces withdrew from Jericho and Arafat returned at last to Palestinian territory, as chairman of a Palestine National Authority (PNA) set up under the 1993 peace agreement.

On 20 January 1996, Arafat was overwhelmingly elected first president of the Palestinian Authority's legislative body, the 88-seat Palestinian Legislative Council. Arafat also acts as head of government, appointing a cabinet formally responsible to the Council. Governing the Gaza Strip and those areas of the West Bank from which the Israelis withdrew, he was widely regarded, and treated, as head of state.

He held off, however, from a formal declaration of Palestinian statehood, recognising that this could be an inflammatory step and prejudicial to the continuing – even if apparently deadlocked – talks with Israel. Arafat resisted the temptation to abandon the "peace process", despite the evident lack of any real commitment to progress on the part of the right-wing Israeli government led by **Benjamin Netanyahu** from May 1996 to May 1999. Arafat recognised that he now had no real alternative but to cultivate support internationally, receive signs of US favour, which culminated in President **Clinton**'s visit to Gaza in late 1998, and await a change in the Israeli stance. Meanwhile he came under fire from critics within the Palestinian movement, including former supporters such as **Hanan Ashrawi**, for the way he kept a firm grip on political control in the Palestinian self-government area, and the extensive use of his police force to suppress dissent.

Hanan **Ashrawi**

A Palestinian woman with a high international profile, strong credentials as a feminist and human rights activist, and the independence of spirit to criticise the shortcomings of **Yassir Arafat***'s administration, Hanan Ashrawi stands for much which has yet to be resolved on the future of Palestine. She became a prominent figure explaining the Palestinian cause in the media during the* intifada *(uprising) which began in the occupied territories in 1988, and made headlines in the early 1990s when she starred as the leading Palestinian representative at the Madrid conference on the Middle East. Although she went on to help facilitate the Oslo peace agreement, she was uncomfortable as part of Arafat's cabinet in the resulting Palestinian self-rule areas and resigned in 1998 to give herself greater critical freedom.*

Hanan Mikhail was born on 8 October 1946 in the town of Nablus in what was then still British-administered Palestine (Nablus being within the West Bank area, which was not made part of the state of Israel in 1948 but which came under Israeli occupation in 1967). The Mikhail family were non-practising Anglican Christians. Hanan's father, Daud Mikhail, who came originally from the mainly

Christian town of Ramallah just north of Jerusalem, was a wealthy doctor and said to be one of the founders of the Palestine Liberation Organization (PLO). Her mother was a nurse who shared her husband's left-wing politics.

After the creation of Israel in May 1948, the family led a peripatetic existence, moving to Amman, the Jordanian capital, coming back to Ramallah, and then going to Beirut. At the time of the Six-Day Arab–Israeli war in June 1967, Hanan was an undergraduate at the American University in Beirut. In Beirut she became involved in the burgeoning Palestinian movement which she helped support by working with Palestinian refugees and playing an active part in the Union of Palestinian Students. During this time she is reported to have had her first meeting with **Yassir Arafat**, leader of the PLO. In 1968 she completed her degree in English literature at the American University in Beirut and went to the University of Virginia in Charlottesville, USA, where she was awarded a doctorate in 1973. Later that year she returned to Ramallah, taking up a senior teaching position at Bir Zeit University. In 1975 she married Emile Ashrawi, with whom she has had two daughters.

Having been chair of the department of English at Bir Zeit from 1973 to 1984, Hanan Ashrawi was appointed dean of the university's faculty of arts in 1986. She retained this post until 1990, and remained a faculty member of Bir Zeit University until 1996, when she became a minister in the Palestinian government.

During the 1970s and 1980s Ashrawi successfully combined her academic career with her engagement in Palestinian politics. As a student in the USA, she actively promoted the cause of Palestinian nationalism by forming the American Friends of Free Palestine. She also pursued a feminist agenda by highlighting the joint concerns of Palestinian and Israeli women. Upon her return to Israel in 1973, she continued her political activities which within months of her arrival led to her first arrest and trial on charges of sedition. Although convicted and sentenced to a six-month prison term, she was released after her employers at Bir Zeit University agreed to pay a US$120 fine in exchange for her freedom. The experience sharpened Ashrawi's sense of injustice against the Israeli authorities and triggered her lifelong commitment to human rights. In 1974 she founded the Bir Zeit University Legal Aid Committee and Human Rights Documentation Centre, an organisation she headed until 1995.

The outbreak of the Palestinian *intifada* in 1988 intensified Ashrawi's involvement in Palestinian politics. As one of the most articulate exponents of the Palestinian cause, she was regularly courted by the international media and in demand as a guest speaker at home and abroad. In 1988 she was named a member of the PLO's political committee, and in 1990 was included in its diplomatic committee. Her international profile rose sharply in 1991 when, as official spokesperson of the Palestinian delegation to the Madrid peace conference, she upstaged her Israeli counterpart, **Benjamin Netanyahu**, by her measured yet impassioned defence of the Palestinian position.

The Oslo peace accords in 1993, which Ashrawi helped to facilitate, provided a framework for Palestinian self-rule (in the Gaza Strip and Jericho from 1994, and with the "Oslo B" agreement in 1995 supposedly establishing a timetable for further self-rule areas in the West Bank). The beginning of self-rule marked a turning point for Ashrawi herself. Many had welcomed her rise to prominence in the late 1980s and early 1990s, a charismatic figure

bringing fresh impetus to the PLO's quest for statehood. Despite her effectiveness under the media spotlight, however, she never fitted in easily alongside the "old guard" around Arafat, who kept a tight rein on the day-to-day running of the Palestinian movement. It now became apparent that, while still as committed as ever to the objectives of the PLO, she was growing increasingly disillusioned with Arafat's leadership. In 1993 she resigned as PLO spokesperson, and she refused to join Arafat's first "cabinet" (the Palestine National Authority – PNA) when it was announced in May 1994. Instead she resumed her activities as a human rights campaigner, forming the Palestinian Independent Commission for Citizens' Rights, one of the first groups to monitor human rights under Palestinian self-rule. This was a mission of particular sensitivity, as Arafat's administration was drawn increasingly into controversial action to keep the security situation under control in the face of militant Palestinian hostility to continuing Israeli occupation and the extension of Jewish settlements.

Ashrawi returned to a formal political role in January 1996 when she was elected a member of the Palestinian Legislative Council to represent a Jerusalem constituency. In June of that year she was named minister for higher education in Arafat's government and worked hard to increase the number of young people, especially women, in tertiary education. In August 1998 Ashrawi resigned from the government shortly after the announcement of a cabinet reshuffle which switched her ministerial portfolio from education to tourism. She stressed that her resignation was not a protest against ministerial changes, but a means of drawing attention to the government's failure to introduce reforms. Nevertheless, the conclusion was widely drawn that Ashrawi, by now an outspoken critic of official mismanagement, was seeking to distance herself from an increasingly corrupt administration.

Hafez al-**Assad**

Assad has dominated the political scene in Syria for the three decades since he first seized power in a bloodless coup on 15 October 1970. His position as president is confirmed at regular intervals in unopposed referendums, most recently in February 1999, although his frail health has recently focused attention on the question of the succession, particularly since the death of his elder son and heir apparent, Bassil, in a car accident in 1994. Assad runs a single-party regime which has dealt effectively and ruthlessly with any opposition. Formerly the closest Middle East ally of the former Soviet Union, he has come to be viewed with less hostility by the USA and other Western governments in the 1990s, principally because of his stance against Iraq at the time of the 1991 Gulf war.

Hafez al-Assad was born in 1930 in Qardaha, near the coastal town of Latakia in northwest Syria. The family was originally called al-Wahsh, meaning "son of the boar", but Hafez later changed this to al-Assad or "son of the lion". He was one of nine children of a poor farming family of Alawite Muslims, a traditionally downtrodden religious minority in predominantly Sunni Muslim Syria, but closely associated with the Ba'ath party which came to power in 1963.

Attending local schools, Assad became involved in politics as head of the students' committee organising demonstrations against French rule. He joined the Arab Socialist (Ba'ath) party when he was 16. Between 1952 and 1955 he attended the Air Force College at the military academy in Homs, after which he entered the air force with the rank of lieutenant. In 1958 he went to the Soviet Union for further training. On his return in 1959 he was posted to lead a night-combat squadron in Cairo at the time of the union of Syria and Egypt as the United Arab Republic. While there he helped to form the Ba'athist Military Committee, which opposed the secession of Syria from the union in 1961, costing Assad his commission.

On 8 March 1963 the military committee seized power in Syria. Assad, promoted to general, became commander of the air force and minister of defence. He held these posts at the time of the Arab–Israeli Six-Day war in June 1967 in which Syria was heavily defeated and suffered the humiliating loss of the Golan Heights. Assad continued to develop his power base within the military, however, and to identify with a nationalistic faction in the Ba'ath party, which grew increasingly disillusioned with the more doctrinaire Marxist policies of its civilian leadership.

In 1970, having refused to commit his air force in an abortive attempt to come to the aid of Palestinians in Jordan, Assad used this fiasco as a pretext for a military-based coup, seizing power on 13 November as leader of the "Rectification Movement". He became prime minister and secretary-general of the Ba'ath party, and his election as president was confirmed by a national referendum the following March.

In an initial process of apparent liberalisation, he allowed more scope in the economy for private enterprise and trade, relaxed laws on freedom of speech and travel, and re-established the People's Council. Elections held in 1973 under a new constitution (defining Syria as a democratic, socialist state) resulted in an overwhelming victory for the Ba'ath-dominated National Progressive Front.

Externally, Assad promoted an effectively stillborn Federation of Arab Republics with Egypt and Libya, and in 1973 joined other Arab states in attacking Israel in an unsuccessful attempt to reclaim the territory lost in 1967. This conflict, together with Assad's strong backing at this time for the Palestine Liberation Organization (PLO) and for other Arab groups engaging in acts of violence, contributed to Western governments' condemnation of Assad's regime as a supporter of terrorism.

Assad was meanwhile establishing a reputation for the ruthless suppression of opposition within Syria. The Muslim Brotherhood, a fundamentalist movement among the majority Sunni population, conducted a protracted insurgency against the Ba'athist regime until it was effectively crushed by the massacre at Hama in February 1982, in which thousands of people were killed. Assad's internal security structures have been designed to divide power between a handful of men in charge of well-separated segments, so that only he has overall control. His initial reliance on family members was reduced after 1983, when he suffered a heart attack as a result of his diabetes and suspected his brother Rifaat of using this to plot against him. Until 1994 his son Bassil, a charismatic figure particularly popular with the armed forces, was generally seen as the heir apparent. Bassil's death in a car accident in 1994 left the question of the succession wide open, raising the likelihood of some kind of collective leadership so that the Alawi elite could incorporate key figures from the Sunni majority population. However, another of Assad's four sons, Bashar, returned to Syria upon his elder brother's death and has been given an army post and, more recently, responsibility for Syrian interests in Lebanon, amid signs that he could be an eventual successor.

Assad maintains a strongly anti-Zionist line, and there has been little relaxation in the mutual hostility between Syria and Israel, particularly during Israel's period of heavy military involvement in Lebanon in the 1980s. The return of the Israeli-occupied Golan Heights remains Assad's irreducible "land for peace" demand to unblock this aspect of the Middle East peace process. However, there has been a significant change in the way Assad's regime is perceived, in the USA and France in particular. One factor in this has been successful Syrian involvement in Lebanon to end the faction-based conflict there. Another is the ending of the cold war, during which Syria had been identified as a pro-Soviet state. Most importantly, Assad has long opposed the aspirations of Iraqi leader **Saddam Hussein** for regional dominance. He backed Iran in the Iran–Iraq war of the 1980s, and his anti-Iraqi stance in the 1991 Gulf war went so far as the hitherto unthinkable decision to commit Syrian forces on the side of the US-led coalition. US aid to Syria remained for the most part debarred, however, by the retention of Syria on the list of states supporting terrorism.

Aung San Suu Kyi

Frail in appearance but steadfast in her determination, Aung San Suu Kyi has gained worldwide recognition as a symbol of hope for Burma's pro-democracy campaign. She gave up the life of an expatriate academic in 1988, drawn to a movement which valued the association with her father Aung San, Burma's pre-independence leader. Suu Kyi became a founder and leader of the National League for Democracy (NLD), putting pressure on the repressive military regime until elections were held in May 1990. The NLD was prevented from forming a government after its sweeping victory, however, by a fresh military clampdown. Frequently isolated and under house arrest until 1995, Suu Kyi has made herself impossible to ignore, and has continued to rally international condemnation of the regime. She has refused the temptation of recent offers to allow her to go abroad – even when her husband was dying in England – because of the likelihood of being prevented from returning to her people.

Daw Aung San Suu Kyi was born on 19 June 1945 in Rangoon, Burma. She is a member of one of the country's most eminent political families. Her father, Gen. Aung San, had been leader of the Burmese independence movement, but was assassinated in July 1947, the year before independence. Her mother, Daw Khin Kyi, was a diplomat who served as Burma's ambassador to India in 1961. Suu Kyi was educated in Rangoon until the age of 15 and then in Delhi, where she attended the St Francis Convent, the Methodist English High School and Delhi University's Lady Shri Ram College. From 1964 to 1967 she studied at St Hugh's College, Oxford, from where she graduated with a degree in politics, philosophy and economics. In 1969 she was appointed to the UN secretariat in New York as assistant secretary to the administrative committee, leaving in 1971 to take up a post as research officer at the ministry of foreign affairs in Thimpu, Bhutan.

After her marriage to a British academic in 1972, she returned to the UK where she settled for several years in London and Oxford. Her husband Michael Aris, with whom she has two sons, pursued his academic career, teaching Tibetan studies at Oxford University, and they raised their family, while Suu Kyi also conducted research, working on a biography of her father and his wartime activities in Japan. In 1985 she won a visiting fellowship to the Centre of Southeast Asian Studies at Kyoto University, and in 1987 was named a fellow of the Indian Institute of Advanced Studies in Simla.

It was during one of her many brief and frequent visits to Rangoon in March 1988 that Suu Kyi's life was irrevocably changed. Intending to care for her ailing mother and open a library in her father's name, she was instead propelled to the forefront of a pro-democracy movement that had suddenly erupted following the resignation of Burma's military dictator, Gen. Ne Win, as head of the ruling Burma Socialist Programme Party. The movement escalated, and in early August a brutal crackdown by the regime led to the killing of thousands of protesters. Suu Kyi joined the demonstrations, revolted by the government's actions and inspired by the faith of her supporters, many of whom were admirers of her father. On 26 August she addressed a mass rally attended by an estimated 500,000 people in front of Rangoon's famous Shwedagon Pagoda where she called for the restoration of democracy. Her appeal was harshly rejected by the ruling military junta which on 18 September re-established itself as the State Law and Order Restoration Council (SLORC) and ordered a fresh crackdown on protesters, killing hundreds more.

Faced with the imperative need for organised resistance to the regime, Suu Kyi mobilised her followers and on 24 September announced the formation of the National League for Democracy (NLD), of which she became general secretary. For the next ten months she toured the country waging a non-violent campaign against what she termed the "fascist government". On 20 July 1989 she was arrested under martial law regulations and placed under house arrest.

The arrest of Suu Kyi provoked international outrage and forced the military junta, under threat of severe economic sanctions, to organise elections in May 1990. The NLD was overwhelmingly successful at the polls, winning by a landslide, which would have given it a clear majority in the parliament. However, the regime refused to honour the results and suppressed all dissent. Suu Kyi herself remained under house arrest, forbidden from communicating with her family, but defiantly refusing all suggestions from the regime that she should leave Burma or abandon her movement in order to obtain her personal liberty. Her courage and resilience won her widespread international support and a host of human rights awards, including the 1991 Nobel Peace Prize.

Mounting international pressure and Burma's dependence on foreign aid compelled the regime to open talks with Suu Kyi in late 1994. On 10 July 1995 she was released from house arrest but remained under heavy guard, denied access to journalists and allowed only limited contacts with foreign diplomats and party members. Nevertheless, she defied the junta by denouncing its plans for a constitutional convention and calling on the international community to boycott Burma until the inauguration of the parliament which had been elected back in 1990. In October 1996 she won the backing of US President **Bill Clinton**, who announced his support for a congressional bill to ban US investment in Burma if the military authorities continued to harass Suu Kyi.

More recently, as in her latest stand-off with the regime from August 1998 onwards over restrictions to her freedom of movement, such harassment has compounded fears that Suu Kyi's state of health may have been permanently damaged. In 1999 her husband, himself suffering from prostate cancer, unsuccessfully sought permission to visit her in Burma, where the authorities played an apparently cynical game by offering her instead the chance to go to the UK to see him. Her fortitude in refusing this, lest she be denied re-entry to Burma afterwards, had the tragic outcome that Michael Aris died on 23 March 1999 without seeing her again.

Author amongst other books of *Freedom from Fear and Other Writings*, which was published in the year she won the Nobel Prize, Suu Kyi has been a resolute advocate of the power of persuasion rather than violence to overcome the regime she has opposed with such determination.

Silvio **Berlusconi**

Silvio Berlusconi first made his name as Italy's foremost media magnate, then built a political career on the back of his business success. Initially he seemed unstoppable, becoming prime minister in 1994 at the head of a right-wing alliance within months of first forming his Forza Italia *party. His government lasted a mere nine months, however, tearing itself apart over economic policy and collapsing in disputes with his neo-fascist coalition partners. Having presented* Forza Italia *as a fresh and dynamic alternative to the old and terminally corrupt party system, Berlusconi was himself caught up in the web of political funding corruption. In opposition, he retains the leadership of his party, but his effectiveness is much impaired by his preoccupation with fighting a conviction for bribery and other criminal charges. In 1999 he still ranked among Europe's top ten richest men and the world's top 50, with a fortune of some US$7 billion.*

Silvio Berlusconi was born on 29 September 1936 in Milan, the son of a banker. His entrepreneurial skills were already evident at school where he did homework for fellow pupils, charging for his services on a sliding scale depending upon the marks awarded. As a student of law at the University of Milan, his close friends included Bettino Craxi, who was later to become leader of the socialist party and prime

minister. Milan remains Berlusconi's home, where he now lives with his second wife, the actress Veronica Bartolini; he has three children by this marriage and two from his first marriage.

After graduation Berlusconi established his own construction and property companies, Cantieri Riuniti Milanesi and Edilnord, in the early 1960s. With these he built up significant property holdings, including the Milan suburb known as Milano 2, on which he began construction in 1969 and which eventually housed 10,000 people.

In the 1970s his business career began to focus increasingly on the media interests for which he was to become best known. In 1974 he founded the cable television company Telemilano, which serviced Milano 2, and the following year he set up Fininvest as the holding company for his growing empire. To circumvent legislation under which only the state-run television service RAI was permitted to broadcast nationally, he set up a network of regional companies, which achieved *de facto* nationwide coverage by broadcasting the same programmes simultaneously. His own television channel, Canale 5, began broadcasting in 1980. He bought Italy's other two main private television stations, Italia Uno and Rete 4, in 1983 and 1984 respectively.

Having also moved successfully into the advertising business and built up Publitalia to make it the largest advertising agency in Europe, Berlusconi diversified his holdings during the 1980s to include the print media, publishing (including the country's largest publishing concern, Mondadori), the film industry (including the largest cinema chain, Cinema 5), retailing (including the largest chain of department stores, La Standa), insurance, financial services, and the football team AC Milan. His success in business was based on the combination of commercial acumen and ruthlessness, backed up by an ability to operate the political system to advantage and good high-level connections. His opponents allege that this extended to exploiting links with the freemasons and the Mafia. Berlusconi was a member of the notorious clandestine P-2 masonic lodge, uncovered in 1981 and subsequently outlawed, although he has denied being actively involved in its dealings.

The opportunity for Berlusconi the business phenomenon to become Berlusconi the political leader came with the upheavals of the early 1990s. Ever-widening judicial investigations mounted by magistrates into kick-back payments and related scandals began to unravel the web of endemic corruption and bribery through which the traditional parties, both socialist and Christian democratic, had wielded power at the local and national level. The impact of the so-called *mani pulite* (clean hands) operation was to discredit the old parties and thus to transform the political landscape. Berlusconi entered the fray with the formation in January 1994 of *Forza Italia*, a political party named after the Italian football supporters' chant, which translates loosely as "Come on, Italy!". He proceeded to form a right-wing Freedom Alliance for the March 1994 general election, embracing *Forza Italia*, the separatist Northern League, the neo-fascist National Alliance and other smaller right-wing parties.

Berlusconi's successful populist campaign was greatly strengthened by his ownership of 85 per cent of commercial television and 20 per cent of the domestic publishing market. The Freedom Alliance secured a majority of seats in the Chamber of Deputies and Berlusconi, as leader of its largest party, was able to form a coalition government in May 1994.

His coalition proved divisive and short-lived, however. He was criticised for appointing his own nominees to key public positions. In July he was obliged after a public outcry to withdraw a decree which ended the preventive detention of corruption and bribery suspects (who by then included Berlusconi's brother and a Fininvest director).

He also failed to tackle economic problems, including reducing the public debt and reorganising the public sector. The draft budget, which focused on cuts in pensions and health care and thus penalised the lower paid, provoked widespread protests and a sharp fall in the value of the lira and of the Milan stock exchange in November. Further, Berlusconi received a summons in November in connection with his alleged bribery of tax inspectors, finally prompting the increasingly disaffected Northern League to withdraw from the coalition and obliging Berlusconi to resign in December 1994.

Since his resignation as prime minister Berlusconi has remained at the head of *Forza Italia*. The party saw its support fall slightly in the April 1996 general election, which brought to power a centre-left coalition of the Olive Tree Alliance led by the moderate **Romano Prodi**.

Berlusconi's political position has been undermined further by the progress of corruption investigations implicating him personally. In December 1997 he was convicted on charges of false accounting over a 1987 film company deal and given a 16-month suspended sentence. In two judgements delivered in July 1998 he was found guilty of bribing tax inspectors and of illegally funding Craxi's socialists during the 1980s to the tune of 22 billion lire. He was sentenced to over five years' imprisonment and a fine of 10 billion lire (£3 million) but remains free pending the outcome of appeals. He still faces other corruption charges, as well as allegations of money laundering for the Mafia.

Benazir **Bhutto**

Twice prime minister of Pakistan and still only in her forties, Benazir Bhutto has had a political career of extraordinary vicissitudes. Groomed for politics with an elite education, but instead plunged into a protest struggle when her father's regime was overthrown, she came to power – via prison and exile – on a wave of popular support as the first ever female head of government in an Islamic country. Undermined in office by persistent accusations of corruption and removed from power by presidential intervention, she gradually recovered the political ascendancy, only to lose her way in government once again. Ousted for a second time, and trounced at the polls in 1997, her ability to make yet another comeback cannot be discounted, despite the seriousness of corruption charges and the threat of a death penalty against her widely unpopular husband.

Benazir Bhutto was born into a wealthy land-owning family on 21 June 1953 in Karachi, Pakistan, the eldest daughter of prominent politician Zulfiqar Ali Bhutto, who later founded the Pakistan People's Party (PPP) and became prime minister in 1971. Benazir enjoyed a privileged upbringing in Pakistan, attending the Presentation Convent School, before going abroad to be educated at Radcliffe College in the USA and at Oxford University in the UK. In 1973 she was elected president of the Oxford Union and in 1977 was awarded a degree in international law.

Benazir Bhutto's entry into politics, for which she had been groomed by her father, was precipitated by a military coup in July 1977 and the imposition of a death sentence on her father. Within days she returned to Pakistan, launching a campaign that failed ultimately to prevent his execution in 1979. She went on to play a critical role in founding the Movement for the Restoration for Democracy, announced in 1981. In December 1993 she inherited her father's mantle by becoming leader of the PPP outright, having shared the post with her mother, Nusrat Bhutto, since 1977.

Repeatedly incarcerated by the military authorities between 1977 and 1984, she nevertheless continued to press for fresh elections and an end to martial law. Her courage and resilience in the face of a particularly harsh regime won her support and admiration at home and abroad. In 1985 her failing health forced the military regime to grant her permission to seek medical treatment abroad. From exile she continued her campaign and won the support of several Western governments, including that of the USA.

In April 1986 she returned to Pakistan and embarked on a campaign of agitation that resulted in some of the largest pro-democracy rallies ever witnessed in the country. In August 1988 Gen. Zia ul-Haq, head of the military regime and Bhutto's bitter opponent, died in a plane crash. The event opened the way for a rapid transfer of power from military to civilian hands. A general election held in November 1988 produced a PPP majority, propelling Benazir Bhutto into power as prime minister for the first time.

In office from 1988 to 1990, Bhutto's government was hailed at the outset for its "modern" outlook and its rejection of the hardline Islamic policies pursued by the former military regime. Her equivocal stance on socialist principles, generally identified with the PPP, also won her the backing of the feudal and industrial elite in the provinces of Sind and Punjab. However, the euphoria was short-lived. The administration was soon mired in controversy as allegations surfaced of rampant corruption in official circles. At the centre of the scandal was Bhutto's businessman husband, Asif Ali Zardari, the father of her three children, whom she had married in 1987 and whose involvement in a series of dubious land deals had earned him the nickname "Mr 10 per cent". Bhutto's own vulnerability was compounded by her strained relations with the army and her alienation from large sections of the PPP. In August 1990 she was removed from office by a presidential decree and charged with corruption and the abuse of power.

Although none of the allegations were substantiated, they contributed decisively to the PPP's defeat in the general election held in October 1990. Bhutto retained her own seat in parliament, however, and in opposition she rapidly regained her political ground, aided by an emerging constitutional struggle between the new prime minister, Nawaz Sharif, and President Ghulam Ishaq Khan. In July 1993 Khan dismissed Sharif's government. This provided Bhutto with an opportunity to make a fresh bid for power; a general election in October returned the PPP with a slender majority and she became prime minister for the second time (1993–96).

Pressures mounted quickly as her government battled to control a spiral of vicious ethnic violence in Sind, to counter renewed allegations of corruption involving Zardari (now nicknamed "Mr 40 per cent"), and to head off a leadership challenge mounted by her brother Murtaza Bhutto. Murtaza was killed in a shoot-out with police in September 1996. In November 1996 Bhutto's virtually paralysed administration was dismissed from office by President Farooq Leghari. The PPP's loss of popular support was reflected in its massive electoral defeat in February 1997.

Out of office, Benazir Bhutto faced an uncertain future as she prepared to stand trial on charges of corruption, and to weigh the consequences of a possible death penalty for her husband, who was jailed in 1997 on charges of organising the murder of Murtaza. She chose to stay abroad when the high court in Lahore charged her and her husband in October 1998 with taking large "commissions" in return for giving contracts to two Swiss companies, SGS and Cotecna. Although she denied the charges, describing them as a politically motivated attempt to ruin her career, a Swiss court had already indicted Zardari and officials of the two companies for taking commissions and for money laundering. In April 1999 the Pakistani courts sentenced her and her husband to five years' imprisonment on the first of a series of charges. Bhutto, in London at the time, declared her intention of returning to Pakistan to challenge the verdict of what she described as a political witch-hunt.

Tony **Blair**

Tony Blair, prime minister of the UK since May 1997, represents a new generation in the country's top leadership. His election victory followed his effective refashioning of the Labour Party into a disciplined political movement of the centre, to which he consistently refers as New Labour to emphasise the move away from class-based politics. In government Blair has encouraged the idea of a "Third Way", based on aligning the free market with social welfare objectives. His success has changed the political balance in the UK, encouraged emulators abroad, and allowed him to assume a prominent role in international affairs, most evident in his promotion of Western military action against Yugoslavia over the Kosovo crisis.

Anthony Charles Lynton Blair was born on 6 May 1953 in Edinburgh. For three years in the mid-1950s his family lived in Australia. After their return, his father, a law lecturer and industrial tribunal chairman, held a university post in Durham, where Tony attended Durham Cathedral School. His father suffered a stroke in 1963 while campaigning as a Conservative candidate for a seat in parliament, and

thereafter, as Blair said in a 1994 interview, "transferred his ambitions on to his kids". Tony Blair went to Fettes College, Edinburgh, and then to Oxford, where he studied law at St John's College, graduating in 1975.

During his time in Oxford he was lead singer and bass guitarist in a college rock band called Ugly Rumours, and he then worked briefly in Paris as a bartender and insurance clerk before resuming his legal training. Called to the Bar at Lincoln's Inn in 1976, he practised as a barrister until 1983, specialising in employment and industrial law. Tony Blair met Cherie Booth when they were both working in the barristers' chambers headed by Alexander (Derry) Irvine, later the Lord Chancellor. He and Cherie married in 1980; she is a barrister and a Queen's Counsel, and she and Tony have two sons, born respectively in 1984 and 1986, and a daughter born in 1989. Blair has been a committed Christian since his student days, his religious faith being an integral element in his political beliefs. A member of the Anglican Church, he also frequently attends mass in the Catholic Church to which his wife Cherie belongs, and in which their three children have been brought up.

Blair joined the Labour Party in 1975 and was elected to parliament in June 1983, the year the party suffered the heaviest defeat in its history. He held his seat, in the traditionally safe Labour constituency of Sedgefield in County Durham, at successive elections in 1987, 1992 and 1997, increasing his majority from some 8,200 in 1983 to over 25,000 in 1997.

Between 1984 and 1994, when he became Labour Party leader, Blair held a series of posts as "shadow" spokesman, representing the Labour Party (as the official opposition in parliament) on issues dealt with by specific government departments, and in 1988 was elected to the shadow cabinet. From 1984 to 1987 he was treasury spokesman, with special responsibility for consumer affairs and the City (London's financial sector). From 1987 to 1988 he was trade and industry spokesman. In 1988 he became shadow secretary of state for energy, then for employment (1989–92), in which role he forged a new industrial relations policy, ending Labour's support for the so-called "closed shop" or compulsory union membership in particular workplaces. After the Labour defeat in the 1992 election Blair was promoted to shadow secretary of state for home affairs under a new party leader, John Smith.

Shortly after Labour's 1992 election defeat Blair and the then shadow chancellor of the exchequer, Gordon Brown, visited the USA on a fact-finding mission, holding discussions with Democratic Party campaign chiefs to discuss tactics for getting the Labour Party elected to government. During his time as shadow secretary of state for home affairs Blair coined the phrase "Tough on crime, tough on the causes of crime", which was used as a key Labour campaign theme.

In September 1992 Blair was elected to Labour's national executive committee, the ruling body of the party. Together with John Prescott, he led the drive to turn Labour into a mass membership party (whereas in the past the Labour membership had been dominated by affiliated trade unions, wielding "block" votes at party conferences proportionate to their size). By 1997 Labour had more than 400,000 individual members, making it one of the fastest-growing parties in Europe.

In May 1994 John Smith died suddenly of a heart attack. An election for the leadership and deputy leadership of the party followed. Blair put himself forward as a candidate for the leadership, despite what was reportedly an earlier informal understanding between himself and Gordon Brown that he would back a Brown candidacy if the leadership became vacant. Brown stood aside from the contest and Blair came top of the poll, ahead of John Prescott (who became deputy leader).

Tony Blair thus became Labour leader on 21 July 1994 at the age of 41, the youngest leader of the party in its history. He immediately grasped the symbolic nettle in terms of modernising the party's policy platform, proposing at the party conference that October the abolition of Clause IV in the party constitution, on the nationalisation of the key elements of the economy. The abolition of Clause IV was approved in 1995. The way the party agonised over this issue foreshadowed the first of the disagreements between so-called "Old Labour" and "New Labour" within the party in government – disagreements which first came into the open in late 1997 over proposed reforms in the welfare benefits system, which were criticised as damaging vulnerable groups such as single mothers and the disabled.

Blair brought a youthful image and a reorganised structure to his party, tightening up its discipline and placing stronger emphasis on presentation and on the "market testing" of policy initiatives. He constantly referred to the party as New Labour, in order to emphasise the distance it had travelled from the days when it was perceived as a union-dominated, pro-welfare socialist party defending the interests of the working class. Having published a manifesto with a highly personalised statement promising "a new and distinctive approach ... that differs from the old left and the Conservative right", and the use of modern means to deliver on a ten-point "contract with the people", Blair led his Labour Party to a landslide victory in the 1 May 1997 general election. After 18 years of Conservative government, the first Labour administration to hold power since 1979 took office amid a wave of optimistic enthusiasm. In government Blair continued to stress the notion of Britain as a "young country", while identifying its institutions and public services as belonging to the people, notwithstanding the role of private enterprise in running and delivering them.

Measures introduced by the Blair government in its first months in power included plans to create a Scottish Parliament and a Welsh Assembly; a decision to adhere to the social chapter of the Maastricht Treaty on European Union, relating to conditions of employment, but to defer until after the next election any decision on joining a single European currency; and controversial changes in the arrangements for providing financial support to university students, whereby they would be required to pay a proportion of their tuition fees. Having placed much emphasis on presentation, the government began to be pilloried in the press for apparent flaws in its image, notably over its handling of welfare reform, the use of an offshore investment tax shelter by one of its economics ministers, and the acceptance from a motor racing company of a large contribution to party funds. The contribution was subsequently returned to rebut the charge that it had had any connection with the exclusion of motor racing from new rules which barred tobacco companies from advertising at, or sponsoring, sporting events.

Blair himself, however, retained remarkably high personal popularity throughout the first two years of his premiership. This remained apparently unaffected by the occasional adverse publicity for his party or government, or by the accusation of hypocrisy on education when his elder son was enrolled in a grant-maintained Catholic school in another part of London, rather than the state secondary school local to his family home in Islington. Nor did there prove to be much mileage in the efforts of commentators to create "divided New Labour" headlines out of any signs of past or present rivalries or political differences between him and Chancellor of the Exchequer Gordon Brown.

The main achievements with which Blair was personally most identified during this period included providing the impetus to drive the Northern Ireland peace process forward, to the point where the Good Friday agreement was signed by the various parties in April 1998 (although subsequently it became mired in protracted disagreements about implementation).

Referendums were also successfully held on the establishment of the Scottish Parliament and Welsh Assembly, both duly elected in May 1999.

The measure of Blair's political strength, however, appeared to be not so much the sum of the achievements of his government, but the credibility with which he cultivated his quasi-presidential image. In this regard, two aspects stood out. The first was his presentation of New Labour's political philosophy as part of the evolution of a "Third Way", essentially the yoking of free-market economics with social welfare considerations, promoted by public–private sector partnerships and guided by consultation with "stakeholder" groups. Referring back to his manifesto promise of "a new and distinctive approach...that differs from the old left and the Conservative right", exponents of the "Third Way" also welcomed the ascendancy of like-minded politicians (notably **Gerhard Schröder**, the German chancellor elected in 1998) across western Europe.

The second and increasingly important aspect of Blair's leadership image was his enhanced role on the world stage. This involved a shift in the balance of his relationship with US President **Bill Clinton**, coinciding with the erosion of the latter's claim to moral authority as a result of his entanglement in sordid domestic scandal. Blair's emphatic espousal of a Western military response in March/June 1999, to compel Serbian forces to withdraw from Kosovo and thus to end the "ethnic cleansing" and refugee crisis there, was reinforced by his high level of confidence that sustained bombing was necessary and right. By contrast with Clinton, he also showed confidence in the judgement that an invasion by ground forces, if it proved necessary, would command widespread support. His unequivocal commitment to this policy was described by some commentators as marking his assumption of the mantle of leader of the Atlantic Alliance, however nonsensical that notion might be in terms of the relative strength of the UK and the USA.

Boutros **Boutros Ghali**

For years a top foreign policy specialist in the Egyptian government, and credited with a major role in shaping the 1978 Camp David agreement with Israel, Boutros Boutros Ghali reached the summit of his career with a five-year term as UN secretary-general (1992–96). The first Arab – and the first from the African continent – to hold this post, the multilingual Boutros Ghali is from his country's minority Coptic Christian community, while his second wife Leia Maria is the daughter of a Jewish rabbi. Boutros Ghali's term of office saw him increasingly at odds with US policy, during a new phase in international relations where the USA was the sole global superpower. Moreover, his sometimes disdainful manner made him enemies at UN headquarters, where he was also criticised for failing to take a sufficient grip on organisational reform. These tensions, and friction over the cash crisis at the UN, led to the USA openly opposing his reappointment, and he eventually withdrew his candidacy for a second term.

Boutros Boutros Ghali was born in Cairo, Egypt, on 14 November 1922. His grandfather, Boutros Ghali Pasha, was Egypt's first Coptic prime minister and one of the three Egyptian prime ministers to be assassinated in office, in 1910. His father, Youssef Boutros Ghali, was a prominent member of Egypt's landed gentry. The young Boutros received his early education in French at a succession of exclusive *lycées* in Cairo, administered by Jesuit priests. He is also fluent in English and Arabic. In 1946 he graduated with a degree in law from Cairo University and in 1949 was awarded a doctorate in international law from the University of Paris (Sorbonne).

From 1949 to 1977 Boutros Boutros Ghali was professor of international law at Cairo University. During this lengthy period he also held the posts of Fulbright research scholar at Columbia University in New York (1954/55), director of the Centre for Research of the Hague Academy of International Law, and visiting professor at the faculty of law at the Sorbonne (1967/68). In addition to his academic career, Boutros Ghali was a successful journalist who founded the publication *Al Ahram Iqtisadi*, which he edited from 1960 to 1975, and the quarterly *Al Siyasa al Dawlia*, which he edited until December 1991.

In October 1977 he entered government, serving as minister of state for foreign affairs until 1991. However, his political career was really launched when, following the resignation of the then foreign minister, Ismail Fahmi, he was called upon to act as his replacement and accompany President Sadat on his historic visit to Israel in November 1977. There his skills as a diplomat made a lasting impression which was to propel him to the very centre of the Arab–Israeli peace process. In September 1978 he attended the summit conference at Camp David in the USA which brought together President Sadat,

Israeli Prime Minister Menachem Begin and US President Jimmy Carter. He played a key role in framing the so-called Camp David peace accords signed at this time between Egypt and Israel.

In 1980 he consolidated his position within the Egyptian political establishment by being appointed to the secretariat of the ruling National Democratic Party. As Egypt's most prominent diplomat he also enjoyed a high international profile, representing his country at meetings of the Organization of African Unity (OAU) and the Non-aligned Movement, as well as leading Egypt's delegation to the UN General Assembly in 1979, 1982 and 1990. In 1987 he became a member of parliament and in May 1991 he was named deputy prime minister with responsibility for foreign affairs.

He was nominated by the UN Security Council in November 1991, and approved by the General Assembly in December, as the UN's sixth secretary-general, in succession to **Javier Pérez de Cuéllar**. One of the most important tasks facing Boutros Ghali at the start of his five-year tenure in January 1992 was the administrative and financial reform of the UN and the reappraisal of the UN's role in the post-cold-war era. His handling of both issues was dogged by controversy. Although he introduced some reforms, especially financial ones, he was criticised for not going far enough to curb waste, corruption and mismanagement within the UN. Similarly, while he was clearly committed to expanding the UN's influence through its peacekeeping activities, the organisation's credibility in this role was severely damaged by high-profile failures, such as the debacle of being unable to protect the so-called "safe havens" in Bosnia-Herzegovina, and the opprobrium of being sidelined and unable to take action to halt genocide in

Rwanda. Boutros Ghali's endorsement of military intervention in Somalia in 1992 also ended up seriously undermining his standing when the UN was forced to abort that mission in 1994. His pro-Western reputation among third world countries was insufficient to endear him to the USA, with which he clashed repeatedly over Middle East policy and over US arrears of payment due the UN.

The USA's growing hostility to Boutros Ghali came to a head in July 1996 when it formally announced that it would veto his candidacy for a second term, citing his failure to pursue reform. The threatened US veto was duly implemented on 19 November in a formal vote in the Security Council. Although he had initially been prepared to defy the US threat by seeking the support of his most powerful backer on the Security Council, France, and its allies, Boutros Ghali recognised defeat and withdrew his candidacy in early December 1996. In January 1997 he was succeeded by the Ghanaian **Kofi Annan**.

A prolongation of his career on the international diplomatic stage, albeit in a role with a lower profile, was ensured when in November 1997, two days after his 75th birthday, he was chosen as the first secretary-general of the group of Francophone countries (La Francophonie). His nomination, at the movement's summit meeting in Hanoi, was accepted by consensus after the withdrawal of a rival candidate from Benin, and he was at pains to dismiss suggestions that his candidacy had been foisted on the conference with the personal support of French President **Jacques Chirac**. Charged with helping the movement gain a more permanent role in the international arena as the expression of distinctive Francophone perspectives, he was to serve a four-year term heading its new Paris-based secretariat.

Richard **Branson**

Richard Branson frequently features in UK opinion polls as the business executive most admired by the younger generation, and even as a hypothetical candidate for the presidency if the monarchy were abolished. An entrepreneur with a talent for showmanship, he has maintained his informal and glamorous image, recently manifested in his hot-air ballooning adventures, since he first achieved national notice in the record business in the early 1970s. Branson's Virgin Group is an international conglomerate with an annual turnover of several billion pounds, and he himself is a billionaire. Virgin, built around music retailing and travel, has branched out into various other areas, notably financial services, but has nevertheless retained a strong brand image closely associated with Branson's own persona. Its growth owes much to his astuteness in identifying markets where Virgin can compete favourably in terms of delivering consumer satisfaction, although there have been setbacks; recently, his venture into rail services has proven problematic.

Richard Charles Nicholas Branson was born on 18 July 1950 in Shamley Green, Surrey, the son of Edward James Branson. After a privileged but rebellious school career, ending at Stowe School, he decided against going to university. Instead, following up on his experience with *The Student* (a national newspaper for school students), he started a mail-order record company, Virgin Mail Order (1970). The postal strikes of 1971 almost doomed his new business before it had a chance to start, and so he quickly opened a small record shop in London's Oxford Street as an alternative sales outlet. In 1972 the first Virgin recording studio opened in Oxfordshire, and in 1973 Branson founded the Virgin record label, which scored an early success with its first recording, Mike Oldfield's *Tubular Bells*, the biggest-selling record of the 1970s. Virgin Music later went on to sign up such leading artists as the Rolling Stones, the Sex Pistols, Janet Jackson and Phil Collins.

By the early 1980s Virgin had expanded its activities to include the Virgin Games software publishing company and Virgin Vision, a film and video distributor which later went on to become a TV and film producer in its own right. Many of its record stores had expanded into Virgin Megastores (selling software, videos and merchandised products as well as records), and Virgin was also operating several nightclubs. It had entertainment subsidiaries in many other countries.

Branson, by now thinking of business possibilities outside the entertainment sector, opened a property development company in 1983, Vanson Developments, which specialised in retail, commercial and residential property. The following year the company bought interests in luxury hotels – initially in Majorca and later in the Caribbean. More significantly, 1984 also saw the launch of Virgin Atlantic Airways and Virgin Cargo. Beginning with services between London, New York, Tokyo, Orlando and Los Angeles, the new long-haul carrier made a rapid impact with its high-class services to Hong Kong, Miami, Boston, Johannesburg and Athens.

(Virgin does not cover short-haul destinations.) However, Virgin Atlantic quickly became embroiled in a bitter courtroom dispute with British Airways. Branson accused BA of using "dirty tricks" to divert potential Virgin customers on to its own air routes, in an apparent effort to drive its new challenger out of business. Although the affair eventually ended in a £610,000 libel award to Branson and Virgin, the undeniable financial pressures which Virgin Atlantic suffered as a result eventually forced Branson to sell the Virgin Music Group (recordings, music publishing and recording studios) to the Thorn EMI entertainment group for US$1 billion.

Branson has also promoted the development of the Virgin name on the Internet, creating a low-cost Internet service provider aimed mainly at household users. Virgin's own brands of cola and of condoms have been making major inroads into their respective UK markets, and Virgin Radio/Ginger Media (in partnership with the radio and television presenter Chris Evans) have been highly successful within the broadcasting field. More significant in the long term, perhaps, has been the development since 1996 of Virgin Direct financial services, which now sells pensions, tax-efficient savings plans and index-tracker investments.

Undeterred by the apparently shapeless spread of his conglomerate empire (which currently comprises over 180 companies), Branson has recently taken the Virgin Group into UK rail services. The deregulation of Britain's rail network in the mid-1990s opened up an opportunity for Virgin to bid successfully for two regional rail franchises, which between them account for about 15 per cent of the national service network. By late 1998 the newly created Virgin Rail was the UK's second-largest rail service company, serving more than 100 towns and cities, although it was attracting negative publicity over service standards. Branson continued to pursue his flagship rail project, the restoration of the neglected west coast rail route between London and Scotland, including the provision of high-speed tilting trains between 2000 and 2002.

Branson has proved himself to be a natural self-publicist, and his love of physical adventure has created many opportunities to promote the Virgin brand. In 1986 his powerboat, Virgin Atlantic Challenger II, crossed the Atlantic in world record time. In 1987 his hot-air balloon, Virgin Atlantic Flyer, became the first such balloon to cross the Atlantic, and in 1991 he crossed the Pacific Ocean from Japan to Canada, his balloon covering the 6,700 miles at speeds of up to 245 miles per hour. However, his ballooning exploits have not been without drama; on more than one occasion, most recently in 1998, technical failures during his record-breaking attempts almost cost him his life, and in 1999 the achievement he had coveted, the first non-stop round-the-world balloon flight, went to a rival team.

Branson has been married twice – first to Kristen Branson (1969–71), and second to Joan Templeman in 1989. He has one son, Sam, and one daughter, Holly. His leisure interests, apart from ballooning, include sailing and, inevitably, rock music. In 1998 he published an autobiography entitled *Losing My Virginity*, and was enough of an exhibitionist to pose apparently naked in publicity shots with the book positioned to hide his private parts. Other Virgin advertising campaigns have also played on his "anti-establishment" hair style and penchant for colourfully patterned sweaters, to personalise the branding of products and services and to reinforce his own image for fun-loving irreverence.

Gro Harlem **Brundtland**

*Gro Harlem Brundtland is probably second only to **Margaret Thatcher** as the most prominent woman politician in Europe in the last quarter of the 20th century. Prime minister of Norway for over ten years between 1980 and 1996, and enormously popular in her own country, she became internationally known for chairing the UN's "Brundtland Commission", whose 1987 report,* Our Common Future, *linked the global themes of environment and development through the concept of sustainability. In 1998 she returned to global issues as director-general of the World Health Organization (WHO), having already been touted once as a potential candidate for the secretary-generalship of the UN itself.*

Gro Harlem was born on 20 April 1939 in Oslo, Norway, the daughter of Gudmund and Inga Harlem. Her father, a doctor specialising in rehabilitation medicine, also held government office as a cabinet minister between 1955 and 1965, as minister of social affairs and then of defence. During Gro's childhood the family lived in both the USA and Egypt, as her father took up a Rockefeller scholarship and then worked as a UN expert on rehabilitation. She was politically involved from a very early age, joining the children's section of the Norwegian Labour Movement at the age of seven.

While studying medicine at Oslo University, she was married in 1960 to Arne Olav Brundtland, a leading member of the Conservative Party who went on to become director of studies of foreign and security policy and senior research fellow at the Norwegian Institute of International Affairs (NUPI) in Oslo. They had three sons and one daughter, and there are now eight grandchildren.

Gro Harlem Brundtland qualified as a doctor in 1963 and gained a master's degree in public health from Harvard University two years later. Returning to Oslo, she worked as a consultant for the health and social affairs ministry from 1965 to 1967, advising on children's health, breastfeeding and cancer prevention. She also worked in the children's department in the national hospital and Oslo city hospital and became director of health for schoolchildren in the capital. During this time she also brought up her own family and began to develop a political profile, joining the Labour Party in 1969.

The political side of her career took off in 1974 when she joined the government to become minister of the environment, a post she was to hold until 1979. Stressing the links between environment and health issues, she successfully built a reputation both at home and abroad. She became deputy chair of the Labour Party in 1975 and was elected to parliament in 1977, continuing as an MP for the next 20 years. As such she led the Labour parliamentary group between 1981 and 1986 and again in 1989/90, served on the standing committees on finance and on foreign affairs, and chaired the standing committees on foreign affairs and on the constitution in 1980, from 1981 to 1986 and from 1989 to 1990.

In February 1981, when Odvar Nordli resigned as party leader and prime minister, she took on both posts, becoming the country's first woman prime minister at the age of 41. She was, however, obliged to resign as prime minister in October of the same year after the party performed poorly in the general election.

While in opposition, and still chairing the Labour Party, she was invited to set up and chair the World Commission on Environment and Development, which published its influential report entitled *Our Common Future* in April 1987. Her work on the Commission helped to establish the concept of sustainable development, and its recommendations eventually resulted in the holding of the UN's 1992 Earth Summit in Rio de Janeiro, Brazil.

Brundtland had two further periods as prime minister of Norway, from May 1986 to October 1989 and from November 1990 to October 1996. In all she held office for over a decade. She strongly supported Norwegian integration into the European Union, and in November 1992 submitted the country's second application for membership, although this application was rejected in a referendum in 1994, as the first had been two decades earlier.

In October 1996, notwithstanding her popularity with the Norwegian people, Brundtland stepped down as prime minister. She had previously made clear her intention of resigning, and her successor, Thorbjoern Jagland, had already taken over the Labour Party leadership from her in 1992, when she reduced her workload following the suicide of her youngest son. The timing of her resignation, however, fuelled speculation that she might be seeking election as UN secretary-general. This came to nothing, but it was not long before she did move on to the international stage again. Nominated as WHO director-general in January 1998, she was elected in May and took up office on 21 July 1998 as the organisation's first woman director-general.

The WHO post presented a particular challenge in view of the extent to which the organisation's reputation had deteriorated over the previous ten years, through poor management and incoherent policies. Brundtland immediately appointed a new ten-member team of executive directors (comprising six women, including herself, and four men, and drawn in equal numbers from countries of the developed North and the global South). She also introduced a code of conduct obliging all high-level staff to declare outside financial interests if they affected their independence.

Gro Harlem Brundtland is also first vice-president of the Socialist International and was a member of the UN's Independent Commission on Disarmament and Security Issues (the Palme Commission).

Warren **Buffett**

The world's biggest investor, Warren Buffett is a US financier with major holdings in globally recognised consumer product groups such as Gillette and Coca-Cola. He is the third richest man in America and fourth in the world, with a fortune valued at around US$30 billion. The diversified company through which he operates, Berkshire Hathaway, had a market capitalisation of US$110 billion as of April 1999. Buffett has a track record of perspicacity in share dealings which has earned him the nickname "the Sage of Omaha", his mid-West native town. His growing reputation as a shrewd and extremely wealthy speculator has elevated his public profile to a plane shared only by George Soros – one in which the global financial markets can be moved even by the rumour that he is about to act. Such is the weight of money at his disposal that Buffett's investment moves, especially when imitated by his many avid followers, may drive share prices in the direction from which he benefits most.

Warren Edward Buffett was born on 30 August 1930 in Omaha, Nebraska, the son of investment broker Howard H. Buffett, who was a four-term Republican member of Congress from Nebraska's 2nd District between 1943 and 1954. Educated at high school in Washington D.C., then at the Wharton School of Finance at the University of Pennsylvania (1947–49), he went on to obtain business degrees at the University of Nebraska (1950) and Columbia University (1951) before starting work as an investment salesman for his father's company. After a brief spell as a securities analyst with the New-York-based Graham-Newman Corporation (1954–56) he returned to Omaha, where he has been based ever since.

The Buffett Partnership, which Buffett inaugurated in 1956, quickly became famous for its success in handling general investment funds on behalf of its clients. A turning point in his career came during the 1960s when Buffett bought a small textile company known as Berkshire Hathaway. He quickly turned his new acquisition into a leading speculative venture company which traded on its own behalf. Buffett used the Berkshire Hathaway vehicle to make takeover bids, usually hostile, for other companies. As it accumulated banks, insurance companies, steel companies, food manufacturers, department stores and news organisations, it was already taking on the characteristics of a self-sufficient, integrated empire with powerful connections in minerals and commodities, news distribution and international speculative ventures. The company was repeatedly accused of letting itself get too close to the operational centres of various commodity trading scandals, but its reputation suffered no lasting harm; on the contrary, most investors took the view that its extraordinary investment record spoke for itself.

A further change of direction came in the mid-1980s, as a wave of corporate mergers and acquisitions swept the USA. Berkshire Hathaway quickly became a leading broker in merger arbitrage (greenmailing), often taking risky short-term shareholding positions in its efforts to promote company takeovers by third parties. On the strength of this extraordinarily predatory habit, Berkshire Hathaway managed to build up a body of 150,000 private investors who were prepared to pay well over book value for their shares in the company, placing their trust completely in Buffett's personal tactical abilities.

One such takeover battle, between American Broadcasting Companies (ABC) and Capital Cities, in 1985 left Buffett's company controlling a sizeable part of the resulting company. When ABC/Capital Cities fell to the Walt Disney Corporation for US$19 billion in 1995, his shareholders felt that they had good reason to value his negotiating skills.

Buffett found that he could make money even when he was defending other companies against takeover bids. A merger battle in 1987, in which he successfully defended the New-York-based Salomon Brothers from corporate raiders, left him with 12 per cent of that influential company's shares, and he then went on to become interim chairman and chief executive of Salomon in 1991/92, during a hiatus which was prompted by an investigation into illegal bond dealings by the company. Shrewd manoeuvrings in 1989 also left Buffett as the second-largest shareholder in the Coca-Cola Company, one of his core long-term stocks along with Gillette and *The Washington Post*.

Buffett's most recent major coup came in June 1998 with the announcement that Berkshire Hathaway was buying General Re, the largest reinsurance group in the USA, in a US$22 billion deal. The acquisition took Berkshire Hathaway's market value above US$100 billion – and, in the process, made it one of the five largest companies in the USA. A large part of the deal was financed by issuing Berkshire Hathaway shares to General Re.

Typical of the extent to which Buffett's dealings attract the attention of analysts and investors was the flurry of speculation which surrounded his decision in late 1998 to buy a substantial amount of silver. On the other hand, a foray into the volatile commodity markets seemed at odds with his advice to look at core investments in terms of their long-term potential rather than seeking short-term gains. As usual, Buffett gave away little in public statements; he is rarely available for interview. One theme which he had been stressing in 1998, however, was that investors could not expect continuing returns as high as those of the previous ten years, when the expanding US economy and low interest rates had provided what he called "an enormous tailwind" to help drive the rise in stock values.

Buffett married Susan Thompson in April 1952, and they have one daughter and two sons. A Democrat with some left-of-centre views who notably opposed abolition of capital gains tax, he is a supporter of the Planned Parenthood organisation which provides advice on contraception and, more controversially, on abortion.

George **Bush**

*A single-term US president (from January 1989 to January 1993), George Bush held office between the two-term presidencies of Ronald Reagan (the Republican in whose administration he was vice-president) and **Bill Clinton** (the Democrat who defeated him when he stood for re-election in 1992). Although he had been successful in the oil business in Texas, his background was a privileged New England upbringing, and he was notably lacking in public charisma; Bush's supporters never really took him to their hearts in the way the right loved Reagan. Nor was he able to engineer any electoral advantage from the sluggish economy in a period of severe budget deficit problems. Bush thus left office with his stature diminished, less than a year after reaching the pinnacle of his popularity during the Gulf war. His presidency, like his previous political career, had its high points in foreign affairs, coinciding as it did with the collapse of communism and the emergence of the USA as the world's unrivalled superpower.*

George Herbert Walker Bush was born on 12 June 1924 in Milton, Massachusetts. His father, Prescott Bush, a partner in a Wall Street investment firm, was active in Republican politics and was elected to the US Senate from Connecticut from 1952 to 1963. On his 18th birthday Bush graduated from the elite Phillips Academy in Andover and joined the US navy, becoming its youngest pilot and gaining a DFC in action in the Pacific war. In January 1945 he married Barbara Pierce and the strength of the family that they founded proved to be a durable political asset in his later career. Following his discharge from the navy, Bush studied economics at Yale University. After his graduation in 1948 the family moved to Texas, where Bush entered the oil industry, first as a salesman, then as co-founder of the Bush-Overbey Oil Development Company (1951), the Zapata Petroleum Corporation (1953) and Zapata Offshore (1954). He was president of Zapata Offshore from 1956 to 1964 and its chairman until 1966.

In 1964 Bush faced his first major political contest when he stood for the Senate as a strongly conservative Republican candidate. Although ultimately unsuccessful, he polled the highest vote ever achieved by a Republican in Texas. He also failed at his second attempt to enter the Senate in 1970. In the interim he served two terms (1966–68 and 1968–70) in the House of Representatives for 7th District, Texas, showing himself as naturally a more moderate political figure, in particular braving the hostility of many constituents to support a national open housing bill.

Appointed by President Nixon as ambassador to the UN from 1971 to 1973, Bush then returned to the centre of Republican politics as chair of the

Republican national committee (1973–74), with the difficult task of steering his party through the political fallout from the Watergate scandal. He enhanced his international reputation during a spell in Beijing as chief of the US liaison office (1974–76), during the period when Sino-US relations were being restored. From 1976 to 1977 Bush was director of the CIA.

In 1980 Bush ran against Ronald Reagan for the party's presidential nomination. He memorably disparaged Reagan's more right-wing policies as "voodoo economics" but Reagan soon dominated the primaries and Bush withdrew from the race. However, Reagan asked him to be his running mate and, following victory in the November 1980 election, Bush was sworn in on 20 January 1981 as vice-president. During his two terms in this office Bush chaired the crisis management team and task forces against terrorism, against drugs and on federal deregulation, but claimed he was "out of the loop" when allegations were cast at him of involvement in the so-called Iran–Contra affair – the illegal sale of weapons to Iran and use of the profits to fund right-wing anti-government forces in Nicaragua. Representing the US abroad on many occasions, Bush was building up the experience which would underlie his claim that he was uniquely well qualified for the presidential role.

Bush won the party's 1988 presidential nomination, voicing less moderate views to gain both financial and electoral support, and to dispel his reputation for weakness and indecision and his image as an over-privileged, wealthy Texan. In the ensuing campaign his negative tactics destroyed the chances of Democrat Michael Dukakis. Bush was sworn in as the 41st US president on 20 January 1989.

As president, Bush excelled on the global stage. His first test came in December 1989 with the successful use of force in Panama to oust Gen. Noriega, whom Bush denounced as an anti-democratic narco-criminal and a threat to the US-controlled canal. His summit meetings with Soviet leader **Mikhail Gorbachev** brought unprecedented agreements on arms reductions. He also negotiated the North American Free Trade Agreement (NAFTA) and formulated a position for the US in the new world that was emerging, following the break-up of the Soviet Union and the reunification of Germany.

The major challenge of Bush's career began on 2 August 1990 when Iraq invaded Kuwait. He determined to send in a large US-led coalition force, with global backing, and to push **Saddam Hussein**'s troops out of Kuwait if withdrawal did not occur before a strict deadline. His expertise in negotiations with foreign powers and his tough stance during the actual fighting, which led to victory after just 43 days, strengthened his image as a man of action.

However, on the home front Bush was handicapped by Democrat majorities in both houses and he was anxious to placate the right wing of his own party. His popularity waned due to his lack of attention to internal policy, indecisiveness and poor public speaking skills, often stammering or using comments that returned to haunt him. His notorious disparaging remarks about broccoli provoked growers to inundate him with protests and produce, while his "Watch my lips – no new taxes" campaign pledge was broken in 1990 as he struggled to reduce the growing budget deficit. As incumbent president he faced little challenge for the party's 1992 presidential nomination but the electorate rejected him in the November elections in favour of the Democrat candidate, Bill Clinton.

George Bush now lives in Texas and Maine, where he is actively involved with the Episcopalian Church. Since leaving office he has visited many countries as an unofficial ambassador and also works to raise money for charity. He and his wife had six children (one of whom died in childhood) and have 14 grandchildren. Their sons, George W. Bush Jr (the eldest) and Jeb Bush are respectively governor of Texas (since 1995) and of Florida (since 1998), and George Jr is widely regarded as a likely Republican candidate for the presidency in the 2000 elections.

Michel **Camdessus**

The seventh head of the International Monetary Fund (IMF), and the first in its history to serve three terms as managing director, Michel Camdessus has seen his own profile rise along with that of the IMF in the latter part of the 1990s. As world leaders struggled to avert the danger of a global crash and to contain the crisis of investor confidence which hit East Asia in 1997/98 and Russia in mid-1998, the IMF was identified as best placed to oversee both regulation and emergency credit reserves on a much increased scale. Camdessus already has a track record of assertiveness in expanding the role of the IMF in policy implementation. He has indicated a commitment to social justice over tackling the debt burden of the poorest countries, but is generally acknowledged as a tough negotiator beneath an affable exterior.

Michel Jean Camdessus was born on 1 May 1933 in Bayonne, southwest France, the son of Alfred Camdessus, a journalist, and Madeleine Cassembon. He studied law at the University of Paris, later gaining postgraduate degrees in economics at the elite Institut d'Etudes Politiques and the Ecole Nationale d'Administration (ENA). He married Brigitte d'Arcy in 1957 and they have two sons and four daughters.

Camdessus joined the French civil service in 1960, working for the first six years at the treasury in the ministry of finance and economic policies. He then spent two years in Brussels as the financial attaché to the French delegation at the European Economic Community (EEC) before returning to the treasury. Climbing up the ranks he became assistant director in 1971, deputy director in 1974 and director from February 1982. During this time he was also chair of the Paris Club of creditor nations (1978–84) and chair of the EEC's monetary committee (1982–84). In August 1984 he was appointed deputy governor of the Banque de France, the French central bank, rising to governor in November 1984.

Two years later he was elected to succeed fellow countryman Jacques de Larosière as managing director and chair of the executive board at the IMF. He took up his post on 16 January 1987, was elected to a second five-year term starting in 1992, and was unanimously re-elected in late 1996 for an unprecedented third term, which began on 16 January 1997.

After a low-profile first term, Camdessus has done much in the 1990s to build up the power and prestige of the IMF. The charge that it has become an international super-agency, acting without democratic supervision in prescribing economic "adjustments" for would-be borrowers, is a criticism which has been levied frequently for decades by the left in the developing world. However, under Camdessus the IMF also encountered the accusation of empire-building, this time from the leading industrialised countries, over his campaign in the early to mid-1990s for a major expansion of global credit reserves. His proposal envisaged creating some US$50 billion worth of extra IMF special drawing rights (SDRs), primarily to help address serious external payments problems of developing countries. The Group of Seven (G7) industrialised countries, concerned at the inflationary implications of this plan, put forward a much less ambitious compromise scheme – which Camdessus opposed – when the debate came to a head in 1994. Camdessus defended his stance with the reflection: "I'm possibly too immodest, but I am the managing director of the IMF. ... My duty is not to look at what the industrial countries think. My duty is to give a judgment on what is in the global need."

In the East Asian financial crisis of 1997/98, Camdessus was perceived as both saviour and tormentor by the governments of what had hitherto been the region's fast-growing "tiger economies". The magazine *Asia Week* acknowledged the importance of his role by naming him ahead of any national leader as number one in its 1997 "Power 50". An imperturbable diplomat and ruthless negotiator, operating from a position of strength even with such once powerful figures as Indonesia's Gen. **Suharto**, he insisted on tough fiscal conditions – and much more open regulatory systems – if the crisis-affected countries were to qualify for IMF support. Higher interest rates were also essential in the short term, he

argued, if confidence was to be re-established and investment capital attracted back to the region.

Although Camdessus has consistently defended his organisation's insistence on the importance of balanced budgets, the financial crises of 1997/98 have brought some significant admissions from the IMF that the free-market tenets of international liberal capitalism must sometimes allow for exceptional measures. The 1998 IMF annual report conceded that controls on inward movements of capital could sometimes be useful and that the premature opening of emerging economies to free capital flows represented "an accident waiting to happen". Camdessus was also strongly behind the decision to provide Russia with an additional US$11.2 billion loan in July 1998, when he declared that it was "important that the international community as a whole, both public and private sectors, show solidarity for Russia at this difficult time".

Within the IMF, Michel Camdessus is generally credited with making the organisation more open in its workings. A practising Catholic, he is considered personally affable and seen by his colleagues as approachable, notwithstanding the unrelenting upward trajectory of his own career path from France's elite *grandes écoles* via the treasury and central bank.

Naomi **Campbell**

Naomi Campbell combines that late-20th-century phenomenon, the supermodel, with the message which has made her a role model for her generation – a black, working-class girl from south London can make it to the top via the world of fashion. Her closest confidante is her mother, who, she has said, helps her to keep her feet on the ground – and who recently launched a career of her own as a fashion model. Dubbed "the goddess of the catwalk", Naomi is noted for not suppressing her views and emotions. She has built on her success as a model to branch out into other high-profile activities as co-owner of a fashionable café business, author, singer, film actress, and worker for humanitarian causes and children worldwide.

Naomi Campbell was born on 22 May 1970, in Streatham, London. Despite limited means, Naomi's mother Valerie Morris enrolled her in the Barbara Speake Stage School and then for ballet training at the prestigious Italia Conti School. She was just 15 when she was "discovered" while out shopping with girlfriends in Covent Garden.

It was the fairytale beginning to a career which, within three years, saw her on the cover of French *Vogue* magazine. In 1989, she also became the first black model to appear on the cover of American *Vogue*, a coup she repeated with British *Vogue* and with *Time* magazine. She and her fellow supermodels, Elle Macpherson and Claudia Schiffer, capitalising on the "buzz" which their every move attracted, developed a business spin-off with the Fashion Café, the first of which was launched with great publicity in New York.

Naomi Campbell's success made her a role model for young black women. Proud of her Afro-Caribbean ethnic origin, she had conquered a fashion industry notorious for favouring "blonde goddesses" as the ideal of feminine beauty. Many of her own particular idols reinforce her association with black pride, among them the American novelist Toni Morrison, the singers Aretha Franklin, Grace Jones and Josephine Baker, the Somali-born model Iman, and South Africa's President **Nelson Mandela**, whom she met in a famous mid-1990s photo opportunity. Her tastes also reflect her exposure to influences from continental Europe; she is a fluent French speaker, and admires especially the films of Fellini and the paintings of Matisse.

A temporary falling-out in 1993 with the Elite model agency, amid accusations that she was manipulative,

rude and an "impossible little madam", did nothing to dent her success, and she and Elite were subsequently reconciled. In 1994 she made US$2.1 million, and showed the world new abilities away from the catwalk, with both a novel and her debut as a recording artist. The book, *Swan*, was a thriller about five supermodels, which she later admitted was largely ghost-written. The album, *Babywoman*, released by Sony Epic with a video shot by film-maker Anton Corbijn in Spain, was followed by *Love and Tears*, while *La, La, La Love Song*, recorded with the Japanese star Toshi, reached number one in the Tokyo charts. She has also appeared in a number of other artists' music videos, including Michael Jackson's steamy *In The Closet*, and **Madonna**'s even steamier *Erotica*.

On the silver screen, Naomi Campbell co-starred with Madonna in Spike Lee's *Girl 6*, appeared in *Miami Rhapsody* opposite Antonio Banderas, and played small parts in *Cool as Ice* and Tony Hickox's *Invasion of Privacy*. She has also played cameo roles in episodes of television shows like *NY Undercover*, *Fresh Prince of Bel Air* and *The Cosby Show*.

Although she continues to work for Elite in London, she has latterly been based mainly in New York, attracted to that city because of its verve and sense of energy. She has modelled for Galliano, **Versace** and Lagerfeldt, but her favourite designer is Azzedine Alaïa, a kind of "father figure" to Naomi from the outset, who is said to reserve his best creations for her – one dress, made from feathers and taffeta, reportedly took six months to prepare.

As a model, Naomi Campbell may be envied for her stunning looks – she stands 5 feet 10 inches, always appears sleek and svelte, and her legs and alluring eyes are regarded as her finest physical features – but it is part of her public persona that she never diets or exercises, and likes to smoke and drink. Her jewellery includes an amethyst and an emerald adorning her navel, testimony to her role as one of the popularisers of the fashion for body-piercing.

She has sometimes appeared to be courting controversy, on a number of fronts. Her role as figurehead for an animal rights organisation, People for the Ethical Treatment of Animals (PETA), ended abruptly when she modelled clothes using fur in 1997. In 1998 she and another supermodel, Kate Moss, had a meeting in Havana with **Fidel Castro**, at a time when campaigns for the lifting of the US trade embargo on Cuba were hitting the headlines. Later that same year it was her role as employer and her personal behaviour which were called into question, by an apparently disgruntled former personal assistant who accused Naomi of assaulting her, and sued for US$2 million in damages.

Passionate, impulsive and somewhat scatty, her timekeeping is notoriously bad, and journalists also lambasted her for allegedly boasting that she would "not get out of bed" for less than several thousand pounds. On top of the earlier spat with Elite, at the beginning of 1999 she had a well-publicised run-in with the Versace fashion house, whose founder Gianni Versace had done much to promote her career from the early days, and with whom she had remained closely associated until his murder in 1997. It was not immediately clear what lay behind the decision that she would not be on the catwalk for the latest Versace winter show, beyond her complaint that she was no longer treated as "one of the family" under the regime of Donatella and Santo Versace, and the suggestion that they considered her fees excessive.

The media like to highlight spoilt and frivolous behaviour, but Naomi Campbell also dedicates considerable effort to humanitarian causes. She joined the **Dalai Lama** to raise funds for kindergartens in deprived communities worldwide, one of which was built in Jamaica in her name. She also sang before a crowd of 16,000 in Paris to support the fight against AIDS, and gave the proceeds from a photo book, *Naomi*, with images from photographers Richard Avedon, Steve Meisel, Herb Ritts and others, to the Red Cross Somalia Relief Fund. In 1998 she won plaudits for her spontaneous empathy when she visited children with HIV and AIDS in Bucharest, Romania, in a special hospital ward which is now named after her.

Fernando **Cardoso**

A sociologist with an international academic reputation, Fernando Cardoso is the first Brazilian head of state this century to secure a second term of office, having opened the way to seek re-election by means of a constitutional amendment in 1997. Actively involved in politics with centrist parties since the early 1980s, he first claimed credit as saviour of the economy after the success of his "Real Plan", establishing a stable currency, when he was economy minister in 1993/94. Cardoso was widely seen as the leader best able to avert economic catastrophe a second time when Brazil became the focus of intense speculation on international currency and stock markets in 1998. With him at the helm, Brazil's economy recovered the confidence of investors to a remarkable extent the following year.

Fernando Henrique Cardoso was born on 18 June 1931 in Rio de Janeiro, the son of a general. He gained a doctorate from the University of São Paulo in 1961, and in 1962/63 studied industrial sociology at the University of Paris. Becoming known as a leading young leftist academic in Brazil, he was forced into exile in 1964 when the military dictatorship took power, but he continued teaching abroad, while writing critical articles about the military regime. During this period he was professor of developmental sociology in Chile and deputy director of the CEPAL centre for economics and planning (1964–67), and then taught sociological theory at the University of Paris–Nanterre (1967/68).

On his return to Brazil in 1968 he set up a social sciences think-tank and took over the directorship of the department of social sciences at the University of São Paulo (1968/69). During this period his research centre was bombed by right-wing terrorists, and he was banned from teaching in 1969, arrested, and interrogated by military intelligence agents. In 1972 he left Brazil again for a lengthy period, holding professorships notably at Stanford (1972), Cambridge (1976/77) and Paris (1977 and 1980/81). From 1973 until 1976 he was a member of the Latin American committee of the New-York-based Social Science Research Council, and from 1976 onwards a member of the governing body of the Institute for Latin American Studies at Santiago, Chile.

In 1980 Cardoso revived his São Paulo think-tank, the Brazilian Centre for Analysis and Planning (CEBRAP), of which he was president until 1982. Also in 1980 he helped found the centrist Christian Democratic Party of the Brazilian Democratic Movement (PMDB), which pursued a broad pro-

democracy campaign, and in 1982 he entered the Brazilian Senate as a PMDB senator for the state of São Paulo. After the end of the era of military rule, and the PMDB's success in the 1986 elections, Cardoso rose to the position of government leader in the Senate, and took part in the work of the National Constituent Assembly to frame the more liberal 1988 constitution.

Cardoso resigned as leader of the PMDB in June 1988 in order to found (with others) the new Brazilian Social Democratic Party (PSDB), which condemned the then President Sarney for clinging to office without a real mandate and for indulging in what Cardoso called "corruption with impunity". After several years in opposition, and the eventual impeachment of Sarney's successor President **Collor**, Cardoso was appointed by his successor Itamar Franco as minister of foreign affairs in October 1992. Moving over to become minister of finance and economy in May 1993, and thereby accepting what many in his party believed was an impossible brief, Cardoso made his political reputation with the success of his plan to regain control over the economy, tackling Brazil's rampant inflation and implementing a currency reform, the so-called "Real Plan".

In the presidential elections of 3 October 1994 he overcame a strong challenge from the Workers' Party candidate, who had a massive early opinion poll lead, and took over 54 per cent of the vote on the first round. His three-party centrist coalition also established a strong position in the concurrent legislative elections.

Cardoso was sworn in as president for a four-year term on 1 January 1995. He vowed to democratise the country, to limit human rights abuses within the police force and to reduce the sharp disparities of wealth currently characteristic of Brazilian society. His free-market economic philosophy made him an enthusiastic proponent of the privatisation of state-run monopolies and the removal of trade restrictions, but his social welfare promises ran into difficulties, and on human rights and environmental protection his government made limited real progress beyond the framing of policies and programmes.

In June 1997 the Senate finally approved a constitutional amendment for which Cardoso had

been pressing, to remove the prohibition on an incumbent president standing for re-election. The price he paid for getting this through Congress was to soft-pedal on some of the more politically sensitive aspects of his programme to cut the cost of Brazil's over-staffed bureaucracy, at regional as well as at federal level. The imperative of reducing public sector expenditure, however, became even more pressing as a collapse in confidence among international investors spread from Asia and Russia to place Brazil's currency and economy in danger by the latter part of 1998. Since this crisis coincided with the federal elections, Cardoso took the courageous decision to make it clear to the voters that he saw no alternative to the introduction of greater budgetary austerity.

Cardoso's reputation for guiding the country through its previous period of economic turmoil served him well at the polls on 4 October 1998, and he was returned for a second term of office with just over 53 per cent of the vote, while his PMDB did better than expected in the simultaneous elections to Congress, the five-party government coalition retaining a three-fifths majority. Within a fortnight of beginning his new presidential term on 1 January 1999, however, and despite having secured international backing for his economic programme, Cardoso was compelled by international speculative pressure to abandon his long-standing hostility to devaluation of the currency, the real.

Cardoso has retained an active interest in the study of political and sociological issues and alternative paths to development, having first established his reputation internationally in the late 1960s as co-author of *Dependency and Development in Latin America*. He is president of several foundations and has been a member since 1990 of the New World Dialogue initiative at the World Resources Institute in Washington D.C. He is married to Ruth Corrêa Leite and they have three children.

Fidel **Castro**

Targeted as an object of particular hatred by successive US administrations, Fidel Castro survives in power as a lone remnant from the gallery of internationally known communist figures of the cold war era. The leader of the Cuban revolution in 1959, he has been in power longer than any other current non-hereditary ruler in the world, and was most recently re-elected (unopposed) by the Cuban parliament in February 1998 for a further five-year presidential term. Castro presents himself in spite of his age as the fatigue-clad bearded revolutionary. He still runs a one-party state, but the pope's visit in January 1998 marked the beginning of an improvement in his regime's international relations, and its partial emergence from the isolation it had suffered since the collapse of communism elsewhere.

Fidel Castro Ruz was born on 13 August 1926 in Birán in the Oriente region of southeast Cuba. His father Angel Castro, who had arrived as an immigrant farm labourer from Galicia in Spain, owned a 23,000-acre sugar plantation. One of seven children, Fidel had a strict upbringing in a large Catholic family, although he was later to be excommunicated. After the local primary school he went to Jesuit schools in Santiago and Havana, and graduated in law from the University of Havana in 1949. He practised as a lawyer in Havana, and planned to stand for parliament, until Gen. Batista seized power in 1952.

After first attempting unsuccessfully to use the law to oppose Batista, by bringing a suit against the dictator for contravening the constitution, Castro became involved in underground resistance. On 26 July 1952 he led an assault on the Moncada barracks in Oriente. Half of his force were killed and both Fidel Castro and his brother Raúl were captured and sentenced to 15 years in prison. Defending himself at the trial, Castro closed his defence with the much-quoted words, "History will absolve me". His marriage to Mirta Diaz-Bilart, with whom he had one son, ended with her divorcing him while he was in prison.

Released under a general amnesty in May 1955, Castro fled to Mexico and then on to the USA. He returned to Cuba aboard the *Granma* on 2 December 1956 as leader of an 82-man group of Cuban exiles calling themselves the 26 July Revolutionary Movement. Batista's troops killed 70 of them soon after they landed, leaving the Castro brothers, Che Guevara and just nine others to form the nucleus of a guerrilla movement in the mountainous Sierra Maestra region. Gathering strength over the next two years, the guerrilla army marched on Havana and put

Batista to flight on 1 January 1959. The USA recognised Castro's government on 7 January and on 16 February Castro declared himself prime minister.

It was the expropriation of US-owned firms which underlay the rapid deterioration in relations with the USA. Castro responded to Soviet overtures by concluding deals on trade, oil, food and credit, while the USA retaliated on the expropriation issue by imposing an economic embargo. Fearing a Marxist and pro-Soviet state "in its back yard", the new Kennedy administration in the USA gave the go-ahead for a disastrous attempted invasion of Cuba by CIA-backed Cuban exiles, who were wiped out at the Bay of Pigs in April 1961. In 1962 Castro agreed to a Soviet nuclear weapons base being established on the island. Global nuclear war seemed imminent as the USA imposed a naval blockade to stop the missiles reaching their new base. Superpower negotiation between presidents Kennedy and Khrushchev ended the crisis, with the Soviet ships turning back with their cargo of missiles, but from then on Castro's government was viewed with even more hostility by the USA and several attempts were made to assassinate Castro.

Castro had declared Cuba a communist single-party state in December 1961, the year in which he was awarded the Lenin Peace Prize. His regime pressed ahead with the nationalisation of industry, setting up farm collectives and appropriating property from the wealthy or from foreigners. Thousands of opponents of his regime were imprisoned or executed and many of the middle and upper classes left Cuba, forming a substantial community of exiles in Miami.

In 1963 Castro became first secretary of the United Party of the Cuban Socialist Revolution (PURSC), which became the Cuban Communist Party in 1965. He did not formally join the party's politburo, however, until 1976. In that year, when Cuba approved its first constitution, instead of prime minister Castro then officially became head of state and government as president of the council of state and the council of ministers. Since then he has been re-elected to the presidency a number of times, most recently by the parliament in February 1998 when he began a new five-year term in office. He also retains the leadership of the party as its first secretary, and in 1992 became in addition chair of the national defence council.

From the 1960s until the 1990s Castro governed Cuba on strict Marxist lines. Within Cuba he pointed with particular pride to achievements in the national education and health services. Keen to export the Cuban example, he was active in the Non-aligned Movement and supported revolutions in Latin America, Ethiopia and Angola, with substantial commitments of military hardware, training and troops.

In the 1990s Castro has insisted on maintaining Cuba's Marxist identity, and has come under criticism for the suppression of dissent as well as for his cautious approach on economic reform. The loss of the once substantial Soviet aid and the ending of preferential trade deals has contributed to the problems of the economy, as has above all the maintenance of the US trade embargo. There have been some concessions to free enterprise since 1993, such as the introduction of farmers' markets, and a foreign investment law in 1995, but in December of that year, during a visit to China, Castro reinforced his own reputation for last-ditch resistance by praising his hosts for holding out against capitalism. In March 1996 a rare meeting of the communist party's central committee was called, at which Castro announced stronger measures to restrict private business ventures, emphasising again his hardline stance.

On the issue of religious freedom, however, the unprecedented visit to Cuba by **Pope John Paul II** in January 1998 helped to encourage the regime's loosening of controls over the Catholic Church, which was even given time for broadcasts on state television, and Christmas was reinstated as a national holiday. Reports continued to emerge of plots among Cuban exiles to assassinate Castro, while in July 1998 the matter of his health hit the headlines, with officials denying the claim made by a Cuban surgeon and recent defector that she had been part of a team which had operated on him for a serious brain condition the previous October.

Viktor **Chernomyrdin**

An engineer in the oil industry and then for many years a government minister in the energy sector during the Soviet era, Chernomyrdin is noted for his absence of charisma, but represents a powerful constituency of former communist industrial managers. Chernomyrdin is still considered a likely contender, if not winner, in any contest to succeed President Yeltsin. A would-be occupant of the problematic middle ground in Russia's recurring disputes between economic reformers and conservatives, Chernomyrdin founded in May 1995 the centrist movement Our Home is Russia, which became the third-largest bloc in the Russian parliament elected in December of that year. Discarded by Yeltsin as prime minister in March 1998, he was then rejected by the parliament when Yeltsin wanted to bring him back five months later. He was back in favour to some extent in 1999 when Yeltsin appointed him as his representative on the Kosovo crisis, a choice generally welcomed by NATO countries keen to avoid a confrontation over their military action against the Yugoslav regime.

Viktor Stepanovich Chernomyrdin was born on 9 April 1938 in Chernyy Otrog in the Orenburg district of Russia. Educated at the Kybyshev Polytechnic in Samara, he served in the army between 1957 and 1960. He spent seven years as an operator in an oil refinery, and in the late 1960s and early 1970s was an official in Orsk for the Communist Party of the Soviet Union (CPSU), which he had joined in 1961. Deputy chief engineer at the gas works in Orenburg from 1973 until 1978, he then worked for the CPSU central committee until 1982, when he became a deputy minister for the gas industry. In charge of developing the Tyumen gas field at this time, he was promoted to full minister in 1985, and sat on the CPSU central committee between 1986 and 1990, as well as being elected as a deputy to the Supreme Soviet (parliament) in 1987. Between 1989 and 1992, as the Soviet Union was disintegrating and the independent Russian state coming into existence, he was running the huge state-owned gas concern Gasprom. Chernomyrdin is married and has two sons.

Chernomyrdin was brought into the Russian government by Boris Yeltsin, a long-time friend, in late May 1992. Initially a deputy premier in charge of food and energy, he was still seen very much as the representative of the industrialists' lobby when he was nominated for prime minister that December. At that time the prime minister was nominated by the then legislature, the Congress of People's Deputies, in a complex interim arrangement on the respective powers of the legislature and presidency. Yeltsin had asked for the approval of the legislature for the retention of leading reformer Yegor Gaidar as premier, but accepted Chernomyrdin as the best available compromise, and the new government was sworn in on 14 December.

As prime minister, Chernomyrdin remained formally head of government under the December 1993 constitution, but the president was empowered to make the nomination, and to call fresh elections if the legislature did not give its approval. He scored a notable success in mid-1995, after taking control of the handling of a hostage-taking drama in Chechnya, by negotiating the safe release of the hostages.

An opponent of rapid privatisation, Chernomyrdin advocated a more gradual process of economic reform, with particular emphasis on improving Russia's self-reliance in key areas. The volatile nature of his ministerial team prevented the emergence of any consistent long-term policy, however, with Yeltsin sometimes making appointments to encourage more rapid reform, and at other times dismissing leading reformers because of their manifest unpopularity.

Although Chernomyrdin was largely preoccupied with the problems of economic management during his term as prime minister, he remained a loyal supporter of Yeltsin against any moves to oust him from power. This was particularly significant when he was required to run the government on occasions when Yeltsin was too unwell, as he was for a lengthy period in late 1996 and early 1997, when he underwent major heart surgery, and again in late 1997 and early 1998. Chernomyrdin's star was apparently in the ascendant before the first of these interludes, his rival Gen. **Lebed** having just been dismissed and a four-member committee established, including Chernomyrdin, to try to make the administration function in a more coherent manner. This did not save Chernomyrdin from bearing the brunt of Yeltsin's criticisms when he recovered from illness and delivered his annual address to parliament in March 1997. Yeltsin's main charge on this occasion, that Chernomyrdin had failed to control the spread of corruption or to halt the slide in the living standards of the Russian people, was renewed with a vengeance in March 1998. On this occasion Chernomyrdin was summarily dismissed, despite having only recently strengthened his authority vis-à-vis the leading reformists and in addition taken charge of the media and energy policy, as the increasingly erratic Yeltsin demanded the reinvigoration of free-market economic reforms.

Within five months, in an extraordinary about-turn, Chernomyrdin's virtues as an experienced "heavyweight" were being extolled again, and Yeltsin was presenting him to parliament as the prime minister Russia needed to cope with its most acute economic crisis yet. The parliament, however, recognising that this issue was a trial of strength between its authority and the president's, twice blocked Chernomyrdin's appointment. Yeltsin was eventually compelled to put forward a candidate more acceptable to the large communist contingent in the parliament. The man on whom the choice now fell, former foreign minister Yevgeny Primakov, thereby became Yeltsin's most likely successor and an increasingly important power broker, whereas Chernomyrdin's prospects correspondingly faded. Still a possible candidate for the presidency, however, he was known to be favoured by many of the country's most powerful business and financial "oligarchs". Chernomyrdin's appointment as Russian envoy to deal with the major international crisis over Kosovo in early 1999 was further proof that his experience and unglamorous political skills were still highly regarded.

Jacques **Chirac**

*Jacques Chirac has become western Europe's elder statesman since the departure from office of former German Chancellor **Helmut Kohl**. As president of France since 1995, Chirac has far-reaching political powers under the constitution framed by de Gaulle in 1958, in particular with regard to external relations, holding referendums, issuing decrees and declaring states of emergency. He has been a prominent Gaullist politician for 30 years, and twice prime minister during that time, but the workings of the French political system have obliged him to share power since 1997 in a so-called "cohabitation" with socialist Prime Minister Lionel Jospin. Chirac is strongly identified with Paris, where he was mayor from 1977 to 1995.*

Jacques Chirac was born in the fifth *arrondissement* of Paris on 29 November 1932. His father François was a bank clerk and later a company director. Jacques attended two prestigious Parisian *lycées*, went on to the Institut d'Études Politiques in Paris, and attended Harvard University summer school in 1953. As a junior officer with the French army he was wounded in Algeria in the mid-1950s. In 1956 he married Bernadette Chodron de Courcel; they have two daughters, Laurence and Claude.

Between 1957 and 1959 Chirac was a student at France's elite civil service training institution, the Ecole Nationale d'Administration (ENA). Upon graduation he began his political career as an auditor in the government's finance office. In 1962 he became *chargé de mission* within the government of Georges Pompidou, soon moving from the government secretariat to a three-year spell as adviser in Pompidou's private office. He became a junior minister in 1967, with responsibility first for employment and, from 1968 to 1971, for economy and finance. He was also public auditor at the Cour des Comptes from 1965, a member of the Corrèze municipal council from 1965 to 1967, was first elected National Assembly deputy for Corrèze in 1967, and chaired the Corrèze general council from 1970 to 1979.

Chirac gained ministerial experience in the early 1970s at the ministry of agriculture and rural development (1972–74) and briefly as minister of the interior. When Giscard d'Estaing won the presidency in May 1974, Chirac at first prospered, as a leading Gaullist in Giscard's centre-right alliance. In addition to the post of prime minister from May 1974, he took on the general secretaryship of the Gaullist party, the

Union of Democrats for the Republic (UDR) from December. The two fell out, however, less over policy than because of friction between their two dominant personalities. Chirac resigned from the government in August 1976, and in December established his dominance within the Gaullist movement, transforming the UDR into the Rally for the Republic (RPR) with himself as its president. The following March he won election for the first time as mayor of Paris, using this power base to keep himself in the political forefront; he retained both the RPR leadership and the Paris mayorship until he launched his successful bid for the presidency in the mid-1990s.

In the run-up to the 1981 presidential election, Chirac increasingly distanced the RPR leadership from the Giscard government, seeking to project himself rather than the president as the leader of the centre-right "majority". In the election, the first of his three bids for the presidency, he split the centre-right vote on the first round but finished a poor third behind the incumbent Giscard and the eventually successful **Mitterrand**.

The honeymoon of the left in government soon gave way to acrimonious divisions and a reversal of direction on the economy, and in 1986 the centre-right came back strongly in the legislative elections. Chirac's RPR, its leadership rejuvenated by him in the years in opposition, performed so well that Mitterrand had little option but to make him prime minister. Thus began the first so-called "cohabitation", a two-year test of some hitherto unexplored aspects of the division of powers under the Fifth Republic's constitution. The experiment was made to work, but Chirac's economic policies – based on a radical privatisation programme – proved less successful with the electorate, and his party was divided on how to deal with the challenge of the National Front from the extreme right, a minority favouring some form of alliance.

Challenging Mitterrand for the presidency in April/May 1988, Chirac this time went through to the run-off, but finished second, with just under 46 per cent of the vote. The general election the following month restored a centre-left majority, while also tilting the balance on the right away from Chirac towards Giscard.

Chirac favoured a "yes" vote in the 1992 referendum on the Maastricht Treaty on European Union. Although his RPR was divided on this issue, it gained fresh momentum in the 1993 legislative elections,

again becoming the largest party in a united centre-right grouping which won a landslide victory. Chirac, remaining aloof to prepare a third presidential bid, put forward fellow party member Edouard Balladur as prime minister for the second "cohabitation" government, little expecting that his loyal colleague would emerge as a rival for the presidency in 1995. Balladur's candidacy was backed by the centre-right Union for French Democracy (UDF), Giscard having decided against standing himself. Chirac overtook Balladur by campaigning strongly with populist calls to tackle unemployment and "social exclusion". Second in the first ballot in April, with socialist Lionel Jospin unexpectedly leading the poll, Chirac picked up most of the Balladur votes in the second round on 7 May, ending with 52.6 per cent, and was sworn in as president for a seven-year term on 17 May 1995.

Two years into his own presidency, Chirac found himself in a third "cohabitation", this time on the other side, when the pendulum in the legislative elections (called early by Chirac in the hope of a vote of confidence) swung back to the left. With Jospin as prime minister, the new socialist-led government in office since June 1997 has been in the forefront of dealing with tensions over the state of the economy. To some extent this has taken the spotlight off Chirac, who had been criticised for neglecting his presidential campaign promises in pursuit of austerity policies to prepare for European monetary union.

In a Gaullist gesture asserting French independence on the world stage, Chirac caused particular controversy soon after taking office with a six-month programme of nuclear tests in the Pacific. On controversial issues such as relations with Iraq, he has showed a marked unwillingness to accept any notion of US leadership. Fundamentally, however, his approach to foreign policy is based around the Franco-German alliance at the core of European Union integration, and the improvement in France's relations with NATO countries was marked by its full involvement as a NATO member country in military action against Yugoslavia when the crisis over Kosovo erupted in early 1999.

Tansu **Çiller**

In a meteoric political career which only began in 1990, the abrasive US-educated economist Tansu Çiller made history as Turkey's first woman prime minister (1993–95), but emerged as the eventual loser from two subsequent and unsuccessful attempts at power sharing. The second and most controversial of these brought Turkey's Islamists to power for the first time, a challenge to secularism which the military establishment found intolerable. Ousted in mid-1997, Çiller retained the leadership of her right-of-centre party. She has escaped the fate of her erstwhile Islamist allies, who are now outlawed from politics, but faces the prospect of being called to account for alleged self-enrichment and corruption during her time in office.

Tansu Çiller was born on 24 May 1946, the daughter of a local official in Mugla, southwest Turkey. She studied economics at Bogazici University, Istanbul, before moving to the USA. There she gained a master's degree in economics from the University of New Hampshire and a doctorate in economics from the University of Connecticut, going on to post-doctoral studies at Yale University and work as a consultant with the World Bank.

Returning to Turkey, she became an associate professor at Bogazici University in 1978 and, in 1983, professor and chair of the economics department. She is married to a wealthy businessman – whom, unusually, she persuaded to take her surname – and they have two children.

Çiller entered politics in 1990, joining the True Path Party (DYP) and becoming an adviser to Süleyman Demirel, then prime minister. She entered parliament at the October 1991 general election and was minister of state for the economy in the new Demirel government, a coalition of the DYP and the Social Democratic People's Party (SHP). Her chance of a bid for the party leadership – and the premiership – came when Demirel moved up to the presidency in May 1993, after the death of incumbent President Özal. At a DYP special convention in June Çiller outpolled Ismet Sezgin of the party's conservative wing on the first ballot and was elected unopposed on the second. On 14 June Demirel asked her officially to form a government. Her ministerial appointments strengthened the role of her own more radical free-market oriented wing of the DYP, while retaining the SHP as coalition partners.

Over the ensuing two and a half years in government, Çiller sought to contain public spending, and to boost government finances by an energetic privatisation programme. She encountered problems, however, with getting some of her more unpopular policies through parliament – despite the coalition's nominal majority. Circumventing parliament and introducing key economic measures by decree, she then ran into opposition from the constitutional court, notably over privatisation in the telecommunications industry. An austerity programme was introduced in April 1994, enabling Turkey to obtain a much-needed IMF stand-by loan, but tensions within the coalition continued to undermine Çiller's efforts on this front, until she eventually called early elections for December 1995.

Meanwhile the Çiller government, although pro-Western in its stance, was gaining some international notoriety over its treatment of Kurdish militants. Deferring to military pressure and nationalist fervour, Çiller adopted a tough line on the continuing Kurdish rebellion in southeast Turkey. The Kurdish nationalist Democracy Party was disbanded in 1994 and heavy prison sentences were imposed on eight of its parliamentary deputies. On other issues, however, her regime had a more liberal face. Changes to the constitution during this period, including enhanced trade union rights and political rights for civil servants, were sufficient to persuade the European Parliament to approve the implementation of a much-delayed EU–Turkey customs union from January 1996.

The December 1995 general election, far from providing a clear-cut outcome, left the political arena more complicated than ever. Manoeuvring to retain her hold on office – without which she faced the prospect of investigations for alleged corruption – Çiller was pushed into the expedient of a power-sharing deal with her bitter rival and critic Mesut Yilmaz, leader of the centre-right Motherland Party (ANAP). The rationale for the ANAP–DYP coalition, eventually formed in March 1996, was that it offered the only way to block the rise of Necmettin Erbakan's Islamist Welfare Party (RP), which had secured the largest share of seats in the election. The intended formula was for Yilmaz to be prime minister until the end of the year, and then to give way to Çiller. This deal was aborted, however, when Yilmaz allowed a parliamentary investigation to be set up to look into the corruption allegations against Çiller.

Having pulled out of the coalition and forced Yilmaz's resignation, Çiller now argued the necessity of an agreement with the Islamists – even though she had fought the 1995 election on the basis of combating the Islamist challenge. Despite rumblings within her own party, she accordingly entered an RP–DYP coalition in June 1996. Erbakan became prime minister at the outset – the Turkish Republic's first ever avowedly Islamist head of government – and Çiller began as deputy premier and foreign minister, with plans to alternate with Erbakan in the top job.

This arrangement encountered the hostility of the powerful military and political establishment, which viewed an Islamist-led government as an affront to Turkey's secular identity. While Erbakan came under heavy pressure to distance himself from the growing fundamentalism of his grassroots supporters, Çiller faced a series of defections from her party and demands that she should withdraw from the coalition. The situation came to a head in June 1997. Erbakan called for early elections, announcing that Çiller's turn as premier would accordingly begin later that same month, but by mid-June the intensified pressure from the military had compelled him to offer the government's resignation. President Demirel, instead of turning first to Çiller, thereupon adopted the army's preferred solution by asking Yilmaz to form a government. Refusing even to discuss co-operation under her rival's leadership, Çiller described Yilmaz's appointment as undemocratic and took her remaining DYP supporters into opposition.

Since her departure from government Tansu Çiller has faced allegations that she has worked for the US Central Intelligence Agency (CIA), accusations of financial impropriety and offending the military, and the suggestion that she was implicated in the 1996 murder of a casino owner. In May 1998 the Ankara assizes court gave her husband Özer Çiller a five-month suspended prison sentence and a nominal fine for forging official documents for the parliamentary investigation into how she had amassed a personal fortune.

Bill **Clinton**

Bill Clinton would wish to be remembered as the two-term Democratic president who led the American people in a period of unparalleled prosperity and sustained economic growth. Indeed, the booming economy did ensure him some remarkable popularity ratings. His name is more immediately associated, however, with his most obvious negative legacy – the damage he did to the remaining moral authority of his office, not just by his sexual conduct but by his failure to be candid about it when caught. The so-called Lewinsky affair, named after a young intern with whom he held secret White House assignations, provided the ammunition for Clinton's Republican opponents to have him impeached. Their lack of a sufficient Senate majority, and the groundswell of public feeling against impeachment, doomed those proceedings to eventual failure in February 1999, but Clinton, once regarded as the ultimate political survivor, was left fatally damaged just half way through his second term in the world's most powerful political post.

Bill Clinton was born William Jefferson Blythe III on 19 August 1946 in Hope, Arkansas. His father was killed in a car accident three months before he was born, and his mother Virginia remarried, to Roger Clinton, in 1950. While his mother was in New Orleans training as a nurse, Bill's Baptist upbringing as a young child was primarily the responsibility of his grandparents, Eldridge and Edith Cassidy. When he was 15 and his half-brother (born in 1956) reached school age, Bill had his name changed legally to the family surname Clinton. He had an unhappy relationship with his stepfather, and as a teenager found himself assuming responsibility for holding the family together, protecting his mother from her husband's abuse.

Bill Clinton attended Hot Springs High School and went on to Georgetown University where he graduated in 1968 in international affairs. From 1968 to 1970 he was a Rhodes scholar at University College, Oxford. In 1973 he completed law school at Yale University and became a junior professor at the University of Arkansas School of Law. In 1975 Clinton married Hillary Rodham, a lawyer whom he met while studying at Yale. They have one daughter, Chelsea, born in 1980.

Interested in politics from his childhood onwards, and inspired by meeting the then President Kennedy at a "Boys Nation" youth leadership conference in Washington D.C. in 1962, Clinton registered as a Democrat, and first sought electoral office himself in 1974. He was narrowly defeated in a bid to unseat the Republican incumbent for an Arkansas seat in the US House of Representatives. Retaining his law professorship, he was in addition chair of the local housing development corporation in 1975/76. In 1976 he took a leading role in the Carter presidential campaign in Arkansas, and also won public office himself, as state attorney-general, holding this post for two years until his election as state governor of Arkansas.

Clinton was thus only 32 when he was inaugurated for the first time in January 1979 as state governor, the youngest governor in the country. His relative political inexperience told against him when he failed to win re-election at the end of his first two-year term, being branded as a high spender because of increases in highway taxes intended to finance the reform of public services. After two years with the law firm of Wright, Lindsey, and Jennings, he came back to win re-election as governor in November 1982, taking office the following January and winning successive terms until his successful bid for the US presidency ten years later. His main achievements as governor centred around the improvement of the education system, the introduction of systematic testing of attainment standards for school students, and the raising of teachers' salaries. Additional responsibilities which he held at national level during this period included in 1987 the chair of the National Governors' Association and co-chair of the Education Commission of the States, and in 1990/91 co-chair of the Task Force on Education and chair of the Democratic Leadership Council.

In 1991 Clinton declared his candidacy for the Democratic Party nomination for the US presidency. His early position as front runner was damaged by allegations about an extra-marital affair, and the suggestion that as a student he had managed to defer being drafted for military service at the time of the Vietnam war by making a promise which he did not fulfil about joining a reserve officers' training programme (the draft later being replaced by a lottery system in which his name did not come up). His ability to overcome such reverses in his campaign attracted the nickname "the comeback kid", but opponents continued to regard the "character issue" as the most vulnerable point on which to attack him.

Winning the nomination and choosing Tennessee senator Al Gore at the Democratic Party convention to be his vice-presidential running mate on a youthful and relatively liberal ticket, Clinton campaigned successfully for the presidency, his ability to strike the right note on a range of issues being contrasted with the more aloof personality of Republican incumbent **George Bush**. In the 3 November 1992 poll Clinton took 43 per cent of the popular vote and won 370 of the 538 electoral college votes, defeating Bush, the

independent Ross Perot and several minor candidates. On 20 January 1993 he took office officially as the 42nd president of the USA.

Clinton's first term of office was marked by the launching of several ambitious reform initiatives, on health and education in particular, which foundered on determined conservative opposition. Right-wing critics attacked his apparent preference for an active government role in social issues, whereas the previous 12 years of Republican administration had emphasised the need to "roll back" the government's involvement to "get it off the backs of the American people". The mid-term elections in November 1994 produced a severe anti-Clinton backlash in which the Democrats lost control of Congress to a Republican Party with a pronounced right-wing agenda, codified as a "contract with America". Clinton showed his political flexibility in conceding an immediate round of tax cuts, beginning to win back the political centre ground. He managed to turn to his advantage a lengthy stalemate with Congress over the federal budget, presenting his Republican opponents as doctrinaire and obstructive, and came back strongly enough to win a further presidential term in the November 1996 elections, much assisted by the recently recovered buoyancy of the economy. He was able in addition to point to a positive balance on his foreign policy record. Initially marked by the failure of US intervention in Somalia, this record now included the fostering of an Israeli-Palestinian agreement, the Dayton agreement on former Yugoslavia signed in November 1995, the US intervention to restore democratic government in Haiti, and the conclusion of the North American Free Trade Agreement with Canada and Mexico.

The poll on 5 November 1996 gave Clinton 49.2 per cent of the popular vote and 379 of the 538 electoral college votes, against 40.8 per cent for Republican candidate Bob Dole, and 8.5 per cent for Perot. During the campaign Clinton had once again faced attack more on his character than on his record in office. In particular, he was unable to free himself from the long-running Whitewater affair. A federal investigation into this scandal centred on his role and that of his wife Hillary in a failed property venture while he was governor of Arkansas, and questioned the veracity of their accounts of this and apparently related events. Renewed allegations of sexual impropriety, the claim that he had used Arkansas state troopers to procure numerous female sexual partners for him, and efforts by former Arkansas state employee Paula Jones to bring a law suit against him for sexual harassment ensured that the "character issue" remained at the forefront of US politics in the year following his inauguration for a second term on 20 January 1997. Clinton's popularity, however, remained high throughout the first year of his second term, in spite of several setbacks, in particular over the continuing Whitewater investigations.

It was in the following year, 1998, that he came badly unstuck on the "character" front, although even when he was brought to the brink of impeachment he continued to enjoy remarkable poll ratings in terms of how well he was doing his job as president. In January 1998 his opponents, doggedly pursuing fresh leads on the Paula Jones affair, enjoyed his humiliation of having to testify on oath as a defendant in that case, and facing allegations about relations with other women as Jones's lawyers sought to establish a "pattern of behaviour". Within four days, the scope had widened dramatically. Clinton was forced to deny both that he had had sexual relations with Monica Lewinsky, in an affair dating from 1995 when she was a 21-year-old intern at the White House, and that he had persuaded Lewinsky to lie to Jones's lawyers about it. The Whitewater special prosecutor Kenneth Starr, authorised to extend his investigations into the question of whether Clinton was guilty of perjury and suborning a witness, took on the case with determination, amid initial suggestions that Clinton could be about to resign. True to his nickname of "the comeback kid", however, Clinton went on television to give an emphatic repetition of his denial, while **Hillary Clinton** spoke publicly of the need for a battle against what she described as a "vast right-wing conspiracy against him".

The details of the affair emerged over the subsequent months, with accounts of their meetings, the gifts they

had exchanged, their intimate conversations and oral sex (which Clinton, as it later transpired, apparently did not regard as constituting full sexual intercourse). Although the Paula Jones case was dismissed in April (and Clinton later offered her a substantial payment to settle in advance of an appeal), this new scandal overshadowed all other political events, even raising the accusation that crucial US actions in the sphere of foreign affairs were being orchestrated to counteract the negative impact of the Lewinsky affair on Clinton. The public support he received from Hillary Clinton throughout this time, however, had a notable positive effect on his (and especially on her) standing. In August, hoping that he could bring the issue to a close, Clinton gave five hours of evidence which was relayed by television to a grand jury investigating him for possible perjury, conspiracy to obstruct justice, and attempting to suborn a witness. While still denying having pressured Lewinsky to lie "or to take any other unlawful act", in a television address he gave his first semi-apology, admitting having had a relationship with Lewinsky which "was not appropriate. In fact it was wrong."

The following month, as the affair gained fresh momentum from dissatisfaction at such prevarication, the enormously detailed Starr report was delivered. The Senate's decision to make its contents public – including Lewinsky's own evidence to the grand jury, delivered under an immunity agreement – and the televised screening of Clinton's evidence, threatened to bury the White House in sordid details.

Clinton certainly forfeited dignity and popular respect as his character failings were exposed, but the opinion polls showed him still getting high "job approval" ratings as president. Disregarding these warning signs that most people wanted to see the matter closed, his political opponents decided to go ahead with impeachment.

No US president had ever been successfully impeached. Andrew Johnson in 1868 had articles of impeachment voted against him by the House of Representatives, but survived the ensuing Senate trial. More recently, Richard Nixon in 1974 had resigned before the House voted. Despite poor prospects of success, and although the Republicans were further deflated by not achieving the successes they expected in mid-term elections in November 1998, the House of Representatives nevertheless voted two of the proposed articles of impeachment against Clinton (for perjury and for obstruction of justice) in December. In February 1999 Clinton survived the Senate impeachment trial. As widely expected, the necessary two-thirds majority was not obtained, the perjury charge actually being defeated by 55 to 45 on 12 February while the obstruction-of-justice charge ended in a 50:50 tied vote.

Notwithstanding Clinton's brave-sounding words about "a time of reconciliation and renewal" after the affair was laid to rest, it was already clear that US politicians would now regard association with him as a liability. Such a calculation was becoming increasingly urgent for them – and even for Hillary Clinton if she were to seek a Senate seat – as the election year of 2000 approached. Nor was Clinton able to restore his standing with achievements in foreign affairs. Apart from British backing, he had already found himself increasingly isolated over the launching of air strikes against Iraq in 1998/99, in a confrontation in which the Iraqis refused to give any further access to UN weapons inspectors. The 1999 conflict with Yugoslavia over the latter's repression in Kosovo, in which the USA provided the majority of the air power used in a sustained NATO bombing campaign from March to June, saw the mantle of forthright leadership of the Atlantic Alliance apparently passing to the UK prime minister **Tony Blair**. The latter's air of conviction about the need to act – and preparedness if necessary to contemplate a ground war – contrasted with Clinton's own hesitation about risking US casualties in a foreign engagement.

Hillary **Clinton**

The most politically committed US president's wife since Eleanor Roosevelt, Hillary Rodham Clinton has only latterly begun to win wide public acceptance as an independent figure of real stature. A high-flying commercial lawyer, and identified especially with women's rights, children's issues and education, she was loathed by conservatives and the radical right at the outset of the Clinton presidency as an assertive, outspoken liberal and manipulative career woman. Improbably, it was when her husband's moral authority reached its lowest point, with the House of Representatives voting to impeach him over the Lewinsky sex scandal in late 1998, that her own political prospects and popularity recovered. Overcoming the rebuff she had received as instigator of the administration's abortive health reform plans of 1993/94, and the buffeting she suffered during investigations into the complex Whitewater affair, she was acclaimed for showing strength of character and the skill and determination to see him through the crisis.

Hillary Diane Rodham was born on 26 October 1947 in Chicago, where her father Hugh Rodham owned a fabric store. She had a strong Methodist upbringing and her mother Dorothy, nurturing high ambitions for her daughter, encouraged Hillary to be forthright about her goals − although she was rebuffed in an early desire to be an astronaut, told by NASA that "women could not apply". She distinguished herself at Wellesley College, where *Life* magazine reported the speech she made as the first student ever to give the commencement address. After graduating in 1969 Hillary went on to study law at Yale, where she wrote her thesis on children's rights, and also met her future husband **Bill Clinton**. In 1973/74 she worked for the Children's Defense Fund, founded by her mentor Marian Wright Edelman.

Chosen for a US House of Representatives panel to investigate the Watergate scandal in 1974, Hillary nevertheless left the opportunities opening up for her in Washington D.C., to join Bill Clinton at the University of Arkansas. There she taught law, and she and Bill set up a scheme to begin to teach pre-school children from under-privileged families how to read and write. They were married on 11 October 1975 and have one daughter, Chelsea, born in 1980.

In 1977 Hillary joined the Rose law firm in Little Rock, rising to become senior partner by 1992 and specialising in cases involving patent infringement and intellectual property. Bill Clinton meanwhile launched his own political career, becoming governor of Arkansas in 1978. Hillary, retaining her own surname and her high-profile career, was criticised for not being a traditional state "first lady", instead involving herself with policies as an outspoken liberal. Some saw her role as one reason for Clinton losing

office in the 1980 election, although he returned in 1982 and held the governorship for the next ten years. During this time the couple invested heavily in property, including as partners from 1978 in the Whitewater Development Corporation, Hillary also being the firm's lawyer.

Deeply involved with education and child welfare reforms in Arkansas, Hillary also founded Arkansas

Advocates for Children and Families (1977), was named as Woman of the Year in Arkansas in 1983 and was the state's Young Mother of the Year in 1984. She also served on the board of the Southern Development Bancorporation (1986). At national level, she was prominent in the National Center on Education and the Economy (1987) and the Children's TV Workshop (1990). A member of the American Bar Association's committee on women in the legal profession from 1987 to 1991, she was listed in both 1988 and 1991 as one of the most influential lawyers in America.

Bill Clinton's transition from governor of a small state to Democratic Party candidate for the US presidency in 1992 brought a searching appraisal of Hillary Rodham's role. She initially encouraged his candidacy on the basis that she would be closely involved, offering voters a "two-for-one" proposition, but the campaign soon began to see this notion as damaging because of her unpopularity with sections of the electorate. Her forceful personality and the fact that she had a successful career of her own were controversial for traditionalists, heightening the focus on the changing role of women in society. Softening her image to assuage these fears, she began styling herself Hillary Clinton (later reinstating Rodham as a middle name), and even competed for plaudits as a cookie-baking mom against her rival as prospective First Lady, the "incumbent" Barbara Bush.

Once in the White House, Bill Clinton acknowledged Hillary's real abilities with her appointment to chair the healthcare commission, the Clinton administration's first major domestic policy initiative. To the delight of her critics, the commission's reforms were rejected by a hostile Congress in 1994, the whole project was shelved and Hillary was forced into retreat, out of the public eye. However influential her political advice to her husband may have been in private, her public role for the ensuing four years was largely confined to an attempt to measure up as a more traditional First Lady, complete with makeovers of her hair style and wardrobe. Her political statements have mainly been on issues centred on women and children, although

even in these areas she has not escaped controversy, continuing to express her liberal views on abortion rights and employment for women, and leading the US delegation at the UN's Fourth World Conference on Women in September 1995, when she unsparingly criticised the conference host country, China, for its human rights record. She also began writing a newspaper column and completed a best-selling book about children, *It Takes a Village and Other Lessons Children Teach Us*.

Increasingly embroiled in the long-running battles over the Whitewater property company's allegedly corrupt affairs in Arkansas in the 1980s, and related conflict of interest, financial impropriety and concealment-of-evidence issues, Hillary became in January 1996 the only First Lady ever to testify before a grand jury. Although not charged with criminal wrongdoing, she was subpoenaed at the instigation of Whitewater special prosecutor Kenneth Starr in connection with the rediscovery of records of her legal billings, which had mysteriously gone missing from the Rose law firm's offices some years beforehand. A highly critical report published in June 1996 by a Senate inquiry, described by its Republican head as having uncovered "a pattern of deep deception and arrogance", but by her lawyer as "the pre-ordained verdict of a kangaroo court", further diminished her popularity. Also damaging to Hillary's standing at this time was another scandal centring on her role in the dismissal of the White House travel staff.

Hillary was once again drawn into the complex world of political scandals when Bill Clinton's second presidential term (from January 1997) was plagued with allegations about instances of sexual harassment, and about his conduct in concealing an affair with young White House intern Monica Lewinsky. This time, however, Hillary's role won her new respect across the nation. Unstinting in her public support for her husband (despite rumours of bitter family rows in private), Hillary was also one of the key figures in finding a legal basis for defending the president's conduct, at successive stages of the unravelling Lewinsky affair throughout 1998. The public perception grew that, throughout their marriage, Hillary had always been there with the power to drag Bill back from scandals and affairs, while trying to rise above the sordid details.

Although the bringing of (ultimately unsuccessful) impeachment charges against Bill Clinton confirmed that association with him would be a political liability after his second presidential term ended in December 2000, the fresh respect accorded to Hillary for her strength of character and acute intelligence can be expected to open up possibilities for her on her own account. Internationally, ambassadorial roles have been suggested on issues such as women's rights, education and the Northern Ireland peace process. She is involved with charities such as Cancer Research and AIDS Awareness. Meanwhile, her outstanding popularity ratings as of early 1999 made it appealing for Democratic candidates for electoral office to enlist her support, and she herself was considering running in the state of New York as a candidate for the US Senate – with some even speculating that this could be a springboard for a future presidential candidacy.

Fernando **Collor**

Fernando Collor rose meteorically to power in 1989, emerging at the age of 40 as Brazil's first directly elected president since the transition from military rule. A right-winger advocating a dose of free-market economics, Collor's prescription for Brazil's economic crisis at that time involved reducing the burden of the overblown public sector and using shock tactics to control the scourge of inflation. During less than three years in office he achieved some initial successes but at the cost of social unrest and political unpopularity. He fell, as rapidly as he had risen, over allegations of corruption that brought him to the very verge of impeachment, forestalled only by his resignation in December 1992.

Fernando Affonso Collor de Mello was born in 1949 in Rio de Janeiro. His father, a businessman and politician, rose to be governor of the northeast state of Alagoas. Fernando Collor graduated in economics and journalism from the University of Brasilia. He married Lilibeth Monteiro de Carvalho in 1975 and they had two sons, but were divorced in 1981. Collor married his second wife, Rosane Malta, in 1984.

President of his family's media group by 1978, he then followed his father into politics, making his mark before he was 30 as mayor of Maceio (the capital of Alagoas). Elected to the National Congress as a deputy for Alagoas in 1982, he became the state's youngest-ever governor in 1987.

Despite the remoteness of Alagoas, Collor attracted attention at national level for his radical economic reforms, which included an overhaul of the state civil service and cuts in the inflated salaries of top officials. Brazil at this time was emerging from two decades of military-dominated government, but struggling with acute economic problems of soaring inflation and foreign debt which the centre-left transitional government failed to tackle. As the 1989 presidential elections approached, Collor entered the race himself, founding the conservative National Reconstruction Party (PRN) and benefiting from the support of Robert Marinho, president of O Globo television network. Television proved the ideal medium for the dashing young Collor to appeal to a poorly educated population, promising sweeping reforms to revitalise the economy.

Having headed the first-round ballot on 15 November, Collor defeated popular unionist leader Lula da Silva of the Workers' Party in the run-off on 17 December. Collor won 53 per cent of the vote, mainly among businessmen and in small towns, city slums and rural areas. His campaign played up Lula's "red" image and, despite his anti-corruption platform, resorted to "dirty tricks", including bribing Lula's ex-girlfriend to slander him on television. The Workers' Party was sufficiently incensed to reject any suggestion of joining a broad government coalition in Congress, where Collor lacked a power base since his PRN had won only a handful of seats.

Taking office on 15 March 1990, Collor that day introduced the *Brasil Nuevo* austerity plan, bringing in a new currency – the cruzeiro – and aiming to get inflation down from 80 per cent per month to just 10 per cent within six months. The plan instigated drastic cuts in state institutions, reducing wages, laying off public employees and cutting the number of state-owned companies. After initial successes, however, inflation quickly rose again and the recessionary measures of the plan were to prove highly unpopular.

The economy remained the key issue throughout Collor's short-lived presidency (1990–92). His basic thrust was to encourage closely controlled free-market reforms, with an emphasis on raising efficiency and productivity. He repeatedly found himself struggling to build the support to get his tough policies accepted by Congress, and if unsuccessful, resorting to imposing them by presidential decree. Seeking greater flexibility in the options available for economic reform, Collor even tried to change the constitution, but failed in this attempt, thereby weakening his government further. Two years of liquidity "squeezes", cuts in subsidies, price and wage freezes, tax increases and privatisation measures met with resistance within the working population, a spate of strikes, and other signs of social unrest.

Despite the economic difficulties that preoccupied his administration at home, Collor used his presidency to pursue an active role on the international stage. He promoted the formation in 1991 of Mercosur, the common market with Argentina, Uruguay and Paraguay. He also took major steps in renegotiating Brazil's foreign debt and repayment schemes, including innovative "debt for nature" swaps which released money to fund environmental protection schemes. In the environmental arena he suspended Brazil's nuclear power programme and took steps to improve its negative image over the destruction of the Amazonian rainforests, an issue of global concern. The situation continued to deteriorate, however, despite the announcement of measures to improve the conservation of habitat and to protect indigenous forest people from the impact of logging, ranching and mining.

The pinnacle of Collor's presidency was hosting the UN Earth Summit held in Rio de Janeiro in June 1992. However, even this was overshadowed by the allegations of corruption against him. The month before the Earth Summit, his own brother, Pedro Collor de Mello, accused him of involvement in the embezzlement of public funds, worth millions of dollars, by his 1989 election campaign manager P.C. Farias. Part of the money, it was claimed, had gone to create a tropical garden at Collor's home in Brasilia. On 27 May 1992 a commission was set up to investigate the claims.

This was the first direct evidence of corruption involving the president himself, although charges had plagued his cabinet throughout its term, and various reshuffles had attempted to freshen its image. Collor's wife Rosane had been forced to resign as head of the government drought relief agency in August 1991 after accusations that she had given large payments to her already wealthy family.

The commission's findings, which uncovered a web of influence-peddling centring on Farias, led to an overwhelming vote by the Chamber of Deputies on 29 September 1992 to impeach Collor, suspending him from official duties for 180 days while proceedings were held. Criminal charges were also brought against him on 12 November for "passive corruption and criminal association", although he could not be tried for activities which occurred while he was president unless he were to be successfully impeached.

On 29 December 1992 Collor resigned, minutes before the start of the impeachment trial by the Federal Senate. The Senate still proceeded with the trial, and voted two days later by 76 votes to 3 to debar him from political or public office for eight years. No longer immune from criminal prosecution, Collor faced a lengthy investigation, but the case collapsed suddenly and dramatically in December 1994 when much of the prosecution evidence was ruled inadmissible because it had been seized without a court order. The Supreme Federal Tribunal thereupon voted to dismiss the charges due to lack of evidence, a move seen as opening the possibility of Collor returning to active politics once his eight-year ban ended.

Dalai Lama

The Dalai Lama has been in exile from Tibet for most of his adult life, having fled in 1959 after an unsuccessful uprising against Chinese rule. He continues to be held in the highest esteem by his religious followers as the focus of Tibetan Buddhism, while also providing an enduring symbol of non-violent commitment to human rights and the cause of the Tibetan people. Winner of the Nobel Peace Prize in 1989, he has impressed the many political and religious leaders he has met around the world by his personal charm and serenity, combined with the evident sincerity of his concern to end Chinese oppression. However, his willingness to compromise over the issue of sovereignty has yet to convince the Chinese government that it would be worth making concessions to secure agreement with him.

Tenzin Gyatso was born in a peasant family in the small village of Takster in northeast Tibet on 6 July 1935. As a small boy of two, he was first recognised in 1937 as the reincarnation of the 13th Dalai Lama, and he was consequently enthroned in Lhasa as the 14th Dalai Lama in 1940. (The Tibetan Buddhist followers of the teachings of the Bodhisattva of Compassion believe that successive Dalai Lamas are his reincarnations, and they accordingly venerate the Dalai Lama as their spiritual leader, as well as recognising him as temporal ruler of Tibet.) His authority was exercised by a regency until 1950, when he assumed political power.

The forces of the recently established communist People's Republic of China invaded Tibet that year and the Dalai Lama fled briefly to southern Tibet after abortive resistance. He negotiated an agreement with the Chinese in 1951, and continued throughout the 1950s to attempt to reach an accommodation with them. As part of this strategy he participated as vice-chair of the standing committee of the Chinese People's Political Consultative Conference between 1951 and 1959, and chaired the preparatory committee for the Autonomous Region of Tibet from 1955 to 1959. At the same time he pursued his studies in Buddhist philosophy, completing a doctorate in 1959 after working in Tibet's monastic universities.

When a doomed Tibetan national uprising in 1959 was crushed by the Chinese, the Dalai Lama and his government fled to Dharamsala, India. This remains his base in exile and is sometimes referred to as "Little Lhasa". The UN passed resolutions in 1959, 1961 and 1965 calling for China's withdrawal, but the Chinese government regards Tibet as an integral part of its territory, reaffirming in 1964 its status as an autonomous region.

In exile, the Dalai Lama sought to work by peaceful means towards the goal of a free and independent Tibet, with the interim objective of establishing a more representative form of government under the Chinese. Initiatives which he put forward in this respect included the draft constitution he drew up in 1963. Significantly, a five-point peace plan he advanced in 1987, and further elaborated in a speech in Strasbourg in 1988, effectively dropped the demand for full independence. It proposed creating a self-governing democratic Tibet "in association with the People's Republic of China", as well as an end to Beijing's policy of large-scale settlement of Tibet by ethnic Chinese, and a halt to nuclear dumping there.

In a notable contrast with his predecessors' remoteness from the Western world, the 14th Dalai Lama has travelled widely throughout the world since the 1970s, meeting religious and political leaders, discussing both spiritual and human rights issues, and working for the resettlement of Tibetan refugees. His books include *My Land and People* (1962), *A Human Approach to World Peace* (1984) and his autobiographical *Freedom in Exile* (1991). In addition to the 1989 Nobel Peace Prize, he has also received the Congressional Human Rights Award (1989) and the US Freedom Award (1991).

In the 1990s the Chinese authorities took fresh steps to suppress any displays of support for the Dalai Lama within Tibet, and intensified their criticisms of him. China also identified, and enthroned in late 1995, its own candidate for the position of Panchen Lama, the second-ranking figure in the Tibetan religious and political hierarchy. The small boy identified by the Dalai Lama and named in May 1995 to succeed the previous Panchen Lama (who died in 1989) was meanwhile kept under arrest by the Chinese authorities.

Amid increased Western media interest in the Tibetan issue following the release of a popular film about it, there was speculation in 1998 about some possibilities for compromise. In June of that year Chinese President **Jiang Zemin** said, during a Beijing press conference with US President **Bill Clinton**, that the way to negotiation would be open if the Dalai Lama made a public statement recognising Tibet as an inalienable part of China (and also accepting that Taiwan was part of China, a political issue on which the Dalai Lama had studiously refrained from commenting). The Dalai Lama, recognising his lack of power and the real limits of likely Western support, was widely reported in November to be considering a "very positive response", in the hope of making it possible for him to return to Tibet and to obtain religious freedom, the release of political prisoners and reinstatement of the Tibetan language. However, later that month any optimism was dampened by renewed Chinese denunciations of the Dalai Lama.

F.W. **De Klerk**

F.W. De Klerk, the leader of South Africa's National Party from the end of the 1980s until 1997, was the last state president of the apartheid *regime. More importantly, he was the leader who took the historic decision to end the regime's confrontational stance against the demands of the black majority. By accepting the need to free **Nelson Mandela**, and by negotiating with him a transition to majority rule over the space of four years, De Klerk claimed credit (and was awarded a joint Nobel Peace Prize) for a process whose outcome delighted the watching world. Avoiding a bloodbath, he thus helped turn the white population from a racist ruling minority to a still-privileged interest group with much of its economic power intact. A consummately skilful and cool political operator who carried little ideological baggage, he had sufficient vision and confidence to see through his high-risk political strategy, although not without recriminations from the past victims of his regime.*

Frederik Willem De Klerk was born on 18 March 1936 in Johannesburg. His Afrikaner family had been prominent in politics for three generations. His schoolteacher father, Jan De Klerk, became a cabinet minister under the architect of formal *apartheid*, Hendrik Verwoerd, while F.W.'s brother Willem later co-founded the Democratic Party. He was educated at the Monument School in Krugersdorp and at Potchefstroom University, where he ran the campus newspaper and graduated in law in 1958. He attended the Dutch Reform Church and was a member of the youth section of the National Party (NP) and of the *Broederbond*, the all-pervasive secret network of the white elite. While at university he met Marike Willemse, whom he married in 1959. They had two sons and one daughter, but the marriage ended in divorce in November 1998 after he fell in love with Elita Giorgiades, the wife of a Greek shipping magnate and 16 years his junior.

Having completed his qualification in law in Pretoria, De Klerk earned a reputation as an astute lawyer in Vereeniging between 1961 and 1972, as well as participating in community affairs and the local NP branch. In 1972 he accepted the offer of a professorship in administrative law at Potchefstroom, but never took up the post because that same November he entered parliament, winning a by-election in the Vereeniging constituency which he has represented ever since.

From 1978 onwards De Klerk held a series of ministerial posts, under J.B. Vorster and then P.W. Botha. Leader of the NP in Transvaal from 1982, at national level he moved from the ministry of internal affairs to the national education portfolio in 1984. It was here – and as leader of the (white) House of Assembly – that he really began to make his political mark. Perceived as a cautious right-winger and opponent of reform, he advocated maintaining racial segregation within schools and universities, and responded to campus riots with threats of cuts in subsidies unless the universities policed and controlled their students. Violent clashes increased as students rallied against De Klerk's hardline stance, and the courts ultimately ruled that his subsidy cuts were invalid.

By the end of the 1980s the strength of internal dissent against the *apartheid* regime, and the application of international sanctions, had brought some within the NP to the view that basic reforms were needed. This question became a major theme in the unexpected party leadership election on 2 February 1989. Occasioned by P.W. Botha's stroke, the contest saw De Klerk emerge as a narrow winner in the third round, ahead of the candidate preferred by the more reform-minded members of the NP caucus, Barend Du Plessis.

Within the space of exactly one year, De Klerk had taken the NP and the government further down the reform path than any had predicted. It has been suggested that he encouraged his party to view him as relatively right wing as a device to help him secure the leadership; indeed he himself said in a 1999 interview that he was "unfairly characterised as conservative" whereas his real views were more liberal. His first major speech upon winning the party leadership was a balancing act between advocating "renewal and change", and warning that the idea of "one man, one vote" would be "catastrophic" for the country. His initial preoccupation, however, was with establishing his leadership vis-à-vis his predecessor, P.W. Botha, who remained state president and was an increasingly bitter rival until the party finally forced him to resign in August 1989. Only after a general election (which saw the NP returned to power by the white electorate, albeit with a reduced majority) was De Klerk finally sworn in as state president, on 20 September 1989.

Now in a position to embark on the long road of reform, De Klerk's initial steps were undramatic, but on 2 February 1990, at the opening of Parliament, he announced the legalisation of the African National Congress (ANC) and the unconditional release of Nelson Mandela. The unexpectedness of these moves created an upsurge of support. De Klerk used this momentum to rush bills through parliament within weeks to repeal the "petty *apartheid*" acts, including the Separate Amenities Act of 1953, and NP membership was opened to all races. In April 1990,

leaders from all parties met, many for the first time, and talks began on the future of the nation.

De Klerk was treading a narrow path. When he first opened up the possibility of far-reaching peaceful change, the support he received, even among the black population, was so striking that a few NP members even believed he might win in a democratic election. ANC radicals, however, declared he was insincere in his calls for reform, whereas the far right called him a traitor to the Afrikaner *Volk* (nation). De Klerk and Mandela each needed the co-operation of the other to achieve a transition with peace and unity, but they disagreed on how much power would remain in Afrikaner hands. For the ruling white minority, undiluted majority rule on a "one person, one vote" basis could mean exchanging a monopoly of power for a marginal political role, but for three years De Klerk engaged in long debate with Mandela to secure more protection for white interests. At no time would he admit *apartheid* was wrong, since this would have removed all claims of validity for the NP's past role. Careful to prepare the ground to take his party with him on major issues, De Klerk was known for his cool, pragmatic approach, but occasionally tempers flared, and in his 1999 autobiography, *The Last Trek, A New Beginning*, De Klerk revealed that the outward unity with Mandela had belied hostile relations between them.

Ranged against reform were conservatives in De Klerk's own party, still controlling much of the NP's decentralised power base. Meanwhile the police and security forces, operating within the "securocrat" system set up by P.W. Botha, set out to highlight the supposed perils of black rule. It remains disputed how much De Klerk knew of the involvement of security forces in assassinations, massacres and the encouragement of fighting between rival black communities, but it is certain that he was slow to dismantle the "securocrat" system. As delays and suspicions eroded whatever faith the black community had placed in him, white voters too began drifting away from the NP. Putting his career on the line, De Klerk called a referendum in March 1992 to measure white support for the reform process, a bold step which won him approval from over two-thirds of the voters.

1993 saw the announcement of plans for a five-year national unity government to be elected by all races the following year – and the joint award of the Nobel Peace Prize to De Klerk and Mandela. As the chair of the Nobel Peace Prize Committee noted: "These are not saints. They are politicians in a complicated reality."

When democratic elections were held at last in April 1994 the ANC dominated the black vote while the NP retained enough support, mainly among white voters, to make it the second largest party. Implementing the agreement between them, Mandela as the new president appointed De Klerk as one of two deputy presidents within a coalition government. Tempestuous policy arguments between the parties over the next two years led De Klerk to withdraw the NP from this national unity government in June 1996, three years before the end of its intended five-year life – although both he and Mandela managed the split with diplomatic grace, De Klerk declaring that it was for the good of the emerging democracy that a proper opposition should exist.

After one year as leader of this opposition, De Klerk announced his retirement from active politics at the end of August 1997. The Truth and Reconciliation Commission, during its lengthy hearings between 1996 and 1998, drew from him the admission that crimes against humanity had occurred during the *apartheid* era, and an apology for these crimes in general terms. Concerning his own specific responsibility, however, he denied having known at the time of police involvement in the violence, or that he was an "accessory after the fact", and he went to court to prevent publication in October 1998 of the section of the Commission's report on these matters.

Jacques **Delors**

Jacques Delors is the Frenchman most firmly associated with Brussels and with strengthening the federal nature of the European Union (EU), where he was Commission president for ten years from 1985. He raised the profile of the Commission in EU decision-making, and played a prominent role in the completion of the single internal market and the Maastricht Treaty on European Union. Remaining in office until the process of European economic and monetary union was well under way, he was then touted as a possible presidential candidate for the French Socialist Party (PS) at the 1995 elections. However, he declined to put his name forward for what was generally agreed to be a lost cause – despite his credentials and his government experience as economy minister in the PS-led government of the early 1980s.

Jacques Lucien Jean Delors was born on 20 July 1925 in Paris. His father Louis was an employee of the Banque de France (the French central bank), where he himself also worked between 1945 and 1962. Only later did he study law and economics at the University of Paris.

Having been involved during his teenage years with progressive Catholic youth movements, Delors became an active (but always moderate) trade unionist while working at the Banque de France. In 1962 he moved on from the Banque, holding various senior civil service posts, notably as head of the social affairs section at the Commissariat Général du Plan. In 1969 he was appointed general secretary of the inter-ministerial committee for vocational training and social promotion, a position he held until 1973. He also had his first taste of government office, as adviser to Prime Minister Jacques Chaban-Delmas from 1969, initially on social and cultural affairs and then more broadly on economic, financial and social questions. From 1973 to 1979 he was a member of the board of directors of the Banque de France.

Delors's active involvement in party politics began in 1974 when he joined the recently unified Socialist Party (PS). Within two years he had become the party's spokesperson on international economic affairs, and in 1979 he joined the PS executive committee. That June he was elected on the PS list as a member of the European Parliament, where he became chair of the economic and monetary committee. Unlike many French politicians he lacks a strong regional base, his only experience of local government coming when he was briefly mayor of Clichy in 1983/84.

The victory of the French left in 1981, however, provided a promising opening for Delors in national politics. In the heady early days of the **Mitterrand** presidency he held a key cabinet post as minister of economy and finance (adding the budget portfolio in 1983), but was the first to call for a change of course as the country faced increasing economic instability and crisis. Delors was the chief architect of the March

1983 austerity plan, announced the day after he took on the budget portfolio. This plan effectively marked the end of the initial spate of radical economic reforms under which key industries and financial services had been nationalised and social welfare provisions improved. The economic policy "U-turn" created strains within the broad left coalition which finally saw the communists withdraw from government in July 1984 – coincidentally, just as Delors too was leaving the cabinet, having been nominated to become president of the European Commission.

Taking office as successor to the Luxembourgeois Gaston Thorn in January 1985, Delors held office as Commission president for ten years in all (being nominated for a second four-year term in 1988 and for a further two years in 1992). He brought fresh vision and energy to the role, raising the profile of the Commission itself and moving it to the centre of European Community (EC) policy-making. His considerable international reputation as an advocate of greater European integration derives from his achievements in helping to set the agenda and himself presenting a series of key proposals.

Principal among his proposals in his first term of office were the crucial February 1987 white paper on completion of the single internal market (which largely shaped the Single European Act approved by member states in 1987) and the budgetary reforms approved in 1988 (providing for multi-year budgets rather than annual battles over EC spending, tackling the problem of the UK's net budgetary contributions,

reforming agricultural pricing mechanisms, and doubling the regional development spending under the structural funds, with increased targeting on the most disadvantaged regions). Building on his involvement in social issues in France, Delors was also strongly committed to the "social dimension" of European integration process.

Turning his attention to economic and monetary union (EMU), Delors persuaded the EC Council of Ministers to establish in June 1988 the "Delors committee" of central bankers and experts to investigate the prospects for the introduction of EMU. The resulting report identified a three-stage process which formed the basis of the 1992 Maastricht Treaty on European Union – although the eventual agreement fell short of his more far-reaching integrationist plans, with compromises such as the provisions under which the UK and Denmark were to opt out of initial participation in the single European currency.

Delors has chaired for UNESCO since October 1992 the international commission on education for the 21st century. In 1996 he was appointed president of the newly founded, Paris-based study and research association, *Notre Europe*.

Jacques Delors married Marie Lephaille in 1948. Their son Jean-Paul died of leukaemia in 1982. Their daughter Martine Aubry has made her own career in politics, serving as labour minister in the French socialist-led government of 1991–93 and as minister for employment and solidarity from June 1997.

Deng Xiaoping

Deng Xiaoping held no official position in the fast-changing China of the 1990s, yet tiny, aged and frail, he was its dominant figure for two decades until his death in 1997. A veteran communist from the generation who made the Long March with Mao in the 1930s, he was by turns military strategist, deputy premier, influential party official, and – through most of the Cultural Revolution – vilified "capitalist-roader". Fully rehabilitated only after Mao's death, Deng then took on the role of China's New Helmsman, determined to oversee economic change and achieve greater prosperity without major disorder by retaining an iron grip on political power. His commitment to the single-party system allowed no scope for dissent, and Deng was denounced by liberal opinion across the world as the Butcher of Tiananmen after the massacre of pro-democracy activists in 1989.

Deng was born in China under the Manchu dynasty, on 22 August 1904, the eldest son of the wealthiest landowner in Paifang village in Sichuan. His mother died when he was young, and in 1920 he went to work and study in France, having spent some time in preparation for this at the special Chongqing school. He quickly became disenchanted, however, as the scarcity of jobs in France forced him into low-paid factory work, which offered him little in terms of gaining industrial expertise and left few opportunities for study. Like other young Chinese intellectuals in Europe, he became attracted to Marxism and joined first the Chinese Socialist Youth League (where he met Zhou Enlai), then in 1924 the Chinese Communist Party (CCP). Forced to flee France in 1926 because of his communist beliefs, he went first to the Soviet Union, attending the Sun Yat-Sen University in Moscow, then back to China in 1927.

With China riven by factional struggles, Deng's new role as chief political adviser at the training college of Kuomintang warlord Feng Yuxiang was soon rendered untenable by the crumbling of the CCP–Kuomintang alliance. Escaping to the CCP headquarters in Wuhan, he was appointed a secretary to the central committee, changed the second part of his name from Xixian to Xiaoping (meaning "small peace"), and soon transferred to Shanghai, a major focus of CCP–Kuomintang fighting.

In 1928 Deng married Zhang Xiyuan, but when she died from a miscarriage two years later he did not attend the funeral; the revolution had to come first. Head of a successful uprising in Guangxi, he led his forces east in a march on Canton, but was defeated and fled northwards to the communist base in Jiangxi. It was here that Deng became a close follower of the

regional leader Mao Zedong. When Mao's policies fell temporarily from favour within the CCP in 1932, Deng was also accused of anti-party propaganda, and he lost his second wife Jin Weiying to his main accuser. Mao's renewed ascendancy, however, saw Deng appointed as editor of the party paper *The Red Star*. Taking part in the legendary Long March from Jiangxi to Yanan in 1934/35, he nearly died of typhoid en route.

Throughout the next decade and a half he proved himself a proficient military commander and political commissar in northern China, fighting forces of the Kuomintang and the Japanese invasion, and taking front-line commands in the full-scale civil war of 1945–49. He returned to the party base in Yanan only occasionally, including in 1939, when he married for the third time. Deng and his wife Pu Chiungying, who changed her name to Zhuo Lin, had three daughters and two sons.

Although the capture of Beijing by the communists allowed Mao to proclaim the People's Republic of China in October 1949, Deng was involved in three more years of fighting, in southwest China and Tibet, until Kuomintang forces were driven completely from the mainland. He then returned to Beijing, where he took on government responsibilities, as deputy premier and then finance minister, in addition to his party roles. He was elected to the CCP central committee in 1954 and joined the politburo the following year. In 1956 he became a member of the politburo standing committee and party general secretary. Influential in both foreign and domestic policy, Deng was the last senior Chinese negotiator to visit the Soviet Union before the final Sino-Soviet rift in 1960; he set up the scientific body which developed China's first nuclear bomb; and he controlled party appointments, thereby building himself a strong power base.

As a believer in total adherence to the communist single-party state, Deng was appalled by Mao's "Hundred Flowers Movement" of 1957, when intellectuals were encouraged to criticise the system, and it was he who spearheaded the backlash "Anti-Rightist Campaign". Deng was also highly sceptical about extreme leftism, however, and especially doubted the wisdom of the "Great Leap Forward", pushed through at Mao's instigation from 1958 in a disastrous attempt to accelerate industrialisation. He and Zhou Enlai promoted pragmatic measures in the early 1960s to repair the damage and to counter widespread famine, permitting some private peasant cultivation and a (limited) use of rural markets. Deng's pragmatism was frequently embodied in folksy slogans, most famously his dictum that "it

doesn't matter whether it's a black cat or a white cat, as long as it catches mice".

Deng's career appeared to reach an abrupt end in the great upheaval of the Cultural Revolution, launched in 1966 as Mao's ideologically motivated response to what he saw as a threatened revival of capitalism. Stripped of all his posts, branded the "number two capitalist-roader", paraded on a jeep through Beijing wearing a dunce's cap, ridiculed for his love of bridge and mah-jong, and forced to sign a self-criticism, Deng was imprisoned for two years before being sent to work in a tractor factory in remote Jiangxi. His family were terrorised; his son jumped from a window, leaving him paralysed, and his brother committed suicide.

Deng's own life was spared only by interventions from Zhou Enlai, who managed to survive in office as prime minister, and Mao himself. When eventually Mao accepted the need to pull China back from its economic and social turmoil, the prompting of Zhou Enlai secured Deng's temporary rehabilitation. Restored as deputy premier in 1973, and to the politburo the following year, he was appointed vice-chair of the central committee, chief of the general staff and acting premier in 1975. Expected to succeed Zhou on the latter's death in January 1976, he instead fell victim once again to ideological rivalries within the party. When Zhou's funeral provoked pro-Deng demonstrations in Tiananmen Square, he was blamed for the demonstrators' hostility to the radical Gang of Four, led by Mao's wife Jiang Qing. Vilified for his attempts to correct the "great achievements" of the Cultural Revolution, he was once again purged of all his positions and placed under house arrest.

The pendulum swung back after Mao's death that September, as the party central committee woke up to the extremism of the radical "Leftists". The arrest of the Gang of Four marked the end of the Cultural Revolution. Hua Guofeng, Mao's successor, grudgingly bowed to popular pressure and the lobbying of Deng's old army comrades, allowing Deng to return to office in July 1977. Outflanking Hua, Deng had by 1980 manoeuvred his own current protégés, Zhao Ziyang and Hu Yaobang, into key posts in a restructured leadership as, respectively, prime minister and CCP general secretary. Deng himself preferred to guide policy from behind the scenes, allowing prospective successors to jockey for position and compete for his favour. As the "New Helmsman", Deng was China's paramount leader until his death in 1997, although his official leadership posts were few – he resigned his vice-premiership in 1980, chaired the party's central military commission only until 1989, and the state military commission until April 1990. He even resigned from the party politburo, central committee and central advisory committee in 1987.

Although Deng had drawn support in 1977 from among the intelligentsia, in the expectation that he would favour greater democratisation, the crushing of the Democracy Wall movement in 1979 showed how ruthless he could be when criticised. This was to be a recurring feature of Deng's approach to "socialist modernisation" in China, most notoriously demonstrated by the massacre of pro-democracy student demonstrators in Tiananmen Square in June 1989. Whether or not Deng himself gave the order to shoot to kill, that brutal act of repression was his responsibility – and the message it sent was one he stood by. In politics, the party was to retain complete control. His encouragement to "seek truth from facts" was intended for the economic sphere alone.

The economic changes which Deng encouraged were, however, far-reaching indeed. "To grow rich is glorious", he told the Chinese people. Private enterprise, powered by the profit motive, would make the country more productive, and it was progressively introduced in place of the command economy. Here too, however, there were draconian policies – on crime and, most notably, on population control. It was Deng who instigated the one-child policy, overriding any concern about infanticide and other human rights implications because he was determined that economic growth should not be rendered impossible by the rapid expansion of the population.

The agricultural sector was the first in line for Deng's modernisation. Decollectivisation led to private leasing of land and individual responsibility for its development, and subsidies encouraged cottage industries to manufacture everyday consumer goods. In 1984 Deng turned his attention to the reform of industry, setting up enterprise zones on the coast as experiments in foreign investment of money and technology. The success of these, creating a massive export industry, and the privatisation of much of the state sector were intended to stimulate industry throughout China, but in fact the disparity between rich and poor became heightened and the inland economy remained based on agriculture except in the major cities.

Under Deng's leadership, China reduced defence spending, fully re-opened relations with the USA, and improved ties with Japan and the Soviet Union, while seeking to expand trade and attract foreign investment in Chinese industry. Deng's "one country, two systems" formula, elaborated in 1984, also opened the way for the return of Hong Kong (achieved in 1997) and Macau to Chinese rule, although reunification with Taiwan remained elusive.

A hardened smoker, Deng suffered at the end of his life from breathing problems, and he was increasingly affected by Parkinson's disease. He died on 19 February 1997 at the age of 92, before he could see his cherished dream of the return of Chinese rule over Hong Kong. The *Selected Thoughts of Deng Xiaoping* and other ideological works remain as important documents of his times; his "theory of building socialism with Chinese characteristics" was hailed by his effective successor **Jiang Zemin** as ranking alongside Mao Zedong Thought in China's guiding ideology.

Diana, Princess of Wales

"Princess Di", the tabloids called her. Media attention dominated her marriage, divorce, public role and private life. Her death in a Paris car crash in August 1997, pursued by photographers keen to capture her new affair with Dodi al-Fayed, focused further attention on the nature and paradoxes of her celebrity. A pretty but quite unexceptional girl from an English aristocratic family who became a "fairytale princess" with her glamorous wedding to the heir to the throne in 1981, Diana had quickly charmed the public and produced two sons. However, her loneliness behind the public role, and the emotional vulnerability which contributed to the eventual breakdown of her marriage, combined to give her a sense of special affinity with victims, the damaged and the distressed. Divorced in 1996, she had then sought more scope to put her glamour to compassionate purpose as a "queen of hearts", bringing comfort to children and the sick and fronting an international campaign against landmines.

Lady Diana Frances Spencer was born on 1 July 1961, the youngest of four children of Edward Spencer, Viscount Althorp – equerry to both George VI and Elizabeth II – and his wife Frances. Brought up at Park House on the royal estate at Sandringham, the Spencer children often played with the Queen's younger sons, Andrew and Edward. Diana was six when her mother left in an acrimonious separation. Her father won the

ensuing custody battle. He remarried in 1976, having moved into Althorp, the ancestral mansion, the previous year after acceding to the title as the 8th Earl Spencer on his own father's death.

Diana went from Riddlesworth Hall preparatory school to boarding school at West Heath, Kent, in 1974, leaving with no O-levels in 1977 and spending a year at a Swiss finishing school, the Institut Alpin Videmanette. Too tall to pursue her ambition to become a ballerina, she took a variety of jobs, as a nanny, a cook and then as a nursery school assistant at the Young England School in London.

As a teenager, Diana reputedly had a crush on Charles, Prince of Wales, whom she had taught to tap dance when he visited her sister Sarah to shoot at Althorp in 1977. In 1980, her life was altered irrevocably when she met him again. Charles, aged 31 and in search of a prospective wife of noble lineage with a spotless past, now saw her as both an attractive young woman and a suitable bride. The tabloid press got wind of blossoming romance and camped outside her London flat to capture shots of the future princess. The following year, on 29 July 1981, their "fairytale wedding" in St Paul's Cathedral was watched by millions worldwide.

At first shy and terrified by her sudden celebrity, Diana would be pursued for the rest of her life by cameras prying for every secret, snatched shot or scoop – although she quickly learnt to use the media spotlight too, for her own ends and for causes she supported. Photogenic, high-spirited and with a strong sense of style, she was to become a supreme international icon, whose image could sell any magazine or paper.

Diana's first solo overseas engagement was in 1982 as the Queen's representative at the funeral of Princess Grace of Monaco, killed in a car crash. The rounds of royal appearances confirmed Diana's popularity, charm and natural ease with the people she met. Within a year, too, she had fulfilled her own desire to start a family, and the need for a royal heir, by giving birth to a son, William, on 21 June 1982. Her second son, Harry, followed on 15 September 1984. Striving to give her sons a stable, loving family life, however, she began to chafe at some aspects of the long-established royal role, notably insisting on taking the infant Prince William when she toured Australia with Charles in 1983. The royal family appeared to close ranks, resisting the implied challenge to its traditions and jealous of Diana's ability to woo the public and the media. Nor, it later emerged, did her life with Charles live up to her ideals – and the popular image – of the romantic and perfect marriage. Even as she evolved into a svelte beauty, whose elegance helped revitalise the world of fashion, Diana was feeling isolated and lonely within the royal establishment, suffering from bulimia and making several half-hearted suicide attempts in desperate cries for help.

In the early 1990s press speculation soared as Charles and Diana themselves made oblique public statements about their growing estrangement. In mid-1992 her perspective on the marriage was revealed sensationally by the publication of *Diana: Her True Story*, a best-selling book written by Andrew Morton. In December 1992 the couple announced a formal separation. One year later, Diana decided to withdraw from public life while she determined her new role on the fringes of the monarchy. She resigned from most of her charities, retaining only those particularly important to her and whose profiles were benefiting most from the prestige of her patronage. These were mainly unglamorous causes relating to the outcasts of society, including the disabled, AIDS and leprosy sufferers, abused children and the homeless.

The tabloid revelations and rumours continued, fuelled in 1994 by an unprecedented television interview in which Charles admitted to extra-marital relations with "old flame" Camilla Parker-Bowles. In

a highly dramatic television interview of her own in 1995 Diana also admitted adultery, claiming she had been forced to seek consolation and comfort elsewhere by the presence of Camilla throughout her marriage and the lack of her acceptance in the royal family. Shortly after the interview the Queen asked the couple to reconsider divorce. Diana had hitherto ruled this out, not wanting to follow the same path as her own parents, but in February 1996 she relented and a divorce was granted on 28 August. The settlement left her with around £15 million plus annual maintenance for her private office. She could keep all her jewels, but lost her "HRH" prefix to become "Diana, Princess of Wales".

Now outside the royal family, but even more in the public eye, Diana started playing an informal "ambassadorial" role for particular causes which would give substance to the aspiration she had expressed in her 1995 interview to become "the queen of people's hearts". In this last phase of her life, which was to last just one year before her tragic death, she auctioned many of her outfits for charity, and in January 1997 visited Angola to highlight the Red Cross campaign to ban landmines. Typically, her contribution centred on compassion and a touching sympathy with victims – and it won enormous popular approval, despite criticism from some politicians that she had crossed the boundary into making political statements.

She continued to promote the anti-landmine campaign during a visit to Bosnia in August 1997, before flying to Sardinia with her new companion Dodi al-Fayed, son of the owner of London's prestigious Harrods department store, Egyptian billionaire businessman Mohamed al-Fayed. As usual the press were on her heels, speculating on their relationship and scavenging for shots of a kiss. On 30 August the couple concluded their holiday with dinner at the Ritz in Paris. Speeding away afterwards, with the paparazzi cameramen in pursuit on motorbikes, their chauffeur-driven Mercedes crashed into the wall of an underpass. Dodi al-Fayed and the driver died at the scene, and Diana, fatally injured, died at La Pitie Salpetriere Hospital at 4am.

Rumours, reports and reconstructions of the sequence of events generally ascribed the high-speed crash to drunkenness on the part of the driver, although others – including Mohammed al-Fayed – suggested more sinister causes. An official French police inquiry concluded in January 1999 but delayed the release of its findings.

Diana's funeral brought out to an extraordinary degree the emotional significance vested in her by millions of people in Britain and beyond. Held in Westminster Abbey on 6 September 1997, it was preceded by press criticism of the Queen for not mourning openly in public. The funeral procession (in which Charles walked behind the coffin with their two sons, her brother, and Prince Philip) and the service itself were watched on television by nearly half the world's population. Carpets of flowers led to every public building, and millions queued to sign hundreds of condolence books. Praise was heaped on Diana's humanitarian work and capacity to reach out to "ordinary" people, even as her brother attacked the way the press had hounded her and denied her privacy.

Criticised in life by the traditionalists, for lowering the dignity of the royal family and destroying the aura it needed to remain "special", Diana was applauded by others for modernising the monarchy and bringing it into contact with normal people. She continued to dominate that debate for months after her death, as the Queen sought to reassess the identity, the meaning and the role the monarchy should have in the future.

Wim **Duisenberg**

Dutch banker Wim Duisenberg is the first head of the new European Central Bank – the custodian of rectitude in monetary policy, entrusted with vital powers by the European Union member states involved in the launching of a single European currency. No dour technocrat, the chain-smoking Duisenburg enjoys, on the contrary, something of a reputation as a bon viveur. *He is generally pragmatic about resolving political differences, but as a central banker he has placed himself firmly in the camp of monetary orthodoxy. His 15-year stint as president of the Dutch central bank (1982–97) established his inflation-controlling credentials and his identification with the creed of "sound money", although in his earlier spell as finance minister in the Dutch labour government of the mid-1970s he had followed a more Keynesian approach to promoting economic growth.*

Willem (Wim) Frederik Duisenberg was born on 9 July 1935 in Heerenveen, Friesland, in the Netherlands. He studied economics at the University of Groningen, gaining his degree with distinction in 1961 and going on to research his doctorate, which was awarded in 1965, on the economic consequences of disarmament. Duisenberg has been married twice and has two sons and one daughter by his first marriage. He married his second wife, Gretta Nieuwenhuizen, in 1987.

Between 1965 and 1969 Duisenberg worked for the International Monetary Fund (IMF) in Washington D.C. He returned to the Netherlands as an adviser to the governing board of De Nederlandsche Bank, the Dutch central bank, and in 1970 took up an academic post as professor of macroeconomics at the University of Amsterdam.

A member of the socialist *Partij van de Arbeid* (PvdA), Duisenberg joined the centre-left government of Joop den Uyl as minister of finance in 1973. The policies that he pursued in response to the oil shock of that year, like those adopted by other European governments, were based on a Keynesian approach, using public expenditure as a demand-side tool to promote economic recovery. The consequent rise in the budget deficit, resulting especially from the growing burden of the welfare system, culminated in what economists came to call "the Dutch disease".

Duisenberg left office in 1977 when the multiparty coalition collapsed, but retained a seat as a PvdA deputy in the general election of that year. In 1978 he left parliament to become vice-chair of the executive board of the co-operative Rabobank Nederland, and in 1981 moved to the central bank as executive

director. A year later he was appointed president of the bank, a post he held for the next 15 years.

A pragmatist rather than a dogmatist, Duisenberg now adopted a thoroughly different approach from the one he had advocated as finance minister, based on a strong guilder, budgetary austerity, and the reform of welfare spending. In 1983 he fixed the guilder to the deutschmark, the benchmark of monetary stability in Europe. In the early 1990s, when the Dutch economy was stronger than that of Germany, Duisenberg was even confident enough to act ahead of the German Bundesbank on occasion when taking decisions on lowering interest rates.

As head of the Dutch central bank Duisenberg was a member of the board of directors of the Bank for International Settlements (BIS) in Basle, and acted as chair of the board and BIS president from January 1988 to December 1990 and from January 1994 to June 1997. He also chaired the committee of central bank governors of the member states of the EEC for the 1993 calendar year, and was a member of the council of the European Monetary Institute (EMI) in Frankfurt from its inception in January 1994.

In June 1997 he was appointed to succeed Alexandre Lamfalussy as president of the EMI – the precursor to the European Central Bank (ECB), which was due to come into existence with the introduction of the euro from 1 January 1999. It was accordingly widely assumed that Duisenberg was in line to become president of the European Central Bank for an eight-year term from 1999. However, when the time came to make the ECB appointment, the French government pressed hard in support of its own preferred candidate, Jean-Claude Trichet, and it became necessary to find a compromise solution. Duisenberg was accordingly nominated in May 1998 for an initial period of only four years. The apparent understanding that he would then "voluntarily" step down to make way for Trichet has since been called into question, with Duisenberg expressing the view that he could decide to serve a full eight years. He was sworn in as president of the European Central Bank on 1 June 1998.

Duisenberg has welcomed the German-inspired "stability pact", concluded among EU member countries, which sets out to limit budget deficits. He argues that the introduction of the euro will speed up the structural changes to labour and product markets needed for the introduction of economic and monetary union. In mid-1998 he gave an optimistic assessment of the economic outlook for the EU as a whole, projecting real growth of around 3 per cent in both 1998 and 1999, although by the autumn he had conceded that the turmoil on world financial markets, provoked by the crises in Asia, Russia and Latin America, would have a "dampening effect" on global growth.

Michael **Eisner**

The head of the Walt Disney Company for the last 15 years, Michael Eisner has been described by the New York Times *as "the man who can shape culture on a global basis like perhaps no other person in history". He is a successful corporate boss who plays up the glamour of the high-rolling world, and his celebrity status has helped foster the US media cult of the top business leader, complete with awards, razzmatazz and self-promoting autobiography. Very much "hands on" and identifying with all things Disney, Eisner is an enthusiast with a firm belief in keeping concepts simple, combining this with an equally firm grasp of financial management and how to drive a tough bargain. He is both politically and socially conservative, and critics and business rivals have decried him as dictatorial, paranoid and an egomaniac, while his company has been taken to task for shortcomings on ethical issues like requiring suppliers worldwide to meet acceptable employment standards.*

Michael Dammann Eisner was born on 7 March 1942 in Mt Kisco, New York State, and grew up in a well-to-do New York Jewish family, living in prestigious Park Avenue. His father Lester was a property developer with firm ideas about the importance of rules in the upbringing of his children. Michael was educated first at Lawrenceville School, where he did well academically and on the sports field (especially tennis and American football). He then went to Denison University, where he graduated in English and theatre arts in 1964. He took up his first job in the same year with the National Broadcasting Company (NBC), where he was a logging clerk, and then at Columbia Broadcasting Systems, where he worked as a programming engineer. By 1966 he had become assistant to the national programming director at American Broadcasting Companies (ABC), and then ABC's director of programme development for the East Coast. He married Jane Breckenridge in 1967, and their long marriage and strong commitment to their family (of three sons, Breck, Eric and Anders) has become legendary in Hollywood circles.

In 1971 Eisner was appointed ABC's vice-president for daytime programming and then senior vice-president for prime-time production and development. His name was made at ABC by the huge success of the *Happy Days* series and *Roots*.

In 1976 Eisner moved to Paramount Pictures Corporation, where he was president and chief executive officer until 1984. His eight years at Paramount saw a major reversal of the company's lagging role in US film-making, with a succession of blockbuster films (including *Raiders of the Lost Ark*, *Saturday Night Fever* and *Airplane!*) which quickly

propelled the company to the top position among the largest film companies in the USA. Under Eisner, Paramount also quadrupled its network television presence and made an early impact on the fast-growing cable TV market by acquiring a 33 per cent stake in the USA Network.

In 1984 Eisner was appointed to his present position as chairman and chief executive officer of Walt

Disney Productions (known after 1986 as the Walt Disney Company). Just as he had done at Paramount, he joined a company which seemed to have lost its way, and succeeded within a few years in revitalising it. The Eisner administration produced not only a rapid succession of stylish animated features in the traditional Disney cartoon mould (*The Little Mermaid*, 1989; *Beauty and the Beast*, 1991; *Aladdin*, 1992; *The Lion King*, 1994; *Pocahontas*, 1995; *The Hunchback of Notre Dame*, 1996; *Mulan*, 1998), but also a series of technologically adventurous animations which made extensive use of computer-generated animation (*Who Framed Roger Rabbit?*, 1988; *Toy Story*, 1996; *It's a Bug's Life*, 1998).

Eisner did not, however, neglect other forms of film-making. The success of popular mass-market titles such as *Down and Out in Beverly Hills* (1986) and *Three Men and a Baby* (1987) gave Disney the confidence to move into part-ownership of various foreign art-house film companies, some of them the kind of outfits which would certainly not have been acceptable partners in the more obsessively wholesome days of Walt Disney himself. At the same time, television series such as *The Golden Girls* were receiving critical acclaim within their own medium. Eisner was instrumental in Disney's 1996 takeover of his old company, Capital Cities/ABC, which is now a wholly owned subsidiary of Disney. The buyout of ABC and acquisitions like Miramax and the ESPN sports network made Disney the world's largest conglomerate in the field of news and entertainment, and Eisner has also sought to position his empire in the rapidly expanding Internet area, building around ABC's content and the Infoseek search engine as a point of entry.

Meanwhile Eisner has pressed ahead with Disney's drive to develop and expand its network of theme parks around the world. The original Disneyland and Epcot centres were joined by the Disney–MGM Studios Theme Park, the Disney California Adventure, the 5,000-acre Celebration Town and the International Sports Center at Walt Disney World in Florida. Other US-based projects included the Disney Institute, an educational park. A new Disney theme park is being built in Tokyo, adjacent to the existing Tokyo Disneyland park.

Eisner was less immediately successful, however, in his efforts to export the Disneyland concept to Europe. His flagship European project, the EuroDisney theme park near Paris, ran into early problems because of the company's apparent inability to adapt its archetypically American cultural standards to its new European location; indeed, it took many years before EuroDisney overcame the cultural suspicions of French consumers and started to make a profit, but EuroDisney is now the most popular commercial destination in Europe.

It was in this context of Gallic suspicion about Disney's intentions toward French culture that Eisner took the courageous decision to focus two of Disney's most important cartoons, *The Hunchback of Notre Dame* and *Beauty and The Beast*, on French stories. In recognition of his efforts, he was made a chevalier of France's Légion d'honneur. He is a member of the board of directors at Denison University and the California Institute of Arts, and the author, with Tony Schwarz, of a book entitled *Work in Progress*, a "business autobiography" published in early 1999.

King **Fahd**

King Fahd of Saudi Arabia is reputed to be the fifth richest man in the world. His family fortune is calculated to be around US$25 billion, derived from the country's immense oil wealth. He has ruled Saudi Arabia since June 1982, showing his determination to protect his mainly Sunni Muslim kingdom and its Wahhabi orthodoxy from the turbulence of radical Islamic fundamentalism in the wake of the revolution in Iran. Governing according to Islamic law, he adopted in 1986 an additional official title to denote his religious role, the Custodian of the Two Holy Mosques. King Fahd maintains a conservative absolute monarchy in which he is head of government as well as head of state, ruling by decree. Now in his late seventies, he has been frail since a stroke in 1995, and the country faces the possibility of a period of change under his most likely successor.

Prince Fahd ibn Abdul Aziz was born in 1923 in Riyadh, the eldest of the seven sons of King Abdul Aziz ibn Saud, founder of the Saudi state in the modern period, and his favourite wife Hassa. He graduated from the Scientific Institute in Makkah. In 1953 he was appointed (Saudi Arabia's first) minister of education and introduced a series of five-year development plans in an attempt to improve his country's education system. In 1962 he became minister of the interior, and by 1967 was second deputy prime minister. In March 1975, on the accession to the throne of his half-brother Khaled, Fahd was appointed crown prince and deputy prime minister. As crown prince he was the effective ruler of the country and oversaw the implementation of successive five-year development plans.

Since his own accession to the throne on 13 June 1982, following Khaled's death, Fahd has continued to take responsibility himself for the country's subsequent development plans, emphasising the growth of the private sector. On 1 March 1992 he introduced a Basic Law for the System of Government, and later that year restructured the *Majlis ash-Shoura* (the Consultative Council). He has introduced new laws governing the administration of the Saudi provinces and the Council of Ministers.

King Fahd has long taken an active interest in Saudi's international position. In 1977, he met with US officials to discuss solutions to the Arab–Israeli conflict, and in 1981 he outlined his own "eight-point peace plan", which became the basis for the Fez declaration. He called in 1985 for increased US intervention in the Middle East. Under Fahd's leadership, Saudi Arabia attended the 1991 Madrid peace conference and the 1992 Moscow peace talks.

The 1991 Gulf conflict, arising from the Iraqi invasion of Kuwait the previous year, sent shock waves through the conservative monarchies of the region. Fahd permitted the US-led allied forces to operate from Saudi Arabia, a decision for which he was strongly criticised by radicals elsewhere in the Arab world, but the tight grip which his regime maintains on domestic affairs effectively prevented the expression of any dissent.

In 1992 Fahd donated emergency relief funds to Bosnia and established a Supreme Committee for the Collection of Donations for the Muslims of Bosnia.

King Fahd has had six sons. The first of his three wives, Princess Anud, died in March 1999. His half-brother, Prince Abdullah, has been crown prince since Fahd came to the throne and deputised in 1995/96 when Fahd was described officially as resting, having reportedly suffered a stroke. Fahd has been significantly weakened ever since this illness, giving rise to repeated speculation about the succession, which intensified when he underwent hospital treatment again in Riyadh in March and August 1998. However, he was discharged from hospital on 18 August 1998 after a team led by a US surgeon had reportedly successfully completed an operation to remove his gall bladder. Prince Abdullah undertook a world tour the following month, apparently designed to raise his profile internationally, which encouraged speculation about competition between factions of the royal family.

Louis **Farrakhan**

Louis Farrakhan is the controversial proponent of separatism among African–Americans in the USA, involved with the Black Muslim movement from 1955 onwards and leader since 1977 of the Nation of Islam organisation. Often condemned as a racist, he became a "hate figure" across the USA when he offered his backing to Jesse Jackson's presidential campaign in 1984, and outraged all but his own supporters with widely reported remarks about Jews. Disowned by Jackson and shunned by mainstream political groups, he nevertheless built up confidence among African–Americans by backing community businesses and organisations, promoting an image of work, control, pride and discipline which is fostered by his own example and his smartly uniformed followers. The potent appeal of this emphasis on self-respect, which lies at the heart of Farrakhan's separatist ideology, was best demonstrated by the mass participation in his Million Man March in 1995.

Louis Eugene Walcott, as he was originally called, was born in Roxbury, Boston, Massachusetts, on 11 May 1933. He and his brother were brought up, in a neighbourhood then predominantly Jewish, by their mother, an immigrant from St Kitts by way of Bermuda (where the young Louis also spent some of his childhood). Working as a seamstress and housekeeper, she managed to finance music lessons for Louis, who was something of a child prodigy as a violinist; he won a national talent competition at 14 when he was one of the first black musicians to appear on the Ted Mack Amateur Hour.

At home Louis and his brother were encouraged to be hardworking and disciplined, and also to respond to their direct awareness of racial discrimination by studying and discussing ideas about black people's struggle for freedom, justice and equality. Louis graduated at 16 from Boston English High School and gained an athletics scholarship (as a promising sprinter) to Winston-Salem Teacher's College in North Carolina. In 1953 he married his childhood sweetheart, Betsy, during his unfinished senior college year, leaving to support his family by earning money in the Boston area as a calypso singer ("Calypso Gene"). He and his wife have had nine children in the course of their long marriage and their family now extends to many grandchildren and great-grandchildren.

His brief musical career ended with his conversion in 1955 to Elijah Muhammad's Nation of Islam, which taught that black people should take pride in stressing their separate racial identity and reject white-dominated society as an aberration. Louis experienced what he described as a rebirth when he was taken to hear Elijah Muhammad preach at a rally. He adopted

the name Louis X, following a Black Muslim tradition where the "X" stood for the "unknown" true heritage of the African–American, stolen during the slave trade. Taking the decision to dedicate his life to the teachings of Elijah Muhammad, he gave up show business when he was told by Malcolm X, the minister of the Nation's New York temple, that it was not compatible with being a Black Muslim.

In the ensuing years he worked to build up the Nation of Islam temple in Boston and was a captain in the movement's security organisation, the Fruits of Islam. In the bitterness engendered by a split in 1963 between Malcolm X and Elijah Muhammad, he is said to have described Malcolm X as worthy of death, and he has never shaken off rumours that he was involved in Malcolm X's killing in February 1965. (Many years later, however, in January 1995, when Malcolm X's daughter, Qubilah Bahiyah Shabazz, was charged with trying to hire an FBI informant to kill Farrakhan, he publicly defended her, dismissing the affair as an FBI attempt to entrap her.) Moving to New York, he took charge in May 1965 of the Nation's temple in Harlem, formerly led by Malcolm X. It was at this time that he changed his name to Louis Farrakhan, a new surname given to him by Elijah Muhammad. Speaking at rallies across the USA in the ensuing decade, combining the messages of black separatism and economic rebirth, he became known as the movement's national spokesman, noted both for his charisma and his attacks against what he denounced as white and Jewish exploitation and domination.

After Elijah Muhammad died in 1975, Farrakhan disagreed with the direction in which Elijah Muhammad's son and designated successor, Warith Muhammad, began trying to take the movement. Breaking away when Warith Muhammad began accepting whites as members of what he restyled the "World Community of Al-Islam in the West", Farrakhan set up in late 1977 a rival Nation of Islam organisation under his own leadership.

It was the 1984 presidential campaign of Rev. Jesse Jackson which first gained Farrakhan the headline-hitting notoriety among white Americans which made him one of the most controversial political figures in the country. Whereas Black Muslims had generally neither voted nor taken part in mainstream US politics, in line with Elijah Muhammad's definition that they were a separate nation, Farrakhan gave Jackson his enthusiastic support as the first credible African–American presidential candidate. Deploying Fruit of Islam militants as a security force

in response to death threats sent to Jackson by Jewish extremists, Farrakhan went on to cause Jackson severe embarrassment with a series of widely reported and highly inflammatory remarks. These included describing Judaism as a "gutter religion", and asserting his people's "legitimate complaints" against Jews as former slave traders and slave owners, ghetto employers and slum landlords. Most notoriously of all, in a March 1984 radio broadcast, he appeared to relish the idea that Jews called him Hitler, saying: "Well, that's a good name. Hitler was a very great man." Despite Farrakhan's subsequent attempt to explain that he regarded Hitler as "wickedly great", Jackson acted decisively to distance himself and his campaign from the Nation of Islam leader.

Condemned by opponents as anti-semitic, anti-Catholic, anti-white, misogynist and anti-gay, Farrakhan stressed that he preached dignity for the black man; he has also described anti-semitism as driven by "just plain envy" of the achievements of Jewish communities and Jewish enterprise. Returning in 1985 to the theme of building up separate political, social and economic structures (he said in March 1984 that God "doesn't want us mixing ourselves up with the slavemaster's children, whose time of doom has arrived"), Farrakhan launched his POWER programme for black economic development, along with a company selling health and beauty products door-to-door. The Nation of Islam newspaper, *The Final Call*, spread the message of separatism, including in each issue a statement of "What the Muslims Want" which spelled out: "We want our people in America whose parents or grandparents were descendants from slaves to be allowed to establish a separate state or territory of their own – either on this continent or elsewhere. We believe that intermarriage or race-mixing should be prohibited."

Sufficiently successful to repurchase in 1988 the Nation of Islam's former flagship temple building in Chicago, Farrakhan rededicated it as Mosque Maryam, the National Center for Re-training and Re-education of the Black Man and Woman of America and the World. Successive three-year economic programmes sought to establish an economic base for the development of black businesses, with highlights including the 1995 opening of the US$5 million Salaam Restaurant in Chicago. The Nation's annual Saviours' Day celebrations drew growing audiences, with 60,000 people participating in the event in 1992 at the Atlanta Dome. The internationalisation of the Saviours' Day idea was celebrated in October 1994 in Accra, Ghana, where Ghanaian President **Jerry Rawlings** opened a five-day convention marked by the presence of a 2,000-strong African–American delegation led by Farrakhan. The importance which Farrakhan places on the Nation's links back to Africa had already been underlined by the holding of the Second African/African–American Summit in Libreville, Gabon, in May 1993.

Although Nation of Islam membership remained small – some estimates suggest that it has not exceeded 16,000 – Farrakhan grew in political significance in the mid-1990s as the leading voice of separatism and an assertive African–American identity. This coincided with the perception that Jesse Jackson's "rainbow coalition" approach to politics had been sidelined when **Bill Clinton** captured the Democratic Party presidential nomination in 1992, while at the same time **Colin Powell** had emerged as a celebrated "all-American" integrationist role model and leadership figure.

A powerful demonstration that Farrakhan could mobilise an impressive response among African–Americans came when over 800,000 took part in the Million Man March which he organised on 16 October 1995. From across the USA they converged on Washington D.C. for a "holy day of atonement and reconciliation". The event culminated in a two-hour speech by Farrakhan. Condemning doctrines of white supremacy, he urged the participants to commit themselves to self-improvement and to making their communities "safe and decent places to live" in a country which he described as still "two Americas, one black, one white, separate and unequal". Farrakhan re-registered to vote in June 1996, as part of his push for political empowerment. He has since been involved in building a coalition of religious, civic and political organisations, while the Nation of Islam provides employment and training through the businesses it has developed, and runs rehabilitation programmes for prisoners, drug addicts and gang members.

Always controversial within the USA, Farrakhan has been banned from visiting the UK since January 1986, when the government feared that an invitation issued to him by Hackney Black People's Association might spark a resumption of rioting in London. In June 1998 a disturbance involving Nation of Islam militants at hearings in London into the killing of black teenager Stephen Lawrence led to UK Home Secretary Jack Straw renewing the exclusion order against Farrakhan, who was then on a major world tour. During his previous and controversial 18-nation tour of Africa and the Middle East in early 1996, which notably including a meeting with South African President **Nelson Mandela**, Farrakhan caused particular outrage when he joined his hosts in Iran in using the term "the Great Satan", widely used there to describe the USA. An Iranian newspaper quoted him as saying "God will destroy America by the hands of Muslims". The Nation of Islam was also debarred under US anti-terrorism legislation from receiving funding offered by Libyan leader **Moamer al-Kadhafi**, reportedly amounting to US$1 billion.

Alberto **Fujimori**

Alberto Fujimori has effectively monopolised political power in Peru in the 1990s. A former academic and sometime television talk-show host, he prides himself on being the man who saved the country from the terror of the Maoist Shining Path movement. His tough stance against terrorism has carried over into his authoritarian attitude to political opposition in general. The steps he took to extend his own presidential powers in 1992, widely if clumsily described as a "self-coup", were followed by the introduction of a new constitution allowing him to seek a second term of office, and in 1996 Congress produced a controversial interpretation of the rules on re-election allowing him to seek a third term in the year 2000. Fujimori's popularity, however, has been eroded by resentment of his harsh neo-liberal economic measures, especially since rapid economic growth gave way to recession in 1998.

Alberto Keinya Fujimori was born on 28 July 1938 in La Victoria, Lima. The son of Japanese immigrants, he converted to Catholicism. After his schooling in Lima he went to the National Agrarian University in La Molina, graduating in 1961 with a degree in agronomic engineering and joining the teaching staff in the mathematics department. Returning after a period spent studying mathematics abroad (at the

University of Strasbourg in 1964, and then at the University of Wisconsin, where he got a master's degree in 1969), he rose to be dean of the school of sciences, and eventually rector of the university from 1984 to 1989. In 1987 he was elected chair of the National Assembly of University Presidents.

Fujimori gained experience and a reputation as a skilful political analyst during his time as rector, hosting a television talk show, *Getting Together*. In 1989 he launched a political career, co-founding the political movement *Cambio 90* (Change 90) and becoming its candidate for the 1990 presidential election.

His unexpectedly strong performance in the first-round ballot on 8 April 1990 gave him second place and forced a second-round run-off against the novelist Mario Vargas Llosa, who was standing as the candidate of the right-wing Democratic Front (*Fredemo*). In the second ballot on 10 June Fujimori won convincingly, with 56.5 per cent of the votes cast, to his opponent's 34 per cent. This result was seen as a protest vote, supporting the claim of *Cambio 90* to be a new alternative to the traditional parties, and reflecting suspicion of his opponent as a member of the elite. Fujimori successfully projected a populist image, attracting strong support from the rural and urban poor. Known as *El Chinito* (the "little Chinaman"), he was seen by Peruvian Indians and *mestizos* (those of mixed race) as not belonging to the dominant minority who were of European descent.

Fujimori was sworn in on 28 July 1990, confronting an economic crisis, a crippling debt burden and hyperinflation. Upon taking power, he instituted austerity measures whose nature and severity shocked many of his supporters. Despite his populist campaign, his policies once in office were calculated to strengthen the free-market economic system by a combination of deregulation and decentralisation, and to restore confidence among international lenders. This approach did succeed in slowing down the rate of inflation, bringing it gradually below three figures and eventually down to just over 10 per cent by 1995. Meanwhile, between 1991 and 1993, Fujimori paid a series of visits to Japan, other parts of east Asia, Europe, the USA and Latin America, in an attempt to gain support and financial backing for the Peruvian economy.

Equally controversial, but more popular, was his hard line against the Maoist guerrilla insurgency of the Shining Path (*Sendero Luminoso*), whom he has confronted without paying much heed to criticism from human rights organisations. Already given extensive emergency powers by the Congress in 1991, he launched an *autogolpe* or "self-coup" on 5 April 1992 to give himself a free hand, dissolving Congress, suspending the national constitution, and dismissing top-ranking government officials and 13 of the 23 Supreme Court justices. In September, the Shining Path leader Abimael Guzman was captured, and a year later Fujimori announced that he had received a letter sent by Guzman from prison, requesting talks towards an eventual "peace treaty".

Fujimori pushed through in the course of 1993 a new constitution which increased his own powers as president and removed the bar on a second term (enabling him to stand for re-election on 9 April 1995, when he won almost two-thirds of the vote). In 1996, moreover, he got congressional acceptance to seek a further term in 2000, on the grounds that the 1993 constitution allowed two terms, and that his first term did not count because he began it under the previous constitution. An attempt by the opposition to have the matter of a third term referred to referendum was quashed by the pro-Fujimori majority in Congress in September 1998.

The image of Fujimori as a man of action was promoted by his personal direction of operations in early 1995 in a border conflict with Ecuador (which was not formally settled until October 1998). The international spotlight fell on him once again when left-wing *Tupac Amaru* guerrillas seized control of the home of the Japanese ambassador during a reception on 17 December 1996, initiating a long siege. Eventually, adopting a characteristically high-risk strategy, Fujimori on 22 April 1997 ordered in a commando unit which successfully stormed the compound, freeing the hostages (one of whom was killed, along with two of the soldiers) and killing all 14 of the guerrillas. In May 1998 Fujimori again got Congress to give him special legislative powers, this time to spearhead a fight against organised crime, with the backing of new and draconian penalties and the use of military tribunals to deal with suspects.

Fujimori married Susana Higuchi, a civil engineer, on 25 July 1974, and the couple had four children. A public dispute between them in 1994, when he issued a decree to try to prevent her entering politics, led to a high-profile rupture in their marriage, which ended in divorce in November 1995.

Rajiv **Gandhi**

Rajiv Gandhi was assassinated on the election trail in May 1991. He had been campaigning to restore the Congress party to what had hitherto appeared its almost permanent place as India's ruling political party. Although the party did win that election (substantially on a sympathy vote), it subsequently fell apart in government, and in many ways it was Rajiv's death which marked the end of its ascendancy. He had never intended a political career, but succeeded his mother, Indira Gandhi, as both party leader and prime minister when she was assassinated in 1984. Although he appeared to grow into his new role, the "Mr Clean" image with which he spearheaded the Congress election victory that December became tarnished in a series of government corruption scandals, which contributed to its temporary loss of power in 1989. An ill-fated intervention in Sri Lanka's ethnic conflict also contributed to this defeat – and, ultimately, to Rajiv's death, victim of a Tamil Tiger suicide bomber.

businessman who married Indira in 1942 and was later divorced from her.

After receiving his early education at the exclusive Doon's School for Boys in Dehra Dun, Rajiv went to Trinity College, Cambridge, in 1964, where he failed to qualify for an engineering degree. In 1968 he married an Italian, Sonia Maino, whom he had met in Cambridge where she was a student at an English-language school. With few professional qualifications and no political ambition, he decided on a career as an airline pilot with the domestic carrier, Indian Airlines.

In 1980 Gandhi was catapulted into the public arena following the death of his far more politically oriented brother, Sanjay Gandhi, in an air crash. Forced to bow to pressure from his mother and continue the Nehru family's political legacy, in 1981 he entered the *Lok Sabha* (India's lower house of parliament) after successfully contesting a seat from his brother's Amethi constituency. In 1983 he was elected president of the ruling Congress party. The assassination of his mother in 1984 led quickly to his appointment as her successor. In December of that year he led the Congress party to a record electoral victory, campaigning on his reputation as a man with modern ideas untainted by corruption – which earned him the nickname "Mr Clean".

Gandhi introduced a programme of liberal economic reform spearheaded by technocrats. Initially his reforms met with enthusiasm, but by 1987 support for his administration had fallen as reports surfaced of growing factionalism and allegations of corruption. The most damaging of these pertained to claims that the Swedish arms manufacturer, Bofors, had bribed

Rajiv Gandhi was born into a distinguished Kashmiri Brahmin family on 28 August 1944 in Bombay. Grandson of India's first prime minister, Jawaharlal Nehru, he was the elder of two sons of Nehru's daughter, Indira Gandhi, who was also to become prime minister. Rajiv's father, Feroze Gandhi (no relation to Mahatma Gandhi), was a successful senior Congressmen and members of Gandhi's own family in exchange for government contracts. Gandhi's difficulties were also compounded by the upsurge of separatist violence in Punjab and Kashmir and by foreign policy blunders, notably the failure of an Indian peacekeeping mission whose intervention he had foisted upon the government of Sri Lanka, ostensibly to end the civil war there by dealing with the insurgency by Tamil separatists.

In 1989 the Congress party suffered a heavy defeat in the general election although it retained its position as the largest single party in parliament. Gandhi, re-elected as party leader despite this defeat, successfully exploited his role as a power broker in the following two years by contributing to the fall of two successive governments and forcing a fresh general election. The electoral campaign which opened in mid-May 1991 saw him in confident mood, deliberately eschewing heavy security and adopting a more informal style to boost his personal popularity.

On 21 May 1991 Gandhi was assassinated at a mass rally in Sriperumpudar, about 22 miles from Madras in the southern state of Tamil Nadu. The attack, staged by a female suicide bomber belonging to the militant Sri Lankan Tamil organisation, the Liberation Tigers of Tamil Eelam (LTTE), suggested that Gandhi may have been killed on the orders of the LTTE in retaliation for his abortive peace mission in Sri Lanka in 1989. Nevertheless, his assassination triggered a substantial "sympathy vote" which helped return Congress to power in June 1991.

Rajiv Gandhi will be remembered less for his leadership qualities than for his conduct as a scion of the Nehru family who, having reluctantly assumed the responsibilities of power, ensured that the Congress party remained the preserve of India's most eminent political dynasty.

This family legacy put pressure on Rajiv's widow, Sonia Gandhi, to take over as Congress president. Although an unlikely candidate, being a foreigner by birth, she appeared to some to be an acceptable choice, at least until one of her two children could succeed their father. However, Sonia Gandhi's well-known distaste for politics proved an obstacle, prompting her repeatedly to turn down the leadership of the Congress party. At the same time, her cultivation of a "Sphinx-like" personality, seemingly above the fray of party politics, clearly appealed to large sections of the party, eager to restore the party to the position it once enjoyed under Nehru as India's premier "national" party. In August 1998 Sonia Gandhi finally assumed her husband's mantle as party leader. She had already been persuaded to lead Congress's February 1998 general election campaign – a move which failed dismally to prevent the party from being routed, although by the end of the year she was being seen as more of a real electoral asset.

Bill **Gates**

Bill Gates is the richest man in the world, with a personal fortune generally reckoned to amount to between US$50 billion and US$100 billion. Much of his wealth is in the form of stock holdings and options in the phenomenally successful personal computer software giant, Microsoft Corporation, of which Gates is co-founder, chairman and chief executive officer. He combines a genius for programming and an astute grasp of the possibilities of information technology with an intensely competitive nature and a ruthless approach to corporate strategy. While Gates himself frequently cites the dictum that "only the paranoid survive", his critics accuse him of a desire to destroy his competitors, and fear that he is seeking to convert Microsoft's position as industry leader into "world domination".

William Henry Gates III was born on 28 October 1955 in Seattle, Washington, the second child of three (and the only son) in a wealthy family. His father William was an attorney while his mother Mary, originally a schoolteacher, was a forceful and outgoing personality with a high-profile role as board member in various organisations. The young Bill Gates – known always at home by the nickname Trey

– had a number of battles of will with his mother as a child. Educated at a public elementary school and then sent to Seattle's elite private Lakeside School for Boys, Gates was already running a small computer programming business by the age of 13, starting with company payroll systems. By the time he entered Harvard University in 1973, studying mathematics and economics, he was already sufficiently proficient to undertake the development of a new programming language, known as BASIC, for the first true microcomputer, the Altair 8800.

Within 18 months of embarking on his BASIC project, Gates and his former school friend and business partner Paul Allen had perfected the new language to the point where they could license it to the Altair's manufacturers, Micro Instrumentation and Telemetry Systems. Allen encouraged Gates to drop out of college at this point to concentrate on their new company, the Microsoft partnership, based initially in Albuquerque, New Mexico. Although Gates was the main driving force, his initial role was mainly taken up with programming while Allen was more involved on the business side. (The two later split after acrimonious disputes and Allen left Microsoft, but was in time brought back on to the board at Gates's instigation.) Microsoft became a fully incorporated company in 1976, and during the next two years the company went on to develop other versions of the BASIC language for computer systems at General Electric, NCR and Tandy.

Microsoft's most important breakthrough came in 1980, when it was approached by International Business Machines (IBM) in connection with IBM's newly announced personal computer and asked to supply an operating system (a simple programme which makes a computer's electronic circuitry respond to commands from the various "applications" which the computer user may want to run). Gates bought the rights to a third-party operating system and rapidly developed it further under the name MS-DOS (Microsoft Disk Operating System); he then leased the MS-DOS operating system to IBM. It was also in 1980 that Gates brought in a former Harvard classmate, Steve Ballmer, to join Microsoft, a company where the close circle around Gates has always been a major factor, as has the culture of combative argument and creative conflict.

MS-DOS achieved such a dominant position in the personal computer market that IBM and Microsoft were soon forced by the US courts to declare their system architectures as "open standards". For IBM, the ruling meant that the company's competitors would henceforth be permitted to develop "clone" machines that could mirror IBM's hardware architecture, provided that they did not copy it exactly. For Microsoft, it meant being forced to disclose secret technical information that would allow other software developers to integrate their programs more closely with the MS-DOS operating system.

The court ruling was particularly significant, in retrospect, in that it reflected an already growing concern about the commercial power that Microsoft could exercise if it retained exclusive control over its world-beating operating system. By forcing the public disclosure of all the operational "handles" within the IBM PC and within MS-DOS, the court was attempting to head off the possibility that the two companies might try to use their proprietary secrets to monopolise the market for both hardware and third-party application programs. Far from diluting Microsoft's position, however, the "open standards" ruling effectively ensured that the MS-DOS operating system became almost ubiquitous throughout the global personal computer market.

Microsoft did not, however, limit itself solely to the IBM/MS-DOS business nexus. Indeed, it was originally for the rival Apple Macintosh computer system that Gates's company developed its next biggest selling program, the word processing software

Microsoft Word (which was only later developed in a version for use in the MS-DOS environment). The company's next important move, in the mid-1980s, was to develop a mathematical spreadsheet program, called Excel, which quickly established a clear lead over the market leader Lotus 1-2-3. Databases and graphics programs followed.

Meanwhile, Gates's work with Apple had opened his eyes to the limitations of the largely text-based character of the MS-DOS operating system, and particularly to the problem that it was considerably harder for novices to use than the more flexible and graphically oriented Macintosh system. Within a year Gates had started work on the first Microsoft Windows operating system (actually an add-on package for the existing MS-DOS operating system), which proved an instant success with both home and business users because of its visual attractiveness and its multi-tasking flexibility.

Gates was caught uncharacteristically off guard when the Internet, the world's first telephone-based computer network, started to become popular among domestic and business users in the mid-1990s. Having at first dismissed the new phenomenon as a passing trend, he realised belatedly that the networking and linking of computers in many different locations could in fact threaten the autonomy of the stand-alone microcomputer on which his MS-DOS and Windows programs had always been based. In a famous turnaround, he told his company in 1996 that it was to make a big bet on the Internet.

A key move was to restructure the Windows operating system so that it was closely integrated with the company's version of a "browser", the software used to "surf" and interact with computers on the Internet. The way this was done brought government accusations that Microsoft was trying to "appropriate" the Internet. Specifically, an anti-trust case was brought against the company on the grounds of anti-competitive practices, allegedly designed to ensure that various essential Internet access functions could only be made to run within the Windows environment if a user was already using Microsoft's own browser software. The justice department's case against Microsoft became a highly complex one with numerous ramifications, and as of April 1999 was yet to be resolved in the courts.

Gates has often been portrayed by his business rivals as something of a social recluse, with few interests apart from computing, biotechnology (in which he also has business interests), reading, and the occasional round of golf or bridge. Yet his grasp of corporate management and strategy is unrivalled; moreover, his decision to build his company around the protective environment of a so-called "campus" has allowed him to exercise near-total control over the living and working environment of the Microsoft staff. The atmosphere helps sustain the staff's virtually unbreakable commitment to the company, in which Gates himself is closely involved on a day-to-day basis and is the unquestionable intellectual and decision-making focus. His book *The Road Ahead*, setting out his vision of the development of information technology, was a best-seller both when it was first published in 1995, and when a revised edition appeared in paperback in 1996. Gates has also founded the Corbis Corporation, buying up electronic rights in art and photographic images held in museums and private collections worldwide, to develop a huge digital archive.

Gates was married on 1 January 1994 to Melinda French, a former manager at Microsoft. The couple have one daughter, Jennifer Katharine Gates, who was born in 1996. They live in a mansion built in 1997 beside a lake near the Seattle headquarters of Microsoft, where Gates has installed sophisticated electronic controls to run the lighting, air conditioning, security, and music and video entertainment systems. Gates reportedly proposed to his future wife during a visit to the home of stock market investment guru **Warren Buffett**, who is third in the list of the country's wealthiest men. The two billionaires have developed a particular friendship, even though Buffett is more than 20 years older than Gates and their business interests have so far remained separate.

Newt **Gingrich**

*Newt Gingrich dedicated his life to politics from early childhood. Reaching the height of his power in his first year as speaker of the US House of Representatives in 1995, he was the archetype of the ruthless party politician pushing a radical right-wing anti-tax and anti-welfare agenda. Brandishing a ten-point "Contract with America" and overturning the Democrat majority in the 1994 congressional elections, Gingrich forced President **Bill Clinton** to adjust to a Congress in hostile hands. The momentum behind the Gingrich agenda, however, was dissipated in a long conflict over the budget, in which Gingrich came to appear obstructively partisan and personally petulant. Having once again misjudged the mood of the US people over the impeachment of the president in the Lewinsky sex scandal in 1998, Gingrich resigned as speaker in November 1998.*

Newton Leroy McPherson was born on 17 June 1943, in Hummelstown, near Harrisburg, Pennsylvania. His mother Kathleen (Kit) Daugherty, already separated from his father Newton McPherson, took the infant to her mother's home. She divorced McPherson in 1947 to marry Robert Bruce Gingrich, who adopted Newt and gave him his surname. Meanwhile Newt's grandmother taught him to read at four, impressing upon him her belief in education. Newt's stepfather took his family on a series of US army postings, including France and Germany, where Newt started secondary school in Stuttgart. Completing his schooling at Baker High School in Columbus, Georgia, and already determined to become a Republican congressman, Newt Gingrich went to Emory University, graduating in 1965, and then to Tulane University (completing a doctorate in modern European history in 1971). He took a post as an associate professor of history and environment at West Georgia College (1970–78), using the job as a stepping stone to campaign for a seat in Congress.

During his second year at Emory, Gingrich married his former high school maths teacher, Jacqueline Battley, although his stepfather strongly opposed the marriage and boycotted the ceremony. The couple had two daughters, but in 1980 Gingrich demanded a divorce (he was criticised for his callousness in discussing the terms of separation the day after Jackie underwent surgery for uterine cancer), and in 1981 he married Marianne Ginther.

Gingrich's political career was taking off by this time and he was making a reputation as an arrogant and awkward newcomer in Congress, having been elected to the House of Representatives for a suburban

district of Atlanta, Georgia, in 1978 (his third attempt at winning the seat). Gingrich helped form the Conservative Opportunity Society (COS) among right-wing Republicans who, unlike the party's congressional leaders, refused to resign themselves to the long-established Democrat dominance of the House. Their attack on "big government" was generally in tune with the Reagan presidency

(1981–88), but they stood out for their extreme hostility to the welfare state, their persistent, strident demands for tax cuts, and Gingrich's ruthless use of any weapons available, a notable favourite being the charge of corruption, against political opponents.

As newcomers without the seniority and party preferment to obtain influential positions in the House committee system, COS members compensated by taking every chance to speak on the House floor, using the opportunities for publicity presented by the fact that proceedings were now being televised. The efforts of Speaker Tip O'Neill to control this, leading up to his exasperated rebuke of Gingrich's behaviour on a notorious occasion in 1984, enabled Gingrich to seize the opportunity for revenge, and he managed to get O'Neill formally disciplined for making a personal criticism of a House member.

Gingrich's combative stance gained more adherents among Republicans in the House after the 1984 elections. One impetus was their outrage when the Democrat-dominated House awarded election victory to the Democrats in an Indiana district which had gone to repeated re-counts. Gingrich's condemnations contrasted sharply with the apparently affable acceptance of the situation by Republican minority leader Bob Michel. By the time of the 1986 congressional elections, Gingrich had become general chairman of the party action committee, GOPAC, set up to help its candidates in their local contests. He grasped the opportunity to implement his long-held view that a unified message and consistent campaign tactics would deliver better results for the party. He worked determinedly to coach candidates, advising them to avoid problematic issues like abortion, to focus on strategy and "our rhythm and style", and to keep labelling their Democrat opponents with accusations of betrayal, corruption, and adjectives like "sick" and "bizarre".

Between 1987 and 1989 Gingrich led a prolonged and ultimately successful campaign to force the resignation of (Democrat) House Speaker Jim Wright, working through the ethics committee with repeated accusations of corruption relating to a book publishing contract. By the time Wright resigned,

Gingrich had become minority whip – second in the party hierarchy in the House after the minority leader. He used this position in 1990 to co-ordinate a remarkable coup that reinforced his identification with tax-cutting, helping to vote down what he saw as an insufficiently radical budget deficit reduction plan put forward by Republican President **George Bush**.

A bitter opponent of President Clinton (who took office in January 1993), Gingrich had his own triumph with the congressional elections of 1994, when the Republicans, campaigning around his ten-point "Contract with America", won majorities in both houses of Congress. When the new House convened in January 1995 Gingrich was elected as speaker, the first Republican to hold this office for 40 years. Having declared his intention to see the Contract embodied in legislation within 100 days, Gingrich achieved this with all but one of the ten points (the exception being term limits for members of Congress). The effectiveness of his control over Republicans in the House was ensured through the Speaker's Advisory Group, and by the streamlining of the committee structure and the scrapping of the seniority system, so that key committee chairmanships went only to those known to be firmly committed to pushing through the Contract.

Talk-show appearances and daily newspaper headlines made Gingrich's name a household word, but his project, grandiosely described as "Renewing American Civilization", became increasingly bogged down in a bruising confrontation between the legislative and executive branch, as Clinton refused to sign the relevant bills into law. Controversially, Gingrich used the tactic of non-cooperation, to the extent of twice forcing the temporary closure of government business, in an effort to compel Clinton to give assent to the massive budget-balancing bill, and to compel him to fund tax cuts through big reductions in social security spending.

Time magazine named Gingrich as its Man of the Year for 1995, but in fact the opinion polls were showing the tide turning against him well before the year was out. Senate Majority Leader Bob Dole, seeing the Republicans being blamed for the budget crisis and their unwillingness to compromise, began pressing for a more constructive approach and "adult leadership" of the party. Gingrich was eventually won over to Dole's stance, accepting in January 1996 the need to allow through the essential spending bills. Gingrich had by this stage lost much public esteem. He had been made to appear particularly petulant when in November 1995 he said he had taken a tough line partly for personal reasons. He had been angered, he said, because Clinton had snubbed him on the presidential aircraft, when they both attended the funeral of the assassinated Israeli prime minister **Yitzhak Rabin**.

By the time a settlement was eventually reached to enact the balanced-budget legislation in April 1996, it was generally perceived that Clinton had emerged victorious from his battle with an obstructive Congress. That autumn, with elections looming, the House acquiesced in voting through the expenditure for the 1997 fiscal year. Moreover, Gingrich reacted to the November 1996 election outcome – the re-election of a Democrat as president and a Republican Congress – with a promise to move away from confrontation. "We have," he said, "an absolute moral obligation to make this system work. This Congress will be the 'implementation Congress'."

He was by this time under severe pressure himself from the ethics committee, over charges he had initially dismissed as merely an attempt at revenge over his earlier action against Speaker Jim Wright. Criticised over a book deal with publisher **Rupert Murdoch** to the point where he gave up a promised US$4.5 million (accepting instead a US$1 advance, plus royalties), he was then compelled to admit in December 1996 that he had given inaccurate evidence over a matter of political funding connected with GOPAC, having used tax-deductible donations to fund two college courses that he taught on "Renewing American Civilization". His re-election as speaker on 7 January 1997 was a far more muted occasion than in 1995 (when his supporters had loudly cheered the result), marred by opposition from nine Republicans. His speech on taking office, with an apology for having been "too brash, too self-confident or too pushy" and for bringing "controversy or inappropriate attention" to the House, was followed two weeks later by a 395:28 House vote approving the ethics committee's reprimand and a US$300,000 fine – the first such action against a sitting speaker.

Much diminished in his political impact through 1997, Gingrich nevertheless survived a mid-year attempt by the radical right to oust him in favour of someone still wedded to their tax-cutting agenda. In August 1997, when Clinton finally signed a bill requiring a balanced budget by 2002, it was notable more as a reflection of a new bipartisan spirit than as the achievement of a major Gingrich objective. The following year, as the Clinton–Lewinsky sex affair unravelled, Gingrich worked assiduously to publicise the evidence and press for the impeachment of the president, but it became evident that he had again misread the public mood. The November 1998 congressional elections fell far short of his hopes of delivering the deathblow to the Clinton presidency with a Republican landslide. Blamed by some disappointed Republicans as one of the contributing factors in alienating the voters, and by others for having abandoned the radical ideological crusade by which he had mobilised the party in 1994, Gingrich resigned his post as speaker of the House on 6 November 1998, announcing at the same time that he would be resigning his House seat in due course.

Gingrich's interests outside his direct political involvement include wildlife conservation (an issue in which he has been involved since mounting a campaign for a zoo in Harrisburg when he was ten), children's and health charities, and promotion of information technology and the opportunities opened up by the Internet. His books include *Window of Opportunity*, the agenda-setting *Contract With America* and *To Renew America*, and a 1998 political memoir, *Lessons Learned the Hard Way*.

Felipe **González**

Felipe González has been the dominant political figure of the post-Franco era in Spain. A charismatic, skilled and pragmatic politician, he first came to power in 1982 as a representative of a dynamic younger generation, heading the first left-wing government since the civil war of the 1930s. He was in office as prime minister for 14 years (1982–96), helping to consolidate democracy and to promote Spain's integration within Europe. Elected on the promise of a modern approach to socialism, his government came to disillusion its more radical supporters, however, by its apparent acceptance of high social costs in pursuit of economic "realism". Since Spain's vote for change in 1996 González has taken a back seat, giving up the party leadership, but angrily contesting the ongoing investigations into links between his government and "anti-terrorist" hit squads in the 1980s.

He is married to Carmen Romero and they have two sons and a daughter.

In 1964 González joined the Spanish Socialist Workers' Party (PSOE), which was banned under the Franco regime (and thus compelled to hold conferences abroad, usually in France); it was only eventually legalised in early 1977, more than a year after the dictator's death. Elected to the PSOE national committee in 1969, and to the national executive in 1970, González was part of the party's radical internal "renovator" wing, which consisted mainly of young professionals like himself. The renovators gradually gained the ascendancy within the party, successfully challenging the ageing, exiled leadership and winning approval in 1972 for their strategy of working in alliance with other anti-Franco forces.

González was elected in October 1974 as PSOE secretary-general, in which capacity he was a major figure in the broad opposition front in the last days of the Franco regime and the post-Franco transition. The PSOE emerged as the second largest party at the June 1977 general election, four months after it was officially legalised. González himself headed the PSOE list in Madrid, gaining a seat in the *Cortes* (parliament) which he has held ever since.

Between 1977 and 1982 the PSOE provided the main parliamentary opposition to Adolfo Suárez's centrist government. González was meanwhile fighting, and winning, a battle to make the party more electable. Having courted controversy by proposing the removal of the official "Marxist" label (only adopted as recently as 1976), he persuaded an extraordinary congress in September 1979 to adopt a

Felipe González Márquez – commonly referred to by his first name as simply Felipe – was born on 5 March 1942 in Seville. He studied law in Spain and at the Catholic University of Louvain in Belgium, specialising in labour law. He joined the Young Socialists in 1962, and in 1966 opened the first labour law office in Seville to deal with workers' problems.

more anodyne formula, merely recognising the value of Marxism as an analytical tool, and to commit itself to a more moderate manifesto. Re-elected as secretary-general, he led the PSOE into its period of greatest popularity, culminating in a landslide victory in the October 1982 general election. At the age of 40, González became prime minister in Spain's first left-wing government since the civil war.

In power for the next 14 years, González played his part in the stabilisation of Spain's young democracy, winning re-election (albeit with a drop in support for the PSOE each time) in 1986, 1989 and 1993. After Spain's years of isolation under Franco, he also promoted closer integration into western Europe. Spain joined the European Communities in January 1986 and, after initial hesitation, González backed continued Spanish membership of the North Atlantic Treaty Organization (NATO), which was confirmed in a referendum in March 1986. Spain later provided logistical support to US forces en route to the 1991 Gulf war.

The González government's pragmatic policies, to promote economic efficiency and modernise Spanish society, flourished in the rapid economic expansion that characterised much of the 1980s. The monetarist remedies which were then adopted to combat inflation, however, and the high cost they exacted in terms of public-spending cuts and job losses, provoked protests and strikes by left-wing parties, students and disillusioned trade unions. González himself came to be seen as isolated from the electorate, while the country entered a recession and unemployment rose above 20 per cent. His support was also undermined by a series of corruption scandals involving members of his government, PSOE representatives in parliament, and former heads of the paramilitary Civil Guard and of the Bank of Spain.

Re-elected only narrowly in 1993, González's PSOE depended on the support of moderate Basque and Catalan nationalists to get legislation through parliament. This left him obliged to concede further self-rule powers to these regions. Increasingly, however, his government was dogged by allegations that it had been implicated in a "dirty war" waged against Basque separatists between 1983 and 1987. These scandals, combined with the overall feeling that the PSOE and González had been long enough in office, contributed to his party's defeat in the March 1996 general election. In June 1997 González was replaced as party leader by his friend and ally Joaquin Almunia.

Out of government, González continued to be troubled by the "dirty war" issue, and the continuing investigation of the alleged links in the 1980s between his regime and the shadowy Anti-Terrorist Liberation Groups (GAL). The Supreme Court ruled in November 1996 that there was insufficient evidence to implicate him personally and he repeatedly distanced himself from the GAL affair. He was sufficiently incensed, however, by what he regarded as a politically motivated witch-hunt, that he offered his own services as a defence lawyer when his former justice minister was given a ten-year prison sentence in July 1998 for illegal detention and diversion of public funds.

In the international arena, González has been a vice-president of the Socialist International since 1978 and is now president of the organisation's Global Progress Foundation. He was appointed in December 1996 as the representative of the Organization for Security and Co-operation in Europe (OSCE) in the former Yugoslavia, and in 1998 as the European Union's special envoy in Kosovo. In early 1999 it was suggested that he might become president of the European Commission, following the downfall of **Jacques Santer**. In the event, however, the former Italian prime minister **Romano Prodi** emerged as a more widely acceptable compromise, González being too much associated with a socialism which the new generation of "Third Way" politicians found uncomfortable.

Mikhail **Gorbachev**

*Scarcely featuring on the international scene since 1991, and without honour in his own land, Mikhail Gorbachev was nevertheless one of the world leaders of the 1980s who had most impact in shaping the ensuing decade. A reforming communist whom **Margaret Thatcher** memorably identified as "someone we can do business with", Gorbachev turned out to be the last Soviet communist leader (1985–91). He shares responsibility for the peaceful retreat from the cold war, the ending of the iron curtain division of Europe, and the demise of Soviet communism itself – the last of these being something which he had sought to avert by reforming the system, but in which, ultimately, he reluctantly acquiesced.*

Mikhail Sergeyevich Gorbachev was born on 2 March 1931 in Privolnoye village, Krasnogvardeisky district, in the Stavropol region of the north Caucasus. His father Sergei Andreyevich was a machine operator before the Second World War, and an economist and local party official afterwards.

Although he had to work as a tractor driver from the age of 14, Gorbachev gained a place to study law at Moscow University, where he was active in the Komsomol youth movement and joined the Communist Party of the Soviet Union (CPSU) in 1952. He also met Raisa Maksimovna Titarenko, a philosophy student, whom he married in 1953; they have one daughter, Irina.

Upon graduation he returned to Stavropol in 1955 to work first as a Komsomol official, then from 1962 for the CPSU. He became party first secretary for Stavropol in 1966 and first secretary of the regional party committee in 1970. He also studied by correspondence for an agriculture degree, which he completed in 1967.

A member of the CPSU central committee from 1971, Gorbachev moved to Moscow in November 1978 to work as its secretary for agriculture. He became a candidate member of the politburo a year later and a full member from October 1980. When his chief mentor Yury Andropov, who also came from the north Caucasus, became CPSU general secretary after Leonid Brezhnev's death in 1982, Gorbachev came to be seen as a possible successor. In Andropov's temporary absence, it was he who chaired the committee handling the September 1983 Korean airliner crisis. When Andropov died the elderly Konstantin Chernenko became stopgap leader, but his death in March 1985 opened the way for Gorbachev to become general secretary. Unexpectedly, the position of chair of the Supreme Soviet (head of state) was separated from the general secretaryship and given to veteran foreign minister Andrei Gromyko at this time, but Gorbachev succeeded to this office too in October 1988.

Once in power, Gorbachev initiated the twin processes of *perestroika* (restructuring) and *glasnost* (openness). These were intended as reforms within the communist framework, but the momentum led eventually to the collapse of the Soviet system. Starting as an anti-corruption campaign, *glasnost* extended to the release of dissidents and unleashed demands for wider freedom of information, while plans to transform the economic and political system into a "socialist pluralist democracy" resulted in 1989 in competitive elections to a new Congress of People's Deputies. In early 1990 Gorbachev even accepted the demand for recognition of other parties, removing the constitution's reference to the CPSU's "leading role".

Abroad, he began a "charm offensive", seeking relations with the West which would afford the economically failing Soviet Union some relief from the pressure of the arms race. His meeting with US President Ronald Reagan in Geneva in November 1985 was an early breakthrough, the first of a sequence of summits after a six-year gap. The Intermediate Nuclear Forces (INF) treaty, signed in 1987, opened the road to the strategic arms reductions talks (START), the arena for some of Gorbachev's most startlingly original negotiating gambits and the eventual framework for bringing the cold war to an end.

Slower to unfreeze, but no less dramatic in its impact when the thaw did come, was the Soviet sphere of dominance in eastern Europe. Abandoning the "Brezhnev doctrine", Gorbachev made it known among the leaders of the Warsaw Pact member countries in 1989 that there would be no armed intervention to prevent internal change. Taken together with the withdrawal of Soviet troops from Afghanistan, the Soviet disengagement from eastern Europe in the wake of the rapid collapse of the region's communist regimes marked the most dramatic transformation of the geopolitical map for 40 years.

The high-water mark of Gorbachev's popularity in western Europe came in 1989/90, thanks both to real breakthroughs on disarmament and his decision not to give Soviet support to the tottering communist regimes of central and eastern Europe. It was this which had euphoric East German crowds chanting his name.

Acclaimed abroad for his statesmanship, and honoured by the Nobel Peace Prize judges in 1990, Gorbachev faced sustained criticism at home. The old guard saw compromise as fatally weakening the Soviet system, while radicals pressed impatiently for faster change. The Soviet Union itself, in chronic economic crisis, was torn by nationalist and secessionist demands. Gorbachev, having taken on the title of state president in March 1990 as part of a restructuring of Soviet leadership posts, began in April 1991 the so-called "nine-plus-one" talks with other Soviet republics on a new union treaty. He was continually outflanked, however, by demands from the Russian republican leadership and others for more radical reform – and unable to claim the democratic mandate which the popular Russian leader **Boris Yeltsin** was able to evoke as republican president after direct elections in June 1991.

The pace of change, and especially the new draft union treaty which envisaged a reduction in central powers, provoked leading army generals and their conservative allies to attempt to halt the process by force. Gorbachev, unable to harness to his own reformist objectives the more radical demands which had been unleashed within the Soviet Union, now suffered a double ignominy. First his powerlessness was exposed, as the conservatives briefly took over in the August 1991 coup in Moscow; then he was "rescued" by Boris Yeltsin in such a way that Yeltsin all too obviously called the shots thereafter.

That the August coup collapsed was in large part because of Yeltsin's courageous opposition at the Russian parliament building. Gorbachev, absent from Moscow on an ill-timed holiday, dissociated himself from the coup, but his role was the subject of much speculation and his position was terminally damaged. The reversal of the coup made Yeltsin the hero of the hour, thus accelerating the break-up of the Soviet Union. Gorbachev, having resigned as general secretary of the CPSU on 24 August 1991, stepped down as president of the Soviet Union on 25

December 1991, handing over to Yeltsin the command of the armed forces and control of nuclear weapons. By the end of the year the Soviet Union was no more, its successor states more or less loosely associated through a new Commonwealth of Independent States.

Gorbachev has largely disappeared from domestic view since stepping down. When he stood in the Russian Federation's June 1996 presidential election he came seventh, with a derisory 386,000 votes or 0.51 per cent of the poll. He does still make occasional appearances in the Western media, giving his perspective on events such as the accession of three former Warsaw Pact member countries to membership of the NATO alliance in March 1999.

Author of numerous publications, he is also propounding a global environmental charter drawn up by Green Cross International, an organisation which he founded in 1993. He heads a Moscow-based International Foundation for Socio-Economic and Political Studies (the "Gorbachev Fund"), in which he invested some of his own money. However, there was growing uncertainty about the future of the Foundation in the late 1990s, as it became clear that Gorbachev was running out of funds. After resorting to the expedient of appearing in television adverts for a pizza chain, he claimed in a December 1998 German magazine interview that he had lost all his remaining savings, amounting to some £50,000, which had been held in a Russian bank which crashed because of the collapse of the rouble.

Alan **Greenspan**

As chairman of the US Federal Reserve Board since 1987, Alan Greenspan has become the world's most highly regarded, as well as most powerful, central banker. His long period in office has spanned both Republican and Democrat administrations. The importance placed on US monetary policy, together with his own good-humoured unflappability, have lent enormous weight to his views and made stock exchanges around the world highly attentive to his comments and statements. He is perhaps most famously associated with questioning the "irrational exuberance" which was driving up share prices in late 1996, even though this warning was not in itself sufficient to dampen down the prolonged "bull run" in the US markets.

Alan Greenspan was born on 6 March 1926 in New York City, the son of Herbert Greenspan, a stockbroker. A talented young musician, his education included a period at the Juillard School in New York, where he studied the saxophone and clarinet. He moved on in 1945 to New York University (where he was later to teach economics from 1953 to 1955). He also undertook a short period of postgraduate research at Columbia University, but he soon abandoned his thesis to start his own consulting firm, Townsend-Greenspan & Co. His eventual doctorate was conferred by New York University in 1977, as an honorary award.

Townsend-Greenspan's first government-level assignment came in 1968, when Greenspan became an adviser to Republican senator Richard Nixon during his 1968 campaign for the US presidency. He continued to work personally for Nixon after the latter's election in November 1968, but he retained his post at the consulting company until 1974, when he became chairman of the Council of Economic Advisers under the newly appointed president Gerald Ford.

Greenspan's first spell in public life came to an abrupt end in 1977 when Democrat Jimmy Carter became president, effectively forcing Greenspan to return to the board of Townsend-Greenspan. He came back to public office in 1981, however, after Ronald Reagan's Republican victory ended the single-term presidential tenure of the Carter administration. For the next two years Greenspan served under Reagan as chairman of the National Commission on Social Security Reform. In 1987 Reagan appointed him to his first term as chairman of the Federal Reserve (the US central bank) – a post which he was to retain through **George**

Bush's Republican presidency (1988–92) and also through **Bill Clinton**'s Democrat presidency (1992 to the present). His third term of office, which began in June 1996, will take him through to June 2000.

Greenspan's economic ideas have consistently placed him to the left of traditional Republican theory but well to the right of mainstream Democrat thought.

An outspoken advocate of the free market, and of banking deregulation in particular, he has consistently stressed his opposition to the use of government intervention as a fiscal tool. He therefore decisively rejects the lowering of taxes as a means of stimulating the economy during recessionary periods – a view which has brought occasional accusations that he helped to prolonged the economic slump of the early 1990s by refusing to sanction fiscal incentives to US businesses.

Greenspan's unwavering faith in the "rational selfishness" of the free market has taken him on to new ground since the end of 1996. At that time, his first widely publicised public warnings about the "irrational exuberance" of the surging US financial markets were generally interpreted as conveying a growing fear that securities dealers were no longer behaving as logically as a conventional free-market theorist would like to believe. The corollary appeared to be that a serious degree of economic instability might result unless their feet could be quickly returned to earth.

Greenspan has repeated his warnings at regular intervals since then, although his fears seemed to have abated somewhat, as it became apparent by 1998 that the US economy was in good shape, combining low levels of inflation with labour-market stability and high rates of industrial capacity utilisation. In particular, the global "flight to quality" among international investors, which followed the 1997/98 financial collapse in Asia, seemed to confirm that US securities were being held in higher international regard than he had personally supposed. This high level of international trust is, however, a measure of his own success; it is precisely this balance of high growth and low inflation which has always constituted the single most important aim of his economic policy.

At home, although he came under fire and was described as having lost moral authority over the decision in late 1998 to bail out the failing speculators' "hedge fund", Long-Term Capital Management, Greenspan generally enjoys an overwhelmingly high level of approval among senior business leaders. His adroit handling of Federal Reserve policy is widely acknowledged, even if his tight fiscal restraint has at times seemed to place him at odds with US business interests. There were many who felt strongly that he was being too cautious on interest rate cuts, and failing to grasp the scale of the dangers facing stock markets in the second half of 1998, but Greenspan has repeatedly refused to be moved by short-term strategic considerations in determining monetary policy. Ultimately, he remains convinced that if securities markets are overvalued, the eventual and damaging consequence for the economy as a whole will be a kind of "asset inflation".

Greenspan lives in New York and has been married since April 1997 to Andrea Mitchell, a television journalist. He lists his hobbies as listening to classical music, playing tennis and reading the works of the free-market economic philosopher Ayn Rand.

Vaclav **Havel**

The playwright and former leading dissident Vaclav Havel provided Czechoslovakia's 1989 "velvet revolution" with leadership of unusual moral authority. Sometimes described as his country's "philosopher king", with an unassuming and informal manner which belies the strength of his influence, he was president of Czechoslovakia for nearly three years, resigning in disappointment as the Czech and Slovak halves of the country appeared bent on separation, but returning to office in January 1993 as president of the Czech Republic. His official functions are mainly ceremonial but, despite serious illness, he continues to play a significant role in cementing relations with western Europe, in matters affecting civil rights and in his campaign for what he describes as the deepening of democracy.

Vaclav Havel was born on 5 October 1936 in Prague. Because of his bourgeois family background (his father was a prominent businessman), the post-war communist regime initially denied him a university place and he worked instead as a chemical laboratory technician, while studying at evening classes and eventually graduating in 1954. From 1954 to 1957 he attended the economics faculty of the Czech Technical University in Prague. He did his military service from 1957 to 1959.

In 1960 he started working as a stagehand, first at the ABC Theatre and then at the Theatre on the Balustrade in Prague, where he rose to be literary manager and assistant director by 1968. His plays were first performed while he was studying dramatic art theory at the Prague Academy of Performing Arts from 1962 to 1966; he won international acclaim with *The Garden Party* (1963) and subsequent work such as *The Increased Difficulty of Concentration* (1968), *Audience* (1975) and *The Mountain Hotel* (1976).

In 1968, caught up in enthusiasm for the promise of a new liberal communism in the so-called "Prague spring", Havel chaired the Circle of Independent Writers, and was a fierce opponent of the invasion by Warsaw Pact forces that August. The subsequent period of repression saw his work banned in Czechoslovakia, although it circulated as *samizdat* (illegal "self-published" manuscripts) and was published to widespread acclaim in the West. Forced to move to the country and work as a labourer in a brewery, he organised a petition in 1972 pressing for the release of political prisoners, and in 1975 he wrote a critical open letter to President Husak. On 1 January 1977 Havel was a founding signatory of what became the rallying call of the human rights movement, Charter 77.

The spokesperson for the small group of dissident intellectuals behind this original initiative, Havel also helped set up the Committee for the Defence of the Unjustly Prosecuted (VONS) in 1978, and wrote his influential essay, *The Power of the Powerless*. His sustained dissident activity led to his house arrest in 1978/79, and he spent a long period in prison from 1979 to 1983 on a charge of sedition, during which he wrote the famous series of *Letters to Olga* to his wife (he had married Olga Splichalova in 1964).

In January 1989 Havel was again arrested, with a group of human rights demonstrators, and sentenced to nine months' imprisonment for incitement and obstruction. This aroused a major international protest, which embarrassed the regime into releasing him in May.

The astonishingly rapid collapse of communist rule in Czechoslovakia – and elsewhere across central and eastern Europe – in late 1989 propelled Havel into a national leadership role, despite his own ambivalence about direct political involvement. Informally identified as the leader of Civic Forum, which he helped set up in November, he was at the forefront of the protest movement and massive popular demonstrations which swept the old regime from power. On 29 December Havel was elected by the parliament as interim president, pending the holding of general elections the following June; the new Federal Assembly, meeting on 5 July 1990, then confirmed him in office for two years.

The 1990 elections underlined Havel's problems in establishing a neutral non-party presidential role, given his close connections with Civic Forum, his attendance at their rallies and his controversial comment during the campaign that he would be voting for Civic Forum candidates. During his subsequent presidential term, Havel's relations with Slovak nationalist leader Vladimir Meciar were often difficult, while it was common knowledge that he differed with the finance minister and later Czech prime minister Vaclav Klaus over the speed and uncompromising radicalism of the switchover to a free-market economy.

Havel stood down as Czechoslovakia's president at the end of his two-year term in July 1992, when his federalist constitutional proposals had been rejected and it was becoming increasingly unlikely that any form of Czech and Slovak federation would survive the pull of Slovak separatism. When the separation of the two states had been formalised, the parliament of the Czech Republic elected him unopposed to the presidency on 26 January 1993. In May of that year several foreign nationals were arrested after a suspected assassination attempt against him.

Although the presidency was required to be non-partisan, Havel's moral stature gave his role considerable weight in Czech public life and in promoting the country's interests in integration within a democratic Europe. Unexpectedly, it took two rounds of voting (by the members of both houses of the bicameral parliament) for him to win re-election for a further five-year term of office in January 1998. This was principally because of the hostility of supporters of Klaus, angered by Havel's appointment of a non-party prime minister and the relegation of Klaus to an opposition role after his government collapsed in late 1997. Havel's backing of the temporary non-party administration continued until the passage of a constitutional amendment compelled him to call a general election for June 1998. Meanwhile, he took the opportunity of his inaugural speech at the beginning of his second term in February 1998 to rededicate himself to the development of democracy and civic society and to combating the growth of nationalism and xenophobia. On several occasions since then he has decried prejudice and discrimination against the Romany minority, calling for greater tolerance and the renewal of the "spirit of 1989".

Havel's first wife Olga died in January 1996. A year later he married the acclaimed Czech actress Dagmar Veskrnova. His health has on several occasions caused serious alarm. A heavy smoker, he had surgery for lung cancer in December 1996 and suffered a serious bout of pneumonia in October/November 1997. In April 1998 he had surgery again in Austria, and in July/August 1998 an operation to remove his temporary colostomy was followed by emergency surgery to deal with the consequences of the collapse of his right lung.

Bob **Hawke**

Bob Hawke built on a formidable record as a trade unionist to become leader of the Australian Labor Party and win four consecutive general elections between 1983 and 1991. A colourful and charismatic figure with enduring popularity among ordinary Australians, his sometimes embattled party base was the right-wing Labor unity faction and the state Labor Party in Victoria. As prime minister, he constructed a prices-and-incomes policy around agreement with the unions, steered Australia away from links with the British monarchy, and promoted its modern identity as a Pacific power. Late in his career he also took some significant steps on what was to become a defining issue in the 1990s, the land rights of Australia's indigenous people.

Robert James Lee Hawke was born in Bordertown, South Australia, on 9 December 1929, the son of a Congregational minister. Moving to Western Australia, he attended Perth Modern School and read law and economics at the University of Western Australia, then won a Rhodes scholarship to study economics at Brasenose College, Oxford, between 1953 and 1955. In 1956 he married Hazel Masterson, with whom he had three children.

Politics was in the family, his uncle Albert Hawke being Australian Labor Party (ALP) premier of Western Australia from 1953 to 1959. Bob Hawke made his own reputation as a research officer and industrial negotiator for the Melbourne-based Australian Council of Trade Unions (ACTU). Employed there from 1958, he attracted notice as a skilled communicator, a resolver of conflicts and a colourful orator. He was president of ACTU from 1970 to 1980 and also very active in ALP politics, both within the powerful Victoria state party machine and at national level. A member of the national executive and a senior ALP vice-president from 1971, he was president of the party from 1973 to 1978.

It was not until 1980 that he first entered the House of Representatives, representing Wills, Victoria. His lack of parliamentary experience proved no obstacle to his rapid political advance. He was immediately appointed opposition spokesman on employment and industrial relations, and in February 1983 replaced Bill Hayden as leader of the opposition, leading the ALP to victory in the general election the following month.

Under Hawke's leadership the ALP won an unprecedented four consecutive general elections (1983, 1984, 1987 and 1990). His first election

manifesto promised to cut personal income tax, increase pensions, boost public spending and reduce unemployment, and a conference of trade unions during the election campaign produced an accord with the ALP on price and wage fixing. Prices-and-incomes policies, based on negotiated agreement with the unions, were credited with reducing industrial disputes to record low levels. Hawke's position within his party was significantly to the right on most issues, and his identification with the Labor Unity group was frequently a source of inter-factional friction, but he was bolstered by his remarkable personal popularity with the wider Australian public. His image was that of a one-time hard-drinking and roistering "larrikin", who had mended his ways but could still claim "mateship" with the ordinary man.

Hawke's second election campaign, held when he called early elections for December 1984, was in some ways his most controversial. His first spell in government had featured the discovery that the national budget deficit was far greater than had been supposed, the consequent revoking of some of the tax cuts he had promised, and a 10 per cent devaluation of the Australian dollar. Then the leader of the Liberal Party, Andrew Peacock, described him in parliament as a "little crook", but was unable to substantiate accusations that Hawke had obstructed a Royal Commission investigation into organised crime. The acrimonious campaign featured the first Australian television debate between two party leaders, a contest not generally adjudged a success for Hawke. He was returned to office, but with a reduced majority.

Under Bob Hawke's leadership Australia took a series of steps towards cutting formal ties with the UK and becoming a republic. In April 1984 Hawke restored *Advance Australia Fair* as national anthem, displacing *God save the Queen* except when royalty were present. In March 1986 Queen Elizabeth II, visiting the country, signed into law the Australia Act, which gave Australia full legal independence and ended the UK Privy Council's role as the country's highest court of appeal. In 1991 the ALP declared itself in favour of a republic by 2001.

As Australian foreign policy emphasised its Asian–Pacific identity, Hawke was involved in the formation in 1989 of the Asia–Pacific Economic Co-operation forum (APEC). He also supported the declaration of a nuclear-free Pacific, pressing France to abandon its underground nuclear testing at Mururoa Atoll. However, Hawke came under fire from left-wingers for allowing uranium mining to continue, and for lifting (in August 1986) a 1983 ban on its export to France.

By late 1988 Hawke was being challenged for the premiership by his treasurer, **Paul Keating**. In a secret deal later known as the Kirribilli pact, Keating agreed to support Hawke until the 1990 election, if he would thereafter resign and support Keating as his successor. Keating's appointment in April 1990 as deputy prime minister (in addition to treasurer) appeared to confirm him as heir apparent, but in December 1990 Hawke took offence at what he described as Keating's "treacherous comments to the press" concerning his leadership qualities, and reneged on his secret undertaking to step down. The existence of the Kirribilli pact only became public when Keating made a formal challenge for the leadership, forcing a vote in the parliamentary party caucus in June 1991. Although Hawke survived this vote, his credibility was seriously damaged, particularly as during the 1990 election campaign he had repeatedly promised that he would serve the whole term. On 19 December 1991 Keating's supporters forced another caucus vote. Hawke was defeated, whereupon he resigned immediately as prime minister.

Looking back, Hawke could claim that "the Australia of 1991 is a profoundly better place than the one in 1983 that I inherited: more tolerant, more compassionate, more competitive". Having only recently brought in a permanent ban on mining on Aboriginal land at Coronation Hill in the Northern Territory (a move regarded as repayment to ALP left-wingers for their support against Keating's first leadership challenge), his final act as prime minister was to unveil an Aboriginal bark painting in Parliament House, and call for reconciliation between the indigenous Aboriginal community and the rest of the Australian population.

Since resigning the premiership (and, in early 1992, his seat in the House of Representatives), Hawke has written his memoirs. In 1995, having divorced his first wife, he married his biographer, the writer Blanche d'Apulget. He holds honorary professorships at Sydney University and at Stanford University, California, and is a familiar figure at cricket matches.

Stephen **Hawking**

Stephen Hawking, dubbed the Einstein of his generation, is a Cambridge-based theoretical physicist famous worldwide for two things. His book A Brief History of Time, *written to explain his research on "black holes" and the space–time continuum, achieved phenomenal sales and helped make serious science an attractive mass-market publishing proposition. And he goes on working and lecturing to packed auditoriums, although he is paralysed by motor neurone disease and needs technological wizardry to overcome the loss of his voice. On the world stage, he has come to symbolise the power of thought, and was famously seen in a cameo film role in 1993 playing poker with Einstein and Newton in* Star Trek: the Next Generation. *Of his illness, Hawking has said that it has enhanced his career by giving him the freedom to think about physics and the universe. The way he confronts his illness and his communication difficulties is an inspiration for other disabled people, an illustration that success can be achieved with perseverance.*

Stephen William Hawking was born on 8 January 1942, the 300th anniversary of the death of Galileo. His father was a doctor and researcher into tropical diseases, his mother a secretary. His mother left wartime London, where the family then lived, for the greater safety of Oxford to have her baby. In 1950 the Hawkings moved from Highgate to St Albans. From an early age Stephen had a desire to know how things worked, and through this understanding to be able to control their behaviour. He was especially inspired by his mathematics teacher at St Albans School. However, he read natural sciences at university, there being no mathematics course on offer at University College, Oxford, where his father had encouraged him to go – as he had himself – in the hope that Stephen might also take up medicine. Bored with the course and adopting the lethargic attitude fashionable among Oxford students in the early 1960s, Hawking nevertheless graduated in 1962 with a first-class honours degree, specialising in physics.

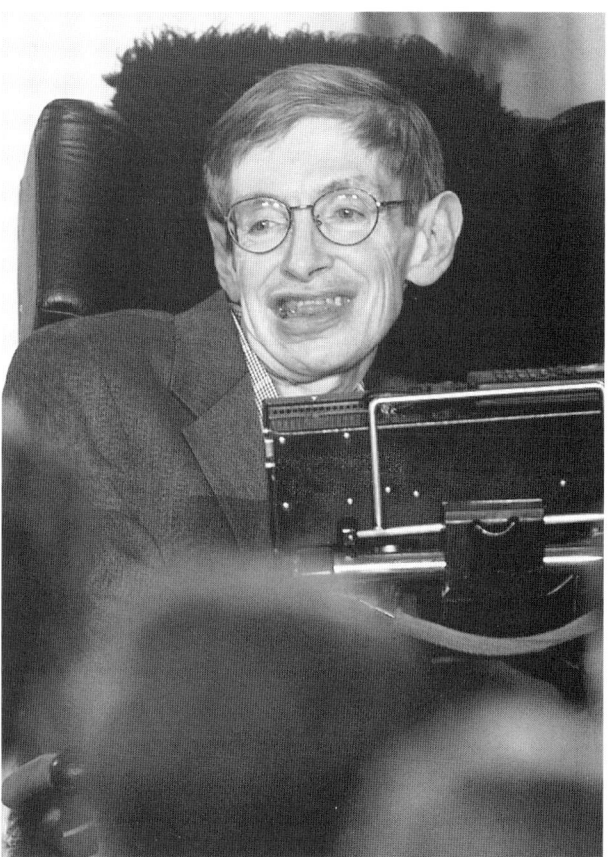

By now his interest had been gripped by cosmology as he strove to understand the workings of the entire universe. No research was being carried out in this field at Oxford, so he moved to Trinity Hall, Cambridge, for postgraduate research. During this period he noticed he was becoming unusually clumsy and occasionally fell. In 1963 came the shattering diagnosis – motor neurone disease or amyotrophic lateral sclerosis (ALS). This disease prevents messages being sent from the brain to muscles, causing them to waste away, prohibiting movement and leading to shortage of breath. Given only a few months to live, and with his body rapidly deteriorating, Hawking was devastated and despairing. However, a slight stabilisation in his decline, and the entrance of fellow student Jane Wilde into his life, made him realise that he should live for the present and for whatever future there was.

Anxious to get a job so that he could marry Jane, he threw himself into his doctorate, and found himself greatly enjoying his research. In 1965, the year of his marriage, he was appointed to a research fellowship at Gonville and Caius College; he became a professorial fellow in 1969. As his research became more theoretical, he left the Institute of Astronomy in 1973 to work in the Department of Applied Mathematics and Theoretical Physics. Here he was promoted to reader in gravitational physics in 1975, by which time he was confined to a wheelchair, requiring constant nursing and support in his research. Appointed professor in 1977, he reached the highest echelon in Cambridge in 1979 with his appointment as Lucasian Professor of Mathematics, the chair once held by Sir Isaac Newton. That year his third child was born (he has two sons and a daughter).

Much of Hawking's work has been to do with "black holes". In the 1960s he began working with Roger Penrose on developing Einstein's General Theory of Relativity. They determined the existence of a singularity in space–time at the beginning of the universe – the Big Bang – at which point none of the laws of science worked. They posited the theory that a corresponding singularity would occur at the end of the universe. Such singularities, or black holes, centre on extremely dense tiny particles, whose pulls of gravity are so great that nothing can escape, not even light – hence their blackness. However, Hawking later realised that a tiny amount of radiation – known as "Hawking radiation" – must be able to escape or the black hole would collapse in on itself. Continuing with this line of research, he conjectured in 1983 that space–time in fact has no boundary, and consequently that singularities cannot exist. This opened up vast fields of investigation. Scientists were able to apply the laws of quantum theory (which govern tiny particles) to apparent singularities, including the Big Bang. Ultimately, Hawking believes, this will unite all the laws of science – from Einstein's laws governing vast universes, to those of quantum theory.

In 1982 Hawking began writing a book to bring his ideas within the grasp of the public, and to raise money to cover his medical costs. Three years later, however, he caught pneumonia while visiting the European Organization for Nuclear Research (CERN) in Switzerland. He was placed on a life support machine, but the doctors believed there was

no hope for him. His wife, however, insisted that he be returned home to Cambridge, where a life-saving tracheotomy was performed – at the cost of his voice. On hearing of his plight two computer companies collaborated to design a portable voice synthesiser. Hawking, who can only move a few facial muscles and one finger, can operate this device to select words one-by-one to build up sentences, allowing him to communicate at a rate of up to 15 words per minute.

When Hawking's book *A Brief History of Time* came out in 1988, it was a publishing sensation. It sold millions of copies in over 30 languages and was also made into an award-winning film. The publicity surrounding his books, and his television and film appearances, have made Hawking – and his synthesised voice – instantly recognisable. In 1993 he published a second book for the general public, *Black Holes and Baby Universes*. The following year saw the finalisation of an acrimonious divorce from Jane Wilde, and in 1995 he married his nurse, Elaine Mason, with whom he had been living since 1990.

A Brief History of Time caused controversy over theories on the origins of the universe which some saw as denying the existence of God. His own view is that "you don't need to appeal to God to set the initial conditions for the universe, but that doesn't prove there is no God – only that he acts through the laws of physics". Never afraid to stand apart from the crowd, Hawking is also outspokenly critical of animal rights activists, and is a patron of Seriously Ill for Medical Research, a charity which contests the view that experimenting on animals is wrong.

Hawking is not eligible to receive a Nobel Prize for physics, as his theories have never been "proved" – nor are they likely to be in the foreseeable future – by supportive experimental observation. However, he has been recognised internationally for his achievements. In 1974 he was elected one of the youngest fellows of the Royal Society, and he is also a member of the National Academy of Sciences of the US. He was appointed CBE in 1982 and Companion of Honour in 1989.

Saddam **Hussein**

In the eyes of Western governments and media, Saddam Hussein was for most of the 1990s the world's most dangerous dictator and most serious threat to peace and stability. In power in Iraq since 1979, he was initially seen as a leader with whom the West should seek constructive engagement, and supported as a counter to the Islamic revolutionary regime in Iran, with which he fought a protracted war in the 1980s. From the time of his invasion of Kuwait in 1990, however, his expansionism, his bellicose attitudes and his effort to become the leading radical voice in the Arab world have been countered by US-led military and diplomatic action. He has remained defiantly in power, surviving defeat by US-led forces in the 1991 Gulf war, uprisings by southern Iraqi Shi'ite Muslims and by separatist Kurds in the north, plots by dissidents, and international sanctions and US-led air strikes intended to compel his regime to comply with UN resolutions on the dismantling of weapons of mass destruction.

Saddam Hussein was born on 28 April 1937 in the city of Tikrit, 120 miles north of Baghdad. Once in power he was to become increasingly reliant on the loyalty of his Tikriti clan, Sunni Muslims bound together by family ties and patronage. Accounts of his childhood suggest that a forceful uncle was the strongest adult influence, and that violence was the key to making a mark within his group of cousins. In 1956 he joined the Iraqi branch of the Arab Ba'ath Socialist Party, involving himself over the next decade in its revolutionist activity and being arrested several times for involvement in attempted coups. Involved in the attempted assassination of Iraqi Prime Minister Gen. Kassem in 1959, he fled the country (later being sentenced to death *in absentia*) and lived in Syria and Egypt until 1963, studying law in 1961 at Cairo University. In 1963 he married Sajida Khairallah; he has two sons and three daughters.

Arrested again in 1964 for plotting the overthrow of President Aref, he was elected while in prison as a member of the Ba'ath leadership, and in 1966, still only in his twenties, became deputy secretary of its Iraqi branch.

Saddam Hussein played an active role in the two Ba'athist coups of July 1968 which brought his fellow Tikriti Gen. Bakr to power, and he was rewarded with the Revolutionary Command Council (RCC) vice-chairmanship the following year. He built up an elaborate network of secret police, aimed at uncovering and suppressing dissent, but also providing the power base which enabled him to push out Gen. Bakr and take over the presidency and party leadership himself in 1979. Turning on those whom he could not count on for loyalty, he purged any possible opponents from within the ruling circle and

crushed a Kurdish rebellion in northern Iraq, gaining international notoriety by the use of chemical weapons against Kurdish villagers.

The Iran–Iraq war was launched by Saddam Hussein in September 1980 ostensibly in an effort to regain territory occupied by Iran since 1973. It developed, however, into a protracted (and in human terms immensely costly) eight-year struggle for ascendancy between the two principal regional powers, setting his Iraqi Arab nationalism against Iran's Shi'ite Muslim clerical leaders and their Islamic revolution. Of these two, Western countries feared Iran most, and supplied much military equipment to Iraq until the war finally ended in a stalemate.

On 2 August 1990 Saddam Hussein provoked a wider crisis when he ordered the occupation of Kuwait, again based on a dispute over territory but offering the opportunity of extending his country's oil wealth. UN demands for a complete withdrawal were ignored, and a US-led alliance initiated heavy air strikes followed up by a land war. This had wide support from Western countries, Soviet acceptance, and backing in the Arab world not just from the conservative monarchies but also from Egypt, Syria and other governments. Saddam Hussein nevertheless invoked the ideas of Muslim *jihad* or holy war, making much of his defiance of the West, and launching missiles at Israel to substantiate the view of himself as a true supporter of the Palestinian cause.

Iraqi forces were overwhelmingly defeated in the field in the January/February 1991 Gulf war, driven out of Kuwait, but saved from the apparent prospect of annihilation when the US-led alliance declared a ceasefire at the end of February, thus rejecting the temptation to expand their limited war aims and press on to take Baghdad. Saddam Hussein had to accept the conditions stipulated by UN resolutions for the ending of hostilities, including the requirement that his regime disclose and destroy any nuclear, chemical and biological warfare facilities and stockpiles. A UN inspections regime was set up to monitor this, with economic sanctions in place pending the certification of Iraqi compliance. The severe impact of these sanctions on the economy, and on the Iraqi people, were only slightly alleviated by a humanitarian provision agreed in late 1996 under which some Iraqi oil could be sold internationally to pay for imports of food and medicine.

Defeat in the Gulf war left Saddam Hussein apparently vulnerable, but he quickly gained the upper hand against rebellions by the Kurdish population in the north and the Shi'ite so-called "marsh Arabs" in the south, and followed up various government reshuffles with purges and executions of military officers in early 1992 and August 1993. In August 1995 divisions opened up within his own family, apparently prompted by the growing power of his son Udai Hussein. Two of his daughters and his sons-in-law, Hussein Kamel and Saddam Kamel, sought political asylum in Jordan and called for the overthrow of the regime. When a supposed reconciliation was effected they returned to Iraq in February 1996, indicating the reassertion of Saddam Hussein's control over any real internal dissent – and shortly afterwards the two sons-in-law were shot and killed by another close family member.

Saddam Hussein maintains a close grip on power, surrounding himself with an elite republican guard and advisers drawn mainly from his own Tikriti clan. He holds a monopoly of top state and party offices – adding the role of prime minister in 1994 to the positions he had held since 1979 as head of the RCC, president, head of the party and head of the armed forces – and was confirmed in the presidency for seven more years by a referendum held in October 1995.

Internationally, Saddam Hussein has survived repeated confrontations in the years since the Gulf war. US and British air power was used from 1992 to enforce "no-fly zones" in southern and northern Iraq, while air strikes were mounted against the Baghdad intelligence headquarters in 1993, to punish an alleged assassination plot against former US President **George Bush**, and US troops and air power were mobilised in quantity in late 1994 to forestall an apparent renewed threat of Iraqi intervention in Kuwait. A serious confrontation in late 1997 led to the withdrawal of UN weapons inspection teams, and a growing crisis over Iraqi non-compliance took Iraq back towards the brink of triggering the military action threatened by the USA and the UK.

This crisis went to the heart of the controversy within the international community about how Saddam Hussein's regime should be handled. Temporarily averted by his renewed assurances about allowing proper facilities for the inspectors, it resumed when he refused them unfettered access to sites designated as presidential palaces. Although UN Secretary-General **Koffi Annan** brokered a compromise in February 1998, further confrontations – notably over charges that traces of chemical weapons had been found – led eventually to the withdrawal of UN inspection teams in December 1998. The USA and UK thereupon launched a series of air strikes, claiming success in inflicting serious damage on Iraqi military installations, but found themselves diplomatically isolated, with France, Russia, China and other countries not accepting their claim of sufficient legal justification for action under a March 1998 UN Security Council resolution warning of extreme consequences if the February compromise were not respected. Thus, although US and British air strikes continued in subsequent months over Iraqi violations of their air exclusion zone, Saddam Hussein emerged with something of a victory, declaring that he would not allow the weapons inspectors to return.

Lee **Iacocca**

Lee Iacocca was the archetype of the hardworking, tough-talking US corporate boss in the pre-Microsoft generation. He was president of Ford for much of the 1970s, but is nevertheless best known as the man who turned round the fortunes of Chrysler, where he moved in 1978. His drive, energy, decisiveness and entrepreneurial ability took him to the top at a time when the hierarchically structured giant motor companies and other industrial and manufacturing companies were the pre-eminent business model in corporate America. The best-selling business autobiographies he published in the 1980s, and his high profile in the media and as a public speaker, helped make him a role model for aspiring business leaders across the industrialised world.

Lido Anthony Iacocca was born on 15 October 1924 in Allentown, Pennsylvania, the son of Italian immigrant Nicola Iacocca. Affected during childhood by pneumonia, which later kept him out of the army, he studied industrial and mechanical engineering at nearby Lehigh University (1943–45), completing his degree in rapid time. He began a further course on a scholarship to Princeton (1946), but then left to join the Ford Motor Company as a trainee engineer. He soon transferred to the sales division, where he was promoted first to assistant sales manager of the Philadelphia district (1953) and then to sales manager in Washington D.C. (1956).

Iacocca's drive and ambition soon became apparent to the senior Ford leadership. He was made vehicle marketing manager for the entire Ford organisation in 1960, then vice-president and general manager later the same year, and became vice-president of the combined Ford car and truck group in 1965, a post he retained until 1969. He was simultaneously executive vice-president at Ford between 1967 and 1969. In 1970 he moved up to take on the coveted presidency of Ford USA.

Iacocca brought a sense of movement and dynamism to Ford which had been largely lacking for most of the post-war era. While embracing new manufacturing technologies such as the weight-saving monocoque chassis, he also dared to tailor the company's products to meet the expectations of an increasingly affluent and youth-oriented buying public – much to the occasional consternation of the ultra-conservative Henry Ford II, who was still technically in control of the company. Motor historians regard the announcement of Iacocca's Ford Mustang sports coupé (1964) as one of the key turning points in the 1960s; its aggressive styling, its light and open structure and its large but unsophisticated engine caught the mood of the time so precisely that it became an instant best-seller.

Yet Iacocca's efforts to modernise the Ford image went down badly with Henry Ford II, who found himself increasingly at odds with his company's president. Ford abruptly ended Iacocca's eight-year rule in 1978, firing him on his 54th birthday. The immediate outcome of this was, however, to launch Iacocca on the second phase of his career in the motor industry, because he was engaged at once by the Chrysler Corporation, where his achievements were to eclipse what he had previously accomplished at Ford.

Although Chrysler had a long tradition and reputation of its own (it had, for example, built the Second World War all-purpose Jeep military vehicle), by 1978 it was facing heavy losses, lacked a strong market image, and suffered high levels of industrial dissatisfaction as a result of a long history of poor management. Iacocca's blunt management style came immediately to the fore as he told the striking workers on his arrival that the company would close unless they accepted redundancies, job restructuring and wage cuts immediately. Having received their grudging assurances of co-operation, he secured what was at that time the largest package of federal government loan assistance ever granted, amounting to US$1.5 billion (which he was able to pay off within five years, so rapid was the turnaround that he achieved). At the same time he initiated a range of new products, including the best-selling Chrysler minivan series and the high-powered Dodge Viper sports car, with the urgent aim of rejuvenating Chrysler's tired product range. Iacocca's very public identification as the man in charge at Chrysler was reinforced by his personal appearances in the company's advertising campaigns during this period.

Iacocca was the first person to perceive that pick-up trucks ("light vans") would eventually sell to urban buyers as well as those in the rural markets where they had hitherto predominated, and that pick-ups would soon acquire a cult status of their own. Thus, by the time that light vans and off-road vehicles came to account for 40 per cent of all American motor sales in the mid-1990s, Chrysler was by far the most prominent company in this burgeoning sector, even though it still lagged behind Ford and General Motors in the saloon car stakes.

Iacocca formally retired from his job at Chrysler at the end of 1992, although he remained head of the company's executive committee for a further year. The period since 1995 has been overshadowed, as far as Chrysler is concerned, by a legal dispute with Iacocca which arose from a US$22.8 billion hostile takeover bid. Iacocca's friend, the prominent speculator Kirk Kerkorian, had originally launched the bid with Iacocca's support in 1995, and the spectacular battle which followed culminated in a US$21 million pay-out to Iacocca, in return for his agreement not to exercise his Chrysler share options.

Iacocca has written two best-selling books, *Iacocca: An Autobiography* (1984) and *Talking Straight* (1988). He has been married three times – first to Mary McCleary (1956), with whom he had two daughters, and then, after her death in 1983, to Peggy Johnson (1986), from whom he was subsequently divorced. He married his third wife, Darrien Earle, in 1991.

Jiang Zemin

*Jiang Zemin established himself in the 1990s as China's most powerful leader, having risen to the top under the patronage of former "elder statesman" leader **Deng Xiaoping**. Described officially as at the centre of the third generation of Chinese communist leaders, he had been mayor of Shanghai in the mid-1980s, general secretary of the ruling Chinese Communist Party since June 1989, and in March 1993 was elected as China's president. Regarded as a reformist, he identified himself with the rapid opening of the economy to private enterprise, but has repeatedly made it clear that the "Chinese road" involved no corresponding liberalisation in the political sphere. The country's economic growth, and the declining influence of conservative former premier **Li Peng**, has left Jiang Zemin with no real rivals for power, particularly in view of his good relations with fellow reformist Zhu Rongji, who succeeded Li Peng as premier (and head of government) in March 1998.*

Jiang Zemin was born on 17 August 1926 in Yangzhou City, west of Shanghai, in Jiangsu province, which remained under Japanese occupation until 1945. The adopted son of a communist revolutionary martyr, he attended an American missionary school, joined the Chinese Communist Party (CCP) himself in 1946, and graduated with a degree in electrical engineering from Jiaotong University in Shanghai in 1947. He is married to Wang Yeping and they have two sons.

In the initial years of the People's Republic of China (proclaimed by Mao Zedong in 1949 after the communist victory in the long civil war), Jiang Zemin was CCP party secretary in a soap factory in Shanghai. In 1955 he went to Moscow as a trainee, working in the Stalin Automobile Plant. Returning in 1956, he moved into the power industry and machine-building, rising through a series of party posts to membership of the central committee in 1982. That year he also became a first deputy minister in the electronics ministry, and he was promoted in 1983 to the rank of minister in the same department, holding the portfolio for two years.

Jiang Zemin first came to wider public notice as mayor of Shanghai, a post he held from 1985 to 1989, and he also became a member of the party politburo during this period (in 1987). When Zhao Ziyang was dismissed as party general secretary and from all his other party posts as a dangerous liberal, in the clampdown which accompanied the June 1989 Tiananmen Square massacre, Jiang was picked to replace him. This was partly on the strength of his own handling of student demonstrations in Shanghai in December 1986, when he had taken a firm line but defused the situation without recourse to military force. He had also endeared himself to the hardliners by his measures in April 1989 to prevent student demonstrations from developing, while impressing others in the party by his record of effective economic management in the relatively go-ahead environment of Shanghai. In November 1989 and April 1990, when **Deng Xiaoping** stepped down as chairman of the central state and party military commissions,

Jiang's appointment confirmed his status as Deng's unofficial heir apparent.

The notion that Jiang might prove no more of a political heavyweight than Deng's previous protégés was dispelled by the success of economic reforms under his leadership, his clarity and determination that there should be no concomitant political liberalisation process, and his steady accumulation of leadership positions. This culminated in his election (with the usual unanimity) by the People's National Assembly on 27 March 1993 as president of the People's Republic for a five-year presidential term, a post to which he was re-elected in March 1998.

Following the death of Deng in February 1997, Jiang Zemin paid particular attention to his relationships with the army, where support for him was apparently less firmly established than among party cadres. On the other hand, at the September 1997 party congress (when he was re-elected as party general secretary) he announced plans to cut the armed forces by 500,000 men, and by mid-1998 he was sufficiently confident of his position to initiate a major and unprecedented attack on members of the armed forces who engaged in smuggling, following this up with an order in July of that year that the armed forces, police and judiciary were to renounce all involvement in business activities.

Jiang's ascendancy, vis-à-vis the more conservative faction associated with Li Peng, had been established in the context of China's rapid economic growth and a reduction in inflation. His promotion of market reforms, including far-reaching privatisation measures approved by the 1997 congress, was accompanied by a firm line against dissident activity and a campaign against corruption. With the thrust of economic policy clearly established by the time of the party congress, Jiang appeared willing to cede much of the responsibility for economic management to Zhu Rongji, who like Jiang was a technocrat, a reformist and a former mayor of Shanghai. (Zhu's appointment in March 1998 as prime minister gave him the formal position of head of government, although he continued to be regarded as number three in the leadership hierarchy after Jiang and Li Peng – and as Jiang's ally rather than potential rival.)

Conversely, a series of high-profile meetings with foreign leaders during 1998 (notably including visits to China by US President **Bill Clinton** and UK Prime Minister **Tony Blair**, and visits by Jiang to both Russia and Japan) marked Jiang's increasing personal control over foreign affairs. The cementing of better relations with the USA was seen as his particular objective, and considerable coverage was given to a speech made by Clinton in Beijing when he praised Jiang as a "man of vision". The desire to foster China's connections with the USA also apparently encouraged Jiang to appear more conciliatory in his stance on the treatment of dissidents. In December 1998, however, there was a fresh crackdown, with Jiang making a distinctly hardline speech in which he stressed that "the Western mode of political systems must never be copied" and pledged to smash opposition to the party.

Pope **John Paul II**

John Paul II (Karol Wojtyla) is the first Polish pope in history and the first non-Italian pope since 1523. In office since 1978, he has become better known worldwide than any of his predecessors, making over 80 foreign trips and clearly revelling in the acclamation he receives. The author of a best-selling popular book as well as of 13 papal encyclicals, he has sought to retain a firm grip on Catholic moral doctrine, anxious to stem the growing acceptance of more liberal ideas on such issues as birth control, abortion, homosexuality and the ordination of women. A convinced anti-communist, he has nevertheless also developed in recent years a critique of global capitalism and the operation of the free market, concerned that it fails to guarantee the global good and the exercise of economic and social rights.

Karol Jozef Wojtyla, the son of Polish army officer Karol Wojtyla and schoolteacher Emilia Kaczorowska, was born on 18 May 1920 in Wadowice, Poland, where he received his early education. His mother died in 1929, followed by his brother three years later. He was confirmed in May 1938 and commenced his studies at the Jagellonian University in Krakow in October. During the Second World War he worked in a variety of manual jobs, earning the name "worker cardinal", and from 1942 studied secretly for the priesthood in Krakow. During these years he was reputedly active in UNIA, the Christian democratic underground organisation, while some authorities have testified that he helped Jews find refuge from the Nazis. He was ordained to the priesthood on 1 November 1946. In 1948, after two years of study in Rome, he received a degree in theology from the Angelicum.

Wojtyla returned to Krakow in 1948, working as a parish priest first in Niefowic, near Gdowo, and then at Saint Florian, in the Krakow diocese. In 1953 he received a doctorate in philosophy from the Jagellonian University in Krakow. He taught moral theology there from 1952 to 1958 and at Lublin from 1954, before he was appointed auxiliary bishop in Krakow in 1958. In 1963 he was nominated as the archbishop of Krakow, and was formally installed on 13 January 1964. Pope Paul VI, whom he had impressed with his 1960 book *Love and Responsibility*, setting out his conservative Catholic views on marriage, appointed him a cardinal in June 1967. He became pope on 16 October 1978 (and simultaneously head of state of the Vatican City, the sovereign mini-state created under the 1929 Lateran Treaty), by virtue of his election by the Sacred College of Cardinals.

Wojtyla took the name John Paul II. In the context of the political upheavals of the times, he was treated by many in his native Poland as a symbol of freedom against the power of the communist state, and his visits to Poland in the ensuing years accordingly took on a special significance. He has also made strong criticisms of the arms trade and the use of the death penalty, on human rights grounds. He used a recent special message before World Peace Day on 1 January 1999 to reinforce his concern about the pernicious effects of consumerism, sounding the alarm about the neglect of the common good, and of economic and social rights, under global free-market capitalism. Theologically, however, he is a conservative, espousing an exclusively male priesthood, while opposing birth control, homosexuality and extra-marital sex. It was especially his stance against birth control, and his implacable hostility to abortion, which placed his doctrinal leadership at odds with more radical proponents of "liberation theology". Pope John Paul II has come to be seen, by many Catholics as well as non-Catholics, as an obstacle in the way of the Church providing moral guidance more practically attuned to the challenges of social conditions and development in the third world. He reaffirmed his authority, however, with a May 1994 apostolic letter rejecting the ordination of women, and a mid-1998 apostolic letter on "obligatory teachings" across a wide range of issues of morality and faith. All practising Catholics were required to show obedience to these teachings, and an existing 1989 oath pledging the clergy and theologians to follow the Vatican line was strengthened by being incorporated into Canon Law.

This aspect of John Paul II's papacy, stressing the papal authority to pronounce infallibly on matters of doctrine, is one side of his dual image. The other side is his personal accessibility and his efforts to find ways of speaking directly to ordinary Catholics, as with the publication in 1994 of his best-selling book, *Crossing the Threshold of Hope*. Until his health began deteriorating markedly in 1994 – with symptoms indicating that he is suffering from Parkinson's disease – he was noted for his vigour and robust appetite, had been a keen sportsman, and was also strongly interested in the theatre, for which he has written several plays. His frequent foreign travels have been undertaken with evident enthusiasm, drawing huge crowds to open-air masses or just to cheer him in his famous "popemobile". Since his election to the papacy, he has made numerous official visits abroad – his high-profile trip to Cuba in early 1998 was the 81st in a series encompassing almost every region of the world. In addition to his personal charisma, he has shown an instinct for the telling gesture and his papacy has been notable for the large number of new saints he has canonised, some of them highly controversial. He has survived two assassination attempts, the first in May 1981 in St Peter's Square, Rome, when he was shot and wounded by a Turkish gunman named Mehmet Ali Agça (whom he later visited in prison and reportedly forgave), and the second a year later in Fatima, Portugal.

The Vatican City's establishment of full diplomatic relations with Israel in June 1994 was hailed as a landmark in efforts made by John Paul II to move the Catholic Church towards reconciliation with the past victims of discrimination and intolerance, although a 1998 statement on the Church's behaviour towards the Jews disappointed those who had hoped to see Catholicism accept partial responsibility for the Holocaust.

In October 1998 Pope John Paul II's 13th encyclical, *Fides et Ratio*, included explicit recognition of the great contributions made by non-Christian philosophy to contemporary thought and faith. Some of his recent statements have also encouraged expectations that during the Holy Year proclaimed for 2000 he could make a clear apology for the Inquisition, the Church's long history of anti-Jewish discrimination, and even for the Crusades mounted against Islam. The Holy Year is intended to include a penitential Ash Wednesday procession in Rome and – his health permitting – a pilgrimage of reconciliation to the Middle East.

Michael **Jordan**

Michael Jordan has been called the greatest basketball player ever, and even the best athlete of all time. His career spanned two Olympic gold medals and an astonishing record in 13 seasons as a professional with the Chicago Bulls. Jordan's fame helped fuel the media-driven explosion in the popularity of basketball, now second only to football (soccer) worldwide and North America's top sport. His sporting prowess, showmanship and attractive personal qualities made him a youth idol and role model, while sports and leisure product manufacturers sought him out for advertising and commercial endorsements. He was especially linked (as "Air Jordan") with trainers sold by Nike, to whose sports shoes, leisurewear sales and company image Jordan's name gave an estimated US$5 billion boost.

Michael Jeffrey Jordan was born on 17 February 1963 in Brooklyn, New York. He was the fourth child of James Jordan, who worked in the US air force, and Deloris Peoples. When he was seven the family moved to Wilmington, North Carolina, where he grew up. Despite a childhood accident in which he cut off part of his big toe with a chopping axe, the young Michael Jordan excelled at sports, especially

baseball. He was the outstanding member of a youth team which won the North Carolina state baseball championships. Maintaining a highly disciplined training regime while still at Laney High School, he made a sudden impact in basketball after a rapid growth spurt which took him to 6 feet 3 inches tall at the age of 16 (he finally stopped growing at 6 feet 6 inches), winning awards at basketball camp the following summer and showing the talent for leaping and skills in shooting a basketball which later made him world-famous. Offered sports scholarships by several universities, he chose the University of North Carolina, where he was a student from 1981 to 1984, leaving at the end of his junior year (the third year in a four-year undergraduate programme). Named twice as college player of the year in basketball, he was picked for the US team which won the gold medal at the Pan American Games in 1983, where he was the leading scorer. The following year Jordan co-captained the gold-medal-winning US basketball team at the Los Angeles Olympics.

The "draft" system under which outstanding college athletes are distributed among professional basketball teams saw Jordan go, as third pick in the first round, to the Chicago Bulls. At the end of his first season, 1984/85, he was named as the National Basketball Association (NBA) Rookie of the Year. In Michael Jordan the hitherto unglamorous Chicago Bulls had acquired a player of exceptional individual brilliance. Moreover, as he gained experience, his achievements transformed the team (which had never won the NBA championships) into six-time champions (1991–93 and 1996–98). Jordan himself was named as the league's most valuable player (MVP) five times, and as MVP of the finals in each of the Bulls' six championship years. He won Olympic gold for the second time in 1992 as part of the US so-called "dream team", which also featured the other top star of the era, Magic Johnson.

A prodigious scorer, Jordan's career aggregate was the third highest ever and his average, 31.5 points per game, the highest in the league's history. His points total of 3,041 in the 1986/87 season was the first time any player had topped 3,000 since Wilt Chamberlain in 1962/63, and he top scored in the league again every year until 1992/93, repeating this feat after a two-year break from the game in 1995/96, 1996/97 and 1997/98. His many records reflected his prowess in defensive play as well as in making telling passes and scoring points. Although not the tallest of players, he was admired by fans for the height he could leap and his apparent ability to float and hang in the air. A natural showman on court, he was also a master of the spectacular "slam dunk", a leap to grab the rim of the basket and score by slamming the ball down from above with the other hand.

Michael Jordan married Juanita Vanoy, a former model four years his senior, in Las Vegas on 2 September 1989. They have three children: Jeffrey Michael, Marcus James and Jasmine.

A nine-year professional basketball career of almost unbroken success, and the pressure of constant media attention, brought Jordan to the point where he felt he had nothing left to prove in the sport he loved. The year 1993 was for him marked by a personal tragedy, the murder of his father, killed by two young robbers. On 6 October 1993, expressing the desire to be remembered by fans at the height of his powers, Michael Jordan stunned the basketball world with the announcement of his retirement from the

professional game. His autobiography, *Rare Air: Michael on Michael*, was published that year, and in 1994 the Chicago Bulls ceremonially "retired" the number 23 jersey with which Jordan was so famously linked. But after two seasons playing minor league professional baseball – a sport he had not played since high school – Jordan was back. Starting on 19 March 1995, he played the remaining games of the 1994/95 NBA season – wearing a number 45 jersey for two months before switching back to number 23 during the play-offs in May. After three more triumphant seasons, he retired for the second time on 13 January 1999 (the 1998/99 season having not yet started, owing to a long wage dispute between players and management).

Forbes magazine's 1999 global rankings of celebrities placed Jordan top of the list in terms of influence and media attention, and in seventh place for total earnings in 1998 with an estimated US$69 million, far outstripping the next-highest-earning sporting personality (racing driver Michael Schumacher with US$38 million). Advertising and commercial endorsements brought in far more than his salary, while his other business interests include ownership of "The Restaurant" in Chicago, equipped with a special glass booth so fans can see him when he eats there. In 1996 his image also hit the big screen in the film *Space Jam*, alongside actor Bill Murray and the cartoon characters from *Looney Tunes* such as Bugs Bunny. Although he can seldom do anything without security guards to protect him, Jordan, for all his fame, retains a friendly and apparently unspoiled personality. Combined with his dedication and fitness, physical courage and team spirit, this makes him a highly attractive role model and the most commercially marketable of athletes.

Laurent **Kabila**

*Since his forces drove out the Zaïrean dictator **Mobutu** in May 1997, Laurent Kabila has disappointed any hopes that this might mark a new beginning for one of Africa's potentially richest but most chronically misgoverned countries. Under Kabila's uncharismatic, divisive and autocratic rule, the newly renamed Democratic Republic of the Congo stands accused of covering up severe and systematic human rights abuses and ethnic violence, and has been plunged into renewed fighting in what has become a major regional conflict involving forces from several neighbouring countries. Kabila, emerging from obscurity less than a year before he took power, had been a lifelong revolutionary and former supporter of Patrice Lumumba, the country's left-wing leader at the time of independence. The concern among prospective foreign-aid donors and investors that he might retain his Marxist orientation has turned out to be the least of their problems.*

independent in 1960. He has also attended military school in China and studied in Tanzania.

Elected as a member of the Katanga regional assembly in the southeast, Kabila was identified as a supporter of Lumumba, who became the country's first prime minister. When Lumumba was killed in a coup, some of his supporters, including Kabila, fled into the jungles of eastern Zaïre. Supported by the Soviet Union and China, they launched successive rebellions against the government subsequently formed by the US-backed coup leader Gen. Mobutu.

In 1964, at the time of the Stanleyville rebellion, forces led by Kabila in the Ruzizi area, near Uvira, were crushed by Mobutu's troops with the aid of mercenaries and Belgian paratroopers. Forced out of the country, the group continued to launch guerrilla raids from Tanzania. Kabila, who was reportedly associated in the mid-1960s with the Latin American revolutionary Che Guevara, set up his own People's Revolutionary Party (PRP) in 1967. Based near Lake Tanganyika, and obtaining Chinese support as well as attracting recruits from among exiled Rwandans of the minority Tutsi ethnic group, the PRP set up its own leftist mini-state in Uvira district. Financed by gold mining and a trade in diamonds and ivory, the party ran collective farms, health clinics and schools.

Laurent-Desiré Kabila was born in Shaba province, in the southern part of what was then the Belgian Congo, on 1 January 1939. A member of the Luba tribe, he was brought up as a Christian and reputedly a teetotaller. Kabila studied political philosophy in France, where he became a Marxist. He returned to his native country just as it was becoming

In 1977 Mobutu's troops once again forced Kabila out across the border into northern Tanzania. The interrelationships between left-wing rebel movements in the region brought him into contact with the forces of future Ugandan leader Yoweri Museveni and with the Rwandan Tutsi leader Paul Kagame, but when his guerrilla group disappeared from view in 1988 it was generally thought that Kabila was dead.

Kabila re-emerged as a rebel leader in October 1996, however, backing a Tutsi struggle against efforts by the Mobutu government to remove them from their land. Leading an Alliance of Democratic Forces for the Liberation of Congo (AFDL), which he had apparently put together four years beforehand as an alliance between Congolese opposition elements and the Tutsi-dominated People's Democratic Alliance, he mounted an insurgency which gathered momentum as Mobutu's forces crumbled before it. With backing from Uganda and other neighbouring countries, by May 1997 the rebels had reached the capital, Kinshasa. South African mediation helped avert large-scale violence at this point, although Kabila showed himself uncompromising in insisting on the departure of Mobutu.

Kabila was sworn in as president on 29 May 1997. Anti-inflation measures, and a three-year plan for the economy, encouraged initial hopes for a new departure in the government of the (now renamed) Congo. These hopes were echoed in public statements by US leaders in particular, although there was a strong current of antipathy to Kabila in France. If US enthusiasm was motivated by hopes of access to the potential wealth of the country, the French conversely feared that its avowedly anglophile new leadership would mean a business backlash against French entrepreneurs who had profited from close association with Mobutu.

International concern about Kabila's attitude to human rights was aroused by his resistance to a UN investigation of the involvement of his forces in a massacre of many thousands of Rwandan Hutu refugees in 1996 in eastern areas under their control. His refusal to assist the investigators became a major obstacle to the resumption of much-needed foreign aid. Meanwhile a supposed root and branch investigation into corruption under Mobutu soon collapsed, amid charges that it was being used not to bring profiteers to account but merely to extort money from them in return for immunity.

Kabila also came under criticism for initially appointing too many of his Tutsi allies to positions of power, and for insensitively echoing Mobutu's despised nepotism by appointing cousins to key ministerial posts and putting his son in charge of his northern military campaign. The Tutsi element, however, was progressively replaced by the appointment of more of Kabila's fellow Katangans, to the extent that Tutsi resentment fostered fears of an imminent Rwandan-backed coup, especially as Rwandan and Ugandan complaints about lack of cross-border security grew more pressing. A rebellion by disaffected Tutsis in the east gathered impetus in mid-1998. The sacking of a number of remaining Tutsis from the government that August effectively drove important sections of Kabila's former ruling coalition into the arms of the rebels. France in particular was quick to give refuge and, increasingly, diplomatic support, to leaders of a growing anti-Kabila rebellion. In desperate straits, Kabila now played the nationalist card with strident denunciations of foreign intervention, directed at Uganda and Rwanda but also effective in mobilising ethnic antagonism against the Tutsis within Congo itself.

By March 1999, although Ugandan- and Rwandan-backed forces in the east were seeking fresh momentum in a drive to oust him, Kabila's regime had survived their initial rapid advances – thanks largely to the backing of Zimbabwe and Angola and the intervention of their troops – and he thus gained some time to build up his own army, effectively from scratch. However, his lack of political skill showed when he missed an opportunity to broaden the basis of his government by offering posts to figures from the political opposition. Instead he announced a reshuffle to create a "government of combat", with new appointments which only reinforced the accusations of cronyism. This was compounded by the award of the economics and industry portfolio to a businessman who had been a prominent part of the Mobutu-era "kleptocracy".

Moamer al-**Kadhafi**

The "Leader of the Revolution" in Libya, Moamer al-Kadhafi has been in power since his 1969 coup. A pan-Arabist who always virulently opposed any manifestation of what he denounced as Western imperialism and Zionism, Kadhafi appeared to have a special talent for the inflammatory gesture. Throughout the 1970s and 1980s his regime attracted particularly strong condemnation from the USA, which encouraged the branding of Libya as an international pariah because of Kadhafi's support for a range of foreign liberation, anti-government and terrorist groups. Latterly he has been less in the spotlight. An Islamic reformist as opposed to a fundamentalist, he sees himself as an innovative thinker and has sought to develop a new kind of model for participative democracy in Libya. At the same time, he retains the apparatus for strict control of any dissident activity.

Moamer al-Kadhafi was born in the Sirte region in 1942, one of three children in a bedouin family. He attended a Koranic elementary school and the high school at Sebha, where his early involvement in politics led to his expulsion. He used a false birth certificate to enrol in another school in Misrata, then studied history and politics at university in Benghazi.

Kadhafi's enthusiasm for the pan-Arabist cause was fired by President Nasser in neighbouring Egypt. In 1963, despite being known as a political activist, he was nevertheless accepted into the Royal Libyan Military Academy in Benghazi. Graduating in 1965, he was commissioned as an officer in the signals corps in Benghazi. A four-month training course in Beaconsfield, England, increased his knowledge of military signalling and armoured vehicle gunnery – and his dislike of the British.

Within the armed forces Kadhafi built up his clandestine Free Officers' Movement, the group that he would lead in a bloodless coup in 1969 to overthrow the conservative regime of King Idris. The intended coup date, twice deferred, was finally set for the early morning of 1 September. Kadhafi was already known to Western intelligence agencies and there has been speculation that they must have known something of his plans. When the date came, everything worked smoothly and efficiently, and military and governmental installations in Benghazi and Tripoli were taken over with little bloodshed. Kadhafi made his first broadcast as head of the new regime within a few hours, and King Idris went into exile. Kadhafi's takeover reportedly pre-empted plans by more senior officers for a coup of their own.

Kadhafi became commander-in-chief of the armed forces, set up a Revolutionary Command Council with himself as president, and, from 1970 to 1972, also held the posts of prime minister and minister for defence. In January 1976 he took the higher military rank of major-general but continued to use the title of colonel. In 1979 he relinquished all official positions, styling himself thereafter "Leader of the Revolution".

Economic, social and political changes after the coup, based on Kadhafi's brand of "natural socialism", included attempts to redistribute the country's oil wealth more equitably, and nationalisation of foreign-owned banks, insurance companies, factories and oil companies. (Some liberalisation of the economy did begin in the late 1980s, as did the development of steel manufacturing to reduce the country's near-total dependence on oil revenue.) Wage labour was declared to be abolished and workers were instead deemed to be partners in industrial ventures.

Instead of building a single-party state through mass membership of the Arab Socialist Union, Kadhafi embarked on the more idiosyncratic project of creating a structure for popular participation through a system of basic people's congresses and committees, with the parliament or General People's Congress at the centre. This was embodied in the 1977 constitution of what was henceforth known officially as the Socialist People's Libyan Arab Jamahiriya. The *Green Book*, published in three volumes between 1976 and 1979, contains Kadhafi's thoughts on what he describes as his "third universal theory" spanning socialism, Islam, development and political systems.

Kadhafi's pan-Arabist aspirations, and his inclination to seek solidarity and involvement with regimes elsewhere which he identified as progressive, led him into several declarations of union between Libya and other Arab and African states. Pan-Arabism also underlay his initial enthusiasm for the Arab Maghreb Union, formed in 1989 with Algeria, Mauritania, Morocco and Tunisia. His relations with neighbouring Egypt in particular have been tense, while his commitment to the Palestinian cause, something of an article of faith, has involved supporting "rejectionist" factions and criticising the mainstream Palestine Liberation Organization's "sell-outs" to Israel.

Palestinian groups are only some among many causes to receive his backing, others have included the British miners' union in its long strike in 1985, the Irish Republican Army, and leftist radicals in many African countries. Kadhafi has himself survived a number of assassination attempts and attempted coups, and has withstood (and bolstered his own defiant image as a result of) actions to "punish" his regime on more than one occasion. The UK broke off diplomatic relations in 1984 over the shooting of a woman police officer at the Libyan embassy in London, and in 1986 the USA launched an air strike on Tripoli and Benghazi after a bomb attack on a West Berlin nightclub frequented by US servicemen. The bomb explosion on a Pan Am airliner over Lockerbie in Scotland in December 1988 was also laid at Kadhafi's door, leading to a long dispute about the extradition of suspects from Libya and the imposition of UN sanctions, which eventually moved a step closer to resolution with a complex arrangement in 1999 under which two Libyans would be tried under Scottish law in the Netherlands.

Col. Moamer al-Kadhafi is married to Safiya Kadhafi. They have seven children of their own and their family also includes a number of adopted children, one of whom was killed in the US air strike against Tripoli in April 1986. Kadhafi has a reclusive aspect in his character and has been prone to spending long periods in a tent out in the desert.

In the 1990s, Kadhafi's regime has been displaced by others as the main targets of Western hostility, and in April 1999 Libya was even taken off the US government's list of countries deemed to support international terrorism. Improvements in external relations included the establishment of diplomatic links with the Vatican in 1997, and Libya has the support of both the Organization of African Unity and the Arab League for the lifting of sanctions. Kadhafi himself has kept a lower profile, having notably remained relatively silent during the Gulf war in 1991.

Radovan **Karadzic**

Radovan Karadzic stands as the most prominent contemporary example of an indicted war criminal living apparently beyond the reach of international law enforcement. Charged in connection with "ethnic cleansing" atrocities, he is protected by his own community to the extent that it is effectively too risky to arrest him. Throughout the war in Bosnia-Herzegovina between 1992 and 1995 he was the president and main political leader of the Bosnian Serbs. A former psychiatrist turned nationalist politician, and sometime poet, he liked to portray himself as a sophisticated intellectual, in marked contrast to the blunt forcefulness of his colleague, the Bosnian Serb military leader Ratko Mladic. As a negotiator his trademark was to appear amenable to compromise, but then to back away from any agreement on the grounds that it would not command popular support.

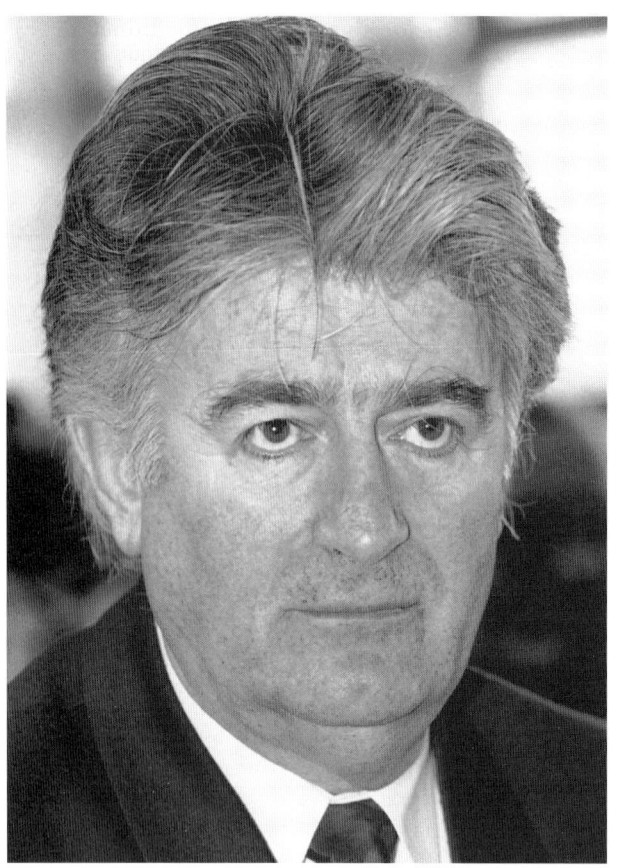

Radovan Karadzic was born on 19 June 1945 in the small village of Petnjica, near Savnik, in the mountains of Montenegro. During the Second World War his father Vuk Karadzic fought with the Chetniks, a nationalist Serb guerrilla force whose initial purpose was to resist the Nazi occupation, but which became increasingly involved in a struggle against the rival communist resistance movement,

Tito's partisans. Vuk Karadzic later served a prison sentence under the Tito regime for his activities during the war.

When Radovan Karadzic was 15, the family moved to Sarajevo to further the children's education. As a university student in Sarajevo, then an ethnically integrated city and the capital of the Bosnian republic within a socialist federal Yugoslavia, he read medicine and psychiatry, wrote poetry, lived the bohemian lifestyle of the 1960s, and married Ljljana Zelen, with whom he has one son and one daughter. His student days also included a year spent in the USA studying psychiatry at Columbia University, New York.

After qualifying as a psychiatrist he worked in various Sarajevo hospitals, including the Kosevo hospital which his Bosnian Serb forces later shelled during the siege of Sarajevo. He was also for a time the psychiatrist for Sarajevo's soccer team. Described by some who knew him during this period as boastful, deceitful and ambitious, he was also alleged to have been involved in various corruption rackets. These included the selling of prescriptions and false medical certificates to allow people to claim benefits, using government building materials for a chicken farm he was constructing in Pale, outside Sarajevo, and misusing funds designated for house loans. In the end he spent several months in prison in the mid-1980s on charges related to these allegations.

In 1990, as Yugoslavia moved towards multiparty elections along increasingly nationalistic lines, Karadzic entered politics through his long-standing friendship with the Serb writer and politician Dobrica Cosic. He was one of the co-founders of the radical Serb nationalist Serbian Democratic Party

(SDS), and was elected president of the party. In elections held in November/December 1990 to a reorganised 240-seat assembly in Bosnia-Herzegovina, polling was clearly along ethnic-national lines and his SDS secured 72 seats; the ruling communists were soundly defeated.

With Yugoslavia fast fragmenting as Croatia and Slovenia seceded, a referendum on Bosnia-Herzegovina's independence was held in February/March 1992. As a close ally of Serbian President **Slobodan Milosevic**, Karadzic declared that he refused to accept an independent Bosnia-Herzegovina, in which ethnic Serbs would be outnumbered. He successfully urged Bosnian Serb voters to boycott the referendum, in which the eventual result was heavily in favour of independence.

Karadzic played a leading role in the outbreak of the civil war in Bosnia-Herzegovina in April 1992, warning Bosnian Muslims that a declaration of Bosnian sovereignty could result in their annihilation. With the outbreak of war he moved the Bosnian Serb administration to Pale and in December 1992 was elected president of the self-proclaimed Serbian Republic of Bosnia-Herzegovina by the territory's assembly.

The Bosnian Serb army held the upper hand until the latter stages of the 1992–95 war, conducting a brutal campaign under Karadzic and military commander-in-chief Mladic, and quickly gaining control of over 70 per cent of the territory of Bosnia-Herzegovina. Karadzic attended a series of abortive peace negotiations in London, Geneva and New York, pretending a willingness to negotiate but never prepared to deliver any settlement in practice, until the Croatian offensive of mid-1995 turned the military tide decisively against the Serbs. Remaining obdurate under growing international pressure even when Milosevic had begun to want a settlement, Karadzic was strongly critical of the November 1995 peace agreement, which eventually resulted from the

negotiations in Dayton, Ohio. He did not attend the Dayton talks himself because of the war crimes charges he faced, but eventually had no choice but to accept the accord under pressure from Milosevic.

The indictment of Karadzic and Mladic for war crimes by the UN War Crimes Tribunal in The Hague was issued in July 1995. These charges concern the crime of genocide, crimes against humanity, and crimes against the civilian population and places of worship throughout Bosnia-Herzegovina between April 1992 and July 1995. In particular they relate to the unlawful detention, murder, rape, sexual assault, torture, beating, robbery and inhumane treatment of thousands of Bosnian Muslim and Bosnian Croat civilians (as part of a programme of "ethnic cleansing"), the killing of civilians in sniper attacks during the siege of Sarajevo and other towns, and the taking of UN peacekeepers as hostages in mid-1995. In November 1995 the two leaders were also indicted on further charges concerning the mass killings of Bosnian Muslims after Bosnian Serb forces overran the so-called "safe area" of Srebrenica in July that year.

In July 1996, as stipulated by the Dayton accord, Karadzic was obliged formally to resign as Bosnian Serb leader and was replaced by his deputy and former ally, Biljana Plavsic. He also resigned as president of the SDS, although he continued to play an influential role behind the scenes, and to be regarded as a symbol of resistance by many Bosnian Serbs resentful of the Dayton settlement.

An international warrant for the arrest of both Karadzic and Mladic was issued in July 1996, and in late 1998 it was reported that the US State Department was offering to pay a bounty of up to US$5 million for their capture, but still both remained at large. Karadzic was believed to be in hiding somewhere in the Pale area in the Republika Srpska, the Serb-run entity within Bosnia-Herzegovina.

Paul **Keating**

*Paul Keating's five-year premiership (1991–96) left its imprint firmly on the Australian political landscape, despite his own retirement after an election defeat. His administration had brought to centre stage the issue of land rights for indigenous peoples, and the question of Australia becoming a republic. Largely self-educated but formidable in his grasp of economics, and deeply involved in politics from an early age, his combative style and cutting wit made him a feared opponent. He was an MP at 25, and at 47 became the youngest-ever Australian prime minister, when he mounted his successful second challenge to oust **Bob Hawke** as leader of the Australian Labor Party (ALP). Outgrowing the image of aloof technocrat which he carried from his long period as treasurer, he famously earned the tabloid newspaper epithet "Lizard of Oz" when he was seen to put his arm around Queen Elizabeth's waist during her 1992 state visit.*

Paul John Keating was born into a working-class family in Sydney, New South Wales, on 18 January 1944. Educated at De La Salle College, Bankstown, he left school at 14 and worked for Sydney city council (and managed a rock band) while continuing to study part-time. Self-educated in economics – the field which later became the strong point in his political armoury – he worked for a Hong Kong

trading company in the late 1960s, then for the Electricity Commission in New South Wales, before joining the Federated Municipal and Shire Council Employees Union of Australia in 1968 as a full-time union official. He married Dutch-born Annita van Iersel in 1975 and they had four children, but separated in 1998.

Keating joined the Australian Labor Party (ALP) at the age of barely 15, rose to be president of the New South Wales youth council in 1966, and was elected in 1969 to the House of Representatives for the federal seat of Blaxland, NSW. Aged only 25, he was the youngest member of the House. He was appointed minister for northern Australia in October 1975 in the ill-fated ALP government of Prime Minister Gough Whitlam, but only held the post for three weeks before the administration was dismissed by the governor-general. He held his parliamentary seat despite his party's defeat in the ensuing general election in December, and spent the next eight years as an opposition spokesman, while also becoming president of the New South Wales branch of the Labor Party in 1976.

It was as federal treasurer in Bob Hawke's ALP governments in the 1980s that Keating really made his name. He was briefly opposition spokesman for treasury matters (having previously been spokesman on agriculture and then on minerals and energy), and was thus appointed treasurer as soon as the party came back into power in the April 1983 elections. He held the post until he challenged for the premiership in mid-1991, and even after that, as prime minister from December 1991, continued to be closely involved in economic policy. Seen as a tough and intellectual economist despite his lack of formal qualifications, he oversaw the devaluation and flotation of the Australian dollar, deregulated the financial sector, extensively reformed the taxation system and retirement incomes policy, and eventually (as prime minister) achieved a budget surplus and a notably low inflation rate, while maintaining the prices-and-incomes policy accord with the trade union movement negotiated by his predecessor.

Although his debating skills made him the party's most formidable performer in parliament, Keating's tough talking was not always well received by the public when he was in government. In May 1986 he made his notorious comment that Australia was in danger of becoming a "banana republic" because of the deterioration in its terms of trade, with a current account deficit of A\$12,000 million over ten months, and falling mineral and primary product prices worldwide. Cuts in government spending and limits on wages would be needed, he said, or Australia would be "basically done for". Hawke publicly reprimanded Keating, but supported the "austerity budget" which Keating presented in August 1986. The treasurer was widely credited with sound handling of the economy in the worst recession since the 1930s – even if he departed from his previous prescriptions of austerity to bring in a politically inspired pre-election budget in 1987, allowing the economy to overheat and making necessary a credit squeeze which temporarily exacerbated the downturn.

The rising star in the Labor government, with powerful associates on the right of the party in his home state of New South Wales, Keating was by 1988 becoming sufficiently confident to press prime minister Hawke about the succession. The two men made a secret agreement (later known as the Kirribilli pact) under which Keating promised to give his support to Hawke until the next election (due in 1990), ensuring that the latter would survive any attempt to unseat him from within the faction-ridden party. Hawke would lead the party in the election campaign, for which his popularity with the public was an indubitable asset. Then he would stand down and support Keating as his successor. The ALP duly won the April 1990 election (despite an unpopular

comment from Keating that the current recession was one that "Australia had to have"), and Keating was immediately appointed deputy prime minister (as well as remaining treasurer). Keating was not the only one to see this as confirmation that he was Hawke's heir apparent.

Hawke's decision in December 1990 against standing down, apparently due to his having taken offence at what he described as Keating's "treacherous comments to the press" about his leadership, precipitated a direct challenge from Keating the following year. Revealing, to considerable public disquiet, the existence of the Kirribilli pact, he failed to win enough support in the party in June 1991 to take over the leadership, and resigned from the cabinet immediately. Six months later, however, his second challenge succeeded as he overcame Hawke in a 56–51 vote by the ALP parliamentary caucus on 19 December 1991. With the party leadership came the office of prime minister, to which Keating was sworn in the following day.

As prime minister Keating continued the micro-economic reform agenda he had set as treasurer, including the deregulation of the airline and telecommunications industries. His foreign policy, like Hawke's, looked more to Asia and the Pacific, and less towards Britain and Europe, and he supported the ALP's generally pro-republican stance. During Queen Elizabeth II's visit to Sydney in 1992 he was criticised (especially in the British press) for a breach of protocol when he put his arm around her waist to guide her, while his wife compounded the apparent informality by failing to curtsey. Keating had also aroused controversy when he suggested shortly before the visit that Australia should drop the Union Jack from the corner of its national flag.

The ALP's general election victory on 13 March 1993 was perhaps Keating's happiest moment in politics. Achieved against the odds at a time of deep economic gloom, thanks to a campaign which demonstrated how far he had broadened his image from that of the grudgingly respected but aloof and unloved treasurer, it was a result which he declared to be a triumph for the "true believers" – all those people who had imagination and faith and believed in a compassionate, forward-thinking and visionary Australia. His second term saw major reforms designed to tackle long-term unemployment, legislation on the land rights of Australia's indigenous people, proposals for constitutional reform to make Australia a republic by the year 2000, the further development of Australia's relations within the Asia–Pacific region, and the conclusion of a historic security agreement with Indonesia.

By the end of his second term of office in 1996 it was assumed that a referendum on the change to a republic would be held before 2000. However, on 2 March 1996 the ALP was defeated in a general election in which his republican views had played a significant part. Keating relinquished the leadership of the parliamentary party and resigned from parliament on 23 April 1996.

In May 1996, Keating was appointed as a visiting professor at the University of New South Wales with a special relationship with the University's Asia–Australia Institute. In the years since leaving office, however, he has become increasingly isolated. No longer looming large in the political milieu or in Sydney society, he moved from fashionable Woollahra into a spare room in his sister's flat when his marriage ended in 1998. In early 1999 Keating faced a possible inquiry into his business dealings, as a documentary broadcast on his long-standing foe Kerry Packer's Channel Nine Network revived public interest in the "piggeries affair". This concerned a pig-rearing business in the Hunter Valley which he had bought into when his political career appeared to be ending (i.e. before his successful premiership challenge in late 1991), and whether he had misled parliament over the terms of its subsequent sale.

Ayatollah **Khamenei**

Seyed Ali Khamenei, a follower of the Ayatollah Khomeini since the 1960s, in 1981 became Iranian president effectively by default, there being a dearth of potential candidates for a post which combined lack of powers with risk of assassination. Holding office until 1989, he then moved up to succeed as the country's Spiritual Leader following Khomeini's death. Khamenei was generally regarded at the time as a comparatively non-partisan figure, without the political impact of his larger-than-life predecessor, and his appointment meant that he relinquished the presidency just as that office took on real powers as head of state and government. His elevation also marked a relaxation of the grip exercised by the theocrats since the Islamic revolution of 1979, and required some retroactive changing of rules since he lacked the religious status expected for the role of Spiritual Leader. However, he has latterly proven to be a conservative influence, restraining the introduction of a more liberal stance by the government of President Khatami.

Seyed Ali Hoseini Khamenei was born in 1939 in Mashhad, in the northeastern Iranian province of Khorasan. He entered a theological school in Mashhad at the age of ten, graduating in 1957 and continuing his studies at Najaf (in Iraq) and in the Iranian holy city of Qom. At the theological school there he studied religious science and came under the influence of Ayatollah Khomeini, who later led the Islamic revolution of 1979. Becoming an outspoken opponent of the regime of the Shah, Khamenei was active in the anti-Shah campaigns led by Khomeini in 1962 and 1963, and was first arrested and briefly detained at this time. Involved thereafter in a combination of religious teaching, pro-Islamic agitation and clandestine militant organisation, he was arrested several more times in the next 15 years, spending a total of three years in prison, and in 1977/78 he was exiled to the town of Iranshahr. As a religious authority, Khamenei had attained the second-rank religious title of *hojatolislam* by the time of the 1979 revolution. He has written several books on Islam and history, such as *The Role of Muslims in the Independence Struggle of India*. He speaks Farsi, Arabic and Azerbaijani Turkish, and is married with six children.

From 1978 Khamenei led the anti-government movement in Mashhad. Moving to Tehran early the following year, he was a founder member of the Foundation of the Oppressed and joined the central council of the Tehran Militant Clergy Association.

After the 1979 revolution Khamenei was appointed Revolutionary Council representative for the army. He was deputy for, and then head of, revolutionary affairs at the national ministry of defence, becoming commander of the Islamic Revolutionary Guard for a

relatively brief period (until February 1980). Elected in 1980 to the Islamic consultative assembly, the *Majlis*, he was secretary-general of the government-sponsored but now defunct Islamic Republican Party, of which he had been a co-founder, and was increasingly seen as one of Ayatollah Khomeini's closest associates. He also held, from January 1980, the influential position of leader of the Friday prayers in Tehran.

Khamenei was wounded in the right hand in an assassination attempt in June 1981, part of a spate of terrorist violence affecting the Islamic regime. In October of that year, following the ousting of President Bani-Sadr and the assassination of his successor Radjai, Khamenei was picked as the regime's candidate to fill the vacant presidency, winning the predictable overwhelming majority against four other candidates in the nationwide poll. He was re-elected, against two opponents, in August 1985.

Generally seen as a conservative rather than a hardline radical in the context of post-revolutionary Iranian politics, Khamenei on occasion came under strong criticism from radical rivals, but as president he avoided identifying himself with any particular faction. He also managed to distance himself from the 1983 defection of his sister to Iraq, where she joined his estranged brother-in-law Sheikh Ali Tehrani, who had fled to Baghdad in 1981 and begun making broadcasts hostile to the Khomeini regime.

In May 1989 Khamenei was made chairman of the secretariat of the Imam (Khomeini), and on 4 June, the day after Khomeini's death, was elected by the Assembly of Experts to succeed him as Iran's new Supreme Spiritual Leader (*Wali-e Faqih*). He was also given the religious title of ayatollah, as being more compatible with his status than the less elevated title *hojatolislam*. Constitutional amendments approved the following month removed the requirement that the Spiritual Leader should hold the religious status of a grand ayatollah or *marja* (source of emulation), Khamenei himself being only a jurist or *motjahed*.

The Spiritual Leader combines supreme religious power with overall political authority, although since the death of Khomeini it is not the Spiritual Leader but the president (previously a mainly ceremonial post) who heads the executive and combines the functions of head of state and head of government. Khamenei's elevation to the post of Spiritual Leader opened the way for the election as president of Hojatolislam **Rafsanjani**, seen as a relative moderate. Rafsanjani and to a greater extent his successor since 1997, Mohammed Khatami, have steered Iran towards a policy of greater liberalisation and openness towards the West. Khamenei for his part, while presenting himself as generally non-partisan, has on key occasions (such as in encouraging the 1996 election of Ali Akbar Nateq-Noori as parliamentary speaker) been identified as more pro-conservative. It was also he who reaffirmed and maintained Khomeini's notorious February 1989 *fatwa* or death sentence against the British writer **Salman Rushdie** over the publication of a novel held to be blasphemous against Islam, in a confrontation with Western liberal values which cast a long shadow until the eventual lifting of the *fatwa* in 1998.

On the ninth anniversary of Khomeini's death, in 1998, Khameini had to cut short a speech, arousing concerns about his health (although he was still only 58) which were, however, quickly dismissed.

Kim Dae Jung

*Kim Dae Jung was hailed as "South Korea's **Nelson Mandela**" when his December 1997 election triumph completed his political journey from prison to presidency. During his 45-year career the veteran opposition leader, renowned for his integrity, had been repeatedly imprisoned or exiled; he was even sentenced to death after the Kwangju rising in 1980. However, at other times he played an active part in politics and had already contested the presidential elections on three previous occasions. Even before his formal inauguration in February 1998, Kim was instrumental in winning agreement on a package of measures to tackle the country's economic crisis. His popularity with ordinary Koreans helped to foster a sense of working together in adversity, although the reforms themselves marked a notable departure from his previous centre-left populism, embracing the need for economic austerity, the liberalisation of investment regulations to attract foreign capital, and the ending of lifetime guaranteed employment for industrial workers.*

Kim Dae Jung was born in southwest Korea at Mokpo, near Kwangju in the Cholla region, on 3 December 1925 (or by some accounts one or even two years earlier). Raised as a strict Catholic, he excelled at school, winning entry to the local school of commerce, but his education was interrupted by the Second World War. The ending of the 40 years of Japanese rule in 1945 brought *de facto* partition of Korea, Soviet forces having liberated the north and US troops the south. By the time the Republic of Korea was declared in 1948, Kim was running the local newspaper in Mokpo.

He fought in the Korean war (1950–53), was captured by the forces of the communist North, and upon his release began a political career, managing in 1960 (on his fifth attempt) to win election to the National Assembly. The legislature was abolished after Gen. Park's military coup in 1961, but elections held in 1963 and 1967 saw Kim again elected and, as a gifted orator, becoming spokesman for the opposition to Park's authoritarian regime. During this period he married for the second time – his first wife having died, leaving him with two children. His second wife, the US-educated Lee Hee Ho, a Protestant doctor's daughter, became his most resolute supporter and political conscience. Kim also found time to attend Kyung-Hee University Business School from 1964, and read economics at the graduate school there in 1970.

For the 1971 presidential elections Kim was chosen as the candidate of the left-of-centre opposition New Democratic Party, with a support base among blue-collar workers and students augmented by Kim's personal popularity in his native Cholla region. Despite the Park government's attempts to discredit him as a communist, and a car accident which many believed was really the first of several assassination attempts against him, he sustained an unexpectedly strong challenge, obtaining 45 per cent of the vote. Refusing an ultimatum to join Park's party, he fled instead to Japan, but in 1973 was abducted from Tokyo (allegedly in a CIA-backed secret service operation) and returned to Seoul under house arrest. Imprisoned again from 1976 to 1978 for his criticisms of the Park regime, Kim became the focus of a pro-democracy campaign in which his wife played a key role, organising choruses of slogans sung after services in the churches by groups of women in hibiscus-coloured shawls.

The May 1980 Kwangju rising, brutally crushed by the army, led to Kim's arrest yet again, this time on charges of plotting to overthrow the government. A death sentence passed on him in September was commuted to life imprisonment as a result of international pressure, and later reduced to 20 years, but in December 1982, due to his ill health, Kim was released in a general amnesty and allowed to travel to the USA for medical treatment.

Effectively exiled to the USA, Kim Dae Jung issued a joint declaration with the other main opposition leader, Kim Young Sam, committing themselves to work together to end the military regime, now led by President Chun Doo Hwan. He was placed under house arrest when he returned to Seoul in 1985 ahead of legislative elections, in which his supporters performed strongly. A merger with Kim Young Sam's party in April 1987 was reversed, however, just one month before the presidential elections which the regime had unexpectedly agreed to hold by direct ballot that December. This debilitating division in the opposition let Chun's successor, Roh Tae Woo, retain power; Kim Dae Jung, as leader of his new Party for Peace and Democracy (PPD), polled almost 27 per cent of the vote and finished third, just behind Kim Young Sam.

In 1989, in the latest of many attempts to portray him as "soft" towards the communist North, Kim was indicted over talks between a PPD representative and the North Korean government. The following year the ruling party achieved a dramatic political coup by absorbing two former opposition groups, co-opting

Kim Young Sam on the understanding that he would succeed Roh as the first government-backed civilian candidate for the presidency in 1992. In that election Kim Dae Jung, having helped create a new Democratic Party in 1991 in an effort to rally the remaining opposition, came second behind Kim Young Sam with 34 per cent of the vote.

Although Kim Dae Jung retired from the political arena in 1993, the growing popular disillusionment with Kim Young Sam's government, and the encouragement of his wife, resulted in his return to the fray in mid-1995. His National Congress for New Politics (NCNP), despite attracting defectors from the Democratic Party, performed unexpectedly poorly in legislative elections in April 1996, when Kim himself failed to win a seat.

In the run-up to the 1997 presidential elections, the NCNP formed an alliance with the United Liberal Democrats, who had split off from the ruling party in 1995. Kim became their joint candidate, and in a closely contested campaign he emerged as the ultimate winner. His 40.3 per cent of the vote in the 18 December poll put him just ahead of the ruling party's candidate, who was damaged by a third candidate splitting the vote. Kim's success, which was the country's first ever opposition election victory, was greeted with particular jubilation in Seoul, and in Kwangju in his native Cholla, as tributes poured in to his character and political rectitude. His promises on the release of political prisoners were followed up with a wide-ranging amnesty which included ex-presidents Chun and Roh, who had both persecuted Kim while in power, and were serving long prison terms for corruption, and in Chun's case for instigating the 1980 Kwangju massacre.

Celebrations of Kim's election were overshadowed, however, by the need for urgent action on the economy. Caught up in the region-wide crisis as foreign investors pulled out in a collective loss of confidence, South Korea faced calls for major reform, including the restructuring and improved regulation of its powerful industrial-financial conglomerates or *chaebols*, and a heavy dose of austerity measures. It was Kim Dae Jung, rather than the outgoing "lame duck" Kim Young Sam, who had to take responsibility for putting together a package of proposals to meet the conditions required by the International Monetary Fund (IMF) for its support.

Once inaugurated as president on 25 February 1998, he also became embroiled in a dispute with parliament, where he lacked a working majority, over his controversial choice of prime minister. His nominee Kim Jong Pil, the leader of a conservative party, had done a deal with Kim Dae Jung to secure this post in return for not standing against him for the presidency, but the opposition considered him too tainted by involvement with the former regime earlier in his career. The president eventually got his way over this appointment in August, however, because of the widely accepted need to press ahead with economic reforms. On this front too Kim Dae Jung could claim real progress by early 1999, with signs of a return to growth after the sharp recession of 1998, and further support being promised by the IMF. The burden of his government's measures, however, fell heavily on industrial workers, and ominous signs of rising labour unrest indicated the end of any "honeymoon period" for the former people's champion.

Kim Il Sung

Kim Il Sung was for almost 46 years the dominant figure in North Korea. Venerated as the "Great Leader", he was both general secretary of the ruling (and sole legal) party, the Korean Workers' Party, and, from 1972 until his death in 1994, state president. It remains disputed how much he owed his initial leadership role to his Soviet backers, but once confirmed in power after the Korean war he became the object of perhaps the world's most overblown cult of personality. Backed by fierce repression of any dissenting voice, and on a war footing as the flames of North–South Korean hostility were kept constantly fanned, his regime supposedly drew inspiration from his so-called Juche ideology of socialist self-reliance. In reality it was a ruthless police state, with the dictatorial Kim Il Sung even succumbing to the dynastic delusion and setting up his son Kim Jong Il as his intended heir.

Kim Il Sung was born Kim Song Ju on 15 April 1912 in Mangyongdae, Pyongyang, North Korea, the eldest of three sons of a peasant couple, Kim Hyonh Jik and Kang Pan Sok. His *nom de guerre* is said to have been adopted in memory of a celebrated anti-Japanese guerrilla fighter.

According to official biographies, Kim received his early education at home, and in 1929 attended the

Yuwen Middle School in Jilin, Manchuria, where he became active in politics as a member of the South Manchurian Communist Youth Association. He was arrested for his anti-imperialist activities against the Japanese and upon his release in 1930 joined the Korean Revolutionary Army. In 1932 he founded his own Korean People's Revolutionary Army which established bases in the Jiandao region of Manchuria, and from there, official biographers maintain, Kim staged guerrilla raids against Japanese installations. His leading role in this struggle continued until the liberation of Korea north of the 38th parallel by Soviet forces in August 1945.

Other, less flattering accounts of Kim's activities during the 1930s and early 1940s suggest that he spent the war years like a Manchurian "bandit" preying on poor Korean farmers who formed nearly 80 per cent of the population in Jiandao. Western observers have also tended to disregard official accounts of Kim's wartime activities, believing that he spent most of his time in the Soviet Union training as a spy.

In August 1946 Kim formed the Korean Workers' Party (KWP – resulting from the merger of the Communist Party of North Korea and the New Democratic Party of Korea) and, with the help of his Soviet allies, proclaimed the Democratic People's Republic of Korea in September 1948. The Korean war (1950–53) perpetuated the division of Korea into two mutually hostile entities, the North supported by the Soviet Union and China and propelled along Kim Il Sung's idiosyncratic "road to socialism", and the South supported by the USA and determinedly anti-communist. Kim Il Sung took advantage of the environment engendered by this conflict to further consolidate his power, ruthlessly crushing political opponents and emerging as the undisputed head of North Korea.

Although he was formally elected president in 1972, Kim's real power base, both before and after he took the title of president, lay in the ruling KWP. Using the vehicle of the single-party state, he promoted an intensely nationalistic economic policy. Predicated on his *Juche* ideology, an amalgam of Marxism–Leninism, it stressed socialist self-reliance and absolute devotion to the party and nation-state. However, North Korea's international isolation, underlined by its hostility to and almost total absence of social and cultural contacts with the outside world, quickly depressed living standards and led to a steady decline in growth. The economic crisis became especially acute towards the very end of Kim's life as he witnessed the collapse of communism in the former Soviet Union and the transformation of the communist regime in his other main erstwhile ally, China.

The most distinctive feature of Kim's regime was the promotion of a quite extraordinary personality cult. Hailed by his people as the "Great Leader" and virtually deified by attributes of infallibility and immortality, he was said to have approved the building of more than 50,000 statues of himself as objects of worship. His portraits hung in every house and more than 20 kinds of Kim Il Sung badges were manufactured for people to wear according to their professional and political status. His 38-volume collected *Works* were made obligatory reading, with the North Korean media also regularly publishing evidence purporting to show people avidly studying them across the world, and he designated his own birthday as "the greatest national holiday".

Kim died of a heart attack in Pyongyang on 8 July 1994. His death unleashed nine days of national mourning, marked by readings from his memoirs on radio and television, which culminated in a state funeral attended by millions of North Koreans. No foreign dignitaries were invited. His body was later embalmed by Russian experts and laid in a coffin at his presidential palace (renamed the Kumsuan Memorial Palace).

Kim was succeeded, after a lengthy interim period lasting over three years, by his son Kim Jong Il as head of the KWP. The younger Kim had been groomed for leadership by his father since the 1970s and was designated officially as his successor in 1974, acquiring the title "Dear Leader" the following year. Even in death, however, Kim Il Sung remained the dominant presence, and amendments to the North Korean constitution in 1998 went so far as to abolish the post of state president, now that he was no longer available to fill it.

Kim Il Sung married twice, according to unofficial sources. Kim Hye Sun, who claimed to be his first wife, was killed by the Japanese in 1940. His second wife, Kim Chong Suk, the mother of Kim Jong Il, died in 1949.

Helmut **Kohl**

Helmut Kohl was head of government for longer than any other chancellor in German history. Responsible for encouraging the rapid reunification of Germany after the collapse of communism in the former German Democratic Republic, he also oversaw the consolidation in the 1980s and 1990s of the Franco-German relationship, at the heart of the process of supranational integration in western Europe. Kohl first took office as federal chancellor of the Federal Republic of Germany in 1982, when it was still West Germany, and won re-election four times, in 1983, 1987, 1990 (for the first time as chancellor of a united Germany) and 1994, before his eventual defeat in September 1998. A Catholic whose original power base was the Rhineland-Palatinate, Kohl led the Christian Democratic Union (CDU), the main right-of-centre party (with its Bavarian sister party the Christian Social Union – CSU), and governed throughout in coalition with the liberal Free Democrats (FDP).

Helmut Kohl was born in Ludwigshafen on 3 April 1930. He studied law, sociology, political science and history at the universities of Frankfurt and Heidelberg, and completed his doctorate after eight years in 1958. Kohl had joined the CDU in 1947, and in 1953 he became a member of the CDU committee in the *Land* (state) of Rhineland-Palatinate. By 1954

he was deputy chairman of its young members' section, and he was a member of the *Land* executive from 1955 to 1966.

After leaving university, Kohl was employed for ten years (1959–69) in the chemical industry, working as a departmental head in the Chemical Industry Association at Ludwigshafen. He married Hannelore Renner in 1960, and they have two sons. During the 1960s he began to build up his power base within the Rhineland-Palatinate, chairing the party group on the Ludwigshafen city council from 1960 until 1967, the CDU group in the *Land* parliament between 1963 and 1969, and the CDU's *Land* executive from 1966 to 1973. Between 1969 and 1976 he was minister president (i.e. regional head of government) of the Rhineland-Palatinate.

In 1969 Kohl entered the CDU national executive, where he was deputy chairman for four years. His strong local support favoured his appointment to the position of CDU federal chairman, succeeding Rainer Barzel in 1973. He was nominated as the CDU/CSU candidate for chancellor in the 1976 elections, but was defeated on that occasion, and not nominated in 1980. However, Kohl managed to retain his position as the chairman of the parliamentary group of the CDU and CSU, and in 1982 he did become chancellor, not by direct election on this occasion but because the FDP was persuaded to abandon its participation in a socialist-led coalition government and to support a "constructive vote of no confidence" against the then chancellor, Helmut Schmidt. Kohl, whose government was sworn in on 4 October 1982, won a convincing victory as chancellor in the general election held the following year.

Consistently underestimated and regarded by his opponents as clumsy and lacking in charisma, Kohl proved himself to be not merely an effective and durable politician, but also unusually adept at interpreting how the mood of the majority of Germans might develop on crucial issues. During more than 15 years continuously in office, he overcame his initial lack of confidence in foreign affairs, which for many years he left largely in the hands of his FDP foreign minister Hans-Dietrich Genscher. It was Kohl who threw his weight decisively behind the policy of encouraging German unification after the fall of the East German communist regime in 1989. He was likewise a major force in promoting European union, built around what he saw as the motor of the Franco-German relationship, and proceeding via the Single European Act of the mid-1980s to the Maastricht Treaty of 1992 and beyond. While he favoured enlargement of the European Union to include former communist countries in central and eastern Europe, in his last term of office it was the project for economic and monetary union that he made his special concern.

With the triumph of German unification behind him, however, his popularity had already fallen by the time of the 1994 elections, as the price paid for that unification exacerbated the problems of Germany's high-cost economy. From the mid-1990s onwards he came in for further criticism, with record levels of unemployment the dominant domestic issue, whereas he was staking his reputation on the goal of European monetary union. Kohl was largely successful in winning over an initially highly apprehensive German

public to the idea that a single European currency could adequately replace the deutschmark, long regarded as the rock of stability on which the country's economic success had been founded. Seeking to obtain one more term as chancellor in 1998 to see this project to fruition, in October 1997 Kohl won the endorsement of 95 per cent of the delegates at the CDU conference to put himself forward as the party's candidate for chancellor in the general election held on 27 September 1998.

In the event it proved to be beyond his reach, as the electorate opted eventually for change rather than continuity, giving his social democrat opponent **Gerhard Schröder** the opportunity to put together a coalition with the environmentalist Greens. Kohl also lost his Ludwigshafen constituency, but retained a seat in the *Bundestag* (the lower house of the federal parliament) by virtue of his position at the top of the CDU party list. He stood down on 7 November 1998 as CDU chairman, at a party congress which then unanimously endorsed his own favoured candidate, Wolfgang Schaüble, as his successor.

Honours conferred upon Kohl include the Grand Cross for Service to the Federal Republic (previously held only by Konrad Adenauer), awarded to him on the day before Schröder was formally sworn in as his successor; the "honorary citizenship of Europe", conferred by the summit meeting of European Union heads of government in Vienna in December 1998, and the highest US civilian award, the Presidential Medal of Freedom, presented to him in April 1999 by **Bill Clinton**, with whom he had enjoyed a particularly good relationship.

Chandrika Bandaranaike **Kumaratunga**

Chandrika Bandaranaike Kumaratunga, who has been in power in Sri Lanka as executive president since 1994, is one of a number of Asian women who have come to office as the daughters or widows of leading politicians. Her membership of this "club" is unique, however, in that she is the daughter of not one but two former prime ministers – and also the widow of a lesser-known figure whose charisma had marked him out as a rising star. Elected on a promise of ending Sri Lanka's protracted ethnic conflict, she has found herself still heavily reliant on the army in a continuing violent struggle, despite her efforts in pushing through devolution proposals. Under her government Sri Lanka has nevertheless achieved significant economic growth, and Kumaratunga has modified her leftist agenda to promote neo-liberal policies.

Chandrika Bandaranaike was born in Colombo on 29 June 1945, and educated initially at St Bridget's Convent in Colombo. Her father Solomon Bandaranaike founded the Sri Lanka Freedom Party (SLFP), leading it to electoral success and becoming prime minister, but was assassinated in 1959. Her mother Sirimavo Bandaranaike, propelled into politics as his widow, took over the party leadership prior to an election campaign in 1960 which resulted in her becoming the first woman in the world to be elected as prime minister. Sirimavo Bandaranaike held that office from 1960 to 1965 and from 1970 to 1977, but was later banned from taking any active part in politics on the grounds of abuse of power; she nevertheless remained the power behind the scenes at the SLFP throughout its nearly two decades in opposition.

Chandrika, meanwhile, spent the latter part of the 1960s in France, training in political journalism with *Le Monde* in Paris, completing degrees in law and political science, and going on to do a doctorate in development economics. This served as preparation for a subsequent career which encompassed teaching and lecturing, research, and work in land reform. Between 1972 and 1976, while her mother was head of government, she helped run the Land Reforms Commission of Sri Lanka, and she then worked as an expert consultant for the UN Food and Agriculture Organization (FAO) until 1979. During this period she published a book entitled *Janawasa Movement: Future Strategies for Development in Sri Lanka*. She chaired the poverty alleviation organisation Jana Savya, and carried out research projects in the fields of food policy, political violence and agrarian reform. In 1974 she became a member of the executive committee of the SLFP's Women's League.

After 1977, with the SLFP cast out into the political wilderness, Chandrika Bandaranaike pursued her press and publishing career, as chairperson and managing director from 1977 to 1985 of the Sinhalese daily newspaper *Dinakara*. By 1980, the year in which her mother was deprived of her political rights, Chandrika was playing a greater role in working to rebuild the fortunes of the SLFP, as a member of both its executive and its working committee. Factional disputes, however, conducted in an atmosphere of heightened tension following the outbreak of what was to become a protracted civil war with the minority ethnic Tamil separatists in the north and east, led to the formation of a separate left-wing socialist Sri Lanka Mahajana Party (SLMP) in January 1984. Chandrika was closely involved with this new party, whose moving spirit was the film idol Vijaya Kumaranatunga, whom she had married in 1978. While he was its national organiser, she was its first vice-president, and from 1986 to 1988 its president.

On 16 February 1988 Vijaya Kumaranatunga was shot dead in Colombo. His killing, like other political attacks at this time, was attributed not to Tamil separatists but to Sinhalese extremists. The widowed Chandrika (who later dropped one of the syllables of her late husband's name, calling herself Chandrika Bandaranaike Kumaratunga) went abroad for three years, attending the Institute of Commonwealth Studies at the University of London as a research fellow, but returned once again to Sri Lanka in 1991.

Realising the futility of an opposition weakened by factional divisions, Chandrika Kumaratunga was instrumental in forming in early 1993 a broader left-wing People's Alliance, encompassing both the SLFP and the United Socialist Alliance (a grouping of which the SLMP had been a member since 1988). In May 1993 this People's Alliance recorded a notable victory in Western Province (which included the capital, Colombo) when elections were held for provincial councils. Chandrika Kumaratunga was sworn in on 21 May as chief minister of the province. Another of the obstacles to effective opposition unity was removed later that year when Chandrika's brother and sometime rival, Anura Bandaranaike, resigned from the SLFP. The general election in August 1994 saw Chandrika campaigning as the Alliance leader, with her mother retaining the leadership of the SLFP itself. Their victory on 16 August opened the way for Chandrika Kumaratunga to become prime minister, and she was duly sworn in three days later.

Following up her general election victory, Chandrika Kumaratunga secured the Alliance's nomination to stand three months later in elections for the country's presidency, the top executive post since a constitutional change in 1978. She won a record 62 per cent of the vote in the November 1994 presidential poll, and was inaugurated for a six-year term on 12 November 1994. Her mother Sirimavo Bandaranaike, despite having harboured her own ambitions for the top job, instead accepted the subordinate role of prime minister. Kumaratunga has since postponed the idea of abolishing the executive presidency and reverting to a prime ministerial form of government.

Chandrika Kumaratunga based her presidential campaign, like the Alliance's general election campaign, around her pledge to restore peace to Sri Lanka. This entailed seeking a rapid end to the ethnic conflict which had divided the majority Sinhalese and minority Tamil populations for over a decade. She launched several initiatives over the succeeding years in efforts to negotiate with the Tamil separatists, pursuing a far-reaching devolution policy to assist in this. However, the initial optimism encouraged by a truce in January 1995 was soon lost amid renewed violence and, beginning with a major army offensive in July 1995, Kumaratunga has repeatedly shown herself prepared to use force in efforts to break the Tamil separatists' military resistance in the north. In 1998, with the fighting still continuing, her government attempted to tighten its grip with the imposition of a formal ban on the main Tamil separatist organisation, followed by press controls on reporting of the war and, later in the year, the declaration of a state of emergency.

Oskar **Lafontaine**

*For years the most prominent advocate of social justice ideals within German social democracy, Oskar Lafontaine spent his political life in power in Saarland, but his party was in opposition until 1998 at federal level. Then, after less than six months as federal finance minister, he resigned in March 1999 in an open rift with Chancellor **Gerhard Schröder**. In that short time he had loomed large in the debate over the direction of economic policy at the national and European level. Lafontaine's vision encompassed higher taxes on business, higher public spending, a strategy to tackle unemployment as the top policy priority, and lower interest rates than those propounded by European central bankers. An internationalist, fluent French-speaker with good English and a reputation as a bon viveur, he was suggested as a possible future president of the European Commission, but became far too controversial to be a realistic candidate. Lafontaine's retirement from politics at 55 took Germany – and Europe – by surprise.*

Oskar Lafontaine was born on 16 September 1943 in Saarlouis. Brought up by his mother, an impoverished war widow, he went to a Jesuit-run school to complete his secondary education in the town of Prüm in the Eifel region. In 1962 he went on to university in Bonn and Saarbrücken, graduating in 1969 with a diploma in physics. Between 1969 and 1974 he worked in Saarbrücken for the local

municipal services and transport company, on whose board he sat from 1971. Lafontaine has been married three times and has two children. Christa Müller, his third wife, is an economist with strong credentials as a political figure in her own right and the co-author with Lafontaine of an influential 1998 book on the impact of globalisation.

Throughout his political career Lafontaine has been strongly identified with the small *Land* (state) of Saarland on the French border. Having first joined the Social Democratic Party of Germany (SPD) in 1966 during his student days, he was first elected to the *Land* parliament in Saarland in 1970 and rose to be the chairman of the SPD in Saarland in 1977, a position he retained for nearly 20 years. He was, in addition, mayor of Saarbrücken from 1976 to 1985 (after two years as deputy mayor), and gained a reputation there as a left-wing radical and pacifist, nicknamed "Red Oskar". As the Saarland state minister president (i.e. regional head of government) from 1985 until 1998, Lafontaine moved towards a more pragmatic and moderate approach; his government was noted, however, for adopting anti-nuclear and other environmentalist policies, a tactic which he evidently favoured over the widely discussed strategy of an SPD alliance with the Green party.

Rising in prominence in the SPD at federal level during this period, he was on the party executive from 1979 and its deputy federal chairman between 1987 and 1995. Considered a more charismatic figure than the party chairman, Johannes Rau, Lafontaine was picked by his party as its candidate for the federal chancellorship at the 1990 elections, which were held in the immediate aftermath of German reunification. During the reunification debate he had spoken out against a rush to one Germany, and made himself unpopular in some quarters with his unwelcome warnings about the likely costs which West Germans would have to bear. Stabbed in the neck and seriously wounded at a campaign meeting in April 1990, Lafontaine resumed his campaign but suffered a crushing defeat at the hands of incumbent Chancellor **Helmut Kohl** of the Christian Democratic Union (CDU). After the elections he returned to the Saarland metaphorically licking his wounds. Despite his continuing role as standard-bearer for the SPD's identification with social justice issues, he announced in June 1993 that he was not a contender to be the party's candidate for the chancellorship at the next federal elections in 1994 (when the new party chairman Rudolf Scharping was similarly unsuccessful in challenging Kohl). However, Lafontaine ousted Scharping as party chairman in November 1995 when he dramatically and unexpectedly forced a vote at the party congress in Mannheim. In his party leadership role he proved highly effective in rallying the demoralised SPD, building up a stronger, more effective party machine, and helping to foster party unity to ensure a successful bid for power in 1998. He also used the SPD's majority in the upper house of the German parliament to frustrate efforts by Kohl to enact a tax reform plan ahead of the elections.

Lafontaine threw his weight behind the decision that Gerhard Schröder rather than he should be SPD candidate for chancellor in 1998, recognising that, for all his popularity with the SPD faithful, he lacked Schröder's broad electoral appeal and was too firmly associated with the left. Schröder, on the other hand, represented the SPD's best chance to oust Kohl in a contest for the political centre ground. The party's victory, on the face of things Schröder's triumph, nevertheless owed much to Lafontaine's efforts as party chairman, and propelled him into a position of tremendous influence. The ministerial portfolio of finance, which he assumed in the new government in October 1998, had so evidently been allowed to extend its authority across the whole area of economic decision-making, and the government's programme was so clearly marked with Lafontaine's imprint that speculation began immediately about power struggles between him and the more "business-friendly" Schröder. Moreover, Lafontaine's enthusiasm for mounting an attack on unemployment as the top policy priority at the European level, working closely with French socialist Prime Minister Lionel Jospin, raised questions about the likely impact on the more narrowly focused "sound money" policies with which Germany's Bundesbank had long been identified. Standing out as a sharp critic of the Bundesbank for failing to cut interest rates, Lafontaine was also sending strong signals that he opposed a similarly restrictive stance by the new European Central Bank, which took over responsibility from the beginning of 1999 for setting interest rates for all EU countries participating in the new single currency.

As the media whipped up the "who really rules Germany" issue, Lafontaine began to be demonised by the British tabloid press, in particular, as a tax-raising old-style socialist and "the most dangerous man in Europe". Within the Schröder government he was increasingly at odds with its more right-wing members, and when criticisms by Schröder himself were leaked to the press in March 1999, Lafontaine announced his resignation. Stepping down simultaneously as SPD chairman, and announcing that he was to resign his parliamentary seat as well, Lafontaine said that the prospect of retirement had been on his mind since the assassination attempt nine years earlier. His departure from government, he said, was because of "poor teamwork", but he urged his party not to forget that its heart "beats to the left".

Jean-Marie **Le Pen**

The most recognisable of Europe's extreme right-wingers, Le Pen is a former French paratrooper who founded the National Front in 1972 and led it for nearly three decades. An old-fashioned populist with an anti-immigrant agenda, he won as much as 15 per cent of the vote in presidential elections with his appeal to disaffected nationalists, but until the mid-1990s his party was marginalised by his extremism and treated as a racist pariah by the mainstream French parties. Younger and more subtle politicians within the Front split the party in early 1999 in a largely successful bid to oust Le Pen, believing that they were more capable than him of cashing in on the Front's core support through electoral bargains with elements of the "respectable" right.

Jean-Marie Le Pen was born on 20 June 1928 in La Trinité-sur-Mer, Brittany. His father, a fisherman, was killed in 1942 by a German mine. Le Pen was expelled from his Jesuit boarding school the following year, and worked as a fisherman and a miner to finance his studies in political science and law at the University of Paris. While a student he was known for his strongly anti-communist views. By some accounts

it was during this period that he lost an eye in a street fight, although the more dignified version is that he lost it fighting in Indochina; he joined a French parachute regiment to fight in Vietnam in 1954, but arrived shortly after the fall of Dien Bien Phu.

In 1956 he won election to the National Assembly (its youngest deputy at that time) as a supporter of the right-wing populist Pierre Poujade. Later the same year he went to fight in Algeria where, like many in the French armed forces, he identified with the French settlers and was strongly critical of what he saw as their betrayal by French President Charles de Gaulle.

In the 1958 general election Le Pen was again elected to the National Assembly, this time as an independent, representing a Paris constituency until 1962. In 1960 he founded the National Front for French Algeria (*Front national pour l'Algérie française*) and at this time was also connected with the extreme nationalist Organisation of the Secret Army (*Organisation de l'armée secrete* – OAS) of French officers who had fought in Algeria. In 1960 he married Pierrette Lalanne, with whom he has three daughters. Following the collapse of this marriage in the 1980s he married Jeanne-Marie ("Jany") Paschos in 1991.

In 1972 Le Pen founded the extreme right-wing National Front (*Front national* – FN), of which he remained undisputed leader until 1999. He got only 0.7 per cent of the vote when he stood in the 1974 presidential elections. A forthright populist, he adopted a strongly nationalist platform, advocating the enforced return of the 3 million immigrants legally settled in France in order to create jobs for French people.

Le Pen's financial position improved when a French industrialist bequeathed him his fortune in 1977, including property in the wealthy Paris suburb of St Cloud. His party commanded little support in the 1970s, however, and in 1981 he was unable to secure the required 500 signatures from elected representatives to validate his candidacy in the presidential poll.

In the early 1980s, with a government of the left in power in France, growing public concerns about immigration provided the breeding ground for the Front's first major political breakthrough. In the 1984 elections to the European Parliament, held under a system of proportional representation, the party won ten seats. Le Pen has had a platform as an MEP ever since, especially between 1984 and 1994, when there were enough extreme right members to constitute a parliamentary group under his leadership. In France, meanwhile, a brief flirtation with proportional representation let in 35 Front deputies to the National Assembly in 1986, Le Pen among them, although all lost their seats in 1988 once the constituency system was restored.

Le Pen's 14–15 per cent support in the 1988 and 1995 presidential elections is broadly comparable with that for his party in recent parliamentary elections (12.4 per cent in 1993 and 14.9 per cent in 1997). The former right-of-centre governing parties, in defeat and disarray in 1997, were torn by disputes over whether to countenance some form of electoral co-operation with the Front, which has generally proven unable to win parliamentary seats without such co-operation. The Front is active at regional level, especially in its heartland in the southeast. Le Pen himself was elected in 1986 as regional councillor in Ile-de-France, and in 1992 and 1998 as a member of the Provence–Alpes–Côte d'Azur regional council.

The author of *Les Français d'abord* (1984) and three other books, Le Pen has provoked outrage with his many outspoken comments. In 1987 he described the Nazi gas chambers as merely "a detail" in the history of the Second World War – an affront for which he later had to pay token damages. He repeated the statement in 1997 in Munich, and MEPs voted in October 1998 to lift his immunity so that he could be brought to trial in Germany under laws prohibiting Holocaust denial. That year he had also outraged many by suggesting that France's national football team lacked commitment because it contained players from a variety of ethnic backgrounds – a piece of ill-judged racism which backfired badly when some of those very players became national heroes for taking France to World Cup victory.

Meanwhile, Le Pen's remaining career was threatened when he was disqualified from voting or standing for public office for two years in an April 1998 conviction for assaulting a female socialist politician while canvassing in a Paris suburb. The ban was reduced to one year by the appeal court judgement in November. A further appeal saved him at least temporarily from having to resign his post as a regional councillor in Provence–Alpes–Côte d'Azur, and was also intended to give him time to head the Front list in the European elections in June 1999.

The question of the party's European list, however, came back to haunt him when he pointedly snubbed Bruno Mégret, his much younger rival within the party, by denying him a prominent place. Mégret, the leading "moderniser" advocating a subtler and less raucous tone for the Front, challenged him directly by calling a special congress for January 1999, at which his faction proclaimed him president instead of Le Pen, thus formalising the party split. Le Pen's humiliation was compounded by the fact that his eldest daughter, Marie-Caroline, was living with one of the leaders of the rival wing.

Aleksander **Lebed**

*Gen. Lebed is repeatedly cited as a likely contender for the Russian presidency after **Yeltsin** goes, although latterly he has been less in the limelight than Prime Minister Yevgeny Primakov and Mayor of Moscow Yuri Luzhkov. His populist nationalist appeal stems from his apparent honesty, patriotism, and image as a man of action, and an aptitude for headline-grabbing "soundbites". However, he has little experience of government – just four months as national security adviser in 1996, and the governorship of Krasnoyarsk in Siberia since May 1998. An atheist and a figure of the authoritarian rather than the traditionalist conservative right, his reputation as a military hero dates back to his days as a paratroop commander in Afghanistan, enhanced by his role in opposing the August 1991 coup in Moscow and in dealing with separatist conflicts in Moldova and Chechnya.*

Aleksander Ivanovich Lebed was born on 20 April 1950 in Novocherkassk, in the Rostov region. His father, a Ukrainian metalworker, was imprisoned in 1937 and fought in a penal battalion during the Second World War; he died in 1978. His mother came from a Don cossack family. Aleksander was the first member of his family to embark upon a military career. He graduated from the Ryazan Higher

Aviation School in 1973 and, after commanding the first battalion of the 345th special paratroops regiment in Afghanistan (1981/82), went on to the Frunze Military Academy. He is married to Inna, a secondary school mathematics teacher, and they have two sons and a daughter.

Lebed passed out from the Academy with distinction in 1985. He was appointed as deputy commander of a paratroop regiment, then as regimental commander in the city of Kostroma, and in 1986 became deputy commander of an airborne division in the city of Pskov. From 1989, and by now a lieutenant-general, he commanded the Tula airborne division. As the Soviet Union began to disintegrate, he was sent to bring various regional troublespots under control, notably Baku in Azerbaijan and Tbilisi in Georgia.

A member of the Communist Party of the Soviet Union (CPSU) since the age of 20, Lebed only became directly involved in political activity when he attended the inaugural conference of the re-founding of the Russian Federation Communist Party in June 1990. He was elected to the party's central committee, which was dominated by conservative figures critical of the reforms being introduced by **Mikhail Gorbachev**. He also attended the 28th congress of the CPSU held the following month. However, when old-guard CPSU communists staged a coup against Gorbachev in August 1991, Lebed backed the popular protesters who resisted them. Russian President Boris Yeltsin, the main figure in the resistance to the August coup, later thanked Lebed personally for the support he had provided by standing guard with a battalion of paratroopers outside the "White House", the Russian parliament building in Moscow.

In 1992 Lebed was sent to command Russian troops in the Dneistr region of Moldova, where he successfully brokered a peace agreement between ethnic Russian separatists and the new Moldovan government. However, his commander Pavel Grachev, the then Russian defence minister, dismissed him in 1995 after differences over his allegedly bullying and high-handed approach and indifference to civilian casualties.

Increasingly identified as a charismatic leader with a reputation for decisiveness, Lebed had by this time begun to attract attention among political analysts of the volatile Russian situation; he is said to be an admirer of Gen. **Colin Powell**, Gen. **Augusto Pinochet** and **Margaret Thatcher**. Moving back into the political arena, he joined the Congress of Russian Communities in April 1995, resigned from the army the following month, and won election to the *Duma* (Russian lower house of parliament) in December as a deputy for Tula. Campaigning on a nationalist platform and promising firm action on law and order, he went on to make a strong showing when he stood in the 1996 Russian presidential elections, coming third in the first round on 16 June with 14.7 per cent of the vote. He was consequently courted by both Yeltsin, the first-round leader, and his communist challenger Gennady Zyuganov. He announced on 18 June that he was throwing his weight behind Yeltsin, who thereupon appointed him secretary of the Russian security council and his personal aide in charge of national security.

Lebed marked his appointment with an immediate surprise announcement that he had acted to forestall a coup attempt. Yeltsin was persuaded to dismiss a number of hardliners, including Lebed's old rival, Defence Minister Grachev. Yeltsin then despatched Lebed to Chechnya, where Russian forces had become mired in a disastrous war against separatists. If this was intended to marginalise him, it failed, because – as in Moldova – Lebed again succeeded in negotiating a peace accord (although his opponents denounced it as a sell-out of Russian interests). In October, nevertheless, Yeltsin dismissed him after only four months in office, amid allegations that Lebed was seeking to establish his own military power base as a prelude to seizing power.

In December 1996 Lebed formed his own party, the Russian Popular Republican Party. Having kept a relatively low profile during 1997, in May 1998 he won election as governor of the Krasnoyarsk region in Siberia with 57 per cent of the vote. In the economic crisis and political uncertainty which beset Russia as a whole, he highlighted the plight of officers in Siberia (who were in charge of batteries of intercontinental nuclear missiles and had not been paid for months) with a headline-grabbing warning to the government in Moscow: "The situation is worse than in 1917. ... Now we have huge stockpiles of poorly guarded nuclear weapons."

With presidential elections due by 2000, but possibly taking place earlier if Yeltsin's health finally gave out, Lebed's position in Siberia was generally regarded as the vantage point from which he would launch a second presidential bid. His governorship ensured him a seat in the upper house of the Russian parliament, the Federation Council, but it also exposed him to the criticism that he lacked the ideas, the organisational skills and the necessary grasp of economics to make a success of regional, let alone national, government.

Li Peng

*Once a protégé of China's long-serving prime minister Zhou Enlai, the conservative communist hardliner Li Peng had himself been prime minister for two years when he signed the 1989 martial law decree to suppress the student protests and, notoriously, applauded the Tiananmen Square massacre of 4 June. After the retirement of **Deng Xiaoping** from active leadership, the fluctuating balance between conservatives and economic reformers evolved gradually to the latter's advantage, but Li Peng remained as number two in the hierarchy behind only State President **Jiang Zemin**. Having recovered from a heart attack in 1993, he commands support throughout the vast state administrative system. Not eligible to retain the premiership when his second term expired in March 1998, he moved over instead to become chairman of the National People's Congress (NPC).*

Li Peng was born on 20 October 1928 in Chengdu City in Sichuan Province. The son of a writer who was executed as a communist rebel in 1930, he was later looked after by Zhou Enlai, and sent to school in Yan'an in 1941. He joined the Chinese Communist Party (CCP) in 1945, and worked between 1946 and 1948 as a technician at the Shanxi-Chahar-Hebei Electricity Company, and as assistant manager and secretary of the party branch at the Harbin Oil and Fats Company, while completing his schooling at the Yan'an Institute of Natural Sciences. He then went to the Soviet Union, where he became chairman of the Chinese students' association while studying from 1948 to 1955 at the hydroelectric engineering department of the Moscow Power Institute.

Returning to China in 1955, six years after the formation of the communist regime, Li Peng married Zhu Lin in 1958, and they have had two sons and one daughter. Working as an engineer and as a party official in the power industry, Li Peng was based from 1966 onwards in the capital, Beijing, where during the cultural revolution he was acting party secretary and chairman of the "revolutionary committee" at the Beijing Electric Power Supply Bureau. In the 1970s he was successively deputy party secretary, deputy director, director, and party secretary, in the city's energy administration. In 1979 he moved into the central government, initially as a deputy minister and then a full minister and party secretary in the power industry. Promoted to the rank of deputy premier in 1983, he took charge of transport and of the state education commission as well as the power industry. Having joined the party central committee in 1982, he was elected to its politburo in September 1985, one of six new members brought in after the retirement of numerous party veterans.

Li's appointment as acting premier in 1987, when he also joined the inner core of the party leadership as a member of the politburo's standing committee, gave him a powerful position as the leading conservative rival to Zhao Ziyang, the former premier who had become party general secretary. Zhao, acting increasingly as Deng Xiaoping's heir apparent, was the instigator of an ambitious economic reform and modernisation programme which had run into serious difficulties with over-spending and rapidly rising inflation. Li Peng, leading a conservative backlash, launched a programme of retrenchment. Confirmed in office as premier for a five-year term by the NPC in 1988, he was subsequently a target of pro-Zhao protests which, crucially, came to be seen by Deng as a threat to the party's monopoly on political power. The eclipse of Zhao, and the brutal suppression of the pro-democracy movement at (and after) the Tiananmen Square massacre in June 1989, set back (without halting) the economic reform process; it also underlined, however, the fact that political reforms would not be part of the Chinese leadership's model for handling the transition to a market economy.

From 1988 to 1990 Li Peng held, concurrently with the premiership, the chair of the state committee for restructuring the economic system. Re-elected as prime minister by the NPC in March 1993, he adopted a more reformist tone in his report on the economy, but again made it a major objective to bring inflation under control. His own illness, however, and the rapid growth of the economy as it began to be opened up to foreign investment in the mid-1990s, made his economic conservatism appear increasingly a rearguard action. The ascendancy of the reformists, championed by president and party leader Jiang Zemin, was underlined by the policies approved at the September 1997 party conference, although Li Peng retained his seat on the politburo and its seven-member standing committee and was confirmed as number two in the party hierarchy. The government reshuffle which followed in March 1998 saw Li Peng vacate the premiership, being ineligible for a third term. His successor, the modernising technocrat and party number three Zhu Rongji, was seen as adding weight in the medium term to the reformist tendency, leaving Li Peng himself more isolated on the conservative wing. However, when the NPC met that same month Li Peng was elected to the important office of NPC chairman – albeit with the embarrassment of a rare show of opposition, as 200 delegates voted against him.

Madonna

Bursting upon the music scene in 1983, Madonna rapidly became the leading female icon of the "MTV generation", with a host of teenage imitators. Many who shared her Catholic Italian–American background were scandalised even by her name, a dramatic clash with the traditional idea of the Madonna. She was celebrated – and condemned – more for her persona and her video presence than for the music which supposedly formed the heart of the package. Adept in adopting and exploiting potent imagery, she could by turns epitomise the liberated woman, then trade unashamedly on her body as an object, courting the accusation of pornography over her notorious book Sex. *Since becoming a mother, Madonna is – in her own words –- still battling male domination, but, rather than being loud and obscene, she now does so with "the power of silence".*

Madonna Louise Veronica Ciccone was born on 16 August 1958 in Bay City, Michigan, USA and grew up in Pontiac, near Detroit. She was the eldest child in a working-class family. Her French Canadian mother Madonna Ciccone (*née* Fortin) died when she was five. Her father Sylvio (Tony) Ciccone remarried, but the young Madonna lived for a while with relatives, a way of escaping her problematic relationship with him and the tensions of the household, which grew to a total of eight children. She soon became ruggedly independent, and her flair for expressiveness and self-publicity found an outlet in dancing and cheerleading.

Although she gained a scholarship to study dance at the University of Michigan, she left after two years, arriving penniless in New York in the late 1970s, and eventually winning a place in the Alvin Ailey Dance Theatre. Drawn to the burgeoning high-energy dance music scene, she moonlighted for a while as a backing singer, but yearned to be a star in her own right. Encouraged by influential New York club DJ Jellybean Benitez, she got her first big break after another club DJ, Mark Kamins, persuaded her to sign a contract with Sire Records. Her debut album, simply entitled *Madonna*, released in 1983, sold a remarkable 7.7 million copies internationally, largely on the basis of three joyous singles, *Holiday*, *Borderline* and *Lucky Star*.

Two features marked Madonna out from the crowd of would-be stars: her extraordinary self-belief and her attention to presentation. She created an image that was to be copied by a generation of teenage girls – the so-called "wannabes" – with her alluring gym singlet, bare midriff and lascivious dancing style. In particular, Madonna realised that rock videos were pivotal to creating her entire aura. The newly established youth music television station, MTV, used Madonna videos to spread her fame worldwide. Fans found her infectious blend of pop, Motown, New Wave and dance irresistible. *Like a Virgin*, released in November 1984, remains her highest-selling album to date in the USA.

Madonna also revealed a penchant for deliberately blurring boundaries. The video for *Like a Virgin*, shot in Venice, counterposed pious Christian imagery of virgin madonnas against the singer's own flirtatious "boy toy" persona. Critics hailed Madonna as a new role model for young women – sexually charged, physically and emotionally strong, always in control – even if she sometimes got into hot water and offended sensibilities with her unguarded remarks.

By 1985, Madonna in her "up-front" mid-1980s incarnation was outselling all other rock artists. Next, she adopted the blonde "material girl" persona (her natural hair colour is dark brown), in both a homage to and pastiche of Marilyn Monroe. Indeed, almost every Madonna album produced for Sire signalled another transformation, either in her physical appearance or musical style – *True Blue* (released in 1986, with sales of 17.3 million worldwide), *You Can Dance* (1987), *Who's That Girl?* (1987), *Like a Prayer* (1989), *I'm Breathless* (1990) and *Immaculate Collection* (1990).

Her CD and video sales were boosted by lavishly stage-managed and physically exhausting tours – *Virgin Tour* (1985), *Who's That Girl?* (1987) and *Blonde Ambition* (1990). These were occasions for Madonna and her crew to sport outlandish garments, created by fashion gurus like Jean-Paul Gaultier (inventor of the infamous breast cones) and **Gianni Versace**. She even pioneered an entirely new dance style, called "vogueing" (after her single, *Vogue*), and popularised navel-piercing.

Madonna's cinematic career, however, has proven somewhat less successful. It really began in 1985 with her leading role in *Desperately Seeking Susan*. Blurring boundaries again, in *Truth or Dare* (released in Europe as *In Bed With Madonna*) she acts herself, with an outrageous portrayal of backstage life.

Increasingly, Madonna has broached serious subjects, like parental abuse, gay rights and religious hypocrisy. Yet her appetite for controversy threatened to overwhelm her career. Many fellow Catholics were offended by her semi-naked cavorting before a black saint and holy icons in her 1989 video for *Like a Prayer*, which was believed to have cost her a lucrative advertising contract with Pepsi-Cola. Others condemned what they saw as thinly veiled pornography, in her best-selling book, *Sex*, the CD *Erotica* (1992), and the *Girlie Show* tour (1993). Her lead role in the film version of the Lloyd Webber musical *Evita* (1996) prompted demonstrations by Argentinian devotees of the late Eva Perón.

In 1992 Madonna signed a seven-year, US$60 million deal with Time Warner. The agreement enabled her to set up her own record label, Maverick, with her manager, Freddy DeMann. Maverick produced three further Madonna albums – *Erotica* (1992), *Bedtime Stories* (1994) and *Something to Remember* (1995); yet also generously promoted new talents, like Alanis Morissette and the British group The Prodigy. Besides her music and cinema careers, Madonna was in the stage play *Goose & Tomtom* in 1986, and (despite some hostile critical notices) appeared again in 1998 in David Mamet's *Speed the Plow*.

Madonna's private life has proved as tempestuous as her public one. She married the actor Sean Penn on 16 August 1985, but their union ended acrimoniously within four years. In 1996 she became pregnant by her personal trainer and current boyfriend, Carlos Leon, and on 14 October 1996 she gave birth to a baby girl, whom she named Lourdes. She has apparently found in motherhood a fulfilling new phase in her life, accompanied by a greater sense of stability and responsibility, which emerges in the more thoughtful and poignant songs found on her latest album, *Ray of Light*, released on the Warner Brothers label in 1998. Her decision to put Lourdes down for a place at Cheltenham Ladies' College, the ultra-respectable English girls' boarding school, attracted much attention, with pundits drawing the contrast between her own iconoclastic career and her aspirations for her daughter. Recent interviews reveal her – once again dark-haired – as less shocking and confrontational, more interested in spirituality, whether this be via Hindu scriptures, yoga, meditation, or the Jewish Kaballah.

Mahathir Mohamed

Head of government in Malaysia since 1981, Prime Minister Mahathir made a name for himself internationally as the most vocal proponent of "Asian values" in political and economic development. While rejecting Western criticisms of his regime's more authoritarian and illiberal characteristics, on the grounds of the importance of political stability, he has latterly been particularly outspoken over the crisis of investor confidence which hit the so-called "Asian tiger" economies of Malaysia and its regional neighbours in late 1997. In typical confrontational style, Mahathir denounced speculators for engineering the crisis and was bitterly critical of international financial organisations for their shortcomings in responding to it. A doctor before he entered full-time politics, who still enjoys being known as "Dr M", Mahathir was facing vocal demands for his resignation by the end of the 1990s, ahead of elections due in the year 2000, as a bruising conflict with his former deputy Anwar Ibrahim laid him open to accusations of political and financial corruption.

Mahathir Mohamed was born on 20 December 1925, the son of a headmaster, in Alor Setar in the state of Kedah in northwest Malaysia, which was then a British protectorate. Having completed his schooling there, at Sultan Abdul Hamid College, he enrolled at the King Edward VII College of Medicine in the University of Malaya in Singapore, where he completed his medical training, going on to be a government medical officer from 1953 to 1957. He set up in private practice in 1957. Mahathir married another doctor, Siti Hasmah, in 1956; they have had four sons and three daughters.

He joined the United Malays National Organisation (UMNO) upon its formation in 1946, while still a student, and sat on the party's supreme council and held a seat in parliament between 1964 and 1969. In that year he lost his seat at the May general election, but attracted notice by publishing a controversial (and subsequently banned) book, criticising the then prime minister, Tengku Abdul Rahman, for his handling of an outbreak of communal rioting in the aftermath of the election. Restored to the party supreme council in 1972, he was appointed as a senator the following year, but in 1974 returned to the House of Representatives, holding his seat there ever since.

Mahathir held ministerial posts between 1974 and 1981, at education and then at trade and industry, and was in addition deputy prime minister from 1976. He rose at the same time in the party leadership, becoming one of three UMNO vice-presidents in 1975, deputy president in 1978, and president in 1981. He took over the leadership of the government in July 1981, as prime minister and also minister of defence, and has led the National Front government since that time; the National Front, in which UMNO is the main constituent, was returned to power in successive general elections in 1982, 1986, 1990 and 1995.

Mahathir risked the charge of ethnic Malay chauvinism in the early stages of his political career and, once in government, emphasised the need for development policies to focus especially on the indigenous Malay people or *bumiputras*. Having thereby done much to create a Malay middle class, he can claim to have redressed an imbalance in the ethnic mix, and now tries to appeal to a wider notion of nationalism embracing also the more prosperous Chinese and other minority groups.

Domestically, Mahathir is known for his forceful approach. He dismisses the accusation of authoritarianism, regarding his own grip on power as beneficial in terms of the political stability it provides. This claim became increasingly difficult for him to justify, however, in the turbulent climate of 1998 and 1999, when − effectively for the first time − he faced a sustained opposition campaign calling for his retirement. The crisis was fuelled by his sudden dismissal in September 1998 of the man widely assumed to be his heir apparent, the deputy prime minister and finance minister Anwar Ibrahim. Anwar's subsequent prosecution on charges of sexual misconduct was backed up by lurid allegations but widely condemned as political manipulation of the judicial system. Anwar had begun to distance himself from Mahathir earlier in the year, favouring a more accommodating stance vis-à-vis the International Monetary Fund (IMF) over economic reforms and expenditure cuts, and he fought back against his dismissal and prosecution by denouncing Mahathir for corruption and demanding that he resign. Until this point, the only serious challenges to Mahathir's leadership had taken the form of contests for the UMNO presidency, which he had overcome in 1987 and successfully forestalled in 1998. Apart from the speculation about his health aroused when he underwent heart surgery in 1989, there had been little question, until the conflict with Anwar, that he would choose the time of his own departure.

Internationally, Mahathir was a driving force behind regional integration in the Association of South East Asian Nations (ASEAN) and the wider Asia–Pacific Economic Co-operation forum (APEC). He helped to popularise the concept of the "tiger economies" of the region, characterised until the economic crisis of 1997 by dramatic rates of growth and industrialisation, but also came under criticism for the emphasis on high-profile projects (many but by no means all of them now suspended) in his "Malaysia 2020" vision of an industrialised society. The abrupt ending of the boom in 1997 may have had its origins in the unsustainability of much of the export-led growth, and weaknesses in financial and corporate regulation, but Mahathir also took it as a personal affront and a calumny on the "Asian model". He famously traded insults with international investment fund manager **George Soros**, whose actions he attacked as typifying the immorality and destructiveness of financial speculators, and has remained trenchant in his criticisms of international organisations such as the IMF and the World Bank for not doing more to avert such crises or, more recently, to help Malaysia and other countries to recover from them.

Nelson **Mandela**

Nelson Mandela was the world's most famous political prisoner under South Africa's racist apartheid *regime, until his eventual release after 27 years in February 1990. Remarkably, he went on from the euphoria of that moment to fulfil the enormous expectations of his people, negotiating the peaceful transition from white minority rule to democratic elections in 1994 and the inauguration of the multiracial "rainbow nation" in place of the* apartheid *state. A man who impressed the world with his sense of responsibility but lack of self-importance, he was chosen unanimously as president of South Africa in May 1994 after the election victory of his African National Congress (ANC). Mandela initially headed a national unity government, and remained throughout his term of office the embodiment of the spirit of national reconciliation. His retirement in June 1999, handing that responsibility to the next generation of ANC leaders as he had planned to do, marked the end of an era.*

Nelson Rolihlahla Mandela was born on 18 July 1918 in the village of Qunu near Umtata, a rural area of the Transkei inhabited by Xhosa pastoralists. He attended Methodist primary and secondary schools, and was simultaneously groomed for tribal duties and leadership. He later entered the University College of Fort Hare and was elected to the student's representative council. He was expelled after his participation in a student strike and went to Johannesburg to complete his degree and study law. In Johannesburg he met Walter Sisulu, Oliver Tambo and others with whom he was instrumental in radicalising the ANC, which Mandela joined in 1942. In 1944 he helped found the ANC Youth League, which quickly became more militant than the old guard of the ANC.

In 1949, the Youth League's Programme of Action, to which Mandela had contributed, was adopted by the ANC. Mandela was elected to the ANC national executive in 1950, and by 1952 was national volunteer-in-chief for the ANC's Campaign for the Defiance of Unjust Laws. He received a suspended sentence for his contributions to this (non violent) campaign. He spent the next 12 years working against *apartheid*, the system of racial segregation imposed by the National Party in 1948. In 1952 he opened a law firm in the centre of Johannesburg with Oliver Tambo, and by the end of that year was president of the ANC Youth League and of the ANC in the Transvaal region. He developed a series of organisational plans intended to mobilise resistance to *apartheid*, especially to the nascent Bantustan policy whereby blacks were assigned to rural "homelands" as a pretext for denying them rights elsewhere in the country. In 1956 he was charged with high treason under the Suppression of Communism Act, together with ANC leader Albert Luthuli, Tambo, Sisulu and others, but the trial on this charge fell through in 1961 due to lack of evidence.

The ANC was banned in 1960. The following year Mandela was released from detention. No longer maintaining his commitment to the use of only peaceful means to resist *apartheid*, he oversaw the founding and first operations of *Umkhonto we Sizwe* (MK), the military branch of the ANC. He left South Africa illegally in 1962, travelling to many African countries, including Algeria for training in guerrilla tactics. He returned before the end of 1962, was swiftly arrested for leaving the country illegally and for incitement to strike, and was jailed for five years from November. While he was in prison, police found the MK headquarters, and he was charged once again with treason. The so-called Rivonia Trial of 1963/64, named after the farm where the police had uncovered the evidence of MK, ended in June 1964 with life sentences for him and seven others. The eloquence of Mandela's final statement from the dock resounded around the world, reiterating his dedication to the struggle of the African people. "I have cherished the ideal of a democratic and free society", he said, "in which all persons live together in harmony and with equal opportunities. It is an ideal which I hope to live for and to achieve. But, if needs be, it is an ideal for which I am prepared to die."

Most of his subsequent imprisonment was spent at the maximum-security prison of Robben Island, just off the coast of Cape Town, where he was held until 1984. While he was in prison, Mandela's situation attracted global attention. He received numerous awards and honours, and thousands of people petitioned for his release during a worldwide campaign launched in the early 1980s. He was offered his freedom several times by President Botha in exchange for a renunciation of violence and acceptance of the Bantustan policy, which he declined, maintaining his refusal to condemn violence despite further government overtures during secret discussions with the minister of justice in 1987 and 1988.

In 1989 Botha was replaced as president by **F.W. De Klerk**, who began a process of repealing many of the laws on which the *apartheid* system rested. De Klerk lifted the ban on the ANC and Nelson Mandela was released on 11 February 1990. He was greeted by scenes of mass jubilation and, although he made it clear that he had accepted no conditions on his release, he did subsequently call for the cessation of violence. In 1991, the ANC held its first national conference for decades inside South Africa, and elected Mandela as its president. Sensitive negotiations were held between him and De Klerk over the dismantling of the *apartheid* state and the creation of conditions in which democratic elections could take place. In 1993 Mandela received, jointly with De Klerk, the Nobel Peace Prize – although the relationship between them, outwardly polite if never warm, was described by De Klerk in his subsequent autobiography as sometimes extremely acrimonious. Mandela's own autobiography, *Long Walk to Freedom*, was published in 1994.

On 26/29 April 1994, when the elections finally took place, the ANC won a landslide victory, with 62.6 per cent of the nationwide vote, and also dominated the poll in seven of the nine provinces. The National Assembly, meeting on 9 May, elected Mandela unanimously as president, and he was sworn in the following day.

A complex power-sharing formula was implemented in the creation of Mandela's first coalition government. Despite the subsequent withdrawal of the (white-backed) National Party, Mandela achieved a large measure of success over the ensuing period in presenting himself and his government as representing the whole "rainbow nation", and in engendering a positive spirit in the face of the awesome task of nation-building. A new constitution was worked out, and finally signed by Mandela on 10 December 1996. Delivering on the popular expectation of rapid economic improvements, however, proved more difficult to achieve, and in March 1996 Mandela announced the closure of the offices of the ambitious reconstruction and development programme, with much of its work of construction, land distribution, educational provision and job creation left to be done by the respective government ministries. A further major problem was the high and rising level of violent crime.

Reaffirming his intention of standing down from the presidency at the end of his term of office to make way for a new generation of leaders, Mandela ceded the ANC leadership to his erstwhile deputy, Thabo Mbeki, in 1997, and became progressively less involved in the day-to-day affairs of government. At the same time, his worldwide stature helped build up South Africa's profile in international affairs and gave the country a new role as mediator in a range of disputes, both regionally and more widely. One notable characteristic of his diplomatic involvement was loyalty to such unfashionable friends as **Fidel Castro** and Col. **Kadhafi** (whose long-running confrontation with the West over the Lockerbie affair he helped to unblock). Mandela also demonstrated the strength of his desire for non-violent resolution of conflicts with vehement condemnations of the resort to force, as in the case of the NATO bombing of Yugoslavia in March/June 1999 in response to repression in Kosovo.

Mandela's last year in office was marked by the celebrations of his 80th birthday in July 1998; his acceptance of the Truth and Reconciliation Committee's report later that year despite its controversial inclusion of strong criticisms of ANC abuses during the period of the liberation struggle; his opening of the parliament for the last time in February 1999; his farewell speech to parliament in March; and his formal retirement and handover to Mbeki on 16 June 1999 after the ANC's election victory. Throughout his extended leave-taking, tributes emphasised his achievements in providing post-*apartheid* South Africa with unifying leadership, a president for all the people. Often, when such praise came from those not part of the ANC, it was accompanied by concern that Mandela was irreplaceable, and that South Africa's serious problems would be tackled by his successors in a more divisive political climate.

Nelson Mandela has been married three times. With his second wife Nomzamo Madikizela (**Winnie**) **Mandela**, whom he married in 1958, he had two daughters, the second born while he was in prison awaiting trial. He and Winnie spent much of their lives apart because of his imprisonment (while she also suffered periods of imprisonment, banning and house arrest). In prison, he held on to his love for her, but they were unable to rebuild their marriage after his release in 1990; they separated in 1992 and were divorced in 1996, becoming increasingly estranged both personally and politically. Helped to overcome his loneliness by the blossoming of a relationship with Graça Machel, the widow of the former Mozambican president Samora Machel, Mandela created a double celebration by marrying her on his 80th birthday in July 1998. They revealed, however, that they would continue to live in their own countries, travelling to see one another as they had during their courtship.

Winnie **Mandela**

An iconic figure of South Africa's anti-apartheid struggle – beautiful, brave, persecuted and cruelly separated from her husband for three decades – Winnie Mandela was both a female role model and "mother of the nation" for a militant younger generation. Tragically, this brought out an arrogant high-handedness, exposed when she and her entourage were implicated in the beating, disappearance and death of a youth they suspected of being an informer. Eventually convicted for kidnapping, she also faced other persistent allegations, both personal and political, which clouded the euphoria surrounding her husband's eventual release and the transition to democracy. Despite the breakdown of her marriage, her dismissal from the post-apartheid government, and the Truth and Reconciliation Commission's reinforcement of criticisms against her, she retains a power base among radical activists disillusioned over the slow pace of social and economic change.

Winnie Mandela was born Nomzamo Nobandla Winnifred Madikizela on 26 September 1936 in Bizana, Pondoland, Transkei in the Eastern Cape. Her mother, Nomathamsanqa Mzaidume, was a domestic science teacher who died when Winnie was only eight years old; her father, Columbus Madikizela, was a teacher and then a minister in the forestry and agriculture department of the Transkei provincial government.

One of eight children, she gained a social work diploma from Jan Hofmeyer School in Johannesburg and became the first black medical social worker at the Baragwanath Hospital in Soweto, working on such issues as infant mortality in the townships. Later she gained a degree in political science at the University of the Witwatersrand, Johannesburg.

In 1957 she met **Nelson Mandela**, a partner in the law firm of her relative Oliver Tambo and a member of the executive of the African National Congress (ANC). The couple married in June 1958 and had two daughters, Zindziwa and Zenani, but could only live together briefly, as Nelson Mandela was arrested in 1960, before Zenani was born. Two years later he was sentenced to life imprisonment.

In marrying Nelson Mandela, Winnie had also married the struggle against *apartheid*. She was first arrested herself within three months of her wedding, for her part in the anti-pass-law protests. She was chair of the Orlando West branch of the ANC and the ANC Women's League prior to the banning of both bodies in 1960, and continued her work thereafter through the Federation of South African Women.

Arrested, detained, banned and harassed on numerous occasions, Winnie Mandela spent 18 months without charge in solitary confinement at Pretoria central prison in 1969/70, before eventually being charged under the Suppression of Communism Act. At first found guilty, she was discharged on appeal. After further shorter terms in prison she was eventually exiled to distant Brandfort, in Orange Free State, in 1977 and obliged to remain there, although she repeatedly broke the banning orders which stipulated where she could live.

After her home in Brandfort was firebombed, she returned to Soweto in 1985, defying banning orders which were subsequently amended and then provisionally withdrawn. Becoming embroiled in the township struggles, in April 1986 she was quoted controversially as having declared that liberation would only be achieved by means of matches and necklaces (a reference to the "necklacing" of informers by placing a burning tyre around their necks), but she later distanced herself from this apparent endorsement of mob violence.

Although her outspoken, fiery brand of politics continued to command widespread support in the townships, her standing elsewhere was seriously undermined in 1989 when her bodyguards, known as the "Mandela united football club", kidnapped and beat up four black youths, one of whom ("Stompie" Moeketse Seipei) was later found dead. While both the United Democratic Front (UDF) and the South African Congress of Trade Unions (Cosatu) were strongly critical of her actions, her husband (finally released after over 27 years in prison in February 1990) was more conciliatory. Winnie Mandela was charged in September 1990 and was sentenced in May 1991 to six years' imprisonment (but released pending an appeal hearing), having been convicted on four counts of kidnapping and of being an accessory to assault.

When new evidence came to light in 1992, she was stripped of a regional position in the ANC Women's League and was obliged to give up her seat on the ANC national executive. Her conviction was upheld on appeal in June 1993, but her prison term was reduced to a two-year suspended term and a fine. Although she was suspended from the ANC Women's League at this time, her continuing support from the radical wing of the ANC provided her with the basis for a political comeback. She was elected as president of the ANC Women's League in December 1993 and returned to the ANC executive committee in 1994.

Winnie Mandela won a seat in parliament as an ANC candidate in the party's historic victory in April 1994, when South Africa's first democratic elections took place. Nelson Mandela, on becoming state president, appointed his by now estranged wife as deputy minister for arts, culture, science and technology. Increasingly, however, she was regarded as a "loose cannon" in the government and she continued to criticise the leadership for not being radical enough. Eventually, as accusations of bribery and corruption mounted, President Mandela was persuaded to dismiss her in April 1995, ostensibly on the grounds that she had gone on a trip to north Africa without first informing the president. Recognising that there was nothing left of their relationship, he filed for divorce in August 1995 and this was finally granted in March 1996. Although the court dismissed Winnie Mandela's claim for half of her ex-husband's wealth, he later offered an unspecified out-of-court settlement in her favour.

Winnie Madikizela-Mandela, as she chooses to be called since her divorce, has remained active on the radical wing of the ANC and was re-elected president of the ANC Women's League for a further term in April 1997. Her continuing prominence within the party attracted strong criticism, however, particularly when she was called to account by the Truth and Reconciliation Commission for her conduct before the demise of the *apartheid* regime. In its October 1998 report the Commission, which had taken evidence after receiving allegations against her, found that she had known about, and possibly participated in, killings and torture carried out by the "Mandela united football club"; that she had been "central" to its creation and that she was accountable, politically and morally, for "gross violations of human rights" committed by it. Nevertheless, in February 1999 she was given tenth position on the ANC's list of candidates for the forthcoming election, in what the party's secretary-general Kgalema Motlanthe described as an expression of confidence reflecting how ANC members felt about her.

Carlos **Menem**

Carlos Menem was first elected president of Argentina in 1989 as leader of the right-of-centre Peronists. In office throughout the 1990s, Menem is identified with turning around an economy in crisis, implementing free-market neo-liberal policies and with linking the currency, the peso, at par with the US dollar. He presented this as a foundation stone for Argentina's striking achievement of rapid growth and effectively zero inflation up to 1998. In 1999 he even proposed strengthening the link and adopting the US dollar as Argentina's currency, to insulate his country from a global crisis in investor confidence. Menem makes a feature of his flamboyant "macho" style, but the Argentine people have never really trusted him or taken him to their hearts. Having needed a constitutional amendment to allow him to serve a second term, he seemed on the verge of trying to push through a further amendment to stand again in 1999. His low personal popularity ratings helped deter him, but did not crush his ambition to return in 2003.

Carlos Saúl Menem was born on 2 July 1930 in Anillaco in La Rioja province. The son of Sunni Muslim immigrants from Syria, he converted to Catholicism, and was active in student politics at university in Córdoba, where he completed a doctorate in law and founded a Peronist youth group. In 1955, the year in which Juan Perón's dictatorship was overthrown, Menem began a 15-year link with the Peronist trade union confederation as a legal adviser. He was also involved from 1955 in defending political prisoners, and became implicated in the abortive attempt to restore Perón to power in 1956, which cost him a brief period in detention.

Menem first stood for election as a provincial deputy in La Rioja in 1958, and was a candidate for deputy governor in 1972, but the intervention of a military coup prevented that election from taking place. Provincial leader of the Peronists (formally known as FREJUPO or the Justicialist Party) in La Rioja from 1963, he was three times provincial governor between 1973 (when Perón made his triumphant return from Spain) and 1989. However, he spent five of these years in prison or under house arrest, from 1976 to 1981, after Perón's widow had been forced out of power by another military coup. The 1983 elections marked the restoration of democratic rule, but with the Radical Civic Union winning power at national level the Peronists became increasingly faction-ridden in opposition.

Menem's nomination as the Peronist presidential candidate for the 1989 election was based on his support among the Peronist trade unions and the "federalism and liberation" faction, against the hostility of a left-wing "renewalist" faction. He won over 47 per cent of the popular vote on 14 May.

Although not due to take over power until the end of the year, he was sworn in early, on 8 July, at the instigation of outgoing President Raúl Alfonsín, who thereby avoided making a decision on an amnesty for human rights violations under military rule. Menem subsequently pardoned many of the former military leaders, attempting to placate the armed forces on this issue in the wake of a military revolt in late 1990.

Once in office, and facing a sharp deterioration in the economy, Menem also made a pronounced shift to the right on economic policy. The third strand in his party, the traditionalist Peronists or so-called "*oficialistas*", criticised this and disagreed with his prescription of neo-liberal free-market policies. In response, however, Menem tended to point to his government's record of economic achievement from 1991 onwards. This success boosted the party's performance in the October 1993 partial legislative elections, encouraging Menem to go ahead with his project for a constituent assembly to reform the constitution. The assembly, elected in April 1994, duly adopted in October of that year a new constitution allowing a president to serve two consecutive terms, now of four years, enabling Menem to seek re-election at the end of 1995.

In the poll on 14 May 1995, Menem won convincingly, receiving 49.8 per cent of the vote, although without a corresponding success in the concurrent legislative election. His lack of a majority in Congress proved less of a handicap in his second term than the social unrest and union opposition aroused by his economic austerity policies, a succession of corruption scandals which saw several of his ministers forced out of office, and the loss of Peronist control over important provincial governments as the opposition parties began working together more effectively. In these circumstances, and with a large part of his own party vociferously opposing him, Menem in mid-1998 abandoned his campaign to get the constitution amended once again so that he could seek a third term.

By this stage his claim to have worked an economic miracle with his free-enterprise revolution was looking less durable. Argentina was threatened by the possible large-scale flight of foreign capital as international speculative investors reacted to a series of recent crises around the world's emerging markets. In 1999 Menem played the currency stability card once again, proposing the adoption of the US dollar in place of the peso for all transactions. Already identified with a strongly pro-US and generally pro-Western stance in foreign relations, Menem was widely believed to be making his "dollarisation" proposal not in terms of imminent policy, but as a way of setting out his stall to return to the political fray at the 2003 presidential elections. During his enforced absence of four years, he calculated, either the opposition parties or his main Peronist rivals would have damaged their popularity through having to grapple with the country's pressing problems.

Carlos Menem was married in 1966 to the equally flamboyant Zulema Fátima Yoma; it was a turbulent relationship which culminated in a lengthy and embarrassing public row in 1991 and eventually ended in divorce and recrimination. He has one son and one daughter, Zulema Menem, who has taken on an unofficial "first lady" role herself, adding glamour to her father's entourage at official receptions and on foreign visits.

Slobodan **Milosevic**

Slobodan Milosevic, the main Serbian leader since 1987, is frequently condemned for suppressing domestic opposition, but chiefly hated as the architect of Serbian aggression and "ethnic cleansing". He rose to prominence on a tide of nationalist feeling that Serbs were being overrun by the ethnic Albanian majority in Kosovo. Milosevic was eventually responsible, as president of the rump Federal Republic of Yugoslavia from 1997, for the brutal campaign launched in 1999 to reclaim Kosovo for the Serb minority. For this he was indicted for war crimes, while his country suffered air bombardment by NATO forces until he agreed to withdraw his repressive forces. By contrast, the Bosnian conflict had seen him tacitly recognised by the West as the person best able to guarantee a lasting settlement – even though his aggressive pursuit of Serbian interests helped precipitate the break-up of former Yugoslavia in 1991/92, and his ambitions for "greater Serbia" at the beginning of the Bosnian conflict did much to encourage the "ethnic cleansing" atrocities of that time.

Slobodan Milosevic was born in the town of Pozarevac in Serbia on 20 August 1941. His father, an orthodox priest and teacher of Montenegrin descent, left home when he was only a child, and he was brought up by his Serbian mother, a primary-school teacher. Both his parents later committed suicide (as did one of his uncles), his father when he was 21 and his mother when he was 32.

While at secondary school in Pozarevac Milosevic met his future wife Mirjana Markovic, one year his junior, who came from a leading Serbian communist family. Forming an intense bond, they both went on to the University of Belgrade; Mirjana subsequently became a professor at the university and a member of the Russian Academy of Social Sciences. She also became a significant political figure in her own right as well as a major force behind her husband's rise to power. They have one son, Marko, and one daughter, Marija.

Active in student politics, Milosevic joined the ruling League of Communists of Yugoslavia (LCY) in Belgrade in 1959. He showed an enthusiasm for party work and made a favourable impression on Ivan Stambolic, the man who was to be his political mentor. Argumentative, intelligent and capable, Milosevic was befriended by Stambolic, and communicated to him his youthful enthusiasm and belief in how much could be achieved by hard work and good organisation.

After graduating in law in 1964, Milosevic began a career in business, working for the national gas extraction company, Tehnogas, in Belgrade. He was also head of the Belgrade Information Service (1966–69), and an adviser on economic affairs to the

mayor of Belgrade. By 1973 he had been promoted to director-general of Tehnogas, a position he held until 1978 when he moved to the presidency of Beogradska Bank. He left the bank in 1983, sat as a member of the presidium of the central committee of the LCY in 1983 and, the following year, became chair of the party's Belgrade committee. Recognised as number two to Stambolic in the party leadership in Serbia, with a reputation as a hardliner, he took over the leadership of the party in that republic in January 1986 when Stambolic moved up to the republican presidency.

Milosevic's adoption as the leader of Serbian nationalism stemmed from a notorious occasion on 24 April 1987 when he addressed a crowd of demonstrators outside the town hall in Kosovo Polje. The gathering was a Serb protest against the concessions being demanded by the majority Albanian population of Kosovo (which at that time had the status of an autonomous republic within Serbia). Nervous at first, he turned the situation to his advantage by reproving the riot police who had acted to restrain the crowd. Milosevic told the protestors: "No one has the right to beat you. No one will ever beat you again." His words struck a chord with the resentful Serbs, playing upon the sense that they were losing their rightful place in Kosovo, the historic cradle of the Serbian nation. Milosevic returned to Belgrade as their hero.

Later that same year, emboldened by his new-found popular support, Milosevic and his fellow hardliners engineered a coup within the Serbian republic's leadership, ousting Stambolic (who bitterly resented this personal betrayal) from the post of president of the collective presidency on the grounds that he was too conciliatory towards the ethnic Albanian agitation in Kosovo. By mid-1989 a new Serbian constitution had abolished the autonomy of Kosovo (and Vojvodina), and Milosevic had himself taken over as president of the collective presidency of Serbia, going on to deliver a stirring nationalist address in Kosovo on the 600th anniversary of the battle of the Field of Black Crows.

In Serbia's first multiparty presidential elections in December 1990, standing as the candidate for the Socialist Party of Serbia (SPS), the renamed communist party, Milosevic won a massive 65 per cent of the vote against 30 other candidates. The SPS simultaneously gained a large majority in the assembly, with 194 out of 250 seats. At his re-election in December 1992, Milosevic received some 57 per cent of the vote. By this time, Serbia was no longer one of six republics under the old Yugoslav structure, but the larger of two (with Montenegro) in a "rump" state, formed in April 1992 as the Federal Republic of Yugoslavia (FRY).

The break-up of former Yugoslavia in 1991/92 began with the secession of Slovenia and Croatia. This represented a setback for Serbian nationalists, who had hoped to preserve a dominant position in a federation which was substantially larger than Serbia itself. A second prize would be a "Greater Serbia", centred on Belgrade but extending west across the Serb-inhabited half of Bosnia and incorporating parts of Croatia on similar ethnic grounds. The bloody conflict in Bosnia, and the retention of Serb control over enclaves within Croatia until 1995/96, was played out against this background. Milosevic's initial backing gave the Bosnian Serbs a military ascendancy, with heavy consequences in killings and "ethnic cleansing". The course of the fighting appeared for a time to encourage Serbian expansionism, but such ambitions were then frustrated both by the inconclusive nature of the fighting and by international efforts to contain the conflict. A marked reduction in military support for the Bosnian Serbs was forced upon Milosevic (who always denied providing any such backing at all). The combined pressure of international sanctions, and the effective intervention of NATO forces, left him anxious to bring the Bosnian conflict to a close by 1995. With the Bosnian Serb leaders under indictment for war crimes, Milosevic represented their interests at the late 1995 peace talks in Dayton, USA, which brought the conflict to an end. Signing the Dayton agreement, he accepted on behalf of the Bosnian Serbs the retention of a Bosnian state, but one within which there would be a Bosnian Serb republic as one of two distinct entities. Until then, he had been unable to convince the Bosnian Serb leadership that this was the best outcome achievable for them.

One thing which Milosevic was able to underline, by accepting the Dayton settlement in Bosnia, was his status as the leader with whom the international community had its principal dealings on the affairs of the region. Hand in hand with this, and crucial for his country's struggling economy, was the promise of progress on ending international sanctions. This was well under way by the end of 1996, when municipal elections were held in Serbia. Milosevic's reputation for holding firm control of Serbian politics was shaken by the aftermath of this poll, when the announcement of a sweeping victory for his SPS brought protestors on to the streets of Belgrade. They held out with impressive courage for nearly two months, proclaiming their demand that Milosevic should go, until a carefully calculated combination of concessions and police action brought the protest to an end.

Nearing the end of his maximum of two terms as president of Serbia, Milosevic decided in 1997 to move across to the federal presidency instead, and was elected unopposed to this post and sworn in on 23 July. The subsequent election of Milan Milutinovic as president of Serbia in December 1997 ensured the continuing control of Milosevic's SPS there, and his skill in playing off and co-opting opponents effectively neutralised the opposition parties. He proved unable to work the same trick in Montenegro, however, and that small republic's president, Milo Djukanovic, progressively strengthened his reputation for taking a stance independent of Belgrade.

Throughout the 1990s, the unresolved problem of Kosovo had remained acute. Milosevic had declared illegal the polls held there by separatists who proclaimed a "Republic of Kosovo", and persisted in representing the problem as an internal matter of dealing with ethnic Albanian terrorism. In March 1998, Serbian forces began a military crackdown against the militant separatist Kosovo Liberation Army, and fighting escalated through the summer.

Repeated Western attempts to broker some agreement produced only a temporary ceasefire in October, following talks involving Milosevic and a US envoy, and the introduction of peace monitors from the Organization for Security and Co-operation in Europe (OSCE). By March 1999, only the Kosovan side had accepted the so-called "Rambouillet plan" drafted by the six-nation "contact group", envisaging a substantial NATO peacekeeping force, the disbanding of all paramilitary groups, a Serbian police withdrawal and substantial regional autonomy. Apparently expecting that a display of resolution would bring the Serbian side into line, NATO began aerial bombing on 24 March against targets throughout the FRY.

Milosevic responded defiantly, and opinion in Serbia (although not Montenegro) rallied initially to him. Moreover, in Kosovo, Serbian police and army units stepped up their action, precipitating a huge outflow of ethnic Albanian refugees fleeing from repression, "ethnic cleansing" and mass killings. By early June, however, Milosevic was ready to accept terms to end the NATO bombing, which had caused far-reaching damage and appeared likely to be backed up by ground troops if the conflict dragged on. Despite his attempts to claim a triumph for Serbian honour, the material damage suffered by the FRY, and the humiliation of having to withdraw from Kosovo, placed him in a politically vulnerable position. This was compounded by his indictment for war crimes by the International Criminal Tribunal for former Yugoslavia on 27 May, based on evidence of his direct responsibility for ethnic-cleansing atrocities in Kosovo. Whether or not he could be brought to trial, he had become irrevocably an international pariah, and the Serbian people were left in no doubt that his removal from power was a precondition of Western aid for much-needed reconstruction.

François **Mitterrand**

*François Mitterrand made his name as the first socialist president of France under the Fifth Republic. He held office for two terms from 1981 to 1995, and during this period was also instrumental in confirming the Franco-German alliance at the heart of European integration, in particular through his close co-operation with **Helmut Kohl**. As the leader who had unified the French socialists, and helped create the alliance of the left which opened the way to government, he was at the peak of his popularity in his first years in office. His Machiavellian machinations, however, had earned him the nicknames "the Florentine" and "the fox", and towards the end of his career he was frequently accused of having no sense of purpose beyond the retention of power.*

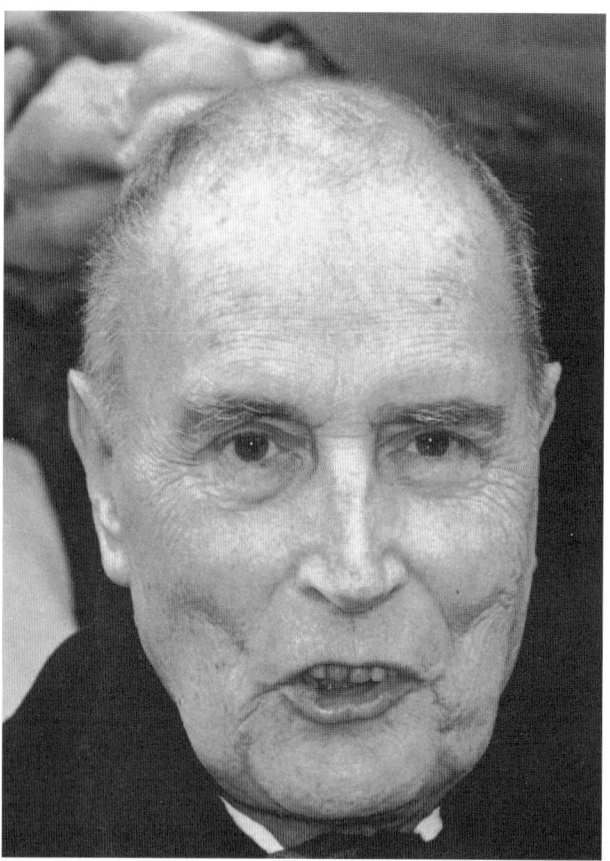

François Maurice Marie Mitterrand was born in a traditional Catholic family on 26 October 1916 in Jarnac in the Charente, southwest France. His father Joseph was a stationmaster, and later went into the vinegar production business started by his wife Yvonne's family.

During the 1930s Mitterrand studied law and politics at the University of Paris, working briefly in journalism before the outbreak of the Second World War. Wounded in 1940 he was taken prisoner but escaped in December 1941 and returned to Vichy France. The extent of his involvement with the collaborationist Vichy regime, where he worked in the prisoners' department, was only revealed in two books published in 1994, although Mitterrand himself stressed that he was subsequently able to use his post as a cover for work with the resistance. A secret meeting with Charles de Gaulle in 1943 in Algiers marked the beginning of a long-standing personal and political rivalry between them.

Mitterrand was first elected to the National Assembly as a centrist in December 1946, and joined the cabinet the following month, initially with responsibility for veterans' affairs and then for overseas *départements*. As interior and then justice minister in the 1950s he took a tough stance against Algerian independence but supported the left on social policy. Already his skill for political manoeuvring was evident, although his career was set back by the return to power of de Gaulle and the "Gaullist" right in 1958.

In 1959 Mitterrand joined the Senate and became mayor of Château-Chinon, gradually moving away from the Catholic Church and political centre, espousing more radical views and seeking to unify the fragmented non-communist left. His strong performance against de Gaulle in the 1965 presidential election presaged his election as leader of a reconstituted Socialist Party (PS) in June 1971. In a second bid for the presidency in 1974 he was narrowly beaten by Valéry Giscard d'Estaing. However, at the third attempt in May 1981 he beat Giscard d'Estaing in the second round to become the country's first socialist president.

Mitterrand's first two years as president, in tandem with a government of the united left, were marked by a series of radical reforms, the nationalisation of key industries and financial services, improved social welfare provision, decentralisation of government and abolition of the death penalty. However, a major U-turn in economic policy in the face of global recession prompted the communists to leave the government amid bitter recriminations in July 1984.

The defeat of what was now a minority socialist government in the 1986 general election made necessary an unprecedented experiment in "cohabitation", in which Mitterrand, a socialist president, shared power with **Jacques Chirac**, a centre-right prime minister. Mitterrand enjoyed extensive powers under the Fifth Republic's constitution and handled this situation adroitly, although his relations with Chirac were often stormy. As Mitterrand concentrated increasingly on European and global affairs, and on a series of monumental architectural schemes in Paris, Chirac's government pursued radical liberal policies of economic deregulation and privatisation.

Mitterrand won a second seven-year presidential term by defeating Chirac in May 1988, concealing from the electorate the knowledge that he already had prostate cancer. He immediately called an early parliamentary election, which brought a PS-led government back to office. During this time Mitterrand's influence in foreign affairs was greatest. He committed French troops to the US-led forces in the 1991 Gulf war, strongly supported the development of the European Union under the Maastricht Treaty and backed its ratification in France's 1992 referendum.

In the final years of his second term Mitterrand's presidency lost its way. He himself was increasingly perceived as out of touch and anxious only to hold on to power. From March 1993 until he left office in May 1995, he was in "cohabitation" with a centre-right government for a second time, the corruption-damaged socialists having suffered a heavy general election defeat.

François Mitterrand died on 8 January 1996, leaving a widow, Danièle Grouze. They had married in 1944 and had two sons, Gilbert and Jean-Christophe, and during his presidency she had established her own role as France's "first lady" and as an advocate of human rights and humanitarian charities. Mitterrand was reputed to have had numerous affairs, and his long-time mistress, Anne Pingeot, was among those present at his funeral, along with their daughter, Mazarine.

Mobutu Sese Seko

Gen. Mobutu was the stereotype of the African post-colonial dictator, writ large. Emerging as an army strongman, he was ruthless, canny and feared. Surrounded by sycophants, he took the vanities of power to extremes, inflating his own military rank (he promoted himself to marshal in 1982) and promoting a cult of personality. His portrait hung everywhere; an opening sequence on state television pictured him descending god-like from the clouds each day, and his mother was compared to the Virgin Mary. Mobutu was the "kleptocrat king", pillaging his country to amass a huge private fortune, to enrich his acolytes and to bribe opponents to his side. In power from 1965 and bolstered by the West as a bulwark against communism, he became an unnecessary embarrassment to such powerful backers once the cold war ended, but could make little pretence of reinventing himself as a leader with a popular mandate. His regime crumbled when rebels mounted a sustained offensive in 1996/97, and he was driven out, dying soon afterwards in exile.

Joseph-Désiré Mobutu was born on 14 October 1930 in what was then the Belgian Congo. His parents were Roman Catholics from the northern Ngbandi tribe; his father worked as a cook and his mother as a chambermaid, in Lisala. Young Joseph, an unruly youth, was sent at the age of eight to a mission school in Coqmilhatville (now Mbandaka), from where in 1949 he was conscripted into the Force Publique, the

Belgian colonial army. A year at an army accountancy and secretarial training school in Luluabourg (now Kananga) was followed by a rapid rise in the accountancy division to the highest rank available to a non-Belgian, sergeant-major.

After leaving the army in 1956 at the end of his seven-year period of conscription, Mobutu went into journalism under the pseudonym José de Banzy. Apprenticed to a Belgian, Pierre Davister, he moved to Léopoldville, the capital, and then in 1959 to Brussels, where he studied at the Institute of Journalism and the Institute of Social Studies. Having joined Patrice Lumumba's National Congolese Movement before his departure for Belgium, Mobutu became Lumumba's representative at the January 1960 negotiations in Brussels, when the Belgians agreed to move as rapidly as possible to an independent Congo, however ill-prepared it might be to function successfully. At the conference Mobutu advanced Lumumba's argument that the new state should have a united central government, rather than be a more diffuse federation of autonomous regions.

On independence in June 1960, the federalist Joseph Kasavubu became president, and his rival Lumumba became prime minister, in a broad coalition with Mobutu as secretary of state and minister of defence. Building a reputation as strongman within this hastily patched together and inexperienced government, Mobutu backed the armed forces commander-in-chief in moves to suppress the mutinies which broke out in the Force Publique within days of independence. Panic was engendered among Europeans by these mutinies, however, prompting intervention by Belgian paratroops, rapidly followed by the dispatch of UN forces, as Moise Tshombe seized the opportunity to launch a separatist rebellion in the mineral-rich Katanga region. Mobutu, having been appointed army chief of staff, took power himself in Léopoldville in September 1960.

Mobutu's 1960 coup was backed by the US Central Intelligence Agency (CIA) and generally approved of in the West as the best prospect of effective government. Gaining Kasavubu's acquiescence, his move was directed mainly against Lumumba, whose readiness to accept Soviet help against the Katanga separatists had horrified the West. The capture and murder of Lumumba in the Katangan capital early in 1961 was later also blamed on Mobutu and the CIA. Mobutu's regime in Léopoldville, however, lacked both public support and effectiveness, and was superseded by a civilian government reinstated in February 1961.

Over the next four years, factional conflict eventually gave way to an unsuccessful attempt at reconciliation between Kasavubu and the secessionist leader Tshombe. Meanwhile Mobutu, now a major-general and commander-in-chief of the armed forces, had built up his position within the military sufficiently to seize power for a second time. His bloodless coup took place on 24 November 1965.

Appointing himself as president, Mobutu drew up a new constitution, initially banning all political parties. In 1967 he formed the Popular Movement of the Revolution (MPR), which he used as the vehicle for creating an authoritarian single-party regime. The West welcomed what it saw as Mobutu's imposition of stability on the vast and turbulent country, as well as the breaking of relations with the Soviet Union, and supported his regime for decades, regarding it as the front line against the perceived threat of communism in Africa.

Internally, "Mobutuism" was a one-party totalitarian system. While suppressing or co-opting opposition, it also incorporated a drive for "Africanisation", self-reliance and sufficiency, and an extravagant cult of his own personality.

One aspect of "Africanisation" or "authenticity", supposed to help build unity among the country's many ethnic groups, involved the removal of the symbols of the ex-colonial powers and the replacement of place-names. Léopoldville became Kinshasa and (in 1971) the Democratic Republic of Congo itself was renamed Zaïre, as was the Congo river. This process merged with the cult of personality when in January 1972 Mobutu ordered all personal names to be Africanised. He adopted for himself the designation Mobutu Sese Seko Kuku Ngbendu wa za Banga, officially translated as "the all-powerful warrior who, because of his inflexible will to win, will go from conquest to conquest leaving fire in his wake". Western-style suits were banned and Mao-style collarless jackets became the fashion, as worn by Mobutu; other self-consciously "African" props included his leopard-skin hat and an ebony, ivory-handled stick said to be so heavy that only he could lift it.

The term "kleptocracy" was coined by critics of Mobutu to describe his rule, devoted as he was to building his own personal fortune, while granting licence for members of his ruling elite to follow his example. His regime became a byword for graft: vast sums of money were stolen from state funds or foreign aid; his fortune was estimated at three times Zaïre's foreign debt; his personal income rose to half the national GDP, and his official salary was a greater proportion of the state budget than was spent on education, health and social services combined. In sharp contrast with the impoverished population of his mineral-rich country, Mobutu lived lavishly, creating a "Versailles of the Jungle" in Gbadolite, his father's tribal village, where he built a marble palace complete with airstrip. He owned ten other palaces in Zaïre alone, besides acquiring luxurious properties in Spain, Portugal, Belgium, Switzerland and France, hotels in South Africa and a luxury river cruiser on the Zaïre.

To prevent the emergence of a power base for potential rivals, Mobutu kept the armed forces weak, except for an elite presidential guard consisting of members of his own tribe. Instead he relied heavily on his foreign backers whenever rebellion broke out. Regarding him as the best bulwark against communism, the USA, France and Belgium overlooked for nearly 30 years the despotic nature of his regime, and in return gained a base for interventions in neighbouring countries such as Angola. With the thawing of the cold war at the end of the 1980s, however, the West became more vocal in condemning his regime's corruption and human rights abuses. Mobutu begrudgingly promised political reforms in May 1990, but that same month saw a hideous massacre of demonstrating students at Lubumbashi University. Years of procrastination followed over the creation of a multiparty framework, as Mobutu tried to manoeuvre himself into an electable position.

In 1994, the refugee crisis precipitated by genocide in neighbouring Rwanda gave Mobutu an opportunity to rehabilitate himself in the eyes of the by now highly critical and hostile West. Briefly his despotism and corruption were forgotten as Zaïre offered one of the few channels for humanitarian assistance. Huge refugee camps grew along the Zaïre–Rwanda border, filling with Rwandan Hutus (the group whose militias had launched the genocide) as they fled the advance of the (mainly ethnic Tutsi) Rwandan Patriotic Front. Two years later, however, it was Rwandan-backed Tutsis, taking action against remaining militiamen in these camps, who provided an essential element of the rebel coalition which was to sweep Mobutu from power. Rebel leader **Laurent Kabila** led the Alliance of Democratic Forces for the Liberation of Congo–Zaïre (AFDL) on a seven-month 1,000-mile fight across Zaïre, meeting with little resistance from Mobutu's feeble, underpaid army.

Mobutu, recently operated on for prostate cancer, returned from Switzerland in December 1996 in a bid to restore his authority. However, it was quickly apparent that the people neither supported him nor feared his power as they had before. As Mobutu's armed forces caved in and his support dwindled, Kabila was emboldened to reject the concessions Mobutu offered at South-African-mediated talks in early May 1997. On 16 May, with Kabila's forces within reach of Kinshasa, Mobutu fled into exile, first to Togo and then to Morocco, the only country prepared to accept him. His Swiss bank accounts, containing an estimated US$5 billion, were frozen. Further surgery could not arrest the spread of his cancer and on 7 September 1997 Mobutu died. He was survived by his second wife, Boby Ladawa, and numerous children; his first wife, Antoinette, had died in 1977.

Hosni **Mubarak**

Hosni Mubarak has been president of Egypt and its dominant political figure for two decades, but lacks the flamboyance and charisma characteristic of his predecessors, Nasser and Sadat. A former air force commander and hero of the 1973 war with Israel, Mubarak was Sadat's vice-president for six years and was standing next to him at the military parade at which Sadat was assassinated by Islamic militants in 1981. Sadat was killed because he had broken ranks with the Arab world, making Egypt the first to conclude a peace agreement with Israel, in 1979. Mubarak, while maintaining that treaty, has based his policies on building a rapprochement *with the other Arab states and, latterly, with the Palestinians. Whereas the USA generally found King Hussein of Jordan a more effective channel than Mubarak for its Middle East diplomacy, and Hussein (often secretly) kept his lines of communication with the Israeli leadership in good repair, Hussein's death in early 1999 opened the way for Mubarak to play a more prominent role in regional affairs.*

Mohammed Hosni Mubarak was born on 4 May 1928 in Kafr al-Musailha, within the Minuffya governorate. From 1947 until 1949 he studied for a degree in military sciences at the Egyptian military academy. Specialising in aviation sciences, he then attended the air force academy and went on to join the Egyptian air force in 1950. Between 1952 and 1959 he lectured at the air force academy, while he also briefly attended the Frunze Military Academy in the Soviet Union.

In the 1950s and 1960s Mubarak was a successful air force pilot, seeing action in the Yemen civil war as a bomber squadron commander and in the 1967 Arab–Israeli war. Later in 1967 he took up a two-year post as director of the aeronautical academy. He was appointed successively air force chief of staff in 1969 and then commander in 1972 (a post he held until 1975). Acclaimed as a war hero after leading a successful air offensive against Israel in the 1973 war, he was promoted in that year to the rank of lieutenant-general. Mubarak is married with two sons.

Mubarak's political rise under the Sadat regime was an exceptionally rapid one. Within three years of his first government appointment, as deputy minister for military affairs in 1972, Sadat made him vice-president. Taking up this post in 1975, he was also given special responsibilities for state security. In 1978 he took charge of the organisation of the newly formed National Democratic Party (NDP), acting as vice-president of the party until 1981 and thereafter as its chairman.

A smooth transfer of power to Mubarak took place following Sadat's assassination on 6 October 1981. He was nominated as the NDP's presidential candidate that same day and endorsed by a nationwide referendum a week later with an approval rating recorded as 98.46 per cent.

When he took office Mubarak was seen as a political moderate, who promised a degree of continuity with Sadat's policies. In the event, his presidency has been notable particularly for the gradual rebuilding of relations with the Arab states which had ostracised Sadat over his Camp David accords with Israel. He has maintained a degree of independence in Egypt's foreign policy, despite heavy reliance on US aid, and has been notably cool in dealings with Israel, which he has visited only once, in 1995. Even this was a condolence call rather than an official visit, on the occasion of the funeral of the Israeli prime minister **Yitzhak Rabin**, on whom many of the hopes for an Israeli–Palestinian peace agreement had rested. His credit with the US government was boosted by his leading role among Arab states in opposing the Iraqi invasion of Kuwait in 1990 and by his decision to commit Egyptian troops to join the US-led forces in the 1991 Gulf war.

Mubarak has been re-elected no less than three times for further presidential terms, in 1987, 1993 and 1999, despite having earlier proclaimed that no president should serve more than two terms. In each case he was nominated as the sole candidate by the National Assembly and endorsed overwhelmingly by national referendum.

He described the central themes of his third term as economic reform and the promotion of a free-market system, combating unemployment and fighting terrorism. He has proved uncompromising in his attitude towards Muslim militant groups in Egypt, and there have been several attempts on his life, most notably on 26 June 1995 when he narrowly escaped assassination during a visit to Addis Ababa, Ethiopia. His clampdown on fundamentalist activity, while incurring criticism from human rights groups over reprisal killings, political trials and the use of torture, has not succeeded in doing more than keeping a lid on a situation that remains tense and potentially explosive.

Rupert **Murdoch**

Rupert Murdoch is one of the world's wealthiest mass media owners, and one of the most controversial. In the UK he is particularly mistrusted among liberals, and hated by the left, because of the combination of his power, his politics, his unashamed commercialism, and his role in the 1980s in breaking the power of the newspaper unions during the move from Fleet Street out to Wapping. The Australian-born Murdoch is now a US citizen with global interests built around the News International flagship and the development of satellite television. Securing television rights to major sporting events has been one of his favourite tactics for breaking into new markets and increasing audience share. His enduring appetite for work and for fresh challenges has frequently impressed even his bitterest enemies.

Keith Rupert Murdoch was born on 11 March 1931 in Melbourne, where his father was chief executive of Australia's largest newspaper chain. He went from grammar school in Geelong, Victoria, to Worcester College, Oxford, and then began working at the *Daily Express* in London, but returned to Australia on his father's death in 1954. Inheriting the ownership of an obscure radio station and two ailing newspapers, he took over the running of the *Adelaide News*, imbuing it with unfettered sensationalism and gaining a huge surge in circulation.

In 1956, ready for further challenges, he bought a Perth Sunday newspaper, then in 1960 acquired the *Sydney Daily Mirror* and *Sunday Mirror*, founding a nationwide alliance of regional publications and, in 1964, starting Australia's first truly national newspaper, *The Australian*. At the same time he was experimenting with the creation of a national radio broadcasting network.

Murdoch's adventures in British newspaper publishing started in 1970 with the purchase of the *News of the World*, a sensationalist Sunday newspaper with a flagging circulation which quickly responded to an injection of Murdoch's trademark journalistic style. Murdoch next launched a successful bid for *The Sun*, a daily tabloid newspaper founded only two years beforehand and already losing most of its readership to the *Daily Mirror*. Introducing a controversial blend of cartoons and nude "page three" pictorials, together with simplistic and sometimes deliberately offensive editorials, *The Sun* shocked many with its down-market approach. However, the newspaper's immediate success showed that it had struck a popular vein. Rival papers began copying the elements of its revolutionary format, but *The Sun* under Murdoch's

ownership remains by far the biggest-selling UK daily, a key reason for politicians to fear its hostility. In 1997, **Tony Blair**'s "New Labour" campaign received a major boost when he won the endorsement of Murdoch's traditionally pro-Conservative press.

Back in 1981, however, Murdoch's successful bid for *The Times*, Britain's oldest daily broadsheet newspaper, unsettled the British establishment. If some readers feared that the barbarians were indeed standing at the gates of the country's most hallowed institutions, Murdoch has since allayed their worst fears for the content of *The Times*, preferring a more hands-off line than had been predicted with regard to its editorial content.

His ownership of *The Times* did, however, help to revolutionise the newspaper industry in another unexpected way. In 1986 the paper closed its London offices in Fleet Street and was relocated, along with *The Sun*, to Canary Wharf, a new high-rise development in Wapping in the east London docklands. Murdoch made this the moment to restructure his workforce, provoking a year-long strike and lock-out. By introducing state-of-the-art electronic presses, dismissing several hundred print operatives and refusing to recognise the trade unions as negotiating partners, Murdoch was using his characteristically blunt personality to drive a brutal path through the old-fashioned and sometimes inefficient ways of doing things. Within a year he had won a tactical victory over the strikers, and other national dailies began to take similar steps to revise and modernise their staffing arrangements.

Murdoch's business talents were less in evidence with the *New York Post*, a tabloid which he had bought in 1976. He eventually sold it at a crippling loss in 1988, and by 1991 he had disposed of nearly all his American magazine holdings to meet his enormous debts in the USA.

In recent years Murdoch's interests have centred on his commitment to satellite and terrestrial digital broadcasting, especially in western Europe and in Asia. His work on the Hong-Kong-based Star satellite broadcasting system (which transmits to 38 countries in east Asia) is still at a loss-making stage, although he is convinced of its value as a strong commercial proposition for the future. It has led him into political controversy on a number of occasions, both when his operations have earned him the disapproval of governments in the region and, conversely, when he has been accused of insisting on an editorial line that will not adversely affect his future business prospects. The latter charge has been levelled at him particularly

over the Murdoch-owned press and television news coverage of China and human rights.

In Britain, Murdoch's satellite television interests centre on British Sky Broadcasting (BSkyB), of which his flagship News International Corporation owns 45 per cent. He has also been working to develop new digital terrestrial systems, but a controversial attempt to buy the Manchester United football club, whose games are a major draw for television viewers, was blocked in early 1999. To develop his satellite broadcasting activities in Germany and Italy, Murdoch formed News Corporation Europe in November 1998, again with the intention of using rights to sporting fixtures to spearhead a drive for subscribers. In the USA he effectively owns the US-based Fox Television Network (founded 1987), and he has been chairman of 20th Century Fox Productions since 1985.

Although Murdoch still considers himself to be an Australian in every functional respect, he adopted US citizenship in 1991, enabling him to comply with US media ownership rules. His main holding company, News Corporation, remains based in Sydney, Australia, although the bulk of its revenues come from abroad; his personal wealth is reckoned to be between US$5 million and US$6 million.

Rupert Murdoch's first marriage, to Patricia Booker, lasted from 1956 until 1965, and they had one daughter. In 1967 he married for the second time, to novelist Anna Maria Torv, with whom he has one daughter, Elisabeth (a senior executive at BSkyB), and two sons, Lachlan (appointed in February 1999 as executive vice-president of News Corporation) and James. Anna initiated divorce proceedings in July 1998, claiming that she had been unable to persuade him to work less hard. The proceedings became increasingly acrimonious when Rupert Murdoch declared his intention of marrying Wendy Deng, a 32-year-old television executive from Hong Kong and vice-president of the Star TV network. Prospects for a settlement were complicated by the legal possibility of Anna Murdoch gaining control of 50 per cent of the media empire, and questions of who would determine the succession among their three children.

Benjamin **Netanyahu**

Benjamin Netanyahu was prime minister of Israel for three years from May 1996, a divisive period in Israeli politics and society during which his lack of constructive policy over the Middle East peace process frustrated earlier hopes of progress towards a lasting settlement with the Palestinians. His right-wing Likud *party was the main element in a multiparty coalition of disparate interests. US-educated and noted for his adept handling of the medium of television, Netanyahu became almost wholly reliant on his tactical skills and short-term political deals, rather than any coherent policy programme, to keep himself in office until his eventual landslide electoral defeat in May 1999. At the international level his repeated prevarication on withdrawing from parts of the occupied West Bank exhausted the patience of Western governments to the extent of forfeiting the goodwill of the US administration.*

Benjamin Netanyahu, widely known as Bibi, was born on 21 October 1949 in Tel Aviv, in a family of Lithuanian immigrant origin, his grandfather having adopted the name Netanyahu (Hebrew for "god's gift") upon his arrival in 1930. When Benjamin was 14 his family moved to the USA, where his father, a militant Zionist, was offered a position as a history professor. He completed high school in Philadelphia, then returned to become a captain in an elite commando unit in the Israeli Defence Force (IDF). Wounded during the operation to end an airline hijacking at Tel Aviv airport, he was discharged from the IDF in 1972. He then returned to the USA for a further four years, studying architecture at Massachusetts Institute of Technology and going on to complete a master's degree in business administration in 1976.

Netanyahu started work as a management consultant with the Boston Consulting Group (1976–78). Returning in 1978 to Israel, he worked as a senior manager of Rim Industries in Jerusalem. To commemorate his brother, who died in the 1976 Israeli commando action to end a hijacking at Entebbe, Uganda, he set up the Jonathan Institute for the study of ways of combating terrorism. His publications on the need to defend the State of Israel, and the high-profile conferences of the Institute, won him a considerable reputation. He went to the USA once again in 1982, as deputy to the Israeli ambassador, Moshe Arens, and then served for four years (1984–88) as his country's ambassador to the UN.

Elected to the *Knesset* (parliament) as a *Likud* member in 1988, Netanyahu was appointed first deputy foreign minister (1988–91), represented Israel abroad during the 1991 Gulf war, and then became deputy minister in the prime minister's office (1991–92). He was a senior member of Israel's delegation at the Middle East peace conference held in Madrid in 1991, and at subsequent peace talks in Washington D.C.

Netanyahu became chairman of the right-wing *Likud* in 1993, defeating the old guard in a party leadership contest in which he benefited from substantial financial backing from US-based Jewish businessmen. His leadership campaign faltered when his stance as a proud young family man (married to his third wife, Sara, and father of three) was threatened by the exposure of his adultery, in a scandal widely nicknamed "Bibigate". He managed to face down his media critics, however, by a televised admission, and Sara, despite low popularity ratings in the opinion polls, subsequently enjoyed a particularly high profile and frequent public appearances at his side. In opposition until 1996, Netanyahu took office following general elections that May. For the first time, the premiership was decided by a separate popular vote, in which he narrowly defeated the Labour leader and incumbent prime minister **Shimon Peres**.

Netanyahu was a severe critic of the peace process with the Palestinians, which had entered a new phase under the Labour government with the creation of a Palestinian entity in the West Bank and Gaza on the basis of agreements in 1993 and 1995. He fought the May 1996 election campaign on a "peace with security" platform which included a refusal to meet Palestinian leader **Yassir Arafat** or to countenance relinquishing Israeli control of the city of Jerusalem. Cultivating popularity particularly among the less-well-off Sephardic community, he advocated Jewish rights to settle in the West Bank territories, which he described as an integral part of the biblical Israeli territory. He subsequently backed down to the extent of meeting Arafat and, under international pressure, went through with the handover of Hebron to Palestinian control, professing himself committed to honouring the previous government's agreements. However, he never tackled the fundamental problem that "land for peace" was incompatible with the demands of the Jewish settlers, to whom his coalition remained beholden and to whose activities he gave both public support and financial backing.

Other initiatives, with less apparently significant purpose, further poisoned the atmosphere – notably

the reopening in 1996 of a tunnel entrance, of archaeological significance but far more inflammatory political import because of its proximity to Islamic holy sites in Jerusalem, and an abortive attempt to assassinate a Palestinian Islamic leader in Jordan in September 1997. Netanyahu held his coalition government together through crisis after crisis by repeated reassurances and promises, and by postponing major decisions. He could not obscure the fact, however, that there were irreconcilable positions within the cabinet, some demanding faster troop withdrawals from the West Bank to restart the peace process, whereas right-wingers threatened to resign to prevent this.

The peace process effectively ground to a halt during his three years in office. The damage to Israel's international position was underlined over the Wye agreement, signed at a summit meeting in Maryland, USA, in October 1998. A last-ditch US-brokered attempt to restart the peace process and establish a new timetable for the progressive handover of West Bank territory to the Palestinians, the Wye agreement required the Palestine National Council to make a fresh renunciation of anti-Israel clauses in the Palestinian national charter, which it duly did, with President **Clinton** in approving attendance, on 10 December 1998. The Israeli side, however, backed away from implementing the required withdrawals from a specified percentage of the West Bank, the cabinet voting to suspend the process on 20 December.

Recognising the eventual failure of Netanyahu's machinations to keep his eight-party coalition together, the *Knesset* on 21 December voted to hold elections within six months. Netanyahu was re-elected as *Likud* leader in January 1999, but faced a growing number of defections. Despite his own confidence in his political skills, and his preparedness to make mutually incompatible promises to different possible allies, he suffered a resounding defeat on 17 May 1999 at the hands of Labour leader Ehud Barak. In the aftermath of the poll he resigned both the premiership and the *Likud* leadership.

Andreas **Papandreou**

In Greek politics until the mid-1990s, two ageing grandees overshadowed the rest: Andreas Papandreou on the non-communist left, and his Cretan rival Constantine Mitsotakis on the centre-right. Papandreou, the founder of the Panhellenic Socialist Party (PASOK), whose two-term government from 1981 to 1989 ended almost 50 years of conservative political dominance, cut the bigger figure on the international stage. An articulate US-educated economist, he made waves with left-wing rhetoric, particularly the unfulfilled threat of pulling Greece out of both NATO and the European Communities (EC). Large-scale EC subsidies placated his hostility and subsidised a high-spending government programme, but the ailing Papandreou's authority was eroded by corruption scandals, and by the spotlight turned on his affair with an airline hostess who became his second wife. An unexpectedly vigorous election campaign in 1993 gave him a further term in office, which drifted without clear direction until his eventual retirement and death in 1996.

Andreas Georgios Papandreou was born on the island of Chios on 5 February 1919. His father Georgios Papandreou was a lawyer and a leading political figure, who was prime minister briefly in 1944, and again in 1963 and 1964/65.

Initially following his father's example, Andreas Papandreou studied law at Athens University. He was arrested in 1939, under the nationalist dictatorship of Metaxas, but was then permitted to go to the USA to continue his studies. Having switched from law to economics, he completed a doctorate at Harvard University in 1943, became a US citizen in 1944, held a series of professorships at American universities, and served in the US navy. While in the USA he married Margaret Chant, with whom he had three sons and a daughter; they were divorced in 1989.

Papandreou returned to Greece and resumed his Greek citizenship in 1959. In 1961 he was appointed director of the Centre of Economic Research in Athens (a post he held until 1964) and adviser to the Bank of Greece (until 1962). His father, Georgios Papandreou, came to power following the 1963 general election and then strengthened his position further in the 1964 election, when Andreas Papandreou secured a seat in parliament as a deputy for Achaia. Papandreou senior appointed his son to the cabinet as minister to the prime minister and then deputy minister in charge of co-ordination, in preference to more senior members of his own republican Centre Union party. The government fell in July 1965.

When Georgios Papadopoulos seized power in April 1967, initiating the five years of repressive military government known as "the regime of the colonels",

Andreas Papandreou was at first arrested and imprisoned, but was then allowed to go into exile in Sweden and then Canada, where he resumed work as an economics professor. In exile he became a prominent campaigner against the colonels, founding and leading the Panhellenic Liberation Movement in 1968. When the regime did eventually collapse in July 1974, Papandreou returned to Greece and founded the Panhellenic Socialist Movement (PASOK) that September.

Between the general elections of 1974 and 1977, Papandreou gradually built up PASOK's popular support, increasing its share of the vote so that it became the main opposition party. PASOK's eventual general election victory in 1981, when it secured 48 per cent of the vote and 172 seats, allowed Papandreou to form a government, in which he was not only prime minister but also minister of defence. He had pledged to withdraw from the European Communities (which the country had just joined in January 1981) and NATO, but did neither when in office, although he did inaugurate lavish spending policies at home.

In the 1985 general election Papandreou successfully secured a second term of office, but his position was undermined by his own poor health (he had several spells in hospital, including two months in the UK in 1988). The opposition also sought to discredit him by linking him to embezzlement scandals concerning the Bank of Crete and the Greek–American businessman Georgios Koskotas. Meanwhile Papandreou announced that he was seeking a divorce so that he could marry Dimitra Liani, a former air hostess half his age, whom he eventually married in 1989 and who held increasing influence over him until his death.

Two sets of elections in 1989 provided no clear winner and two short-lived governments followed, although renewed elections in April 1990 gave Constantine Mitsotakis's conservative New Democracy a clearer majority over the discredited PASOK. Reinvigorated by a spell in opposition, however, and acquitted of involvement in the diversion of funds from the Bank of Crete to PASOK, Papandreou was able to make a strong comeback. In the October 1993 general election he projected his party as a model of 1990s social democracy, playing down its previous radical socialist image.

Papandreou's 1993 victory (PASOK won 47 per cent of the vote) was based partly on his own charisma, but was helped by the unpopularity of the austerity measures of the outgoing government, and by divisions within New Democracy itself. Papandreou went on to form a government, in which his young wife headed the prime minister's private office. (He also appointed his son, Georgios Papandreou, as minister of education and religion in July 1994.) He proceeded to renationalise the Athens bus network, but a year later also announced plans for the partial privatisation of the national telecommunications concern OTE. His position was, however, increasingly undermined by his deteriorating health. He was taken into hospital in late 1995 with pneumonia and kidney failure, and placed in intensive care. He was eventually persuaded to resign as prime minister on 15 January 1996, although he clung on to the leadership of PASOK until his death on 23 June 1996.

Shimon **Peres**

*Shimon Peres, a founder of the Israel Labour Party in 1968, led his party in the mid-1980s into Israel's first Labour–Likud power-sharing agreement, alternating as prime minister with Yitzhak Shamir. Although he was later ousted from the party leadership by his more charismatic rival **Yitzhak Rabin**, it was as Rabin's foreign minister that Peres made his most notable contribution, leading the Israeli government team in the secret peace talks with the Palestinians that produced the so-called Oslo agreement. This won him a Nobel Peace Prize in 1994, jointly with Rabin and **Yassir Arafat**. Returning as prime minister following Rabin's assassination, Peres represented the best hope for Israel to implement the historic "land for peace" settlement, but defeat at the 1996 general election relegated him to the role of elder statesman critic as the peace process foundered.*

Shimon Peres was born Shimon Persky on 21 August 1923 in Vishneva near Minsk (then part of Poland, later annexed by the Soviet Union and now in Belarus). His father, Isaac Persky, took the family to Palestine and settled in Tel Aviv in 1934. There Shimon attended the Guela school and then the Ben Shemen agricultural school. In the late 1930s he began work in the *kibbutzim* (collective farms), becoming active in the Labour Youth Movement of which he was elected secretary in 1943. It was around this time that he modified his surname to Peres. He married Sonya Gelman, and they have had three children.

In 1947 Peres joined the Haganah Defence Forces fighting against the British authorities in Palestine, and was put in charge of arms purchases. In 1949, acting for the newly independent State of Israel, he led a defence ministry arms purchase delegation to the USA, where he also attended night school at the New School for Social Research in New York and completed a course in management at Harvard University. After his return to Israel in 1952, he was named deputy director-general of the ministry of defence, and promoted to be director-general between 1953 and 1959.

Peres's rapid rise in Israeli politics owed much to his close relationship with Israel's first prime minister, David Ben-Gurion. In 1959 Peres was elected to the *Knesset* (parliament) as a member of Ben-Gurion's *Mapai* Labour Party and appointed deputy defence minister in Ben-Gurion's government. In 1965 he joined Ben-Gurion in quitting *Mapai* and forming the *Rafi* party, which he later helped re-integrate into *Mapai* to form the Israel Labour Party in 1968. The following year he was appointed minister for

immigrant absorption in the Labour-led government of Golda Meir, subsequently moving to transport and then to the information portfolio.

In June 1974 Peres suffered his first major setback when his less experienced political rival Yitzhak Rabin was chosen ahead of him as successor to Golda Meir. He regained his political ground when as minister for defence (1974–77) he successfully supervised the 1976 rescue operation at Entebbe, Uganda, which led to the release of more than 100 Jewish and Israeli passengers hijacked by Palestinian militants aboard an Air France flight. By early 1977, Rabin's growing difficulties in maintaining the support of a united Labour Party paved the way for Peres to gain control of the party he had helped create. In April 1977 he took over as party leader (and caretaker prime minister) after Rabin was forced to resign in the midst of a series of political scandals.

Peres was unable to repair the damaged image of the Labour Party before the 1977 general election; defeat forced him into opposition. Defeated again in 1981, he was disappointed when the Labour Party failed to win an absolute majority in 1984. Obliged to share power with the right-wing *Likud* party, he reluctantly agreed to form a government of national unity and took over as prime minister until 1986. From 1986 to 1988 he served as deputy prime minister and foreign minister under *Likud* leader Yitzhak Shamir, although sharp differences divided them over Peres's advocacy of peace talks with moderate Palestinians. The inconclusive result of the 1988 general election forced the Labour Party into another uneasy coalition with the *Likud* party in which Peres served as deputy prime minister and finance minister until its collapse in March 1990.

Peres's failure to make a decisive impact on national policy, especially the Middle East peace process, left him vulnerable to opposing factions in the Labour Party. Never personally popular with the electorate, he suffered under the frequently quoted assessment of his rival Rabin that he was a "tireless schemer", and in February 1992 he lost the party leadership to Rabin. The blow was softened when, following Labour's victory in the 1992 general election, Rabin made him foreign minister. In this role he helped frame and begin implementing the 1993 Oslo peace accord with the Palestine Liberation Organization (PLO). His role as one of the chief architects of the peace process was recognised in December 1994 when he, Rabin and the PLO leader, Yassir Arafat, were jointly awarded the Nobel Peace Prize.

Peres returned to the leadership of the Labour Party in traumatic circumstances, when Rabin was assassinated by a fanatical Jewish opponent of the Oslo peace deal on 5 November 1995. Taking over also as prime minister, he held this post only for seven months, however. Peres renounced the opportunistic option of an immediate dash to the polls to take advantage of a sympathy vote over Rabin's death. Instead he pressed ahead with the first stage of withdrawals from the West Bank to get the Oslo peace process fully under way – only to see this approach undermined when the Palestinian rejectionists in *Hamas* and Islamic *Jihad* launched their notorious suicide attacks on buses in Jerusalem and Tel Aviv. Peres's Labour Party, its support fatally compromised by popular revulsion against this carnage, narrowly lost the general election in May 1996 and he was displaced as prime minister by *Likud* leader **Benjamin Netanyahu**.

Under Netanyahu there were repeated setbacks to the hopes invested in the peace process, with Peres in the "elder statesman" role, the architect of an agreement which he criticised his successor for failing to advance. As Netanyahu's coalition began to unwind, and with early elections called for May 1999, Peres took a back seat in party politics to new Labour leader Ehud Baruk, but spoke out in favour of a new national unity government as the best way to get the peace process back on track. He was enthusiastically received at the Palestinian parliament in Ramallah in January 1999 when he spoke of the need for Jews and Palestinians to treat each other as partners, accepting the need for a Palestinian state and emphasising Israel's interest in its prosperity.

Javier **Pérez de Cuéllar**

Former Peruvian diplomat Pérez de Cuéllar was the fifth holder of the post of UN secretary-general. In office for two terms from the beginning of 1982 until the end of 1991, he brought a quiet diplomatic approach to the job, which he understood from the inside, having spent much of the previous decade working for the UN. His greatest achievement was to help bring to an end the Iran–Iraq war, while his ten-year tenure as secretary-general spanned the period of the ending of the cold war. He thus left office amid considerable optimism that the UN could play a more effective part in international peacekeeping, but with many organisational problems still unresolved. His soft-spoken manner did not transfer well into domestic politics, where his bid for the Peruvian presidency in 1995 ended in failure.

Javier Pérez de Cuéllar was born on 19 January 1920, in Lima, Peru. His father, a businessman, died four years later and the young Javier was left in the care of his extended family. He received his early education in his native city, and went on to the Catholic University there, graduating with a degree in law. In 1940 he joined the ministry of foreign affairs, and in 1944 entered the diplomatic service as a junior diplomat serving in the Peruvian embassies in France, the UK, Bolivia and Brazil; he also represented his country as a member of the Peruvian delegation to the first session of the UN General Assembly in 1946. In 1961 he returned to Lima as a senior administrator in the foreign service and the following year was promoted to the rank of ambassador, serving in Switzerland, the Soviet Union, Poland and Venezuela. He is married to Marcela Temple and they have two children.

Involvement with the UN dominated his career from 1971, when he was appointed as Peru's permanent representative. From 1973 to 1975 he served as president of the UN Security Council, during which time his handling of the partition crisis in Cyprus won him the admiration of his peers. It also led to his being appointed in 1975 as the UN secretary-general's special representative to Cyprus, a role he fulfilled until his return to Lima in December 1977. In 1979 he was recalled to the UN where he served as under-secretary-general for political affairs and, concurrently from April 1981, as the secretary-general's personal representative to Afghanistan. In this capacity he was, albeit briefly, in charge of peace negotiations to end the civil war between the Soviet-backed regime and *mujaheddin* groups.

In December 1981 Pérez de Cuéllar was nominated by the Security Council to take over as the UN's fifth

secretary-general. Although he was widely respected for his diligence and discretion, his candidacy was closely contested, with many (particularly in the third world) arguing in favour of the more dynamic Tanzanian diplomat, Salim Ahmed Salim. The need for a robust approach was especially underlined during Pérez de Cuéllar's first term in office. On two occasions in particular, however, his skills as a peacemaker failed to prevent armed conflict: Argentina and the UK sidelined his efforts and went to war over the Falkland Islands in 1982, and in the same year he was unable to establish a strong enough UN role in southern Lebanon either to prevent the invasion by Israeli troops or to stabilise the situation thereafter.

Recovering from these early setbacks enough to have his first term as UN secretary-general accounted a qualified success, Pérez de Cuéllar was re-elected unopposed for a second five-year term, starting in January 1987. The achievements of his second term in office were significant, involving the end of the bloody Iran–Iraq war in 1988, negotiations leading to the independence of Namibia in 1990, and substantial progress in resolving regional and civil conflicts in Afghanistan, Cambodia, Cyprus, El Salvador and Western Sahara. His commitment to collective security under the auspices of the UN was also most effectively demonstrated during his second term, which witnessed the emergence of a broad-based international coalition against Iraq following its invasion of Kuwait in August 1990. Pérez de Cuéllar's

other notable success was the release in 1991 of Western hostages held by the Muslim *Hezbollah* group in Lebanon.

After declining to stand for a third term as UN secretary-general, Pérez de Cuéllar decided to enter national politics in Peru. In 1994 he declared his candidacy for the following year's presidential election, but finished a poor second, with just under 22 per cent of the first-round vote on 9 April 1995. He had been expected to mount a more convincing challenge to the incumbent, **Alberto Fujimori**. He had formed a new political grouping known as the Union for Peru (UPP) to support his stance as an independent who would respect Fujimori's economic achievements but offer a stronger commitment to democracy. The UPP became the second-largest group in Congress as a result of elections held concurrently with the presidential poll, but Fujimori, re-elected to the presidency, continued to dominate the Peruvian political scene and Pérez de Cuéllar's party has been unable to make a major impact.

Augusto **Pinochet**

The Chilean military dictator whose authoritarian regime from 1973 to 1990 was notorious for the use of torture and abuse of human rights, Pinochet retained the role of head of the army for eight years after giving up the presidency. By securing the status of senator for life thereafter, he appeared to have made himself safe from prosecution, while his supporters in the army and in right-wing political circles continued to regard him as the saviour of his country from the Marxist regime he had overthrown. His arrest in Britain in late 1998, however, and the decision that he should face extradition to Spain for trial on human rights charges, fuelled the international debate about the treatment of war criminals and those held to have committed crimes against humanity.

Augusto Pinochet Ugarte was born on 25 November 1915 in Valparaiso, where he attended a Catholic seminary school, the (Marist) Quillota Institute and the College of the French Fathers. Deciding on an army career, he entered military school in 1933, then joined the infantry. In 1943 he married Lucia Hiriart Rodriguez, with whom he had three daughters and two sons. A lengthy period as student and teacher of geopolitics at military college, interspersed with tours of regimental duty, saw him posted abroad between 1956 and 1959 on a mission with the Ecuador military academy in Quito, and he was appointed deputy director of the War Academy in 1963. A devout Catholic and fitness fanatic, he was regarded by subordinates as a strict disciplinarian with a commanding manner and a widely feared temper.

In January 1971, having been promoted to general, Pinochet was placed in command of the Santiago-based second army division. Authoritarian but apparently unpolitical, he rose rapidly under President Allende's left-wing Popular Unity government (first elected in 1970), becoming army chief of staff in 1972, and – shortly after putting down a minor anti-Allende coup attempt – army commander-in-chief on 23 August 1973. This was the position he held when he and the other armed forces chiefs mounted their own coup on 11 September 1973. Their five-member junta formally took over power after Allende's death later that day, moving rapidly and ruthlessly to suppress all opposition.

Pinochet justified the coup on the grounds that Allende's government was destroying Chilean unity, damaging the economy and fomenting class struggle with "false ideas alien to our concepts", and that in the

period of crisis prior to the coup it had fallen into "flagrant illegitimacy". Marxist political parties were banned immediately, and a ban on all political parties was maintained between 1977 and 1987. Named as president in 1974, Pinochet dominated the junta, which ruled by decree under a state of siege until the introduction of a new constitution in March 1981. This provided that Pinochet should have an eight-year presidential term, with a plebiscite in 1988 which could confirm him in power for a further term.

Internationally, the Pinochet regime aroused special hostility. Liberal as well as left-wing opinion was outraged by its abuse of human rights – the rounding up and killing of political opponents at the time of the 1973 coup, and then the widespread use of political killings, "disappearances", arrests, and forcible removal of young children for adoption. The feared DINA secret police, reporting daily to Pinochet himself, maintained an all-pervading surveillance, and detention centres became notorious for the extensive use of torture and sadistic sexual and psychological abuse of prisoners.

In overthrowing Allende, Pinochet put an end to a democratically elected Marxist-led government and thus removed an example in which the left had invested great hopes. Within two years he had not only reversed Allende's nationalisations and social welfare measures, but begun implementing the most fundamental monetarist experiment, paving the way for the creation of a free-market economy on neo-liberal principles. This prescription, framed under the advice of the so-called Chicago Boys, radical right-wing "supply-side" economists from the University of Chicago, did produce a period of high growth and price stability in the late 1970s. At the same time, however, Chile was running up external debts, running down its welfare provisions, and creating large-scale unemployment by pulling the plug on uncompetitive industries. The international recession of the early 1980s brought social protest and conflict to the fore, as the economy shrank dramatically, but Pinochet survived this challenge, and a 1986 assassination attempt, to pursue his objective of securing his hold on power for eight more years. Only the incontrovertible "No" vote of the October 1988 plebiscite, and defeat in the general election the following year at the hands of a broad coalition of recently unbanned opposition parties, persuaded him to hand over power to an elected government in 1990.

The terms on which Pinochet retired as president, on 11 March 1990, left him with the guarantee of a continuing powerful role as army commander-in-chief (which he retained until March 1998), and the post of senator for life thereafter. Regarded by his supporters as Chile's saviour from Marxism, he was shielded from prosecution for human rights abuses by the constitutional device of the life senatorship, giving him parliamentary immunity, although attempts were made to challenge this. While still head of the army he made a number of trips abroad in connection with arms procurement. These trips included visits to Britain, where he was held in particular favour by former Prime Minister **Margaret Thatcher** because of his regime's pro-British attitude during the 1982 Falklands conflict (Chile having also been embroiled in a territorial dispute with the UK's adversary of that time, Argentina). In October 1998, however, while in London for medical treatment, he was arrested – a Spanish judge having sought his extradition to face charges there over the killing and torture of Spanish nationals.

Pinochet's arrest gave rise to much controversy, firstly over whether Britain should treat him as a bloody ex-dictator or (in Thatcher's view) a good friend, secondly over whether he was immune from prosecution for murder and torture because he had been a head of state at the time, and thirdly over whether holding him to account for human rights abuses was a matter solely for the now democratically governed Chile to decide. A November 1998 ruling by the House of Lords, upholding his arrest, was set aside after one of the judges was found to have connections with Amnesty International. In March 1999 a second House of Lords panel ruled that he was not immune and should face extradition. This second ruling, however, discounted 27 of the 30 charges so far brought by the Spanish judge, for the technical reason that they related to the period before September 1988; only then had UK legislation incorporated "extraterritoriality" so that torture was considered an offence wherever in the world it was committed.

Pol Pot

Under Pol Pot's leadership, the Khmer Rouge *regime in Cambodia in the late 1970s perpetrated atrocities never since equalled in scale, even in Rwanda, although widespread systematic killings elsewhere have attracted more attention in international affairs. Cambodia's killing fields were instruments not of ethnic oppression or attempted genocide, but of a fanatical ideological drive to purge a whole society and rebuild from the "Year Zero". Ousted by Vietnamese intervention in 1979, Pol Pot still controlled a guerrilla army, ran large border areas and exercised influence internationally through the Western-backed exile coalition government of which the* Khmers Rouges *were a part. Too embarrassing a partner for the West, he took a back seat only as a diplomatic palliative. The UN-brokered peace deal in 1993, however, left the* Khmers Rouges *isolated and increasingly hard pressed in their guerrilla camps. Pol Pot himself fell prey to factional divisions, apparently committing suicide in 1998 after his arrest by a rival commander.*

Pol Pot is in fact the best-known *nom de guerre* of Saloth Sar (also known as Pol Porth or Tol Saut), who was born on 19 May 1925 in what was then the French protectorate of Cambodia. His family were prosperous peasant farmers in Kompong Thom province, 80 miles north of Phnom Penh. Sent away to be educated as a monk in a Buddhist monastery for six years, he then spent a year studying carpentry at a technical school in Phnom Penh. In the early 1940s he joined the anti-French resistance movement led by the Vietnamese leader, Ho Chi Minh, and in 1946 became a member of the outlawed Indo-Chinese Communist Party.

Leaving Cambodia in 1949 on a government scholarship to study radio electronics in Paris, he became active in a circle of Cambodian Marxists led by his fellow Cambodian student Ieng Sary. Absorbed in left-wing politics, he failed his exams and lost his scholarship. On his return to Cambodia he joined the underground movement against the French and, after independence in 1953, helped establish the Cambodian Communist Party, of which he became secretary-general in 1963. In the meantime he earned his living by teaching history, geography and morals at a private school in Phnom Penh. Pol Pot was married twice and acknowledged having one daughter.

An anti-communist crackdown by Prince **Sihanouk**'s government forced Pol Pot to leave Phnom Penh in 1963. Together with Ieng Sary he created an armed guerrilla movement known as the *Khmers Rouges* (Red Cambodians) which established bases in the jungles of Cambodia and gained control of the countryside. Aided by China and Vietnam, it waged a relentless armed campaign in the 1960s and early 1970s against the governments of Prince Sihanouk (who later joined the guerrillas after being overthrown by a coup in 1970) and the US-backed prime minister, Lon Nol. On 17 April 1975 the *Khmers Rouges* entered the Cambodian capital, Phnom Penh, and declared themselves to be the government of the country, which they renamed Kampuchea. Pol Pot became prime minister, part of an inner circle which included President Khieu Samphan, Foreign Minister Ieng Sary and Defence Minister Son Sen.

The new *Khmer Rouge* regime immediately expelled all foreigners and sealed off the country, marking the new era as "Year Zero". It introduced a system of rigid agrarian communism, inspired by Maoist principles, and rejected all aspects of modern urban life; money was abolished, communal kitchens opened and schools and temples shut. Thousands of Cambodians were evacuated at gunpoint from cities to the countryside and forced to engage in agricultural labour. Between 2 and 4 million Cambodians were estimated to have died in the mass exodus through imprisonment, torture, starvation or execution, evidence of which was later unearthed in mass graves that came to be known as the "killing fields". Especially targeted were the middle classes, including scientists, engineers, writers, teachers, doctors and civil servants, whose activities were regarded as anti-revolutionary. Members of religious and ethnic minorities were also persecuted and killed; those with links to Vietnam were the victims of a series of brutal massacres in 1977. *Khmer Rouge* hostility to Vietnam derived in part from Cambodia's historical fear of the territorial ambitions of its larger neighbour. Despite the fact that both regimes described themselves as communist, Vietnam was by now firmly in the Soviet rather than the pro-Chinese camp. In December 1978 Vietnam invaded Cambodia, citing a border dispute; Vietnamese forces drove Pol Pot's regime out of the capital, and in January 1979 installed a new communist government led by *Khmer Rouge* defectors.

Pol Pot retreated to western Cambodia from where he directed a fresh campaign against the Vietnamese-backed regime, joining forces in 1982 in a tripartite coalition with opposition leaders Prince Sihanouk and former Prime Minister Son Sann. In 1985 he formally resigned as *Khmer Rouge* commander, apparently to placate the international community still outraged by the brutality of the *Khmer Rouge* regime. Although still effectively in command of *Khmer Rouge* operations along the Thai border, Pol Pot maintained a low profile through much of the early 1990s while *Khmer Rouge* representatives and their royalist allies concluded a peace treaty with the Vietnamese-backed government. The *Khmers Rouges* later renounced this agreement by resuming hostilities and boycotting the UN-supervised 1993 elections. By the mid-1990s Pol Pot faced imminent defeat, weakened by mass defections and bloody factional fighting within the *Khmers Rouges*. In July 1997 he was taken prisoner near the Thai border in northern Cambodia by *Khmer Rouge* guerrillas led by rival commander Ta Mok, after losing a power struggle unleashed by the murder of the former defence minister, Son Sen, who had been holding secret peace talks with the Cambodian government.

Pol Pot died in his sleep while under arrest in his jungle stronghold on 15 April 1998. The cause of death was stated to be a heart attack, and the body was cremated without autopsy, but it was reported soon afterwards that he had in fact committed suicide by taking an overdose of valium and the anti-malaria drug chloroquinine. According to this version of events, his suicide was motivated by the fear that Ta Mok was on the point of turning him over to the USA, and that he would then face trial for crimes against humanity.

Colin **Powell**

Colin Powell personifies the values of success through hard work, commitment to public service, and faith in strong and simple principles, which many Americans want to look to in their country's leaders. His attractive optimism, unassuming charm and calm authority made a strong impression on the public during the 1991 Gulf conflict, in which he played a leading military role as chairman of the US joint chiefs of staff, the first African–American and youngest-ever holder of this post. The repeated speculation that he might seek elective office at the highest political level, although not fulfilled either in 1992 or 1996, has persisted as he has built up his reputation on youth initiatives since his retirement from the armed forces.

Colin Luther Powell was born on 5 April 1937 in Harlem, New York City, where his parents, Jamaican immigrants Luther and Maud Powell, worked in a clothing factory. His loving family, and the Episcopalian faith in which he was brought up, instilled in him a strong sense of moral values, and he is a powerful advocate of the importance of providing this type of background for children today. Growing up in the South Bronx he attended the New York City public schools but on leaving Morris High School in 1955 he was unsure about his future career. As was expected, he followed the footsteps of his older sister by going to college, studying geology at the City College of New York.

While at college he joined the Reserve Officers' Training Corps, thriving in the spirit of adventure and camaraderie within the unit. Setting his heart on a career in the army, he heeded his parents' advice to aim high and to seek to excel as far as he could. He graduated top of his military class in June 1958, and was commissioned as second lieutenant in the US army after a short period of basic training at Fort Benning, Georgia. After an overseas posting in Germany he got married, in August 1962, to Alma Johnson. Then came a posting to Vietnam, as one of the US personnel involved there at this time as "military advisers". He returned to the USA after a year, having injured his foot when he stepped on a booby trap in the jungle while leading a group of South Vietnamese soldiers.

Back at Fort Benning, in the heart of the racially divided southern USA, he was appalled by the discrimination he encountered in the nearby town. Excluded from many places and treated as an inferior citizen, he contrasted this with how he was treated

within the army, as the equal of white soldiers, equally prepared to risk their life for their country. His sense of indignation heightened his determination to succeed in his military career. This was also one of the few periods of his life when he had any apparent party political leanings, doing campaigning work for the re-election of President Lyndon Johnson in 1964.

In 1968 Powell began a second tour of duty in Vietnam. He was awarded the Soldier's Medal for rescuing comrades from a burning helicopter, despite a broken ankle and other injuries sustained in the crash. Back in the USA he gained a master's degree in business administration from George Washington University in 1971. Promoted to major, he was appointed in December 1971 as a White House fellow at the Office of Management and Budget (OMB).

From this point onwards, his career was to alternate frequently between periods of active duty and work within government in Washington D.C. He rose steadily in military rank, from colonel in 1973 (promoted during a period on active duty as a battalion commander in Korea) to lieutenant-general by July 1986 (when he was posted to Germany as commander of V Corps), via home-based postings as commander of 2nd Brigade, 101st Airborne Division (1976) and assistant division commander for operations and training at Fort Carson, Colorado (1981–83).

Powell's rise to prominence in Washington, where he eventually became the president's national security adviser in 1987, was boosted by the impression he made in the early 1970s on Caspar Weinberger, then the OMB director, and Frank Carlucci, his deputy. He held a staff job in the Pentagon from 1974 to 1975, and returned to Washington in 1979 as executive assistant to the energy secretary, soon transferring to become senior military assistant to the deputy defence secretary (1979–81), spanning the transition in January 1981 from the outgoing Carter administration to the new Reagan administration, under which Weinberger and Carlucci became defence secretary and deputy secretary respectively. Between 1983 and 1986 he worked as senior military assistant to Defence Secretary Weinberger, whom he advised during US military interventions in Libya and Grenada.

When a scandal broke in Washington in November 1986 over the illegal sale of arms to Iran, and the use of the proceeds for funding anti-government right-wing "contra" forces in Nicaragua, Powell was

questioned about his involvement in it, but he was cleared and appointed early the following year as deputy to Carlucci, the president's new national security adviser. Together they began the daunting job of restoring the credibility of the National Security Council, severely damaged by the so-called Iran–Contra affair. Carlucci was transferred to the post of defence secretary when Weinberger resigned in November 1987, and it was at this stage that Powell himself was promoted to national security adviser, a post he held until the end of 1988, when the Reagan administration's second term of office ended.

In April 1989 Powell became a four-star general and commander-in-chief of Forces Command at Fort McPherson, Georgia. On 1 October 1989, aged 52, he reached the pinnacle of the US military command when he took office as chairman of the joint chiefs of staff. His first main responsibility was to co-ordinate the invasion of Panama in December 1989, but his major challenge, where he made his name on the international stage under the focus of intense media attention, was commanding the military dimension of the US response to the Iraqi invasion of Kuwait in August 1990. The ensuing Gulf conflict involved the deployment of 550,000 US troops as the main ingredient of a US-led international force. Operation Desert Storm, launched in January 1991, ended with the defeat of Iraqi forces the following month.

The calm manner in which Gen. Powell exercised his authority in the Gulf conflict won him immense respect. There was speculation that President **Bush**, his own popularity temporarily buoyed up by this military success, might invite him to be his vice-presidential running-mate in the presidential elections due in November 1992, but this speculation was effectively ended by Powell's reappointment as chairman of the joint chiefs of staff in October 1991.

The question of Powell's possible future in politics was renewed, however, after he retired from the US army on 30 September 1993. While he now enjoyed a much more private life at his home in Virginia, he did his reputation no harm with high-profile visits abroad – to attend the inauguration of **Nelson Mandela** as president of South Africa in 1994, and as part of a three-member delegation to Haiti, with former President Carter and senior senator Sam Nunn, to work out proposals for ending military rule there.

By the time he published his autobiography *My American Journey* in September 1995, Powell was the person most widely mentioned as a plausible candidate to be the first African–American US president. Whereas Jesse Jackson's influence in the Democratic Party was seen as on the wane and not central in determining the party's platform, and the Nation of Islam leader **Louis Farrakhan** was seen as commanding support only within his own minority community, Powell by contrast seemed to epitomise the "model" American life, achieving success by hard work with an appeal transcending the race issue. A strong family man, he prided himself on having brought up his two daughters and one son according to the beliefs and moral values which he encompassed in his simply-expressed "13 Rules". An economic conservative, he was nevertheless regarded as politically in the centre, supporting the continuation of affirmative action, pro-choice on abortion, favouring some degree of gun control, but known to have resisted the Clinton administration's line on opening up the army to gay men and lesbians.

Courted by both main parties, Powell declared publicly in November 1995 that he had no intention of standing. He did, however, acknowledge that he favoured the Republicans, at whose party convention the following August he gave the opening address. In April 1997 he chaired the President's Summit for America's Future. This high-profile appointment, and his other continuing work on youth issues, fuelled renewed suggestions that he might ultimately launch a political career. The summit instigated the volunteer youth campaign, America's Promise: the Alliance for Youth, with Powell as chairman, and he lectures widely in this area as well as serving on the board of several other national youth bodies. In November 1998 he visited the UK to help increase army recruitment from ethnic minorities and advise on measures to reduce racism within the forces, and in early 1999 he headed a delegation from the International Republican Institute to Nigeria, to witness the elections there as part of the monitoring effort led by former President Carter.

Romano **Prodi**

In 1999, European Union leaders chose the former Italian prime minister Romano Prodi as the next head of the European Commission. A Catholic northerner and a respected economist, widely known as "Il Professore", with a cheerful demeanour, unchallenged integrity and management experience at the highest level in industry, Prodi was to take charge of the Commission at a crucial period. At stake were both its own credibility – the previous Commission having been compelled to resign early en bloc *over its failure to deal with fraud – and its role in managing the future of European integration. Prodi had held office as Italian prime minister between 1996 and 1998, leading the broad centre-left Olive Tree alliance. His government's signal achievement was the economic programme which ensured Italy's qualification to participate in the European single currency from its launch in 1999.*

Romano Prodi was born on 9 August 1939 in Scandiano, in the north Italian Reggio Emilia region. He graduated in economics and commerce from the Catholic University of Milan in 1961, then studied at the London School of Economics before beginning an academic career as a professor of economics and industrial policy at the University of Bologna and a visiting professor at Harvard University. He has

written many papers on European industrial policies, economic systems and the Italian industrial sector. His research in these fields led to his appointment as chairman of the scientific committee of NOMISMA, the economic research institute in Bologna. Romano Prodi is married to Flavia Prodi Franzoni and they have two sons.

Prodi first entered government for a brief period in the late 1970s. Appointed in November 1978 as minister for industry, he came in as a non-party extra-parliamentary expert but subsequently aligned himself with the Christian democrats. In March 1979 he went back to teaching, then in November 1982 became chairman of the huge industrial and financial state holding company IRI (Istituto per la Ricostruzione Industriale). During his period at IRI he returned the company to operational profit, despite political opposition to his reforms, which included greater private sector investment and the sale of some of its subsidiaries, such as the controversial sale of Alfa Romeo to Fiat in 1987. With the state petroleum company Ente Nazionale Idrocarburi (ENI) being run during this period by another former academic, Franco Reviglio, it became known as the "era of the professors" in Italian business.

Prodi left the IRI in March 1989, returning once again to his professorship at the University of Bologna, teaching industrial organisation and policy. He did, however, retain strong links in the business community, as a consultant and member of the boards of various international companies. In May 1993 he was reappointed as chairman of the IRI by the then prime minister, Carlo Ciampi, remaining there until July 1994.

The elections of April 1996 which brought Prodi to the forefront of national politics took place in a party political landscape dramatically different from that which had existed for most of the post-war period. The "meltdown" had already brought to power in 1994 a tripartite "Freedom Alliance" government headed by media tycoon **Silvio Berlusconi**, comprising his newly formed *Forza Italia* movement, the neo-fascists, and right-wing northern regionalists. The collapse of this coalition was followed by over a year of "technocratic" government devoted mainly to tackling the country's economic problems, until the 1996 election was called. The campaign basically took the form of a contest between the Freedom Alliance, and disparate parties ranging from Christian democrats to ex-communists and environmentalists, grouped within the new Olive Tree alliance. Its outcome was a triumph for Prodi, whose low-key style, emphasis on listening to ordinary people, managerial credentials, and corruption-free reputation helped to rally voters behind the Olive Tree alliance.

Prodi was sworn in as prime minister on 18 May 1996, with his Olive Tree alliance now the largest grouping in both the Senate and the Chamber of Deputies. Although technically a minority government, he was able to govern with external support from the Communist Refoundation Party. In office his government provided Italy with a period of unusual political stability and oversaw a marked improvement in economic performance, bringing the country into line with the requirements for participation in the single European currency in 1999. Prodi retained much of his personal popularity in spite of the impact of his austerity programme. In addition to remedying the budget deficit, his government accelerated the process of privatising state-owned industries and services, strengthened the currency and brought down inflation. Despite these achievements, he fell prey to the fractious nature of Italian politics when he failed to persuade the communists not to bring down his government over the October 1997 budget.

On this occasion he retained power only by resigning, and re-presenting his government for parliamentary approval a few days later, after backtracking on a far-reaching reform of the state pension and social security system and on the privatisation of ENI. It was a trick he resented having to perform, for Prodi was a powerful critic of *trasformismo*, the weakness in the system which allowed small parties to wield so much destructive power by bringing down governments. As leader of what proved to be the second most durable government in post-war Italian history, from May 1996 to October 1998, his views carried considerable weight. Nevertheless, it was in effectively identical circumstances to those of October 1997, and again over the budget, that his government was brought down by the margin of a single vote a year later. Resigning on 9 October 1998, he failed on this occasion in a bid to re-form his government and was instead replaced as prime minister by Massimo D'Alema.

Although his career in Italian politics was widely assumed to be at an end, Prodi unexpectedly emerged in early 1999 with a rival view about the future of the apparently incoherent Olive Tree alliance. Founding in February a new political party, Democrats for the Olive Tree, and aiming to refashion the centre-left into a movement with a disciplined structure, he apparently threatened to precipitate a split between his supporters and the government of D'Alema. The swiftness with which a crisis at the European Commission developed, however, drew Prodi away from domestic politics as it became clear that he commanded powerful support as a new Commission president, notably from German Chancellor **Gerhard Schröder** and UK Prime Minister **Tony Blair**. Shortly after the discredited **Jacques Santer** had accepted the need to resign the post, Prodi was approved unanimously by the European Union heads of government on 24 March 1999 as their choice to become Commission president, subject to approval by the European Parliament due to be elected that coming June.

Yitzhak **Rabin**

At the time of his assassination in November 1995, Yitzhak Rabin was over three years into a term as Israeli prime minister, heading a Labour-led coalition government. He had already held the premiership in the mid-1970s, barely six months after launching a political career founded on his military prowess and the status of hero of the Arab–Israeli Six-Day war of 1967. His unimpeachable credentials as a defender of Israel's national security made it all the more significant that, in 1993, he committed his government to implementing a newly concluded "land for peace" agreement, offering the best prospect for decades of a historic settlement between Israel and the Palestinians. Rabin's death profoundly shocked the divided nation. In the ensuing months a spate of Palestinian terror attacks swayed the mood of the undecided. Revulsion and fear undermined faith in a deal which Israelis just might have trusted Rabin to pull off, thus ensuring defeat for Labour and the pro-peace campaign in the 1996 general election.

Yitzhak Rabin was born in Jerusalem on 1 March 1922. His father, Nehemiah, was an immigrant to Palestine from the USA, and had served as a volunteer in the Jewish Legion during the First World War. His mother, Rosa Cohen, was one of the first members of the *Haganah*, the mainstream Jewish national defence organisation. Both were members of the *Ahdut Ha'avoda*, a precursor of the Israeli Labour Party.

Rabin received his early education in Tel Aviv where he attended the Beit Leyaldei Ovdim, a school for workers' children, before studying at the Kadoorie Agricultural School. In 1940 he joined *Palmach*, the secret elite unit of the *Haganah*, fighting against the British authorities in Palestine, and in 1946 was imprisoned for his activities. After his release in 1947 he fought in the Jewish "War of Independence" (1948–49) against the British, and for the next 20 years, until 1968, rose steadily through the ranks of the Israeli Defence Forces (IDF). He was commanding officer Northern Command (1956–59), then chief of operations and deputy chief of staff (1959–64), and finally chief of staff (1964–68) when he emerged as the hero of the 1967 Arab–Israeli Six-Day war.

In 1968 he retired from military service and was named Israel's ambassador to the USA. At the end of his tenure in 1973, Rabin returned to Israel and became active in politics as a member of the Labour Party. He was elected to the *Knesset* (parliament) in the general election in December 1973, and in April 1974 was appointed labour minister by Prime Minister Golda Meir. On 3 June he defeated his political rival, **Shimon Peres**, to succeed Meir as prime minister and leader of the Labour Party after she was forced to resign following a vote of no confidence. Rabin thus became Israel's first native-born prime minister.

In office Rabin took charge of fighting inflation and strengthening the IDF, which had nearly suffered defeat in the 1973 Arab–Israeli war. He also opened peace talks with neighbouring Arab states, which led in 1975 to an interim agreement with Egypt providing for the withdrawal of Israeli forces from the Sinai Peninsula. In June 1976 his popularity soared after a successful commando operation at Entebbe, Uganda, led to the release of over 100 Israeli and Jewish passengers who had been hijacked by Palestinian militants aboard an Air France flight. By early 1977, however, schisms within the Labour Party and allegations of corruption in government increased pressure on Rabin. On 8 April 1977 he resigned as prime minister and surrendered his party leadership to Peres, amid revelations that his wife Leah had violated currency regulations.

Despite the Labour Party's defeat in the general election of May 1977, Rabin remained influential as a *Knesset* deputy and a member of the parliamentary foreign and defence committee. He returned to national prominence in September 1984 when he joined the newly formed *Likud*–Labour National Unity government as defence minister. He oversaw the withdrawal of Israeli forces from Lebanon and the controversial delineation of a so-called Israeli security zone in the south of that country, designed to protect Israel's northern border from attack by Palestinian guerrillas. With the collapse of the government in March 1990, Rabin returned to the opposition benches where he remained until June 1992. In the interim he regained his position as leader of the Labour Party by defeating Shimon Peres in the party's first nationwide primaries, held in February 1992.

In June 1992 Rabin became prime minister for the second time after a general election returned the Labour Party to power. Prepared to take an uncompromisingly hard line in support of Israeli forces confronting the Palestinian uprising or *intifada* in the occupied West Bank, Rabin nevertheless placed at the top of his agenda the negotiation of a lasting peace settlement with the Palestine Liberation Organization (PLO) and Jordan. Talks held in secret during 1992/93 in the Norwegian capital, Oslo, led to a historic peace accord signed on 13 September 1993 in Washington D.C. by Rabin and PLO leader **Yassir Arafat**, which provided for limited Palestinian self-government in the Gaza Strip and Jericho; a further agreement in September 1995 guaranteed elections for a Palestinian government in the self-governed territories. On 26 October 1994 Rabin also signed a separate peace agreement with King Hussein of Jordan.

The apparent breakthrough in the peace process represented by the Oslo negotiations was recognised by the award of the 1994 Nobel Peace Prize jointly to Rabin, Peres (who had led the Israeli negotiating team) and Arafat. Even as the Nobel ceremony was being held in December 1994, however, the peace initiative was already encountering determined opposition from Jewish settlers and the unremitting hostility of right-wing parties. On 4 November 1995 Yitzhak Rabin was assassinated by a Jewish student and right-wing activist, Yigal Amir, in protest against his policies. He was survived by his widow, Leah Schlossberg, and two children.

Ali Akbar **Rafsanjani**

Former Iranian President Rafsanjani, in office from 1989 to 1997, had the political and religious credentials – and the close association with Ayatollah Khomeini – to make him an influential figure from the outset in Iran's 1979 Islamic revolution. Mainly involved in the 1980s with military affairs, he was credited particularly with a major role in ending (in 1988) the protracted and debilitating eight-year war with Iraq. As president, he consistently favoured a moderate reformist line which attracted some favourable notice internationally. However, it also brought him frequently into sharp confrontation with more hardline conservatives. Rafsanjani's critics saw his steps towards liberalisation and improved relations with the West as a threat to the essence of the theocratic rule established under Khomeini.

Ali Akbar Hashemi Rafsanjani was born in 1934 in the village of Bahraman in the southeastern desert region of Rafsanjan, near Kerman. His father, Ali Hashemi Rafsanjani, was a cleric and prosperous pistachio farmer. In the absence of a primary school in the village, the young Rafsanjani was educated instead by a local religious teacher. In 1948 he travelled to the holy city of Qom where he studied at the renowned theological seminary and came under the influence of Ayatollah Ruhollah Khomeini. By 1956 he had completed all introductory courses in theology, enabling him to qualify as an Islamic jurist (*motjahed*) with a substantial following which was to win him the title *hojatolislam* (Proof of Islam).

Rafsanjani entered active politics in the early 1960s when he was involved in the resistance movement against the Shah's authoritarian modernising regime. In 1963 he was arrested and detained for the first time for his part in the 5 June uprising. He was imprisoned again in 1964 on charges of conspiring to assassinate the then prime minister, Hasan Ali Mansour, and received further prison sentences in 1967, 1971 and 1972. In 1975 he served a jail sentence for co-operating with the banned guerrilla organisation, the *Mujaheddin-i-Khaql.* Upon his release in 1978, he co-founded the Tehran Militant Clergy Association. Curiously, his political activities had little adverse effect on his construction business, the success of which in the 1970s had made him a wealthy property speculator. Rafsanjani is married with five children. His youngest daughter, Faezeh Rafsanjani, was elected to the *Majlis* (legislative assembly) in March 1996.

It was Rafsanjani's close association with Ayatollah Khomeini which accounted for his meteoric rise as one of the leading figures of Iran's Islamic revolution. In 1978, before the overthrow of the Shah, he was appointed by Khomeini as a member of the Council of the Islamic Revolution, with the objective of turning the country from a monarchy to a theocracy. The Shah's fall in February 1979 opened the way for a new government in which Rafsanjani soon established himself, as interior minister, having already co-founded the dominant Islamic Republican Party (IRP) with Khomeini's backing.

He was elected to the *Majlis* as a deputy in the first general election held in 1980 and became speaker, a post he held continuously until 1989. The outbreak of the Iran–Iraq war in 1980 led to his involvement in military affairs. As Khomeini's representative on the Supreme Defence Council, he gained influence that eventually persuaded Khomeini to end the war and, in 1988, to name him deputy commander-in-chief of the armed forces, second only to Khomeini. His position was also consolidated by his membership in 1983 of the Council of Experts (which decides on the succession to the country's supreme spiritual leader), and his appointment in 1984 to the Supreme Council of the Cultural Revolution.

In July 1989 Rafsanjani took almost 95 per cent in a nationwide vote to win election as president, a post endowed under a constitutional amendment with much more power than hitherto. Although as president he was both head of state and head of government, the highest overall authority remained that of the Supreme Spiritual Leader – a role for which the outgoing president, **Ayatollah Khamenei**, had been chosen after the death of Khomeini earlier in the year.

Rafsanjani began by steering his presidency with caution, distancing himself from ultra-conservative factions while taking care not to reject Khomeini's legacy. Thus he pledged to carry on the Islamic revolution while simultaneously purging many Islamic hardliners from the government. Gradually, however, he emerged as a bold and independent leader, especially in foreign policy. His attempts to normalise relations with the West, including the USA, met with stiff opposition from conservative groups and hostility from Ayatollah Khamenei. Undeterred, he continued his programme of reform, liberalising the economy to make it more competitive and diluting the harsher aspects of Islamic law by granting more freedom to women and encouraging intellectual debate.

By the time he was elected to a second term in office in June 1993, Rafsanjani had established his reputation as a supreme pragmatist and consummate politician adept at handling the conflicting interests of religious zealots and modern technocrats. The liberal reforms of his first administration had already wrought significant changes that gave greater influence to the moderate factions which Rafsanjani increasingly favoured. The impact of these changes was most visibly demonstrated in 1997 when, unable to contest a third term as president, Rafsanjani manoeuvred to secure the election of Mohammad Khatami as his successor. Khatami's victory in the nationwide poll in May that year, with a landslide majority backed by a progressive coalition of left-wingers, young men and women and intellectuals, was a milestone for Rafsanjani, signifying the permanence of his legacy to end Iran's international isolation and relax the strict mores of the Islamic revolution.

Jerry **Rawlings**

Jerry Rawlings, who has dominated political life in Ghana for two decades, first came to power as leader of a coup by young officers with a socialist-inspired and anti-corruption agenda. An enigmatic and charismatic figure, he has largely eschewed the temptation of self-enrichment in what was a notoriously venal government culture. Rawlings consistently expresses a strong social message, and has proven pragmatic about policies in pursuit of development, thereby disappointing those who once saw him as a beacon of socialism in Africa. Praised for a transition to civilian government in the 1990s which has seen him twice elected as president, he also – unexpectedly – became a favourite of the World Bank and IMF when he introduced aid-backed market reforms. Rawlings remains notoriously unpredictable about how long he intends to remain at the helm. His current term of office formally expires at the end of the year 2000.

Jerry John Rawlings was born on 22 June 1947 in Accra. He took his name from his Scottish father, and his mixed racial origin was something which some opponents would later try to use against him when he became a national political figure, but his upbringing was primarily the responsibility of his Ghanaian mother, Victoria Agbotui. Her efforts in seeing him through primary school were rewarded when he won a place at Accra's prestigious Achimota School, formerly known as the Prince of Wales School, whose most celebrated former pupil was Ghana's charismatic leader Kwame Nkrumah. Rawlings experienced during his boyhood both an introduction to military disciplines through the school cadet corps, and the passionate enthusiasm of Nkrumah's nationalism and pan-Africanism, his country having become in 1957 the first in Africa to make the transition from colonial status to independence. He also first met his future wife, Nana Konadu Agyeman, while he was at Achimota School. She became a political figure of some significance in her own right as leader of a women's movement. Jerry and Nana Rawlings have one son and three daughters.

Rawlings went on from Achimota to the Ghana Military Academy at Teshie, and enlisted in the Ghana air force in August 1967. In 1969 he became a pilot officer and was promoted in 1978 to the rank of flight lieutenant. During his time as an air force junior officer, Rawlings became increasingly politicised, combining socialist principles with disgust at the rampant corruption, deteriorating morale and indiscipline of the so-called "kleptocracy" under the military government of Gen. Acheampong.

Identified as a charismatic figure and becoming a focus for disaffection with the regime among his circle in the Ghanaian armed forces, Rawlings was arrested in May 1979 and charged with leading a mutiny of junior officers and men of the air force. On 4 June, however, he was freed by his supporters and led a revolt which ousted the ruling Supreme Military Council. Rawlings set up the Armed Forces Revolutionary Council (AFRC) as an interim ruling body, while ensuring that general elections could go ahead under the programme already set in motion before his June coup. The elections were duly held in September, and the AFRC handed over to a civilian government formed by the People's National Party under President Hilla Limann.

Having thus experienced power, but vested his hopes for more accountable government in a return to democracy, Rawlings found it increasingly difficult to remain on the sidelines, with the economy in dire straits and the Limann government patently not addressing the problems of ingrained corruption and mismanagement. On 31 December 1981, denouncing the failures of the civilian regime, Rawlings once again led a revolt within the armed forces. This time he retained power on a more long-term basis, running the country through a Provisional National Defence Council, composed of both civilian and military members, under his own chairmanship. He became the head of state in January 1982 and chief of the defence staff in November 1982.

In power, Rawlings has placed particular emphasis on avoiding the charges of corruption and self-enrichment levelled against his predecessors. His leftist orientation was reflected in some of his reforms of the administration and the judiciary, and also encouraged him to plan for union with neighbouring Burkina Faso until his kindred spirit Thomas Sankara was ousted from power in that country. Ghana's long transition to civilian rule under Rawlings's leadership was accompanied in the latter stages by a programme of economic reform and adjustment, backed by the World Bank and International Monetary Fund (IMF), which resulted in its being widely cited as a rare example of a "success story" among African states. This progress on the economic front, besides providing some vindication of the Bank's developmental prescriptions for Africa, helped towards securing the position of the Rawlings regime in the late 1980s and the beginning of the 1990s, although renewed difficulties since then have driven the government to have recourse to further IMF bail-outs.

Lifting the ban on political activities on 1 May 1992, Rawlings resigned his air force commission, as stipulated in the new constitution, in order to contest the presidency. Standing as the candidate of his recently formed National Democratic Congress (NDC) party, he won 58.34 per cent of the votes cast on 3 November. He was re-elected for a second four-year term on 7 December 1996, winning 57.2 per cent of the vote to defeat two other candidates. This election, and the simultaneous legislative election in which an NDC-led alliance won 130 out of 200 seats, were hailed as the most free and fair ever experienced in Ghana, while his own victory made him the country's first-ever leader to win re-election. As the year 2000 elections approached, there were signs in early 1999 of the hardening of divisions within the NDC, with a reform movement planning to field candidates independent of the pro-government list.

Mary **Robinson**

The victory of a female civil rights lawyer, Mary Robinson, in Ireland's 1990 presidential election signalled a marked change of tone in the country's public life. In a figurehead rather than an executive role, her seven-year presidency nevertheless placed a new emphasis on the values and concerns of a younger generation, assisting Ireland's emergence from the social conservatism of the political and religious establishment. The more outward-looking internationalist character of the new Ireland was underlined by Robinson's subsequent appointment as UN High Commissioner for Human Rights – her name having even been suggested as a possible candidate to be the UN's first female secretary-general.

Mary Bourke was born on 21 May 1944 in a Catholic family in Ballina, Co. Mayo. Both her parents, Aubrey Bourke and Tessa O'Donnell, were medical doctors. She was educated at private schools in Dublin and Paris, and then went to Trinity College, Dublin, traditionally a stronghold of the Protestant minority which had dominated Irish public life before independence. She gained a first-class law degree

from Trinity in 1967, the prestigious master of law degree from Harvard University the following year, and a master's degree from Trinity College in 1970. She qualified for the Bar in Dublin in 1967 and in London in 1973. She married fellow lawyer Nicholas Robinson, a Protestant, in 1970 and has combined her subsequent career with raising their three children, Tessa, William and Aubrey.

In 1969, at the age of only 25, Robinson was appointed Reid Professor of Criminal Law at Trinity College, Dublin. She held this post until 1975, when she became lecturer in European Community (EC) law at Trinity College, Dublin. She served as a member of the International Commission of Jurists from 1987 to 1990 and of the advisory commission of the Inter-Rights organisation from 1984 to 1990. With her husband she also founded the Irish Centre for European Law in 1988, working as its director until 1990. As a prominent civil rights lawyer she championed the decriminalisation of homosexuality in Ireland and the right of inheritance for illegitimate children, and opposed the constitutional ban on the provision of information on abortion.

Mary Robinson's political career began in 1969 when she was elected as a representative of the University of Dublin to the *Seanad Éireann* (upper house of parliament). During this time she served on the parliamentary joint committee on EC secondary legislation (1973–89), and chaired the *Seanad*'s social affairs sub-committee (1977–87), its legal affairs committee (1987–89), and the parliamentary joint committee on marital breakdown (1983–85). She was also a member of Dublin City Council from 1979 until 1983, and stood twice for the Labour Party in elections to the *Dáil* (lower house of parliament).

However, she left the party in 1985 when it supported the Anglo-Irish agreement which she thought took insufficient account of Northern Unionist views.

Nominated by the Labour Party and the small Workers' Party in the November 1990 presidential election, she campaigned on the slogan "You have a voice, I will make it heard". She won support even from the rural women's vote, generally presumed to represent the heartland of Irish traditionalism. Acknowledging the role of women voters in her election success, she memorably declared that the hand that rocked the cradle had rocked the system.

As the country's first woman president, Robinson transformed the role of Irish head of state from a purely ceremonial office to one which reflected a more modern, liberal and dynamic Ireland, both at home and abroad. Acting as both symbol and motor of this change, she worked to promote the equality of women and of socially marginalised groups. Her period of office saw the decriminalisation of homosexuality in 1993, and the legalisation of divorce following a referendum in November 1995.

Perhaps her most controversial initiative was to hold a private meeting with the *Sinn Féin* leader **Gerry Adams** in June 1993, before the announcement of an Irish Republican Army (IRA) ceasefire. She also met privately with Queen Elizabeth II – the first meeting of the British and Irish heads of state since Irish independence in 1922 – during a visit to London earlier that year. Abroad she visited Somalia in 1992, criticising both the UN and the European Communities for their slow response to the crisis. In 1994 she was the first head of state to visit Rwanda in the aftermath of the genocide there.

In March 1997, despite overwhelming support for her position, she decided not to stand for re-election. UN Secretary-General **Kofi Annan** nominated her three months later to the post of UN High Commissioner for Human Rights, which was first created in 1994. She accordingly resigned as president shortly before the end of her term, and took up her new UN post on 12 September 1997.

Since becoming high commissioner, Mary Robinson has committed herself and her small office in Geneva to raising the profile of the issue of human rights protection and making it a mainstream concern throughout the UN system. When she visited Iran in March 1998, she obtained assurances that the government would not carry out Ayatollah Khomeini's controversial 1989 *fatwa* sentencing author **Salman Rushdie** to death, a breakthrough which was followed six months later by confirmation that the Iranian government had formally dissociated itself from the *fatwa*. Robinson also went to China in September 1998 and travelled to Tibet, declaring that, despite rebuffs from government officials, she regarded this visit as the start of a continuing process.

Richard **Rogers**

Few modern architects have had as much impact on urban design as Richard Rogers, who became Lord Rogers of Riverside when he received a life peerage in 1996. Probably best known for two particularly technologically innovative buildings dating from the 1970s, the Pompidou Centre in Paris (designed with Renzo Piano) and the Lloyds building in the City of London, he has latterly become increasingly involved in developing overall urban planning strategies. His proposals for London and other cities, like his buildings, focus on responding to changing patterns of use and the imperative of environmental sustainability. As head of the UK government's urban task force, Rogers is in the forefront of rethinking public policy on the redevelopment of inner cities.

Richard George Rogers was born in Florence, Italy, on 23 July 1933, the son of a British father and an Italian mother. He studied at the Architectural Association in London from 1954 to 1959, and went as a Fulbright scholar to Yale University in the USA, where he completed a master's degree in architecture in 1962. Rogers had three sons with his first wife Su Brumwell, also an architect, whom he married in 1961, and with whom he worked in the Team 4 partnership with Norman and Wendy Foster from 1964 to 1966. In 1973 he married again; he has had two sons with his second wife, Ruth Elias.

It was Rogers's partnership with the Italian architect Renzo Piano, established in 1970, which really projected him to international celebrity status. The design which he and Piano submitted for the Pompidou Centre, Paris, was chosen as the winner of the competition in 1971. Their building, completed in 1976 and also known as the Beaubourg, bears the Rogers trademark, his commitment to creating "people's places" as well as reflecting his modernist aesthetics. Rejecting classicism, it displays an enthusiasm for technology both in its materials and in its expression of the idea of buildings as machines. Similarly, the Lloyds Building in London, designed in 1979 (two years after he first set up the Richard Rogers Partnership, his present practice) and completed in 1986, exuberantly uses technical imagery while aiming for total flexibility and uninterrupted interior spaces. The Richard Rogers Partnership has subsequently been responsible for other radical and sometimes controversial buildings with which the public has struck up strong relationships, including the European Court of Human Rights in Strasbourg and Channel 4's Pimlico headquarters. Other works include the Reuters building in London and major office buildings in Germany and Japan. Rogers has also developed urban master plans for Berlin, the Shanghai financial district of Pu Dong, the ParcBIT in Majorca and, in London, the South Bank Centre and the Greenwich peninsula site.

The emphasis on technology in Rogers's work does not signify a desire to use new techniques and materials for their own sake but a belief that design and technology can help solve social and ecological problems; hence the emphasis in his books, articles, lectures and daily work on concepts of society, sustainability, culture and citizenship. Optimistic and enthusiastic, he is a visionary with strong convictions about the social importance of appropriately designed and rational built environments, and a desire to demonstrate that high population density is compatible with high quality of life. His ideas for London are based around zoning, so that people can live, work and enjoy leisure facilities with a minimum of travel. This basic planning principle must then be backed up with high-quality public services, especially public transport, and a concern for pleasure and beauty in the urban environment, with emphasis on trees, good pavements and facilities like cycle paths. Rogers himself regularly travels by bicycle and is active in promoting cycling by others working at the Partnership.

In 1998 Rogers was appointed to chair a new 14-member task force, set up by the Labour government to develop innovative ideas and identify the best practice for redevelopment of urban areas throughout the UK. A particular requirement for the task force is to demonstrate the full potential for the re-use of previously developed "brownfield" land in cities, to respond to the need for a large increase in the number of homes available across the country over the coming decade, and meet a target of 60 per cent of new residential building on "brownfield" rather than "greenfield" sites.

Rogers was awarded the Royal Gold Medal for Architecture by the Royal Institute of British Architects in 1985. He was knighted in 1991 and created a life peer in 1996, taking the title Lord Rogers of Riverside. His books include *Cities for a Small Planet*, based on the BBC Reith Lectures, which he was invited to give in 1995, the first architect to do so. He has also been involved with arts organisations, as chairman of the Tate Gallery through the 1980s and deputy chairman of the Arts Council for three years in the mid-1990s, and also chairs the Architecture Foundation.

Salman **Rushdie**

A British novelist whose distinctive writing is richly spiced with themes and images drawn from his native India, Salman Rushdie would be one of the most notable contemporary literary celebrities even without the "affair" which projected his name into the arena of international politics. For a whole decade from 1989 onwards, however, his life was taken over as he was driven into hiding by the notorious fatwa, *the pronouncement by the Iranian leader Ayatollah Khomeini that it was the duty of Muslims to kill him for having blasphemed against Islam. The Rushdie affair was not only a long-running impediment to improving relations between Western countries and Iran, but a global cause célèbre in the clash of cultural values. While it exposed the selectivity of a supposedly multicultural British society where blasphemy laws related only to Christianity, its broader significance was in reasserting the liberal values of free speech and artistic expression, notwithstanding the demands of radicalised Islam that its tenets be respected as sacrosanct.*

Salman Ahmed Rushdie was born in India just before partition, on 19 June 1947, into an affluent Muslim family in Bombay. His paternal grandfather was an Urdu poet, and his father a Cambridge-educated businessman. Rushdie received his early education at the Cathedral School in Bombay and, from 1961, at Rugby School in England. In 1964 his parents emigrated to Karachi, Pakistan, while Rushdie went

to King's College, Cambridge, from where he graduated with a degree in history in 1968. From 1968 to 1970 he worked as an actor in London before deciding to earn his living as a freelance advertising copy-editor and take up permanent residence in the UK.

In 1975 he made his debut as an author with the publication of his first novel, *Grimus*. This received little critical attention and sold poorly, but his second novel, *Midnight's Children*, an allegory about the birth of independent India, brought him international fame when it was published in 1981. Lauded by critics as a masterpiece in the best literary tradition of "magical realism", it won Rushdie a clutch of awards including the prestigious Booker McConnell Prize for Fiction (1981); the English Speaking Union Award (1981) and the James Tait Black Memorial Prize (1982). The book also exposed Rushdie to controversy for the first time when it was banned in India for its unflattering portrayal of the then prime minister, Indira Gandhi. Rushdie's third novel, *Shame*, published in 1983, also incurred displeasure, this time of Pakistan's political establishment.

The publication of *The Satanic Verses* in 1988 dramatically altered Rushdie's life and triggered a passionate debate in the media and international literary circles about the limits of free speech and religious tolerance. The novel, which won Rushdie a Whitbread Award, weaves a complex tale around the birth of a religion resembling Islam, whose chief proponent, Mahound, is broadly modelled on the character of the Prophet Mohammad. Muslims were outraged, regarding its representation of Islam and its Prophet as insulting and blasphemous. Angry protests erupted in the UK, where Muslims burned the book on the streets of Bradford. Across Asia, Africa and the Middle East there were violent demonstrations, and several deaths, as governments hastened to ban the novel.

On 14 February 1989 Iran's spiritual leader, Ayatollah Ruhollah Khomeini, issued a religious edict (*fatwa*) declaring the novel blasphemous and sentencing Rushdie and his publishers to death. The Iranian charity, the Khordad Foundation simultaneously offered a "bounty" of US$1 million for the taking of Rushdie's life, later raised to US$2.8 million.

Within hours Rushdie went into hiding and many bookshops across Europe and the USA removed all their copies of *The Satanic Verses* from display. The British government, which granted Rushdie special protection, severed diplomatic ties with Iran in protest against the *fatwa*, while writers and artists rallied to his cause. A protracted campaign for his right to publish was co-ordinated by the London-based anti-censorship organisation Article 19. After Khomeini's death in June 1989, however, his successor **Ayatollah Ali Khamenei** reiterated the decree. Several attacks in the early 1990s relating to the *fatwa* (which asked all Muslims to execute "the author...and all those involved in its publication who were aware of its content") included the killing of the Italian translator of *The Satanic Verses*; the novel's Japanese translator and Norwegian publisher were also seriously injured.

Rushdie sought to appease his Muslim critics by making a statement, entitled *In Good Faith* (1990), in which he declared his intention "to enter into the body of Islam after a lifetime spent outside it". Neither this statement, nor intense diplomatic efforts by the UK and the European Union to persuade Iran to withdraw the *fatwa*, had any effect on successive Iranian governments, which maintained that the *fatwa* was an immutable religious edict.

It was not until May 1997, when the election of Iranian President Mohammad Khatami introduced a distinctly more liberal regime, that the prospects improved for an end to the affair. Iranian officials indicated the following year that they would not sanction any assassination plan against Rushdie, and on 24 September 1998 Iranian Foreign Minister Kamal Kharrazi confirmed in a meeting with his British counterpart Robin Cook that the Iranian government had formally dissociated itself from Khomeini's 1989 *fatwa*.

On 25 September Rushdie emerged from hiding, declaring that "it means everything, it means freedom", and saying that he had no regrets about *The Satanic Verses*, while acknowledging that during his years in hiding "there were times when I attempted to compromise, when I said things that weren't true. I'm not a religious person and I shouldn't have said that I'd rediscovered religion."

It soon became clear, however, that he needed to retain his security arrangements and that his life was still under threat from Muslims worldwide unwilling to repudiate Khomeini's death sentence. Many Iranian clerics continued to regard the *fatwa* as valid, and in October 1998 the Khordad Foundation announced a further increase in the "bounty" on offer for carrying it out.

While in hiding Rushdie published several critically acclaimed novels and essays, including a book for children, *Haroun and the Sea of Stories* (1990), *Imaginary Homelands: Essays and Criticism* (1991) and the novel *The Moor's Last Sigh* (1995). A new novel, *The Ground Beneath Her Feet*, appeared in 1999.

Rushdie has been married three times; in 1975 to Clarissa Luard (the mother of his elder son); in 1988 to the American author Marianne Wiggins, and in 1998 to his third wife, whose identity was not made public to ensure her safety under the *fatwa*, and with whom he has one son.

Jacques **Santer**

Jacques Santer is a classic case of a political figure influential because he occupied a significant office during a key period, rather than because of his achievements or personal attributes. Likeable and conciliatory, he was plucked from the premiership of Luxembourg in 1995 as a compromise candidate for a sensitive European Union (EU) post as president of the Commission. He worked unobtrusively wherever possible to bring the European single currency project to fruition, but had no major initiatives to his name when his term was brought to a premature end in 1999 and was ultimately disgraced by failure to tackle the problem of fraud within the EU bureaucracy. Santer's Commission touched a low point in public esteem and political clout, although he himself retained the backing of his colleagues in national politics.

Jacques Santer was born on 18 May 1937 in Wasserbillig in Luxembourg. He completed his secondary education at the Athénée de Luxembourg before going to study law in France, at the universities of Strasbourg and Paris. Having completed his doctorate, he obtained the certificate of the Institute of Political Science in Paris, and in 1961 became a barrister at the court of appeal in Luxembourg, where he remained until 1965. He is married to Danièle Binot and they have two sons.

His first involvement with government came at the age of only 26, as attaché to the minister for labour and social security, from which he moved on two years later for a brief spell as government attaché. For several years thereafter, he was occupied mainly with his role in the centre-right Christian Social Party (PSC), of which he was successively parliamentary secretary (1966–72), secretary-general (1972–74), and president (1974–82).

He briefly held government office as secretary of state for cultural and social affairs (1972–74). His party was out of power between 1974 and 1979, although he himself held a seat in the national parliament during this period and was an alderman of the city of Luxembourg for three years from 1976. Santer also became a member of the Strasbourg-based European Parliament (MEP) for the first time in 1975, and his three successive terms as an MEP introduced him to a wider stage than the national politics of his own small country. (He was a vice-president of the European Parliament between 1975 and 1977, and in 1987, towards the end of his time in Strasbourg, was chosen to head the European People's Party, the coalition of MEPs from Christian Democratic and Christian Social parties.)

The PSC's return to government after the 1979 Luxembourg general election saw Santer take up the post of minister for finance, labour and social security. Having been chosen to succeed Pierre Werner as PSC leader at the party conference in December 1983, Santer was then the automatic choice to be asked to form a government when the party retained its position as the largest in parliament at the June 1984 general election. In his first cabinet, a coalition with the socialists sworn in on 20 July, he himself retained the finance portfolio as well as holding that of communications.

Santer retained office after the 1989 elections, this time taking on the treasury and cultural affairs portfolios in addition to the premiership. He had just begun a third term when the European Council, the 12 heads of government of the European Union (EU) countries, chose him in July 1994 as a compromise candidate to be president of the European Commission. He had meanwhile picked up experience of international organisations as a governor of the World Bank (1984–89), the International Monetary Fund (1989–94) and the European Bank for Reconstruction and Development (1991–94). He had also had two six-month spells as holder of the rotating presidency of the European Council, in his capacity as prime minister of Luxembourg, in the second half of 1985 and the first half of 1991 – coinciding with two major agreements on European integration, the creation of the single market and the Maastricht Treaty on European Union.

Despite being one of the longer-established heads of government, the Luxembourg prime minister was understandably described as having been "plucked from obscurity" to head the European Commission. He brought to his new task a personality in marked contrast to his dynamic predecessor **Jacques Delors**, who had been the source of successive radical initiatives in the building of an integrated Europe. Affable, self-effacing and schooled in the politics of coalition-building, Santer's skills lay in conciliation and the arts of compromise. His nomination was backed by UK Prime Minister John Major as a more acceptable option than Belgian Prime Minister Jean-Luc Dehaene. In practice, the differences were more symbolic than substantial. Major vetoed Dehaene as unacceptably wedded to a federalist vision of Europe, which he abhorred because of the threat he perceived to national sovereignty. The Santer version placed less emphasis on the centralisation of powers at the EU level, stressing instead that federalism also meant decentralisation and the principle of "subsidiarity", the taking of decisions at the lowest appropriate level of authority.

Santer's candidacy for a five-year term (from January 1995) was endorsed by the European Council at a special meeting on 15 July 1994. It was confirmed, albeit only by a slim majority, by the European Parliament later that month, and he and his new Commission took office on 23 January 1995. Santer's main contribution in his first four years in office was to help steer through the completion of the Maastricht Treaty review process. This duly reached its culmination in 1999 with the introduction of the European single currency, and the entry into force of the Treaty of Amsterdam, redrawing the distribution of powers among EU institutions.

Santer's Commission, however, had meanwhile become engulfed in crisis over accusations that fraud had gone unchecked, within two of the Commission's directorates-general in particular. A vote in the European Parliament on the censure of the Commission as a whole (there being no institutional mechanism to challenge individual commissioners) was only narrowly rejected on 14 January 1999. Faced with the refusal of the most tarnished commissioners to resign, and prevaricating over referring their cases to the European Court of Justice, Santer eventually bowed to the growing demands for a fundamental reform and agreed to leave office without completing his full five-year term. On 17 March 1999 the Commission announced that "we have resigned and we have neither the desire nor the intention to remain in office a moment longer than is necessary", although all remained in a managerial capacity pending the choice of a new president and Commission. Santer himself retained strong backing from the Luxembourg government and from his party, which placed him top of its list of candidates for the European Parliament elections of June 1999.

Gerhard **Schröder**

*Gerhard Schröder is the moderate leader of Germany's Social Democrats, heading a government coalition with the environmentalist Greens. He came to power at the 1998 election, ending **Helmut Kohl**'s 16 years as federal chancellor. Schröder completed his transition from radical young socialist to proponent of the "new centre" as head of the regional government in the northwest German* Land *(state) of Lower Saxony from 1990 to 1998. Ambitious, designer-suited and business-friendly, he is frequently cited with UK Prime Minister **Tony Blair** as representative of a new centrist politics in western Europe. Like Blair, he has left-wing critics in his own party, but he strengthened his position by taking over the party chairmanship in 1999.*

Schröder was obliged to leave school at the age of 14 and work as an apprentice in a china shop. He went to night school to gain his school-leaving certificate, going on to study law at the University of Göttingen, and financing his studies by working on a building site. He joined the Social Democratic Party of Germany (SPD) in 1963, and has been a member of the public service union ÖTV since 1973.

Upon qualifying he set up a legal practice in Hanover in 1978, and in the same year was elected chair of the Young Social Democrats ("Jusos"). He gained an early reputation as a radical firebrand, opposing the stationing of US nuclear weapons on West German soil, courting conservative criticism by appearing without a tie to deliver his maiden speech in the *Bundestag* (the lower house of the federal parliament, where he became a deputy on the SPD list in the October 1980 elections) and, in his law practice, defending former terrorists. A widely circulated – though possibly apocryphal – story told to illustrate Schröder's personal ambition describes him rattling the gates of the chancellor's residence in Bonn after a drinking spree, shortly after Helmut Kohl became federal chancellor in 1982, and shouting, "I want in there!"

Gerhard Fritz Kurt Schröder was born in Mossenberg near Detmold, Westphalia, on 7 April 1944. His father was killed a few days later as German troops withdrew from Romania. His mother Erika, a Protestant and staunch social democrat, did cleaning work to support him and his elder sister; she went on to have three more children by a second marriage.

Although still a *Bundestag* deputy until 1986, it was in regional politics in Lower Saxony that Schröder first really made his mark. In 1984 he was SPD candidate for minister president (i.e. regional head of government); two years later, in June 1986, he became a deputy in the regional parliament (*Landtag*), for which he had to give up his *Bundestag* seat; and he finally became minister president after the 1990 regional election by forming a "red–green" coalition with the environmentalist Greens.

During this period Schröder moved away from the radical stance of his early years in politics, alienating some on the left of his own party but cultivating broader contacts and, importantly, winning the confidence of key business figures. The conservative daily *Frankfurter Allgemeine Zeitung* wrote that he had "undergone an astonishing personality change" after coming to power in Lower Saxony. "The wounded aggressiveness of the opposition leader has become relaxed joviality, the stilted wish to impress has been replaced by the cool, governing style of an unassailable office holder." He dropped the Greens from government in Lower Saxony when the SPD gained a majority of one seat in the 1994 state election.

Although he joined the SPD presidium in 1989, he had an ambivalent relationship with the party apparatus and especially with his contemporaries and rivals: **Oskar Lafontaine**, the former minister president of Saarland who was later to become his minister of finance, and Rudolf Scharping, who was leader of the SPD group in the *Bundestag* and later became defence minister. By turning the tide of a run of poor party results in state elections, and winning 47.9 per cent of the vote and an absolute majority of seats in the Lower Saxony poll on 1 March 1998, Schröder demonstrated that he had the credentials to succeed at federal level, and he secured election the following day as the SPD candidate for chancellor.

The federal election on 27 September 1998 was Schröder's hour of triumph. As a proponent of the "new centre" he campaigned as a 1990s politician seeking a "Third Way" between old conservative and socialist values. Having determinedly made this move to the centre ground to gain electoral support, like his UK counterpart Tony Blair, he encountered criticism during the campaign from observers who questioned where the substance of his policies lay. His detractors portrayed him as a wheeler-dealer and telegenic showman, who had discarded his radical image in favour of centrist rhetoric, fashionable Italian designer clothes and a penchant for fine cigars and champagne. His image as a modern leader, however,

capable of both bold and pragmatic decisions and seeking to reconcile liberal capitalism with social values, appealed to an electorate which was eager for change after 16 years of Chancellor Kohl.

The SPD emerged from the 1998 elections as the largest party, but needed a coalition partner to command a majority in parliament. Schröder put together an agreement with the Greens, who thus entered the federal government for the first time. When Schröder's cabinet was formed in October, however, its image was immediately dented by the withdrawal of his most controversial and business-oriented nominee, computer entrepreneur Jost Stollmann, and by debate about the amount of power he had conceded to Lafontaine, the SPD chairman and standard-bearer of the left, as head of a new financial super-ministry.

In its first six months, the Schröder government had a rude awakening. Battered by disagreements with the Greens, particularly over phasing out nuclear power plants, the SPD suffered badly in state elections in Hesse in early 1999. Bigger drama followed when Lafontaine resigned, following disagreements about monetary issues within the new European single currency, about tax policy, and indeed about the overall direction the SPD was taking in government. Although many still regarded Lafontaine as representing the heart and soul of the party, Schröder assumed the SPD chairmanship himself; his formal election in April 1999 was unopposed, but, unusually, a quarter of the delegates still failed to back him.

Gerhard Schröder has had four marriages. The first, in 1968, was with librarian Eva Schubach, his childhood sweetheart. After leaving her he married schoolteacher Anne Taschenbach in 1971. He benefited during his rise to power from his partnership with his third wife, political scientist Hiltrud ("Hillu") Hampel, whom he married in 1984 and whose two daughters he helped to bring up. In early 1997 he married his fourth wife, the Bavarian journalist Doris Köpf, who also has a daughter.

Eduard **Shevardnadze**

*Among national leaders in post-communist countries who had also held high office under communism, Eduard Shevardnadze stands out. As Georgia's head of state since 1992 he is the pre-eminent statesman of that small and crisis-riven country. His international stature, however, derives from his role between 1985 and 1990 as Soviet foreign minister under **Mikhail Gorbachev**, helping to engineer the Soviet Union's withdrawal from the cold war arms race and from regional hegemony in eastern Europe. Once the police chief and head of the communist security apparatus in Georgia, by the mid-1990s he was showing visible signs of fatigue, but no sign of relinquishing office. Since independence he has once come under artillery fire and twice been targeted by assassination attempts arising from Georgia's internal divisions. Condemned by opponents for a pro-Russian line which he regards as simply an acknowledgement of political realities, he has nevertheless on occasion been a bitter critic of interference by Russia, Georgia's overbearing northern neighbour.*

Eduard Amvrosiyevich Shevardnadze was born on 25 January 1928, the son of a teacher in the village of Mamat in the Lanchkhuti region of Georgia not far from the Black Sea. Heavily involved in youth work and as a teacher and activist in the Komsomol, the communist youth league, he became first secretary of the Komsomol at republic level in Georgia in 1957. Two years later he was first elected to the Supreme Soviet in the republic, and also in 1959 completed a correspondence degree in history at the Kutaisi Pedagogical Institute. A devoted family man, Shevardnadze and his wife Nanuli had one son and one daughter, and later became proud grandparents.

Drafted into the civilian police (MVD) in Georgia, Shevardnadze began to make a name for himself as head of the republic's ministry of public order from 1965 onwards, tackling both unrest and corruption, and clamping down on self-enrichment by government and party officials. He was promoted to minister of the interior and, from 1972, became first secretary of the Georgian communist party. He held this post, the top leadership position in Georgia under Soviet rule, for over a decade and was noted among other things for a relatively sympathetic attitude towards Jews seeking to emigrate to Israel.

Shevardnadze was a member of the central committee of the Communist Party of the Soviet Union (CPSU) from 1976. However, his rapid elevation at central level in 1985, to the CPSU politburo and simultaneously to the post of foreign minister, despite his lack of experience in foreign affairs or central government, came as a result of his political association and growing personal friendship with the new party general secretary Mikhail Gorbachev.

Over the next five years Shevardnadze worked as Gorbachev's right-hand man in transforming Soviet foreign relations. Beginning with the bilateral Soviet–US summits of 1985 and 1986, the new Soviet leadership backed away progressively from the economically ruinous effort to sustain the superpower rivalry of the cold war. Soviet troops had pulled out of Afghanistan by 1989, while a series of agreements on arms control and arms reduction coincided with a loosening of the Soviet grip on what had been the communist bloc. The crowds who welcomed the collapse of communism across the countries of central and eastern Europe hailed Shevardnadze, like Gorbachev, as a hero of democratisation.

At home, however, Shevardnadze felt the growing danger of a military and hardline backlash. Resigning as foreign minister in December 1990, he delivered a dramatic speech warning that "dictatorship is coming", and the August 1991 Moscow coup attempt proved his warnings justified. Joining in efforts to rally support for Gorbachev, he returned briefly to the post of Soviet foreign minister as the Soviet Union was disintegrating in 1991.

He returned in March 1992 to newly independent Georgia, where open conflict between nationalist factions was threatening to destroy a country that was already in serious economic disarray. Appointed within four days as chairman of a military-dominated State Council, he was pitched into a period of overt conflict with the ousted former president Zviad Gamsakhurdia and more seriously with secessionists in Abkhazia, which bordered Russia on the Black Sea coast. On 11 October 1992, he was elected chairman of the parliament of Georgia, and a referendum endorsed him as head of state and commander-in-chief of the armed forces. Under a new constitution three years later, the office of president was reintroduced, with executive powers, and Shevardnadze was elected for a five-year term in a nationwide ballot on 5 November 1995. He won more than three-quarters of the votes cast, ahead of the former communist party first secretary and four minor candidates, and welcomed the outcome as showing that "democracy and reforms have triumphed". Shevardnadze is also chair of the Citizens' Union, which he founded in 1993 as a pro-democracy and free-market-oriented alliance with a strong environmentalist element, and which won a large majority in the November/December 1995 legislative elections.

Meanwhile, the threat of the disintegration of Georgia remained Shevardnadze's most acute and recurring problem. In February 1994 he and Russian President **Boris Yeltsin** signed a treaty of friendship and co-operation, especially controversial in that it allowed for the continuing existence of Russian military bases on Georgian soil. His pro-Russian line, and his decision to take Georgia into the Russian-dominated Commonwealth of Independent States (CIS), reflected his perception of how vulnerable Georgia's position had become, especially after rebel forces gained the upper hand in the northern separatist republic of Abkhazia (where he himself came under heavy shelling during one visit).

The stabilisation of the Abkhazia situation, with a Russian-backed ceasefire in March 1994 and the presence of a Russian-dominated international peacekeeping force thereafter, still left the issue of what to do about a flood of ethnic Georgian refugees. Meanwhile the country faced economic problems so severe that Shevardnadze was forced to announce unpopular food rationing measures. Over the next few years, however, he began to be able to claim some success in tackling chronic instability, although there were renewed flare-ups of the conflict with Abkhazia, and other separatist struggles in other parts of the country. Shevardnadze's own life remains under threat from would-be assassins, his regime having struggled to control the private armies of various nationalist leaders. In August 1995 he survived a car bombing in Tbilisi, and a second attempt was made to kill him in February 1998. Brittle signs of the beginning of economic recovery were damaged in 1998 by drought and a currency crisis, but the long-heralded opening in April 1999 of a pipeline to take oil from the Caspian Sea across Georgia to the Black Sea brought a promise of substantial and much-needed revenue to Shevardnadze's beleaguered government.

King **Sihanouk**

King Norodom Sihanouk has been Cambodia's head of state since the 1991 UN-sponsored peace agreement, having spent the 1980s as head of an anti-Vietnamese coalition government in exile. Elderly, ill, and at odds with the government of rival faction leader Hun Sen, he nevertheless retains significance as a durable expression of Cambodian national identity. Few political careers can have encompassed so much upheaval, but his readiness to see events in a long-term perspective has helped preserve his unique influence. First crowned king at 18, under French colonial administration, he subsequently went into exile as a national figure campaigning for independence, and returned to lead Cambodia along the path of non-alignment. Ousted in a US-backed coup in 1970, he allied himself with Chinese-backed communist insurgents, but was effectively a prisoner of their murderous Khmer Rouge regime between 1975 and 1979.

Norodom Sihanouk was born on 31 October 1922 in Phnom Penh, the capital of Cambodia. The country was at that time under French colonial rule as part of Indochina, and the young prince's early education was in Paris. He returned to Indochina to attend secondary school in Saigon in Vietnam, and later also received military training in France.

Upon the death of his grandfather, Sihanouk was proclaimed king of Cambodia, for the first time, on 26 April 1941. The Vichy government in France supported this choice, anticipating that his inexperience and reputation for high living would make him easy to manipulate. However, Sihanouk proved to be no mere jazz-loving playboy but a subtle and astute political operator, and increasingly significant as a national independence leader. In 1953/54 he mounted a protest against French rule by going into exile, returning only when independence was achieved. By abdicating the throne in favour of his father in 1955 he freed himself to play an unfettered political role. Retaining the title of prince, he effectively controlled internal affairs through his political movement *Sangkum*, while holding office as prime minister and minister of foreign affairs until 1956, and then ambassador at the UN. On his father's death in 1960 he became once again head of state, but he declined to take up the title of king.

A participant at the founding conference of the Non-aligned Movement in Belgrade in 1961, Sihanouk demonstrated great skill in getting aid from both superpowers at the height of the cold war, but ultimately was unable to keep Cambodia isolated from the region's dominant confrontation, the Vietnam war. The US government suspected him of complicity with the North Vietnamese and of allowing them the use of Cambodian territory, and in 1970 he was driven into exile by Lon Nol's US-backed right-wing military coup. Controversially, as Cambodia was being shattered in what the US military cynically regarded as a "sideshow" to their Vietnam war, Sihanouk then allied himself with the Cambodian communist *Khmers Rouges*. Concluding a national unity front agreement (FUNK) in Beijing, he became a figurehead in their insurgency, and was named head of state of Democratic Kampuchea when they took control of Phnom Penh in 1975. Virtually a prisoner in the royal palace, however, Sihanouk resigned the following year, finding to his enduring shame that he had no power to restrain the **Pol Pot** government's genocidal policies. Among perhaps 1–2 million Cambodians killed by the *Khmers Rouges* were five of Sihanouk's own children.

Sihanouk managed to flee in 1979 when the *Khmers Rouges* were ousted by intervention from Vietnam. He spent the next decade in exile, living mainly in Beijing and in the North Korean capital Pyongyang. The *Khmers Rouges*, driven out of Phnom Penh, struck back at the new regime from border areas, in uneasy alliance with non-communist guerrillas. To Sihanouk, the Vietnamese domination of his country was so great an evil that he was tempted back into the expediency of alliance with the *Khmers Rouges* once again. Accordingly, if reluctantly, he agreed in 1982 to join a tripartite anti-Vietnamese coalition, the so-called "Coalition Government of Democratic Kampuchea" (CGDK). The exile government over which he presided received wide international recognition, with Western backing, notwithstanding the fact that the *Khmers Rouges* were militarily its strongest element.

During this period Sihanouk worked to build up the credibility of his own guerrilla forces, founding a National United Front for an Independent, Neutral, Peaceful and Co-operative Kampuchea (known by its French acronym as Funcinpec). In 1989 the CGDK was superseded by a so-called "National Government of Cambodia", with Sihanouk again its president.

In 1991 a UN-brokered peace accord was concluded between the three anti-Vietnamese factions and the Hun Sen government in Phnom Penh, Vietnam having pulled its forces out in 1989. Sihanouk took on the presidency of a new Supreme National Council (SNC) of Cambodia, and elections went ahead in 1993 despite a *Khmer Rouge* withdrawal from the peace process. The June polls were dominated by Sihanouk's royalist supporters on the one hand, and the former Phnom Penh government led by Hun Sen on the other, an outcome which Sihanouk recognised in putting together a power-sharing agreement between them. This formula created a joint premiership between Hun Sen and Sihanouk's son Prince Norodom Ranariddh. (Sihanouk has married six times and has fathered, by his count, 14 children.) A vote in the parliament approved a proposal to restore the monarchy, and Sihanouk thus became king once again, on 24 September 1993.

Suspecting that royalists were promoting reconciliation with the remaining *Khmer Rouge* rebels to tilt the balance of power, Hun Sen in mid-1997 tightened his own grip in what was effectively a coup, driving out Ranariddh and naming a replacement himself. King Sihanouk's response was equivocal, neither outright condemnation nor acquiescence. He was by now old and ill, a distant figure living mainly in Beijing, and once again his behaviour reflected his appreciation of the realities of power. Remaining aloof from the political fray as Hun Sen pushed through with the holding of elections in July 1998, he then offered to mediate to resolve the post-election stalemate, and managed to broker a deal which eventually led to a renewed coalition government.

O.J. Simpson

O. J. Simpson, a former American football star turned broadcaster and one of the USA's most widely liked and admired celebrities, became in 1994 the central figure of a case which held public attention and divided the country on racial lines for years – his extraordinarily high-profile arrest for the murder of his former wife and a friend, his trial in the full glare of live television coverage, the controversial acquittal in October 1995, and the subsequent civil court case which, contradicting this acquittal, found him liable for the two deaths. While the trial highlighted complex social attitudes to the relationship between a successful black man and a much younger white woman, the lasting significance of the O. J. Simpson affair was the doubts it cast on the ability of the US justice system to command respect for impartiality, when events and circumstances were perceived so differently by different racial groups.

Orenthal James Simpson was born in San Francisco on 9 July 1947, the third of four children of Jimmie Lee and Eunice Durden Simpson. Raised in the "projects" of Petrero Hill, a mainly black neighbourhood of high-density housing, he joined a local gang at 13, spending a weekend in youth custody when he was 15, but his mother Eunice was the strongest influence in his upbringing,

encouraging him to persevere at Galileo High School, where he excelled in most sports. Just before his 20th birthday in 1967 he got married for the first time, to his high-school sweetheart Marguerite Whitley; they had three children, one of whom drowned in early childhood in an accident at a swimming pool. Their marriage ended in separation in 1978. Meanwhile Simpson, by now a major sports celebrity and a millionaire, had met his future second wife Nicole Brown, who had recently graduated from high school and was waitressing in a restaurant in Beverly Hills. Simpson and Nicole Brown married in February 1985; they had one daughter and one son, in 1985 and 1988, but separated and divorced in 1992.

Simpson's career was based on his success as a running back in American football, first as a college athlete at the University of Southern California, where he won selection as an All-American in 1967 and 1968 and took the Heisman Trophy as best player in 1968, and then during 11 seasons in the professional game. The first college athlete picked in the professional draft in 1969, by the National Football League team the Buffalo Bills, Simpson became best known by his initials, O.J., and the resulting nickname "the Juice". He set records as the first player to rush for a total of more than 2,000 yards in a single season (1973) and the scorer of most touchdowns in one season (23 in 1975). He played for the Buffalo Bills until 1978, when he moved back to the West Coast and played two seasons with the San Francisco 49ers, retiring because of injuries at the end of the 1979 season.

While playing football, Simpson paved the way for his subsequent media career, with appearances in films such as *The Towering Inferno* (1974) and *The*

Cassandra Crossing (1977), and in advertising campaigns for a wide range of products. He went on to act in the phenomenally successful television series *Roots*, achieved further film stardom in the *Naked Gun* series, and became a highly successful sports broadcaster. His fame and across-the-board popularity made him a frequently cited role model for young African–Americans and an example of the success of racial integration.

In June 1994, national celebrity turned to international notoriety. On 13 June, Los Angeles police discovered the bodies of Nicole Brown Simpson and Ronald Goldman, a friend who worked at the fashionable Mezzaluna restaurant where she had eaten that evening. Both had been stabbed to death at her house. That same night Simpson boarded a plane from Los Angeles to Chicago. A week later, and one day after attending Nicole's funeral, Simpson apparently agreed to surrender to police for questioning, but then changed his mind. He left his Los Angeles mansion by car, but was followed by police. As the news spread, his fans stood by the road shouting encouragement during an extraordinary slow-speed "chase", shown live on television, until Simpson finally returned home and gave himself up.

The O.J. Simpson murder trial was the media event of 1995. Starting that January, it received massive coverage and went out daily on live US television. Judge Lance Ito, the prosecution team led by Marcia Clark, O.J. Simpson's so-called "dream team" of expensive lawyers including Robert Shapiro and Johnnie Cochran, and a range of witnesses all became personalities known to the avid viewers.

The prosecution produced material and forensic evidence connecting Simpson's shoes, clothes, gloves and vehicle with the crime, backed up by evidence from witnesses, including police and neighbours. The trial also trawled through the history of Simpson's marriage to Nicole and incidents before and since

their separation, stressing that Simpson had been convicted of spousal abuse in 1989, when he was placed on probation and ordered to do community service and attend battery counselling sessions. Ultimately, however, the outcome turned on whether the jury (of whom 9 out of 12 were black) was affected by the defence's portrayal of the case as prejudiced by racism. Simpson's prestigious social circle was mainly white, his lifestyle hardly that of a disadvantaged African–American despite his Petrero Hill childhood. Nevertheless, the media reported that most whites believed him guilty of murder, while three-quarters of blacks believed him an innocent victim of prejudice. Cochran made much of exposing racist attitudes in some of the police witnesses. He dwelt in particular on one officer's reputed hatred of mixed-race marriages epitomised by that of Simpson and the blonde-haired younger white woman Nicole Brown.

In October 1995 the jury brought in a controversial verdict of not guilty, and Simpson was released from custody. Incensed that he should walk free, the Brown and Goldman families brought a civil suit, which resulted on 4 February 1997 in the finding that Simpson was indeed liable for the two deaths. He was ordered to pay the families of the two victims US$33.5 million in damages.

Simpson's creditors forced the sale of his mansion in the exclusive Los Angeles suburb of Brentwood (the house was demolished in July 1998), and the auctioning of other assets and sports trophies. Simpson continues to live comfortably on a substantial pension, making appearances on the amateur and celebrity golf tournament circuit, and still maintaining his innocence. His public comments, notably on television programmes such as the celebrity showcase *Ruby Wax Meets...* in 1998, shed no further light on the affair, which has fuelled a publishing spree with some 60 books offering different slants on Simpson's character and theories on the murders.

George **Soros**

The world's best-known currency speculator, the Hungarian-born and US-based international fund manager George Soros has recently become an outspoken critic of the unfettered operation of the global capital markets on which he made his massive fortune. Despite his professorial manner and his claim to be most interested in abstract philosophical ideas such as "reflexivity", it is his canny timing and ability to understand market movements that have formed the basis of his success. Normally urbane and charming, he has proven outspoken in criticising both the Malaysian government and Russian "oligarchs" for their role in exacerbating recent financial crises in those two countries, and robust in defending the propriety of his involvement in such speculative coups as the run on the UK pound in 1992 which forced sterling out of the European exchange rate mechanism. Since he drew back from hands-on fund management in the late 1980s, he has devoted considerable resources to projects designed to build civil society in the former communist world.

George Soros was born in Budapest, Hungary, in 1930, the son of an educated middle-class Hungarian Jewish couple; his father was a lawyer. At the age of 14 he and his family were forced to go into hiding when the Nazis invaded Hungary, signalling the imminent beginning of a policy of extermination towards Hungarian Jews. It was not until 1947, two years after the war had ended, that Soros finally

arrived in Britain, taking up a place to study at the London School of Economics where he was strongly influenced by the political philosopher Karl Popper. After graduating in 1950, he had a brief spell trying to sell holiday souvenirs in Wales before beginning work with merchant bankers Singer & Friedlander. In 1956, however, Soros emigrated to the USA, where he has lived ever since. His first marriage ended in divorce in 1979. He is now married to his second wife, the art magazine publisher Suzan Weber. He has five children, and homes in both Manhattan and London.

Soros's first international investment fund, the Quantum Fund, had its beginnings in 1957, shortly after he arrived in New York and began working on Wall Street, but Quantum was only registered in 1969, in Curaçao in the Netherlands Antilles. Since 1973 he has also been president of the New-York-based Soros Fund Management, and he has created several other specialist investment vehicles using the Quantum branding during the 1990s, such as Quantum Emerging Growth and Quantum Realty Trust.

The original Quantum Fund, like its many successors, has always based some of its investment decisions on an observation of financial market dynamics – rather than seeking primarily to determine the underlying economic fundamentals of any particular market, as most other funds would normally do. Soros showed that he would, in effect, be perfectly willing to back a losing scenario if he felt that he could realise a profit by selling on his holdings to another investor at the correct moment. Expressed simply, his strategy involved looking for information loopholes and inefficiencies in the financial markets and then arbitraging between them for short-term gain.

Soros was also an early exponent of what later became known as the contrarian school of investment. Contrarians held that markets would invariably reach a point during upward economic phases when they became irrationally overvalued, so that a wise investor should be selling off his holdings during those times; conversely, contrarians considered that profitable opportunities for buying could often be found during downward economic phases. Accordingly, at carefully selected moments, Soros would take up an extreme position which he would support using heavily leveraged financial instruments, including futures, options contracts and the increasingly popular leveraged bank finance facilities which characterised the markets of the 1970s and 1980s.

Soros's immediate successes were founded on his sharp personal perceptions of human behaviour, and on his willingness to take audacious risks. As his fame and influence started to spread in the 1980s and early 1990s, however, his prophecies also became self-fulfilling. Whenever Soros bought large volumes of a particular currency, for example, other traders would rush to buy that currency for themselves, believing that Soros must know something they did not. As the level of demand for the currency grew in the following days, it would inevitably strengthen and Soros's gamble would pay off. Despite several well-publicised failures, notably when he lost money on Wall Street's sharp downturn in 1987, he had become one of only a few investors in the world who could move markets by their own actions.

Conversely, a selling panic would often set in whenever Soros sold his holdings in a particular security. This was to make him a highly controversial figure in a number of countries, and to bring him hostile criticism from national governments which resented his detached and mathematical approach to investment. The excessive market power which he was seen as able to deploy was regarded by such critics as a dangerous distorting factor in the investment world.

He was, for example, vilified by the British press for having bet against sterling in 1992, a speculative coup which made him a personal gain of US$1 billion at the time. This involved selling sterling "short" on the currency markets – selling pounds which he did not hold, for future delivery, in the expectation of being able to buy in the necessary amount of sterling at a lower price to fulfil the sales contracts at the appointed time. The effect was to help start a financial stampede which led to a sharp drop in the pound and its withdrawal from the exchange rate mechanism (ERM) of the European Monetary System. On a subsequent occasion, in 1997, Soros was openly blamed by Malaysia's prime minister **Mahathir Mohamed** for allegedly instigating the Asian crisis of confidence by withdrawing money from east Asia in order to invest it in Russia. His own analysis of the Asian financial crisis and its implications was published in late 1998 under the title *The Crisis of Global Communism*; it attracted attention by calling for more restrictions on the kind of speculative international capital movements which he himself exploited so adroitly.

Soros's Russian investments in the late 1990s, however, proved to be his most costly failure so far. Having personally placed some US$20 billion of his Quantum Fund's money in Russian investments during early 1998, Soros alarmed the markets in August 1998 by calling publicly for a 15–25 per cent devaluation of the rouble in order, he said, to restore the balance in Russian trade. Affected by an evaporation of confidence, in an already highly volatile international investment market, the rouble plunged in value by around 65 per cent, tipping the Russian economy into immediate crisis, and Soros was personally believed to have lost up to US$3 billion in the panic.

His losses in Russia appeared particularly ironic in view of his own long-standing commitment to the revival of free-market economies and the building of civil society in central and eastern Europe and the former Soviet Union. Using vehicles such as the Open Society Fund (set up in 1979) and the Soros Foundations, he was increasingly involved throughout the 1980s in projects to promote the flow of information, to support scientific research, to provide scholarships for study in the West and to encourage pluralist institution-building wherever possible within communist societies. He was thus among the first to realise that the collapse of communism between 1989 and 1991 offered mutual opportunities and social-political challenges to both East and West. In addition to such high-profile donations as the US$50 million he gave to the UN for refugee work in Sarajevo in 1992, he has donated over US$1.5 billion through a variety of educational and philanthropic trusts and foundations to projects in the region. Two of his books, *Opening the Soviet System* (1990) and *Underwriting Democracy* (1991), reflect his commitment to this aspect of his work, whereas *Soros on Soros: Staying Ahead of the Curve* (1995) and his earlier book *The Alchemy of Finance* (1987) are primarily about the financial world. At home in the USA he has also been active in supporting social projects involving drug education, poverty, criminal rehabilitation, welfare of immigrants and civil rights.

Steven **Spielberg**

The Hollywood film director and producer Steven Spielberg has become the top-earning and most powerful creative figure in an industry which worships success, and whose products are the dominant cultural artefacts of the era. Over the course of some 25 years Spielberg has had a string of major hits with films including Jaws, Jurassic Park, Schindler's List *and* Saving Private Ryan. *His record of commercial triumphs has enabled him to turn in succession to various themes of real gravity, without losing his sureness of touch in packaging them for further box office success. In 1994 he played a major part in setting up a new Hollywood studio, Dreamworks, in a bid to return more control to the creative side of the film industry.*

Steven Spielberg was born on 18 December 1947, in Cincinnati, Ohio, USA. His father Arnold was an electrical engineer, and his mother Leah a concert pianist. Steven preferred watching television to schoolwork, and developed his passion for cinema after seeing Cecil B. DeMille's epic, *The Greatest Story Ever Told*, when he was four. He would often startle his younger sisters with pranks – a flair for the dramatic which later germinated into some of the best-loved films of all time.

The Spielberg family moved home several times, to New Jersey and Arizona, ending up in Saratoga, California. Steven Spielberg's aptitude for filming first emerged when he shot family home movies. Between the ages of 12 and 18, he also made 15 short amateur films, including one two-hour science fiction epic. Unable to get the necessary grades for film school, he studied English at California State College, Long Beach.

He first bluffed his way on to the Universal Studios set in 1965, spending as much time as he could getting experience of how filming and editing was done there. He became the youngest director to get a long-term contract with a major Hollywood studio when he was officially hired by their television department in 1969 on the strength of a 24-minute short called *Amblin'*, which won numerous festival prizes and supported the popular *Love Story* in mainstream cinemas. Spielberg cut his teeth directing television slots for *Night Gallery*, *The Psychiatrists*, *Columbo* and *Marcus Welby MD*.

Spielberg's first success under his own name was *Duel*, initially released for television in 1971. A gripping tale of a travelling salesman hounded by a demonic

truck, *Duel* was praised as worthy of Alfred Hitchcock – despite its low budget, simple plot and unknown cast. Three years later, Spielberg released his first full-length cinematic feature, *The Sugarland Express*.

It was *Jaws* (1975) which ensured him international fame. Based on a story about a man-eating shark, *Jaws* showed Spielberg's ruthlessly tight editing skills to best effect. It cost US$8.5 million to make, yet grossed US$130 million at its first US release, breaking all previous box office records. Its success gave Spielberg, still only 28, much more freedom to choose among projects and prospective collaborators in Hollywood. Two years later he directed another blockbuster, *Close Encounters of the Third Kind*. Superficially about visiting aliens, it subtly criticised contemporary American values, a theme to which Spielberg would return in later films.

A first attempt at comedy, entitled *1941* and released in 1979, proved less successful. Two years later he directed *Raiders of the Lost Ark*, a fast-paced adventure which skilfully mixed technical wizardry with good old-fashioned storytelling. *Raiders* won Spielberg his second Oscar nomination for best director, and spawned a series of Spielberg films featuring the hero Indiana Jones (played by Harrison Ford).

In 1982 Spielberg created what many call his masterpiece, *ET – The Extra-Terrestrial*. Its heart-tugging tale of a child befriending a lost alien appealed to all ages, and *ET* grossed more at the box office than any previous film. Apart from its brilliant special effects, *ET* was also an intensely personal creation. As Spielberg admitted: "I am 34 and I haven't really grown up". He explained in one interview that he had the idea of an extra-terrestrial character becoming a child's special friend when thinking back to his own emotional needs when his parents were splitting up (they divorced in 1966).

The Color Purple, released in 1985, marked a new departure. An adaptation of Alice Walker's novel, it addressed fundamental and serious issues – racism, lesbianism and wife-beating – and many in the film industry believed that Spielberg was over-reaching himself. Audience reaction proved them wrong. The film took US$100 million in ticket sales, and launched the careers of Whoopi Goldberg and **Oprah Winfrey**. In more lighthearted vein, Spielberg's Amblin Entertainment company produced *Back to the Future* (1985), an escapist science fiction yarn which posed the intriguing question whether, by travelling back in time, it would become possible to change history. *Who Framed*

Roger Rabbit? (1988), which cleverly blended real actors with cartoon characters, was another success for Amblin Entertainment.

By the mid-1980s Spielberg was producing more and directing less. *Empire of the Sun* (1987), another adaptation (from a J.G. Ballard novel) this time done in collaboration with British playwright Tom Stoppard, saw Spielberg again adopting a child's-eye view. But the film's themes – British colonialism, Japanese totalitarianism and the horrors of war – were far from escapist. For some years thereafter Spielberg seemed to mark time, making cartoon and adventure series for television, and *Hook* (1991), a quirky update of the Peter Pan story. Then in 1993 he released two epochal although highly contrasting films.

Jurassic Park, a fantasy about dinosaurs restored to life from fossil DNA, cost US$70 million to make, yet grossed almost a billion dollars in cinemas. However, it was *Schindler's List* which at last established Spielberg as a "serious" director, capable of restrained and sensitive handling of profound moral issues. Shot on location in Poland and based on the Thomas Keneally novel *Schindler's Ark*, it allowed Spielberg to draw on his own Jewish identity, telling the true story of a German industrialist who defied his Nazi colleagues to rescue Jews from the Holocaust. *Schindler's List* won seven Academy awards, including Spielberg's first Oscar for best director.

In October 1994 Steven Spielberg, together with former Disney executive Jeffrey Katzenberg and film and music mogul David Geffen, raised US$2.7 billion to establish the first new Hollywood studio in 65 years. Dreamworks SKG aimed to garner a pool of talent spanning cinema, television, video games, CD-ROMs and the Internet. To some, it symbolised a victory of "artists" over "suits" (i.e. commercially minded executives). However, Dreamworks lacked the established studios' powerful distribution networks and was forced into joint ventures, product tie-ins and revenue sharing. Initial releases – *The Peacemaker, Paulie* and the slavery drama, *Amistad* – proved financially disappointing. By 1998, however, Spielberg had restored his reputation with the Second World War epic, *Saving Private Ryan* – for which he won his second Oscar as best director – and two path-setting cartoon features, *Prince of Egypt* and *Antz*.

Steven Spielberg has directed, produced or executive-produced eight of the top-grossing films of all time. Some critics call his works mawkish, manipulative, formulaic or patronising, but most agree they will stand the test of time. In the "Celebrity 100" listings produced by *Forbes* magazine covering 1998, he ranked third in terms of earnings (US$175 million, behind only Jerry Seinfeld and his co-writer Larry David) and fifth in terms of "buzz factor" or media attention. Commercial considerations aside, he has set new landmarks for cinematic lighting, photography and special effects, and has broached topics that other Hollywood directors had shunned, like the Holocaust and slavery. Spielberg's films feature recurring themes, which possibly reflect his own somewhat mythologised life story – childhood loneliness, the problems of parenthood, and the triumph of imagination over establishment perspectives. A fundamentally private person, he can be dictatorial on set, but also encourages others' ideas. He married for the first time in 1985, to the actress Amy Irving, with whom he had one son. This marriage ended in 1989, and two years later he married Kate Capshaw, also an actress, with whom he has had one child and adopted others from different ethnic backgrounds.

Suharto

Gen. Suharto ruled Indonesia for over 30 years. An army officer whose career dated back to the pre-1949 struggle for independence, he emerged gradually as the key figure in the armed forces leadership which took over in 1965/66. Polite, formal and soft-spoken, autocratic in style, and a shrewd operator behind a public image of simplicity, Suharto was an enigma to the outside world. He faced sustained criticism internationally over the brutal annexation of East Timor, the former Portuguese colony occupied by Indonesian forces in 1975, and the forcible suppression of separatist opposition there and in Aceh and Irian Jaya. Until the latter part of the 1990s, however, Suharto's regime was generally thought to be delivering economic success. The 1997 economic crisis exposed the shallow roots of the Indonesian boom and its rampant "cronyism", the manipulation of rules and contracts to benefit his family and friends. The strength of feeling against Suharto became apparent in massive demonstrations which brought about his rapid fall from power.

Thojib N. J. Suharto was born on 8 June 1921 in Kemuju near Jogjakarta, on the island of Java, into a peasant family of tenant farmers. One of 11 children, he left school in his early teens, and by 18 had enlisted in the colonial Royal Dutch Indies Army. During the Second World War the Japanese encouraged the growth of Indonesian nationalism and sponsored the formation of an Indonesian

guerrilla army to fight the Dutch, in which Suharto became a commander. Pursuing the nationalist and anti-colonial struggle after the end of the Second World War, he distinguished himself by leading an attack on Dutch forces occupying Jogjakarta, shortly before independence in 1949. His career flourished in the post-independence Indonesian army; by the mid-1950s he was commanding central Java's Diponegoro division, and in 1962/63, promoted to the rank of major-general, he led the campaign to wrest Irian Jaya from the Dutch. He was then called to the capital, Jakarta, and placed in charge of the low-profile army strategic reserve.

Having apparently fallen out with the top armed forces leadership over business dealings, Suharto was not included in a "death list" of those at the centre of power whom communist insurgents planned to assassinate in their abortive October 1965 coup attempt. He led the forces who retook control of strategic locations in the capital, and soon emerged as the key figure in the military leadership which effectively sidelined President Sukarno. The communist threat was ruthlessly eliminated in a nationwide purge costing many hundreds of thousands of lives.

On 11 March 1966 Sukarno formally handed executive powers to Gen. Suharto in the so-called "Supersemar" decree, a play on the Indonesian words for 11 March Order and the name Semar, the legendary founding father of the Javanese. Suharto consciously identified himself with the pragmatic side of the Semar folk myth, rather than with the nationalist rhetoric of his predecessor Sukarno, and focused his regime's efforts on providing stability to develop Indonesia's poor but resource-endowed economy. Named acting president in 1967, he was elected to a full presidential term by the People's Consultative Assembly in 1968, and re-elected thereafter at successive five-year intervals. His sixth term accordingly began with the Assembly's (unanimous) approval on 10 March 1993.

The dominant political organisation, *Golkar* (the Joint Secretariat of Functional Groups), became under Suharto's leadership a civilian vehicle for the military regime; and from 1973 to 1975 the other political organisations then in existence were required to merge into two new parties to create a formal three-party system, within which all criticism of the government was banned. In 1984 Suharto (himself a Muslim like the majority of Indonesians) decreed that all political groups should base themselves upon the official five-point secular state ideology of Pancasila – monotheism, humanitarianism, national unity, consensus democracy and social justice. On the economic front, development programmes were funded by a combination of Indonesia's oil revenues and foreign lending. An impressive growth rate of around 6 per cent per year was maintained well into the 1990s, although the increased foreign investment which accompanied the deregulation of the financial sector from 1988 ultimately left the country more vulnerable to the vagaries of investor confidence which proved so damaging when the crash came in 1997.

The political stability which had encouraged Suharto in a brief experiment with liberalisation in the early 1990s had given way by 1994 to the renewed enforcement of controls on the media. As he approached a possible seventh presidential term from March 1998, the reins were tightened further, to prevent the emergence of political rivals.

Suharto's wife Siti Hartinah (nicknamed Mrs Tien), whom he married in 1947, died in April 1996 aged 72. Reports of Suharto's subsequent depression were augmented by speculation about his health, apparently confirmed when he visited Germany for medical attention in July 1996. Business rivalries among his six children became more overt, with Mrs Tien no longer there as arbiter in feuds within the so-called "first family". His eldest son Sigit

Harjoyudanto and eldest daughter Siti Hardiyanti Rukmana (nicknamed Tutut) were particularly involved in banking, while sons Bambang Trihatmodjo and Hutomo Mandala Putra (nicknamed Tommy) competed fiercely in automobiles and cellular phones, though coexisted relatively peacefully in the airline and petrochemical sectors. Four of the six children also ran for office in the June 1997 parliamentary elections under the *Golkar* banner.

Although the authoritarian system severely restricted the scope for political differences, this election campaign proved exceptionally bloody, with nearly 300 deaths. A show of force by the regime had already helped to engineer the ousting of former President Sukarno's daughter Megawati from the leadership of the Indonesian Democratic Party, but *Golkar*'s landslide win was still blighted by a strong showing in the capital by the other main opposition group, the Muslim-based United Development Party.

In late 1997, as the effects of the so-called "Asian crisis" on the international financial markets took hold in Indonesia, the Suharto regime suddenly lost its power to placate most ordinary Indonesians by steadily easing the burden of their poverty. As the sudden downturn in the economy fuelled popular unrest against him, so too did the pressure grow from foreign investors and the international financial institutions for more accountable economic management and an end to "cronyism". This, however, would strike directly at his and his family's fortunes, with their current business interests controlling an estimated one-seventh of the national economy. Despite the International Monetary Fund's insistence on reforms, the Suharto family made only modest concessions, although they did give up some of their most blatantly unviable projects.

Indecisive and apparently unwell, Suharto resisted the suggestion that he stand down when his sixth presidential term expired in March 1998 and thereby contribute to an ordered transition to a new government. Instead he had the Assembly once again endorse him in office, for a term not due to end until 2003, and compounded this obstinacy by appointing a government without any convincing credentials for tackling reform and reducing corruption. When student-led riots erupted in Jakarta and other cities two months later, even the army leadership declined to stand firm behind him, and Suharto eventually resigned on 21 May 1998.

Suharto's designated successor, B.J. Habibie, was a lifelong loyal associate, and it was widely believed that Suharto had insisted on guarantees to protect his family interests before agreeing to stand down. However, such was the popular pressure on Habibie's successor regime (which was eventually compelled to accept the status of a mere interim government pending elections in 1999), that within four months an investigation had been set up to "clarify" the mass of complaints about how Suharto's family fortune – estimated by *Forbes* magazine at US$4 billion – had been amassed. Although Suharto denied on television that he had massive savings abroad, and offered in November to surrender the family's control over 7 of its 13 charitable foundations, formal legal proceedings began in December for "corruption, collusion and nepotism practices", raising the possibility that he could be placed under house arrest. Reports in March 1999 revealed that the Suharto family had begun selling some of the luxury property owned by the family in London.

Quentin **Tarantino**

Quentin Tarantino is the self-styled enfant terrible *of US cinema. Internet websites pore over the minutest detail of his screen productions, which receive adulation from audiences of his own generation and within the youth culture. This response is mirrored by the incomprehension and revulsion of others who, whether or not they have seen his films, believe them to be celebrations of nihilistic violence, and fear the possible social and psychological consequences of their popularity. The success of his first two major films,* Reservoir Dogs *and* Pulp Fiction, *which both demonstrate the extent to which Tarantino is immersed in the film history and culture of Hollywood, have ensured his own status within the industry, even if he has yet to produce other work with comparable impact.*

Quentin Jerome Tarantino was born on 27 March 1963 in Knoxville, Tennessee, USA. His father, a law student named Tony Tarantino, left Quentin's 16-year-old mother Connie before her child was born. She moved when Quentin was two to South Bay, near Los Angeles, where he grew up, nourished on a diet of violent movies and Hollywood westerns.

Tarantino left school at 17, and spent five years drifting before finding a job as rental clerk at Video Archives, Manhattan Beach, California. It was there that he first became fascinated by the work of European film directors like François Truffaut and Jean-Luc Godard, whose work was confined largely to the art-house circuit in the USA, while he also became an aficionado of Hong Kong gangster movies directed by John Woo.

Tarantino spent virtually every spare hour scribbling away at his own film scripts, or discussing cinema with his co-worker, Roger Avary. In between, he took acting lessons and landed a few small roles, including one as an Elvis impersonator in *The Golden Girls*. He learnt the rudiments of camera-work on the set of a Dolph Lundgren exercise video. *My Best Friend's Birthday* was his first stab at shooting a movie, in 1986, but he never finished it.

Quentin Tarantino penned his first full script, *True Romance*, in 1987. Unable to raise the capital to actually shoot it, he was forced to sell it in 1990. The same was true of the notoriously violent *Natural Born Killers*, written in 1988 and then sold to the esteemed director Oliver Stone. (It was eventually released in 1994, directed by Oliver Stone, to a mixture of adulation and condemnation.)

In 1990 Tarantino left Video Archives to do rewrites for a small Hollywood production company, CineTel. Through a CineTel co-worker, Lawrence Bender, he met the actor Harvey Keitel, who was so impressed by the young man's passion that he promised to act in his next venture – which turned out to be *Reservoir Dogs*.

Written, produced and directed by Tarantino, aided in large measure by a grant from LIVE Entertainment, *Reservoir Dogs* was shot on 16 mm black-and-white film. Its title is a bastardisation of the French classic *Au Revoir Les Enfants* and Sam Peckinpah's violent and highly controversial 1970s film *Straw Dogs*. It starred Harvey Keitel and Tim Roth, with Tarantino also appearing in it himself – a trademark apparently borrowed from Alfred Hitchcock. *Reservoir Dogs* premiered at the Sundance '92 film festival, where its raw camera work, powerful performances, clever cinematographic allusions and modern sensibility won it an immediate cult following. Soon it was picked for distribution by the Miramax agency. In an industry always keen to identify new vogues and new talent in terms of similarities with established successes, Tarantino was hailed as "the next Martin Scorsese". *Reservoir Dogs* was released in the cinema in the UK in January 1993, but was adjudged unsuitable to be licensed for video release there, fuelling an ongoing debate over issues of censorship and the extent to which delinquent behaviour was imitative of screen violence.

Tarantino's eagerly awaited next film was *Pulp Fiction*, a dark comedy using an unusual non-linear narrative to weave together a number of stories about the Los Angeles underworld. Tarantino trademarks abounded: brilliant casting, pace, "quotations" from earlier films, an evocative soundtrack, and copious amounts of blood. It starred Harvey Keitel, John Travolta, Samuel L. Jackson, Uma Thurman and Tarantino himself. In 1994 *Pulp Fiction* won Tarantino the prestigious Palme D'Or at the Cannes film festival. Nominated for seven Oscars, it won only one, for best screenplay – shared by Tarantino and Avary.

Pulp Fiction grossed more than US$100 million at US box offices and spread Tarantino's reputation globally. He went on to direct episodes of television's *ER* series, was executive producer of Roger Avary's

Killing Zoë (1994), and part-directed the poorly received *Four Rooms* (1995). He then joined Lawrence Bender and Michael Bodnarchek in launching an innovative commercials agency, called "A Band Apart". In 1996 Tarantino executive-produced, wrote and acted in Robert Rodriguez's vampire thriller *From Dusk Till Dawn*.

Miramax permitted Tarantino to form his own independent distribution arm, Rolling Thunder. The company donates a quarter of all its profits to film preservation societies – indicative of the respect Tarantino shows to his cinematographic forebears, despite his much-vaunted "bad boy" image.

Tarantino's most recent film is *Jackie Brown*, which was released on Christmas Day 1997. A crime comedy loosely based on Elmore Leonard's novel *Rum Punch*, it self-consciously parodies early 1970s "blaxploitation" films. *Jackie Brown* immediately sparked controversy, after several African–Americans objected to its liberal usage of the derogatory term "nigger". Tarantino retorted that his work was an authentic tribute to black American subculture, a lifelong source of his artistic inspiration. However, the film delighted audiences, both black and white. It also revived the career of the African–American actress Pam Grier, who starred alongside such established luminaries as Robert de Niro, Samuel L. Jackson, Bridget Fonda and Michael Keaton.

Tarantino has sustained his early promise and won praise for his wit and energy. That said, many condemn his films as gratuitously violent, amoral, nihilistic, or simply too derivative. His private life is often as controversial as his films: he was arrested for shoplifting at 15, touted a fictitious CV in the late 1980s, faced a US$5 million lawsuit for alleged assault in 1995, and ostentatiously dated Hollywood starlet Mira Sorvino from 1996 to 1998. Tarantino acts like a rebel, yet, ironically, his story conforms to that well-established American archetype, success through dogged hard work.

Mother **Teresa**

*The death of Mother Teresa in September 1997, in the same week as **Princess Diana**, deprived the world of a woman popularly regarded as the embodiment of selflessness. She has since been beatified by **Pope John Paul II** and is on a "fast track" towards sainthood. Her lifetime of service as a missionary nun in Calcutta, working in the slums to relieve the suffering of some of the most destitute people on earth, stood out as both an inspiration to others and a rebuke to the materialism of Western culture. At the same time, her devout Catholicism allowed of no compromise on birth control, while her emphasis on caring, and bringing spiritual solace, distanced her from political–humanitarian efforts to focus more on the causes of poverty.*

Agnes Gonxha Bojaxhiu was born on 27 August 1910 in Skopje, in what is now Macedonia. Her parents were Roman Catholics of ethnic Albanian descent; her father, Nicholas Bojaxhiu, was said to be the prosperous co-owner of a construction company, although some reports describe him as a grocer or the manager of a small farm. The young Agnes showed early signs of pursuing a religious vocation. By the age of 12, she had decided on a missionary career, dedicated to helping the poor.

In December 1928 Agnes travelled to Dublin, in Ireland, where she joined a missionary religious order, the Sisters of Loretto, originally founded in the 17th century. In January 1929 she sailed for India, arriving at the Loretto convent in the northeast hill station of Darjeeling, where she took her initial vows as a novice. On 24 May 1931 she adopted the name Teresa in honour of the French saint, Therese of Lisieux. She took her final vows as a nun in 1937.

From 1929 to 1948 she taught at St Mary's High School in Calcutta, run by the Loretto order. She was particularly moved by the plight of the homeless, the sick and the dying on the streets of Calcutta. On 10 September 1946, while aboard a train bound from Calcutta to Darjeeling, Sister Teresa received what she described as a "divine call", persuading her to abandon the relative comfort and security of her post, then as principal of St Mary's, to serve the poor. Later that year, after receiving permission from her archbishop, she established an open-air school for homeless children in Calcutta. Soon she was joined by volunteers and supported by benefactors who donated funds and facilities.

In 1948 Sister Teresa was granted Indian citizenship and permission by Pope Pius XII to live as an independent nun. In 1949 she founded her own sisterhood, the Missionaries of Charity, which she headed as Mother Teresa. The organisation was recognised by the Vatican as a pontifical congregation on 7 October 1950. The distinctive habit adopted by the Missionaries of Charity is a plain white sari with a blue border and simple cross pinned to the left shoulder.

Mother Teresa's first major project was the establishment of the Nirmal Hriday ("pure heart") hospice for the destitute, founded in Calcutta in 1952. With a team of dedicated recruits and basic medical training, acquired while serving with the American Medical Missionaries in Patna, Bihar, in 1949, Mother Teresa cared for people found dying on the streets of Calcutta. In 1953 she opened her first orphanage in Calcutta, and in 1957 established Shanti Nagar (Town of Peace), a leper colony near the city of Asansol, northwest of Calcutta.

By the early 1960s her religious devotion and charity among the poor was winning Mother Teresa wide acclaim. Popularly designated the "Saint of the Gutters", in 1962 she won the first of many awards – the Shri Padma prize for humanitarian effort, bestowed by the Indian government. In 1965 Pope Paul VI recognised her growing importance by bringing the Missionaries of Charity under the control of the papacy and authorising its expansion beyond India. The order quickly developed an international network that spawned more than 550 missions across 120 countries, administering food centres, orphanages, hospices and, in 1988, a home for AIDS patients in San Francisco, California. The Brothers of Charity, the male equivalent of the sisterhood, was established in 1963.

In 1979 Mother Teresa won the Nobel Peace Prize, which she accepted, she said, on behalf of "the unwanted, the unloved and the uncared for". She had already been awarded the so-called "papal peace prize" eight years earlier, and in 1980 she was honoured with India's highest civilian award, the Bharat Ratna.

In later life the diminutive Mother Teresa's apparent personal frailty was compounded by health problems. She suffered a first heart attack in 1983, when on a visit to the Vatican, and eventually gave up the leadership of her order for health reasons in March 1997. On 5 September 1997 she died of a heart attack in Calcutta. Her funeral, a state occasion in Calcutta, was attended by hundreds of dignitaries from more than 20 countries, including heads of state and government. She was succeeded as head of the Missionaries by Sister Nirmala, who had already been elected to the post on 13 March 1997.

Mother Teresa, though widely hailed as a saint in her lifetime, was not above controversy. Her outspoken views against abortion and preference for prayer over politics dismayed many humanitarian and human rights groups. Some critics also accused her of courting political dictators and corrupt businessmen in return for donations, while others alleged that she used her charitable work as a guise to convert vulnerable groups of Hindus and Muslims to Christianity. To those who believed that the Missionaries of Charity should give a higher priority to building hospitals, and concentrate their expenditure on such practical and medical projects, she would reply that this was not her mission; she and her sisters were nuns, rather than nurses or social workers, devoted to bringing comfort to those in both physical and spiritual anguish.

Margaret **Thatcher**

Margaret Thatcher's impact as UK prime minister (1979–90) continued to shape the country's political culture for much of the ensuing decade, while her radical free-market policies left their enduring mark on the economic landscape. "Thatcherism" has also been imitated in various countries across the globe long after her retirement from government. The UK's first woman prime minister, indeed the first (and to date the only) woman to lead any of the country's main political parties, she was noted for her abrasive style of leadership and the indefatigable zeal of her "conviction politics". Her government programme was built around her belief that the road to wealth creation lay via the unfettering of competition and the promotion of self-reliant individualism.

Margaret Hilda Roberts was born on 13 October 1925 in a strongly Methodist family in Grantham, a small town in Lincolnshire in the east of England. She was the second daughter of Alfred Roberts, a grocer, and Beatrice, a dressmaker. She has often cited her father, who was to become borough councillor, alderman, and then mayor of Grantham, as the greatest formative influence on her political ambitions and conservative values.

Educated at Kesteven and Grantham Girls' High School, she won a scholarship to study chemistry at Somerville College, Oxford and, while a student there, was president of the University Conservative Association. Upon graduating she worked as an industrial chemist for four years, while also studying for the Bar. She stood unsuccessfully as Conservative parliamentary candidate for Dartford in 1950 and 1951, the year she married Denis Thatcher, a divorcé and director of a number of major companies. In 1953 she gave birth to twins, Mark and Carol. Called to the Bar in 1954, she specialised in tax law.

In 1959 she was elected to parliament in the safe Conservative constituency of Finchley, north London, where she was to be MP for 33 years. Her first junior post in government was as joint parliamentary secretary in the ministry of pensions and national insurance, from 1961 until the Conservatives were defeated in the 1964 general election. She joined the shadow cabinet in 1967, initially as shadow minister for power, where she came into contact for the first time with the problems of the coal industry and marked herself out as an opponent of public subsidies to keep mines open. Reshuffles of the shadow cabinet saw her move subsequently to the transport and then the education brief. The Conservative victory in the

1970 election opened the way for her to take up a full ministerial post for the first – and, as it turned out, only – time, at the age of 44.

Margaret Thatcher was the only woman cabinet minister in Edward Heath's 1970–74 government, holding throughout this period the job of secretary of state for education and science. She gained some notoriety, and gave notice of her determination not to be deflected from apparently unpopular policies, by abolishing the provision of free milk to schoolchildren – although the abuse of "Maggie Thatcher, milk snatcher" had a little more wit, and less venom, than the protest chants which were to feature her name through the 1980s.

Defeat in the two general elections of 1974 relegated the Conservatives to opposition again. Thatcher seized the opportunity of Heath's weakened position in the party to mount her challenge from the more radical right. Unexpectedly successful in her audacious bid to oust him from the leadership in 1975, she gave a new sense of mission to the Conservative Party in opposition, focusing particularly on the extent to which Labour in office was beholden to the power of the unions.

Leading the Conservatives to victory when the general election eventually came in May 1979, Thatcher became the first woman to be elected head of government in any European country. She was to hold office for the next eleven-and-a-half years, winning three general elections in a row (1979, 1983 and 1987). Proud to call herself a conviction politician, and scornfully equating consensus with feeble "wet" compromise, she demanded loyalty from cabinet members and trusted only those she classed as "one of us". On the international stage she gloried in the epithet "the iron lady". Demanding respect for Britain, she recovered from a serious slump in the opinion polls to strike a popular chord with her determined pursuit of victory in the 1982 Falklands war against Argentina. She also made political capital by the intransigent "handbagging" of other European Community (EC) leaders when she perceived a national interest as opposed to a common one. Her radical domestic policy programme aimed meanwhile to transform the UK economy and society, and to raise up the values of the individual as paramount. Thatcher placed home-ownership and self-reliance at the centre of social policy, and privatisation and monetarism at the centre of economic policy, while relentlessly stripping the trade unions of their power.

It was in her second term of office (1983–87) that "Thatcherism" was at its height. Her first term featured income tax reductions, council house sales, public spending cuts, rising unemployment, and the legislation with which she took on the trade unions, but, until the Falklands war rescued her popularity ratings, the Thatcher government lacked the enormous self-confidence which she gained from the landslide election victory in June 1983.

The privatisation project, starting with local authority housing and key nationalised industries, was really taking hold by 1983, to be accompanied by the deregulation of pensions and further cuts in direct taxation. Describing striking miners in 1984 as "the enemy within", Thatcher did not flinch from large-scale police deployment against them, holding out for "total victory" over the miners' unions and regarding the effective demise of the coal industry as an acceptable price to pay. Her stance on Northern Ireland was hardened by the death of colleagues in attacks by the Irish Republican Army, notably when the Grand Hotel in Brighton was bombed during the Conservative Party conference in 1984, and she was a chief architect of the Anglo-Irish agreement concluded the following year. During this period she also fought successfully to secure a British rebate on contributions to the EC budget, and raised the global profile of the UK in the context of a trans-Atlantic alliance with the USA – which was considerably enhanced by her close personal relations with US President Ronald Reagan.

Apparently more dominant than ever in her own government after the 1987 election, Thatcher brushed aside a nominal challenge to her leadership of the party in 1989. Had she encouraged more independence of judgement among her ministers, however, she might have foreseen the threat she was to face the following year, when two issues came to a head which proved her downfall. The first was public opposition and protest against the poll tax, a controversial per capita "community charge". The poll tax was a Thatcher flagship and she fixed her colours to the mast with typical determination. The second crucial issue was Britain's role in Europe. Having signed the Single European Act and opened the way for sterling to join the European Monetary System, she nevertheless identified federalism as a growing threat to sovereignty, and took every opportunity to denounce it.

The bombshell, from within her cabinet, came from an unexpected source – Sir Geoffrey Howe, whose resignation as foreign secretary was followed up by a statement in parliament criticising her leadership style and her attitude towards Europe. Interpreting this as a challenge to her leadership, her old rival Michael Heseltine declared his candidacy for the post. Thatcher topped the first ballot, but without a sufficient majority to preclude a second round of voting. Advised by her senior ministers that she faced defeat, she resigned rather than lose the ballot, and was replaced by her chancellor of the exchequer, John Major.

Since her departure from government Thatcher has travelled extensively, promoting her policies through the Thatcher Foundation, and has published *The Downing Street Years* (in 1993) and *The Path to Power* (in 1995). In 1992 she was created a life peer as Baroness Thatcher of Kesteven, her husband having been made a baronet in December 1990.

Hans **Tietmeyer**

Something of an eminence grise *of the international financial world, Hans Tietmeyer became president of Germany's Bundesbank in 1993 after long experience in the federal economic and finance ministries. Tietmeyer has a reputation for being a perfectionist and combines missionary enthusiasm with formidable negotiating skills. He is the world's leading exponent of "sound money" policies, and has unparalleled expertise in the formulation and introduction of economic and monetary union, both between East and West Germany in 1990 and at the European Union level. By the end of his term of office at the Bundesbank in August 1999, the main responsibility for monetary policy had passed to the new European Central Bank.*

Hans Tietmeyer was born on 18 August 1931 in Metelen, Westphalia, where his father Bernhard was a local government revenue official. He gained his *Abitur* (school-leaving certificate) from Paulinum grammar school in Münster in 1952 and began further studies in Catholic theology, later switching to economics and social sciences. He graduated with a

degree in economics from the University of Cologne in 1958 and went on to gain a doctorate in economics from the same university in 1960. From 1959 to 1962 he worked for the student aid organisation *Cusanuswerk.*

In 1962 Tietmeyer entered the federal government bureaucracy at the ministry of economics, where he was to work for the next 20 years. By 1967 he had risen to head the division responsible for basic issues of the economic system and of economic policy. In 1970 he moved to head the directorate responsible for the Common Market and relations with other countries. From 1972 he headed the directorate for basic issues of economics, the business cycle and growth policy. Between 1973 and 1982 he was head of the directorate-general which had overall responsibility for economic policy. He was particularly influential as one of the closest advisers to Otto Graf Lambsdorff, who was economics minister from October 1977. During this period he also chaired the economic policy committee of the European Communities (EC), the working party of the Organization for Economic Co-operation and Development (OECD) on positive adjustment policies, and the EC's monetary committee.

The election of **Helmut Kohl** as federal chancellor in October 1982 was the occasion for a switch to the finance ministry for Tietmeyer, himself a member of Kohl's Christian Democratic Union (CDU). As permanent secretary for seven years, he had particular responsibility for basic issues of financial policy, international monetary policy, EC matters and the preparation of Germany's position at world economic summits.

Tietmeyer was appointed with effect from January 1990 to the board of the Bundesbank and to the Central Bank Council, responsible for foreign countries, international monetary issues, organisations and agreements. However, two months later, as the prospect of German unification became apparent, Kohl appointed him as his personal adviser in negotiations with the East German government on the crucial economic and monetary aspects of union. Tietmeyer successfully masterminded the process of securing an agreement in rapid time – his sensitive task made easier by Kohl's political decision that West Germany should accept the high costs involved in using an artificial one-for-one exchange rate to unify the two currencies. Concluded in April and signed in May, the state treaty on the creation of a monetary, economic and social union took effect on 1 July 1990.

A powerful defender of the "sound money" policies traditionally associated with the Bundesbank, where he was vice-president from mid-1991, Tietmeyer was an obvious candidate to succeed to the Bundesbank presidency upon the retirement of Helmut Schlesinger in July 1993. Appointed for a six-year term until August 1999 (with Johann-Wilhelm Gaddum as his vice-president), Tietmeyer is only the seventh holder of the post.

Under Tietmeyer's leadership the Bundesbank has further strengthened its already well-founded reputation for monetary policies designed to ensure low inflation. In May–June 1997 he adopted a tough stance to assert its independence vis-à-vis the German government, when the latter announced plans to revalue the Bundesbank's gold reserves. The government had hoped that this expedient, delivering a cosmetic improvement in the public finances, would assist Germany in meeting the qualifying "convergence criteria" for European economic and monetary union (EMU). In an unprecedented move, however, Tietmeyer publicly opposed the government, declaring that it was in a crisis of its own making, and describing the proposed reserve revaluation as a form of creative accounting. The government was obliged to climb down, and Tietmeyer's prestige in the financial community rose accordingly. When in October 1998 the Group of Seven (G7) industrialised countries endorsed UK Chancellor of the Exchequer Gordon Brown's call for a new regulatory authority to oversee global financial markets, it was the ever-orthodox and sceptical Tietmeyer whom they chose to draw up a report on how to put such a proposal into action. He has also consistently taken a dim view of the idea that third world debt problems require greater willingness to "forgive" debt. Tietmeyer has the classic banker's reflexes, concerned to see obligations honoured once they have been contracted, for the sake of the proper functioning of the financial system, rather than taking a more flexible approach to solve a political and economic impasse.

As head of the most powerful central bank in Europe, Tietmeyer has also repeatedly stressed that the successful creation of a stable common currency at the European Union level will depend on member states adhering strictly to measures to promote economic stability, and respecting the convergence criteria set out in the 1992 Maastricht Treaty on European Union. When Germans reflect on their country's economic achievements since 1945, they commonly place the highest symbolic value on the strength of the deutschmark. Tietmeyer has fought to ensure that the euro, replacing the participating national currencies between 1999 and 2002, will be run on similar "sound money" principles. However, his own main custodial role as Germany's central banker will pass to the European Central Bank under **Wim Duisenberg**.

Tietmeyer's first wife, Marie-Luise, died in 1978 and two years later he married Marie-Therese Kalff. He has a son and a daughter.

David **Trimble**

David Trimble has been, since July 1998, the first minister of the Northern Ireland power-sharing executive. An Ulster Protestant who became leader of the main Unionist party in 1995, his background and previous political career gave little hope that he would be a flexible and imaginative negotiator. Just three years later, however, he was joint winner of the Nobel Peace Prize, praised for his political courage in contributing to the peace process. Something of a loner, determined rather than eloquent in debate, and no great political charmer, he characteristically greeted the Nobel announcement with the dour comment that he hoped it would not prove premature. Although the danger of this grew more pronounced through the first half of 1999, Trimble refused to compromise on his interpretation of the previous year's agreement, maintaining that weapons decommissioning was a precondition for militant republicans – represented by Sinn Féin *– joining the power-sharing executive. Without them, the executive would effectively be an irrelevance.*

David Trimble was born on 15 October 1944, the son of William and Ivy Trimble, whose ancestors had emigrated to Ulster from Northumberland, northern England, in the late 1600s or early 1700s. Growing up in Bangor, Northern Ireland, he attended the local grammar school and then Queen's University, Belfast, graduating in law. He completed his training as a barrister and was appointed a lecturer in the university's law department in 1968. In 1978 he married Daphne Orr; the couple have had two sons and two daughters.

When Trimble first became politically active in the mid-1960s, Northern Ireland was on the verge of a period of major unrest, with civil rights campaigners demanding equal treatment for the large Catholic minority, and Irish republicans pursuing the objective of a united Ireland. Trimble joined what was then effectively the party of the majority Protestant community, the Ulster Unionist Party (UUP), which had dominated the Belfast-based Northern Ireland parliament and government at Stormont Castle since the partition of Ireland in 1921. Trimble was appointed to the UUP's central organisation, the Ulster Unionist Council (UUC).

The British decision in 1972 to abolish the Stormont system and govern the province directly from London produced splits in the Unionist ranks. Trimble joined a newly formed Vanguard Unionist Party, consisting of hardline Unionists who were regarded as close to the views of Protestant "loyalist" paramilitary groups. The Sunningdale agreement of 1973, which created a power-sharing executive and thus brought Catholics into the government structure, was rejected by a self-styled United Ulster Unionist Council, of which Vanguard was one element. Trimble, who became deputy leader of Vanguard, was active in supporting the 1974 strike by Protestant loyalist workers which effectively buried the power-sharing initiative.

The next initiative involved the election of a Northern Ireland Constitutional Convention in 1975, in which Trimble was one of 14 Vanguard members, the third largest party contingent. The convention ended unproductively within a year, with its Unionist majority unwilling to make meaningful concessions. An unexpected suggestion by the Vanguard leader, involving "voluntary power-sharing", had little impact other than to destroy the party's credibility with its hardline supporters. Its membership collapsed, most of them joining the other main hardline grouping, Ian Paisley's Democratic Unionist Party. Trimble, however, had by 1978 rejoined the main party of the Unionist establishment, now known as the Official Unionist Party but retaining the abbreviation UUP.

Pursuing his academic career as a lecturer in law, Trimble rose during the 1980s to become senior lecturer and dean of the faculty at Queen's by 1990. From 1985 he was also chairman of the Lagan Valley Unionist Association and of the Ulster Society, campaigning within the Ulster Clubs pressure group against the 1985 Anglo-Irish agreement. In 1990 he gave up all his positions, including his law lectureship, when he won a convincing by-election victory in the Upper Bann constituency and took up a seat as a UUP member of parliament at Westminster.

At the time of James Molyneaux's resignation as UUP leader in August 1995, Trimble was still a relatively little-known MP. He nevertheless entered the party leadership contest, and emerged as the winner on the third round of voting by the party council on 8 September, his support among loyalist hardliners augmented by backing from newer and less conservative members.

The election of Trimble brought initial concern within the UK and Irish governments, fearing from his reputation that he would hold up the current peace talks and hinder negotiations by holding out against any concessions. However, Trimble swiftly joined the rounds of summits and negotiations, agreeing to meet the Irish prime minister, John Bruton, in Dublin in October 1995, and backing the idea of all-party elections to a new Northern Ireland forum. The UK government quickly realised that, with his loyalist background and hardline reputation,

Trimble might be best placed to deliver Unionist agreement on a peace settlement. During this period (up to the 1997 UK elections) Trimble's UUP held remarkable sway over UK policy because of its ability to boost the Conservative government's minimal parliamentary majority.

Within his own party Trimble moved to restrict the voting rights of the Protestant traditionalist Orange Order on the UUC, but in July 1996 he reinforced his loyalist credentials – and simultaneously outraged the Catholic community – by supporting the right of the Orangemen to hold their annual parade at Drumcree. The Royal Ulster Constabulary refused to let the Orangemen pass, and a five-day "siege" ensued, with Trimble himself prominent at the forefront of the marchers.

The election of a new UK government brought renewed impetus for an agreement on the future of Northern Ireland, and all-party talks began in September 1997 following the declaration of a ceasefire by the Irish Republican Army (IRA) in July. While taking a hardline stance at the talks, and expressing grave concern that promises of the decommissioning of IRA weapons were not being fulfilled, Trimble was fighting hard within his party to find an acceptable way to make the necessary concessions. With the backing of the party council (the UUC), he signed the Good Friday agreement on 10 April 1998. This marked a historic step forward, creating a new Assembly and power-sharing executive which would end direct rule from Westminster. Despite significant dissent within the UUP ranks, the agreement was ratified by a referendum in Northern Ireland in May.

Trimble's position was consolidated when the UUP emerged as the largest party in elections to the new Assembly in June 1998. Its first meeting on 1 July duly elected him to the post of first minister heading the power-sharing executive. In September Trimble met and spoke to, but refused to shake hands with, **Gerry Adams** in the first face-to-face encounter between the leaders of the UUP and *Sinn Féin* for 75 years. He remained adamant, however, that the decommissioning of IRA weapons must be under way before *Sinn Féin* could take up posts on the new executive.

Later in September 1998, Trimble gave a symbolic indication of his commitment to reconciliation, at the risk of outraging hardline Protestants and alienating the Orange Order, by attending a Catholic church service – the funeral mass for some of the children killed in the 15 August Omagh bombing. The bombing, an outrage committed by the splinter "real IRA" faction which killed both Protestants and Catholics in the border town, was the worst single incident of the 30 years of the Northern Ireland "troubles".

The year ended, for Trimble, with the accolade of major honours, but with the unresolved issue of weapons decommissioning continuing to cast its shadow over progress on the peace process. On 16 October 1998 it was announced that he and John Hume, leader of the moderate nationalist Social Democratic and Labour Party, were to be jointly awarded the 1998 Nobel Peace Prize for their efforts to find a solution to the Northern Ireland conflict, the citation praising David Trimble for his "great political courage". In the UK's 1999 New Year's Honours List he was appointed to the Privy Council.

Donald **Trump**

When Donald Trump was ranked by Forbes *magazine in 1997 as the 105th richest person in the USA, with net wealth of over US$1.3 billion, he – typically – disputed the calculation, claiming to be nearly three times richer. Either way, he had achieved a considerable recovery from the edge of bankruptcy seven years earlier. Trump had in some ways personified the speculation-based financial boom of the 1980s. A New York property dealer who promoted his own name as a prestige brand, he and his then wife Ivana had enjoyed their wealth in an ostentatious manner which exercised a kind of fascination for the media. Equally, his detractors revelled in his subsequent fall. The aggressive expansion of his hotels and casinos business once again in the 1990s has shown his resilience and determination to succeed, with his appetite for publicity apparently unaffected by bruising disputes over his divorce settlement with Ivana.*

Donald John Trump was born on 14 June 1946 in Queens, New York, the fourth of five children of house builder and property owner Fred Trump. A prosperous childhood led on to a spell at a military academy and to a degree at the Wharton School of Finance in Pennsylvania. While still at Wharton he began to get involved with property development himself, buying a run-down apartment block in Ohio which he and his father stripped and renovated, using wholly borrowed money. They made a small fortune together when they eventually sold the completed building.

Trump quickly perceived the lucrative prospects for further property speculation in New York City. He cultivated a network of important political contacts there, as well as meeting wealthy potential clients, through his membership of various exclusive clubs. His second important coup in the property business came in 1974, at the age of 28. Having secured an option on the Penn Central railway yards, he succeeded in persuading the New York City authorities that this would make a good site for the construction of a convention centre. He was even better rewarded, financially speaking, by his decision to develop the dilapidated Commodore Hotel, nowadays known as the Grand Hyatt Hotel, whose completion in 1980 firmly established Trump as Manhattan's most audacious and high-spending property developer.

From this basis, Trump launched into the spectacular expansion which characterised his business career in the first half of the 1980s. The first major stage in this

was the construction of the Trump Tower on Fifth Avenue, a building remarkable for its extravagant cost and luxury, as well as for the extent to which the enterprise was leveraged, i.e. financed by borrowing against expected future returns. The key to his success with Trump Tower, as with subsequent prestige projects bearing his name, was that he tapped into the psychology of very wealthy buyers in a way that had not been understood in the property market up until then. His basic trick was to create an aura of success and excitement about what he was offering, putting his apartments on the market at prices so high as to make this a talking-point in itself, even while his business rivals were trying to be competitive by lowering prices on theirs. The strategy fitted perfectly with the conspicuous spending so prevalent in the 1980s. Trump had also grasped a lesson about perceived investment value. As in the contemporary world of record art auction prices and stock exchange bull runs, so in the property market, something that was desirable to own – thanks to the image and "branding" of his apartments – was seen as likely to keep going up in value.

Hard on the heels of Trump Tower, he lost little time in pressing ahead with the construction of Trump Parc, a still more luxurious apartment complex which commanded still higher prices. This in turn became the launchpad for the next expansion phase in his personal financial empire. He was now determined to create a personality cult around his own identity, so that he could use his celebrity status as a tool to forge a selling link across a wide range of differing commercial activities. His fame would also ensure that he always had unlimited access to the bank finance that he would need for his projects.

Thus it was that within five years Trump owned not only the Trump Plaza Hotel and 24,000 rented apartments but also the Trump Shuttle airline (previously part of Eastern Airlines), the New Jersey Generals football team, and several casinos in Atlantic City and New Jersey (including most famously Trump's Castle and the Trump Taj Mahal). He also owned a 282-foot yacht, a riverboat casino in Indiana and numerous holiday parks. He had bought various South American air travel routes from the failed Braniff airline and had sold them at a substantial profit to American Airlines. To round it all off he had written a best-selling book, *Trump: The Art of the Deal*, published in 1987, in which he explained his business ideas.

Yet Trump eventually over-extended himself very badly with his excessive bank borrowing, and when the USA lurched into recession in the late 1980s he was quickly swamped by some US$2 billion of debts which he was unable to service. By 1990, barely five years after his peak, Trump was facing personal bankruptcy, in debt to the tune of almost US$1 billion, and most of his business empire was being sold off to repay his creditors. His second book, *Trump: Surviving at the Top*, was published rather embarrassingly at the height of his financial troubles in 1990. He fought his way back, however, buying a 50 per cent share of the Empire State Building in 1994, purchasing a 70-storey apartment block on Wall Street in 1995 with the intention of renovating it for leasing, and consolidating the Trump Hotels and Casino Resorts company in 1997. That year he published another book, which with typical *chuzpah* he called *Trump: the Art of the Comeback*. In early 1999 he was making headlines once again with controversial plans for a speedway development on New York's Long Island. Estimates of his personal wealth vary widely, according to how the debts are calculated.

Trump has been married twice – between 1977 and 1991 to the Czech-born former beauty queen Ivana Zelnicek, with whom he had two sons, Donny and Eric, and a daughter, Ivanka, and from 1993 to 1997 to Maria Maples, a model, with whom he had a daughter, Tiffany. His divorce from Ivana Trump was highly publicised – not only because of the US$2 billion settlement she sought and the US$25 million she obtained, but because of her own high profile and because it was unusually acrimonious. His separation from Maria Maples, by contrast, was a fairly low-key affair which cost him only a reputed US$5 million.

Ted **Turner**

Ted Turner is chiefly famous as the flamboyant founder of CNN, which made its reputation worldwide by on-the-spot television coverage of the 1991 Gulf war. Turner himself has been a force to reckon with in US cable TV since the 1970s and in the international news media for the last decade. Based in Atlanta, Georgia, and unflatteringly dubbed by some the "Mouth of the South", Turner built up his business, from an unpromising start, with entrepreneurial energy and abrasiveness. Less shrewd in his later forays into corporate acquisition, he continues to attract attention with high-profile philanthropic gestures – and as one half of a celebrated "media couple" with his third wife Jane Fonda, the politically minded film star whom right-wingers once called "Hanoi Jane".

Robert Edward Turner III was born on 19 November 1938 in Cincinnati, Ohio, the son of Robert Turner, who owned a struggling company that rented advertising billboard space. He was educated at McCallie School, Chattanooga, where he failed to make any noticeable academic impression. Moving on to Georgia Military Academy, and then to Brown University, he continued to enjoy a reputation for outspoken and reckless behaviour which eventually led to his expulsion for misconduct.

Turner's unpromising early career came to an abrupt end in 1963, when his father's suicide left him unexpectedly responsible for running the family billboard company. In that year he married Jane Nye, the first of his three wives; his second marriage, to Jane Shirley Smith lasted for 23 years, from 1965 until 1988.

Turner's entry into the broadcasting business came in 1970, when he purchased an ailing Atlanta UHF television broadcasting station; by 1975, however, he had already transformed the station into the nucleus of a nationwide "superstation", the Turner Broadcasting System (WTBS), which broadcast low-cost sports and entertainment programmes to cable TV networks across the USA. Today, the majority of media analysts agree that WTBS provided most of the impetus that drove the development of cable TV in the USA during the 1970s.

By 1980, the rapid growth of the Turner network enabled him to open the country's first 24-hour Cable News Network (CNN), which shot to worldwide prominence, particularly in 1986 after its live coverage of the Challenger space shuttle disaster, and which later went on to achieve fame

through its authoritative on-the-spot coverage of the Gulf war that followed Iraq's invasion of Kuwait in August 1990. *Time* magazine named Turner as its Man of the Year in 1991, in acknowledgement of the contribution that CNN's unrivalled satellite TV coverage had made to worldwide awareness of the Gulf war and its related issues. It was also in 1991 that he began his most celebrated marriage, his third, to actress Jane Fonda. He has three sons and two daughters by his previous marriages.

Despite his commercial successes, Turner has frequently made headlines with his flamboyant and occasionally misconceived penchant for risk-taking in both his personal and his business life. The "Mouth of the South", as he has sometimes been known, still has the ability to offend as well as entertain his business rivals, and consequently his mistakes have generally been well publicised. In 1985 he paid an extraordinarily generous US$1.6 billion for the Metro Goldwyn Mayer/United Artists entertainment company but quickly sold it back, retaining only the MGM film library. In 1986 he made another ill-judged takeover bid for Columbia Broadcasting System (CBS), which eventually passed to Sony instead, and when Sony disposed of the loss-making company in 1995 he tried to launch a second bid for it; instead, however, he was persuaded to sell a majority stake in Turner Broadcasting to Time Warner, the new owner of CBS. Turner is now vice-chairman of Time Warner and head of the Turner Broadcasting unit within Time Warner.

Since the mid-1980s Turner (whose fortune of some US$5 billion puts him among America's 30 richest men) has devoted a good deal of his energy to charitable causes and has become known as a philanthropist. His staging of the 1986 "Goodwill Games" in Moscow might have been dismissed by a large part of the media as a personal publicity stunt, but it also reflected a deep and continuing personal commitment to international peace. The charitable foundation which Turner inaugurated in 1990 has been active in promoting environmental causes, and the personal gift of US$1 billion which he offered in September 1997 to a new foundation for the UN is thought to have been among the largest single donations ever made. Turner is also director of the Martin Luther King Center in Atlanta.

Turner's leisure interests include yachting (he captained the winning vessel in the 1977 Americas Cup and was named Yachtsman of the Year four times), as well as baseball and basketball (he owns the Atlanta Braves and the Atlanta Hawks). He has a cattle ranch in Montana.

Desmond **Tutu**

One of the most influential Christian figures of his generation, courageously and persistently insisting that Christianity was incompatible with the apartheid *system, Bishop Tutu appeared a rare symbol of hope in 1984, the year he won the Nobel Peace Prize. Over the succeeding decade Tutu, as Anglican archbishop of Cape Town, provided a vital bridge between demonstrators, the liberal opposition within the South African system, the Church, and international support for the anti-*apartheid *struggle of the African National Congress (ANC). A former teacher and a passionate speaker, he could be charming and modest to the point of self-deprecation, but maintained a powerful commitment to principle and justice. This came out most recently when, chairing the Truth and Reconciliation Commission, he refused to let its report's less convenient findings be swept under the carpet by the post-*apartheid *ANC-led government. Famous for his infectious humour, Tutu frequently used mischievous jokes to defuse any attempt to cast him as a dangerous troublemaker.*

Desmond Mpilo Tutu was born on 7 October 1931, in Klerksdorp, a small town west of Johannesburg. He grew up, like many black South Africans, in a shack without electricity or sanitation, although his father was a respected figure in the community as a primary school headmaster. In 1937 Desmond nearly died from tuberculosis. During two years spent in hospital he met the English priest Father Trevor Huddleston, who became his lifelong mentor, teaching a Christianity fundamentally at odds with racial discrimination.

Tutu qualified as a teacher in 1954 (financial constraints having forced him to abandon dreams of studying medicine). The next year he married Leah Nomalizo Shenxane, with whom he has had three daughters and one son. He also took his first overt stance against the *apartheid* system of strict racial segregation, incorporated into law by the white supremacist National Party which had swept to power in 1948. Writing to the prime minister, Tutu lambasted the "diabolical system" which reserved jobs for whites, outlawed inter-racial marriage and forced blacks into inferior living quarters.

The situation became even worse for the idealistic young teacher when the Bantu Education Act (1955) barred black children from learning maths or science. Furious at the introduction of this deliberately inferior education system, Tutu left teaching in 1957 to join St Peter's Theological College in Rossettenville, Johannesburg, while completing his degree in theology at the University of South Africa (1958). In 1960 he became an Anglican deacon and he was ordained as a priest in 1961. With political tension rising in South Africa, marked notably by the 1960 Sharpeville massacre, the banning of the ANC and the initiation of its guerrilla war, Desmond Tutu left the country to work and study in the UK, taking up a part-time post as curate in St Albans in September 1962 and studying theology at King's College, London.

Returning five years later to teach at St Peter's College, Alice, in the Cape, he found the situation even more oppressive, under "grand *apartheid*" laws which now corralled blacks into impoverished satellite "homelands" and stripped them of their rights in South Africa proper. Millions still flocked to the cities, giving white-run businesses a pool of cheap labour without citizenship. When students at St Peter's protested in 1968, they were beaten by police.

In 1970, Desmond Tutu took up lectureships at universities in the neighbouring states of Botswana, Lesotho and Swaziland, and began formulating a new doctrine, fusing the Black Consciousness ideas of the townships with the controversial Liberation Theology, developed particularly in Latin America, which emphasised Christianity's duty to fight injustice in this world, rather than hope for salvation in the next. As Tutu's reputation spread beyond South Africa, he became associate director of the Theological Association Fund in London in 1972.

In 1976, the year after he became the first black Anglican dean of Johannesburg, Tutu warned Prime Minister John Vorster that violence would erupt unless the regime abandoned its oppressive policies. On 16 June 1976, police fired upon peacefully demonstrating black schoolchildren in Soweto, thus igniting years of nationwide rioting, police repression and thousands of deaths.

Consecrated as bishop of Lesotho the following month, Tutu used this platform to decry "the cancer of the migratory labour system" which split families apart. It was Tutu who in 1977 delivered the funeral oration for Steve Biko, the young Black Consciousness leader killed while in police detention. Increasingly, he used his clerical immunity to articulate the concerns of blacks whose political leaders were either detained, exiled or killed. As general secretary of the South African Council of Churches (1978–84) he called for punitive sanctions on South Africa, winning support in the West but angering both the South African regime (which withdrew his passport) and Tutu's allies in the white liberal opposition.

Nationwide demonstrations broke out anew in early 1984, in protest against duplicitous constitutional reforms. Once again, Tutu was thrust into a political role, as co-founder of the opposition National Forum and patron of the pro-ANC United Democratic Front. Over succeeding years, he courageously condemned both police violence and the slaying of alleged "collaborators" by some over-zealous township militants.

In December 1984 Desmond Tutu was awarded the Nobel Peace Prize; his international acclaim also brought him scores of other awards and honorary doctorates. Rising to the top of South Africa's Anglican Church hierarchy, as bishop of Johannesburg (February 1985) and then archbishop of Cape Town (July 1986), he worked to make his archdiocese a rare oasis of white and black intermingling in an otherwise racially divided country. In August 1988 the building housing Tutu's offices in Johannesburg was firebombed. Undaunted, he led a "march for peace" to parliament in Cape Town on the day before **F.W. De Klerk** was elected state president, in September 1989. He also helped spearhead the "Soweto People's Delegation", which secured concessions to end a three-year rent strike by township residents.

Nelson Mandela's release from prison and the unbanning of the ANC in 1990 unleashed a new impetus for political reform. Throughout the often tortuous negotiations that ensued, Tutu remained a voice of sanity and reason. Publicly, he ceded the limelight to Mandela and other black politicians; privately, he acted as a crucial bridge between former enemies, and praised De Klerk for his political courage. The best-known of his five books to date, *The Rainbow People of God*, was published in 1994.

Following Nelson Mandela's election as president in 1994, Tutu was appointed in December 1995 to chair the Truth and Reconciliation Commission (TRC), set up with the aim of getting South Africans of all races and political hues to confront their difficult past. It bore Tutu's distinctive imprimatur, not least his controversial insistence on granting amnesty to all who admitted guilt for political crimes.

Desmond Tutu formally retired as archbishop in June 1996, but continued to be consulted by groups across the world on issues as diverse as AIDS, health, ecology, Tibet, disability, welfare, education, war and children's rights. Within post-*apartheid* South Africa itself, the two-and-a-half years of TRC hearings, and the controversy over the publication of its five-volume report in October 1998, kept him in the political limelight. Whereas he called for all South Africans to accept the results of the TRC's work as "an indispensable way to healing", the government resisted the publication of parts of the TRC report, angry that it covered ANC abuses of human rights during the years of struggle alongside its scathing indictment of the *apartheid* regime's crimes. Tutu's determination to give due emphasis to this less politically convenient aspect of the TRC's work, and his vehemence in fighting for its publication, was a further illustration of the devotion to democratic values which has from time to time led him into confrontations even with dear friends such as President Mandela himself.

Atal Bihari **Vajpayee**

When A.B. Vajpayee became Indian prime minister in March 1998, dire warnings abounded about inter-communal tensions being stirred up by right-wing Hindu chauvinism. Vajpayee, the so-called "acceptable face" of the Bharatiya Janata *Party (BJP) and its most distinguished parliamentary orator, commanded respect for his personal qualities and political experience, but the BJP's opponents depicted him as the front man for the resurgence of extremism. During over one year in power, however, until the fractiousness of Indian coalition politics brought his government down in April 1999, there was little sign of the party's militant tendency or extreme right-wing allies dictating policy. Nevertheless, the Vajpayee government was unequal to the task of rooting out corruption, lacked clear direction on running the economy, and became involved in risky confrontations with Pakistan both over nuclear weapons and over Kashmir.*

first degree at Victoria (now Laximbai) College in Gwalior, and a master's degree in law at DAV College in Kanpur, but his progress towards qualification in law was interrupted by partition in 1947, when he decided to work full-time with the RSS, the parent organisation from which right-wing Hindu parties and paramilitary groups developed over the subsequent decades.

In 1951 he helped found the *Jan Sangh* party, of which he was parliamentary leader for 20 years from 1957, president from 1968 to 1973, and representative on the National Integration Council, revived by Prime Minister Indira Gandhi in 1968 "to counter the menace of communalism". For five years (between 1962 and 1967) he sat in the upper house, the *Rajya Sabha*, but with that exception he was a *Lok Sabha* (lower house) member from 1957 until 1984; in 1986 he became a *Rajya Sabha* member again, but was re-elected to the *Lok Sabha* from 1991 onwards. A former journalist, an author of books on foreign policy and on the caste system, and a poet with several well-known publications to his name, Vajpayee is one of the most compelling orators in the Indian parliament. He has never married, but has two adopted children.

Atal Bihari Vajpayee was born on 25 December 1926 in Gwalior, now in Madhya Pradesh, in a high-caste Brahmin family. His elder brother was a member of the Hindu militant *Rashtriya Swayamsewak Sangh* (RSS), which he himself joined through its youth network in 1939. He was arrested in 1942 for his participation in the Quit India movement directed against British rule. He subsequently completed his

Detained along with many other opposition politicians during the period of emergency rule declared by Mrs Gandhi and her Congress (I) regime in 1975, Vajpayee was the leading *Jan Sangh* representative in the broad *Janata* coalition which ousted Congress (I) from power in the 1977 elections. He was minister of external affairs for the three years of *Janata* rule, until 1980. In that year he co-founded the *Bharatiya Janata* Party, whose president he was for six years until 1986, helping it project a relatively moderate image. In 1986 he moved over to be general secretary, with the more confrontationalist veteran Advani becoming BJP president.

The leader of the parliamentary opposition from 1993, Vajpayee found himself on the threshold of power after the general election of April/May 1996. The BJP had campaigned for an independent nuclear weapons policy, a more restrictive stance on foreign investment (by contrast with the outgoing government's recent liberalisation), and the building of a Hindu temple at Ayodhya, on the disputed site where a mosque had been destroyed by Hindu militants over three years previously. Its main rival, the Congress (I) party, accused it of anti-Muslim bigotry and stirring up inter-communal tension. Having won 30 per cent of the seats in the *Lok Sabha*, the BJP claimed the right as the largest party to try to form a government. Named as prime minister on 13 May 1996, Vajpayee was unable to build a coalition which could command a parliamentary majority, and resigned in advance of a no-confidence motion on 28 May. A United Front coalition government was then formed by the left-wing and regional alliance, headed by Deve Gowda as prime minister, with Congress (I) promising its backing (but not participating) to keep the BJP out of power.

Vajpayee got his second chance to form a government in early 1998, when Congress (I) withdrew its support from the United Front and thereby precipitated an inconclusive early general election. This time around, although the BJP increased its own representation only slightly, Vajpayee had a sufficient coalition, albeit an unstable one ranging from *Shiv Sena* to the right of the BJP to regional parties which did not share its nationalist agenda. He was sworn in as prime minister on 19 March 1998.

The central tenet of Vajpayee's political philosophy is a nationalism in which Hindu customs and culture represent the defining features of the Indian national identity. This *Hindutva* culture should, he believes, command the allegiance of all Indians, whether they are by religion Hindu, Muslim or any other creed. In his own words, "Mecca can continue to be holy for the Muslims but India should be holier than the holy for them". His government, however, with its dependence on secular parties for a majority, did little to implement a nationalist cultural programme, apart from an unsuccessful attempt to modify the secular curriculum for state schools to include study of the Sanskrit language and Hindu scripture. Nor was its slogan of "India shall be built by Indians" translated into a vigorous programme of *swadeshi* (self-reliance); only token restrictions were introduced on foreign investment, within a context which effectively continued the process of opening up the economy.

On international affairs, Vajpayee did play the high-risk card of assertiveness on nuclear weapons policy, carrying out five nuclear tests just two months after taking office. He gained considerable popularity within India as a result but triggered "tit-for-tat" tests by Pakistan which caused great alarm across the world and resulted in international sanctions on both countries. Later, however, Vajpayee sent out an unexpectedly conciliatory message towards Pakistan by visiting it in late February 1999, disregarding the opposition of the so-called "saffron fringe" of Hindu fundamentalists to any negotiation. This visit followed the successful sporting reconciliation of a tour of India by the Pakistani cricket team, but was itself soon put into a gloomier perspective by the outbreak of tension and shooting incidents along the *de facto* border in disputed Kashmir.

Always at the mercy of his quarrelsome and personality-fraught coalition partners, Vajpayee lost his majority when one of the southern regional parties pulled out in April 1999. Defeated in an ensuing vote of no confidence, he resigned on 17 April, but remained in office in a caretaker capacity (his Congress (I) rivals having attempted unsuccessfully to form a new coalition government) pending yet another general election.

Gianni **Versace**

The driving force and designing flair behind the Versace fashion empire until he was murdered in Miami in 1997, Gianni Versace was a child of post-war Italy, rising from humble origins to become a megastar among the international glitterati. Personally popular within an industry notorious for its rivalries, he could shape the career of supermodels like **Naomi Campbell***, have his clothes advertised by* **Madonna***, and count* **Princess Diana** *among his friends: more than anyone, Versace symbolised the high status accorded to designer fashion as art form, public statement and aspirational lifestyle in the 1980s and 1990s. His sister and younger brother, partners in his fashion empire, continue to run it since his death.*

Gianni Versace was born on 2 December 1946 in Reggio di Calabria at the southern tip of Italy. His parents, Antonio, an appliances salesman, and Francesca, a dressmaker, struggled to make a living in a region which had always been poor and was only slowly beginning to recover from the devastation of the Second World War. As a young boy, Gianni showed an early flair for fashion, designing his first dress when he was just nine, and beginning work as an apprentice to his mother while he was still in high school in Reggio di Calabria. By 1968 he had abandoned the idea of studying architecture and was working as a travelling fabric buyer for her atelier.

Before long, however, Gianni Versace gravitated towards Milan, the centre of the fashion industry, in a bid to set up on his own. In November 1972 he went to live there, doing designs for ready-to-wear items, and he soon began to get work with fashion houses such as Callaghan, Genny and Complice. His own first "signed collection" of women's wear, which he launched in 1978, showed inklings of what were later to become his stylistic hallmarks – innovation and daring, combined with a unique blend of elegance and femininity. The following year, Versace displayed versatility and commercial acumen, too, by launching a menswear collection, and setting up the first of an eventual 80 boutiques.

Italy's ever-inquisitive fashion pundits were duly impressed, and in 1982 they bestowed upon Versace the first of what would become a string of Occhio d'Oro (Golden Eye) design awards. That same year, he broke new ground by creating lavish costumes for two ballet productions at Milan's celebrated La Scala Theatre, and in 1984 he began a long association with the opera, designing costumes for Donizetti's *Don Pasquale* – again at La Scala. Other fashion awards followed, while in January 1986 President Francesco Cossiga conferred on him the honorary title of Commendatore of the Italian Republic.

Soon the Versace name became synonymous with chic. He was feted by the rich and famous, with Princess Diana, Madonna, Demi Moore, Naomi

Campbell, Sting and Sylvester Stallone among the enthusiasts. Clothes represented just one facet of his involvement with fashion; he also launched a series of perfumes and fragrances, watches and (in 1993) a range of home furnishings. Versace showrooms in London, Paris and Berlin attracted devotees of the "total fashion" lifestyle which this range of products offered. Younger clients were drawn to his less expensive informal ranges, beginning with Istante, which he launched in 1985. Gianni Versace not only kept pace with the ever-changing tastes of international fashion; in many instances, he actually set the trend. He revived those hallmarks of the 1960s, the mini-skirt and catsuit; pioneered the slit skirt; encouraged women to wear leggings and tights as trousers; and even persuaded them to don the normally discreetly hidden bustier as an ostentatious night-time outfit.

A man of extraordinary contrasts, Versace designed the set and costumes for Elton John's world rock tour of 1992, yet still catered for more formal tastes – such as the V2 By Versace range of men's suits in 1990, the Versace Signature menswear collection, launched in Berlin in 1995, and a prize-winning diamond-studded tiara the following year. It was precisely this blending of "high" and "low" art which guaranteed Versace's appeal. Often his work was feted in museums – something unimaginable in previous decades. In 1985 Les Serres d'Auteil, Paris, exhibited artworks inspired by Versace. In 1991 the London Royal College of Art housed an exhibition of his theatrical creations, which later travelled to Genoa and Munich. In keeping with his vision of the "total image", Versace collaborated astutely with photographers – Richard Avedon, Bruce Weber and Helmut Newton – and with the choreographer Maurice Béjart. Gianni Versace's Vanitas series of coffee-table books showcased his (and others') talents.

In 1995 the Versus line spearheaded a Versace assault on the US market, where dozens of Versace outlets soon opened. The globalisation of the Versace name also included exclusive retailing outlets in Japan, run by a Japanese partner. With his sales rocketing, to nearly US$500 million in 1996, Gianni Versace could afford houses in Miami, Paris, New York, Lake Como in north Italy, and his home base, Milan.

A Versace "statement" could make front-page news, like Liz Hurley's famously revealing safety-pin gown. While his earlier collections showed clean, classical lines, he was soon experimenting with brighter colours and metallic finishes – displays of wit and audacity which one fashion critic described as "jubilant vulgarity". As he told a journalist in 1997: "I didn't want to do haute couture as it existed in the 1940s and 1950s. It cannot exist in the same way in the 1990s." Yet despite this assertive modernity, Versace constantly derived inspiration from ancient Greece and Rome, Japan or Byzantium, and reflected his continuing fascination with architecture. Traditional craftsmanship underpinned all his work, for Versace could cut and sew garments himself.

Close-knit family ties remained the foundation for his astounding success. With his sister Donatella and their younger brother Santo, he formed a joint business partnership, and Donatella, a considerable designer in her own right, often modelled his preparatory designs. Confident yet modest in bearing, with greying stubble on his chin, Gianni Versace in the 1990s was a popular figure on catwalks throughout the world. He never hid his homosexuality, even in the staid upper echelons of Catholic Italy. Tragically, it appears that it may have been his sexuality which linked him fatally with former male prostitute Andrew Cunanan, who shot and killed him outside his Miami home on 15 July 1997. The killing precipitated a media furore and a nationwide manhunt until police found that Cunanan, also suspected of four other murders, had not left Miami but had avoided capture by committing suicide on a houseboat where he had been hiding.

Among the many models and celebrities who paid their respects at Versace's funeral, a sobbing Princess Diana was seen being comforted by Elton John – who would sing a tribute at her own funeral less than two months later.

Terry **Waite**

Terry Waite, the archbishop of Canterbury's special envoy abducted in Lebanon while negotiating for the release of hostages, was the "big man" of the Lebanese hostage drama which so gripped the world news agenda of the 1980s and early 1990s. A popular hero for his efforts before his capture, his imposing figure and calm demeanour seemed to symbolise the gravity of his mission, helping deflect the disquieting evidence linking him with US intelligence and its so-called Iran–Contra scandal over "buying out" hostages with illegal arms deals. Waite had no contact with the outside world during most of his own five-year captivity, when only rumour sustained the belief in the West that he was still alive. His release in November 1991, if not quite the emotional "high" of the earlier release of the young journalist John McCarthy, marked the last major dramatic moment of the protracted hostage crisis.

Terence Hardy Waite was born on 31 May 1939 in Bollington, Cheshire, England, the son of Thomas Waite, a policeman, and his wife Lena. Keen to join the navy after being a sea cadet, he persuaded his father to let him leave Wilmslow School at 16. However, his ambitions changed and, after working briefly in Warrington, he joined the Grenadier Guards in 1956. This also proved short-lived, for he was soon discharged due to poor health.

Looking for a new direction, Waite was drawn to the Anglican Church but had no vocation for the priesthood. While working at a hostel for ex-prisoners and the homeless in Middlesbrough, he identified the Church Army as the ideal solution. Selected for its training college in London in 1958, he got his first taste of public speaking as he conducted teaching and preaching programmes around the country, and developed his interest in methods of education and group development.

In London he met his future wife Frances Watters. They were married in her home town of Belfast in May 1964, the year Waite took up his first post as lay education adviser to the Anglican bishop of Bristol. His twin daughters were born in 1965 and another daughter a year later. A son was born after the family's move to Uganda, where Waite was appointed provincial training adviser to the first African Anglican archbishop of Uganda, Rwanda and Burundi in 1969. At a time when the region was in a state of considerable unrest, Waite travelled extensively, often in life-threatening situations (notably during the Idi Amin coup), co-ordinating programmes to provide aid and development, including the Southern Sudan Relief Project.

In 1972 Waite moved to Rome as an international consultant for a Roman Catholic medical order. Programmes on education, health, development and relations took him all over the world for the next eight years. In 1978 the family returned to London, where Waite also worked on the Africa desk of the British Council of Churches.

Appointed assistant for Anglican Communion affairs to Archbishop of Canterbury Robert Runcie in 1980, he was responsible for the archbishop's foreign visits, including the first-ever such visit to China, and for advising on developments in the Anglican community. Continuing to travel throughout the world, he acquired a breadth of experience and diplomatic skills which led to a request for his help as special envoy to the archbishop to free three missionaries taken hostage in Iran. The success of this mission in 1981 brought him into the public eye and he was awarded an MBE the following year. Four civilian hostages were released in Libya following Waite's negotiations with Col. **Kadhafi** in late 1984 and early 1985.

By 1986 Waite was in Lebanon, still officially as the archbishop's special envoy, and mounting an attempt to secure the release of European and US hostages held by an Iranian-backed guerrilla group, the Islamic *Jihad* for the Liberation of Palestine. The situation deteriorated in April following the US bombing of Libya but hope was restored with two releases later in the year. In November 1986 the process suffered another setback with revelations in the USA about the so-called Iran–Contra affair, whose Middle East dimension was the US government's willingness to sell arms to Iran (in contravention of an embargo) to secure the release of hostages. Waite remained committed to his task, despite the evidence that hostages in whose recent release he had been involved had in fact been traded for US arms, and allegations that he was himself a spy and involved with the key US figure in the Iran–Contra affair, Lt.-Col. Oliver North.

While holding talks with the kidnappers in Beirut on 20 January 1987, Waite was himself abducted, held hostage and imprisoned somewhere in Lebanon. Four years of solitary confinement ensued. Chained to a wall in a small windowless cell, he kept himself sane by the combination of strength of character and deep Christian faith. Each night he would save a tiny amount of bread and water so in the morning he could receive Communion. During the day he would remember stories, poems and prayers, and contemplate the language and meaning of the lessons in the Bible, much of which he knew by heart. In the evening he would sing the hymns of Evensong and pray to God, giving him encouragement and hope. After 18 months he was given a copy of the Bible, and human companionship came in early 1991, when he was joined in captivity by the US hostage Thomas Sutherland, a former academic at the American University in Beirut.

After 1,763 days in captivity, Terry Waite was released on 18 November 1991, together with Thomas Sutherland, as part of a UN-mediated Arab–Israeli–Western hostage exchange. Their release, and that of five more people the following month, effectively marked the end of the long Lebanese hostage crisis.

Author of two best-selling books (*Taken on Trust* and *Footfalls in Memory*) about his experiences, Waite found himself in great demand for lectures and broadcasts, both about his captivity and about how his survival skills (such as management of stress and loneliness) relate to normal life, especially in the business world. Appointed a fellow commoner of Trinity Hall, Cambridge, he also recommended his work for Y Care, the international development wing of the YMCA, which he had founded and chaired from 1984 until his capture, and under whose aegis several Terry Waite vocational training centres for street children have been established in India.

Terry Waite is currently writing three new books and campaigning for the release of three US hostages held in Colombia. He supports many charities and organisations working with the homeless, prisoners, the disabled and victims of violent crime.

Lech **Walesa**

Lech Walesa, the best-known opponent of the communist regime in Poland, became his country's first president in the post-communist era. However, his five years in office and his acrimonious defeat when he sought a second term, proved more the coda to his career than its culmination. His impatience, outspokenness and combative style appeared autocratic and divisive, while his anti-communism made his relationship with the post-1993 government of former communists especially problematic. A former shipyard electrician from Gdansk, Walesa's lasting political significance is as leader of the free trade union Solidarity, spawned by the shipyard strikes of 1980. As Solidarity grew into a mass movement which challenged the communist system, Walesa was hailed in the West as an icon of freedom. Arrested as the movement was driven underground, he led its resurgence in 1988 and helped negotiate the dismantling of Poland's one-party state, a key development in precipitating the collapse of communism throughout eastern Europe.

Lech Walesa was born on 29 September 1943 in Popowo, near Lipno in northwest Poland. His father Boleslaw was a carpenter, who died in 1946 after being conscripted by the Nazis to dig ditches during the Second World War. Lech Walesa trained as an electrician, working for a local collective farm administration, before doing military service. In 1967 he moved to Gdansk, on the Baltic coast, finding work as an electrician in the Lenin shipyard. A devout Catholic, he married Danuta in 1969; they have four sons and four daughters.

Walesa's first political involvement came when he led a strike committee at the shipyard in the worker protests of December 1970. Six years later he was sacked from his job after speaking out about working conditions in the yard, and had to find intermittent work in a machine repair shop. When strikers began a sit-in in the shipyard in August 1980, he climbed over the gate and joined them again. Making a strong impression with his fiery oratorical skills, he became leader of the Gdansk inter-factory strike committee, and encouraged the workers to go beyond demanding improved pay and working conditions to demanding the right to strike and form free trade unions. This was a dramatic departure from the concept that all workplace issues would be handled through official unions within the communist structure. However, the impetus behind the strike movement was so powerful that the Polish government agreed to concede its essential demands, in the historic "Gdansk accords" in which Walesa played a major negotiating role, and which were signed at the end of August 1980.

The following month, when *Solidarnosc* (Solidarity) was formed – the first free trade union in the Soviet bloc – Walesa became chairman of its national co-ordinating commission. The movement (granted legal registration in November) caught on with astonishing speed across the country as a whole, among both industrial and agricultural workers, as membership numbers rose rapidly towards a peak of 10 million. Walesa became an international celebrity as well as a national figure. He was feted in the West by the right-wing regimes of both Ronald Reagan in the USA and **Margaret Thatcher** in the UK, who conveniently glossed over his role as a leader of organised labour and focused instead on the image of Solidarity striking a blow for freedom against the totalitarian communist system. Among the high points of this period for Walesa was his personal audience with **Pope John Paul II**, a fellow Pole, in Rome in January 1981.

By September 1981, when Walesa was elected as Solidarity chairman by a national delegate conference, its demands were moving clearly into the political arena, focusing around the call for free elections. The government, by now under the hardline leadership of Gen. Jaruzelski and highly conscious of the imminent danger of Soviet intervention, resolved on its own clampdown. Martial law was declared in November 1981, all trade unions were suspended and strikes banned, and Walesa and other leaders were arrested. He was detained for 11 months until late 1982, returning after his release to work once again in the Lenin shipyard.

Walesa's role in establishing Solidarity earned him the Nobel Peace Prize in 1983 and another audience with the pope, this time in Krakow during a papal visit to Poland. Walesa continued to lead an underground workers' movement throughout the 1980s. The outlook changed with the advent of **Mikhail Gorbachev**'s *glasnost* (openness) in the Soviet Union in the latter part of the decade. The new attitudes of the Soviet leadership raised hopes, as yet untested, that there could be real change in a communist country without the Soviet Union intervening militarily. Another occupation strike in the Gdansk Lenin shipyard in 1988 helped add to the political pressure which constrained the Polish government to concede a series of "round-table" talks. These not only resulted in the re-legalisation of Solidarity, but initiated the democratic reforms which marked the beginning of the collapse of the Soviet bloc.

In the resulting partly free elections in June 1989, the communists suffered a historic defeat at the hands of Solidarity, and Walesa's former aide Tadeusz Mazowiecki was appointed prime minister. Walesa himself refused ministerial office and returned to

trade union issues, becoming increasingly critical of his erstwhile Solidarity allies as they introduced tough economic austerity measures. These differences within Solidarity over strategy became even more evident when Walesa stood against Mazowiecki in the 1990 presidential elections. While Walesa, impatient at the pace of change, called for "permanent war at the top" and faster, broader reforms, Mazowiecki favoured stability and consistency. Walesa emerged the winner in a second round of polling in December, and thereupon resigned as leader of Solidarity to emphasise that his new role stood above party politics.

As president, Walesa, like his fellow head of state and former dissident **Vaclav Havel** in the Czech Republic, used his international celebrity to help press his country's case for early inclusion within the European Union and the North Atlantic Treaty Organization (NATO). He also angrily rejected allegations arising from the selective leaking of communist-era secret police records, which suggested that he had collaborated with the authorities in the early 1980s.

In domestic politics the Walesa presidency was a period of considerable political instability, with three parliaments, six governments, and frequent clashes between him and parliament over the choice of ministers. Seeking opportunities to present himself as a national figure of historical significance, with echoes of the authoritarian inter-war dictator Pilsudski, he formed a Pilsudski-style Non-Party Bloc in Support of Reforms, but this movement performed poorly in the 1993 legislative elections. The former communists returned to office following that poll, a development which exacerbated tensions between government and president. Walesa criticised the prime minister for stalling on privatisation, and stretched the legal limits of his powers to obstruct the new government and veto legislation, notably over liberalising the existing strict anti-abortion legislation.

Walesa's stormy five years in office came to an end with the November 1995 presidential election, when he lost to former communist Aleksander Kwasniewski. Walesa's autocratic style and often intemperate language contributed to undermining his popular support, as did the perception that he was standing on his past achievements whereas his opponent represented a new, younger generation. Tellingly, a new Polish constitution eventually agreed in April 1997 reduced the president's powers of appointment while strengthening those of parliament – not least in reaction to the experiences of Walesa's rule.

Walesa returned to Gdansk upon leaving office, re-emerging in the public eye at the time of the September 1997 general election, whose outcome gave the Solidarity Electoral Alliance the opportunity to return to government. He offered to broker a coalition deal between the winning parties, while denying any aspirations to the premiership himself. The following month, reflecting the extent to which the paths of different Solidarity figures had diverged, Walesa announced the formation of a new political party, Christian Democracy of Poland. Perhaps symbolically, the international media gave greater prominence to his subsequent announcement that he wanted his old job at the shipyard back.

Andrew **Wiles**

Andrew Wiles is the reserved Oxbridge-educated mathematician who astounded the world in 1993 by revealing that he had proved Fermat's Last Theorem. This conjecture had fascinated mathematicians for three-and-a-half centuries. In millions of tests it had not been shown to be false – conclusive enough evidence to constitute a proof in science – but in mathematics nothing is proved until it is shown that it would hold under any test. Wiles had worked on his proof in secret for seven years. This was unheard of in the mathematics community, where open discussion inspires most advances, but Wiles dreaded attracting attention by revealing what he was working on. Propelled into the media spotlight when he announced his success, he then had to work for a further year to repair a flaw, this time with every manoeuvre tracked by the entire mathematics community, until finally completing and publishing his full proof, to international acclaim. Now "at rest", no problem will ever grip him with the same fervour in the remainder of his mathematical research.

Andrew John Wiles was born on 11 April 1953 in Cambridge, England, where his father was chaplain at Ridley Hall and later dean of Clare College. Educated locally, Wiles was intrigued by mathematics and puzzles from an early age. When he was ten, he discovered at his local library a whole book devoted to one particular problem, once scribbled in the margin of a book by the 17th-century French mathematician Fermat. Fermat had claimed to have an amazing proof for the problem, too large to write alongside it, but the rediscovery of this proof had evaded eminent mathematicians for three centuries.

The problem looked simple to Wiles. The equation $x^n + y^n = z^n$ was familiar to him, when $n = 2$, as Pythagoras's theorem. In that form it has whole-number solutions, including $3^2 + 4^2 = 5^2$. Fermat's theorem stated that, when n is greater than 2, there are no (non-trivial) whole-number solutions. Wiles immediately began playing around with the puzzle, armed at ten with much the same array of mathematical techniques as Fermat in the 1600s.

Fascinated by its hidden complexity, Wiles retained a passion for this theorem throughout his education. Graduating in mathematics from Merton College, Oxford, in 1974, he returned to Cambridge to study for a doctorate at Clare College, specialising in number theory. Wiles realised that he could not yet tackle Fermat's Last Theorem, which he might study for years without achieving any results. However, as nobody had managed to prove it using existing mathematical techniques, he determined to study and develop emerging techniques with the hope that these might give him a new insight into the problem. He worked with his supervisor, Professor John Coates, on

elliptic curves, continuing in this field during 1977/78, when he was an assistant professor at Harvard, and completing his doctorate in 1979. He then was appointed as a junior research fellow at Clare. In 1982 he became the Eugene Higgins Professor of Mathematics at Princeton University, USA, a position he has retained except for a short period as a visiting professorial fellow at Merton

College, Oxford (1988–90), during which time he was appointed to the Royal Society.

In his research he had encountered the Taniyama–Shimura conjecture, proposed in 1955, which if true linked two disparate fields of mathematics – elliptic curves and modular forms. Taniyama–Shimura underlay many mathematical results worked on since then. Like Fermat's Last Theorem, it had evaded proof. In 1986 a mathematician showed that if Taniyama–Shimura was true then so was Fermat. Suddenly Wiles found he could pursue Fermat by working on areas of mainstream modern mathematics that would produce useful results, even if they ultimately led nowhere for him.

Unusually for a mathematician, he resolved to work alone and secretly in his attic. He was wary of becoming the subject of intense scrutiny if he talked about his work on such an infamous problem, and unwilling to publish papers on minor results as he went along in case this enabled a competitor to complete the proof before him. Wiles married just after the start of his secret labour, not even telling his wife Nada about his work until their honeymoon. Having recently finished a long paper, he released sections of it over the next few years, so as not to arouse suspicions about what he was doing, and ceased going to conferences so as to focus solidly on the problem. Thinking about it constantly, he broke off only to carry out the necessary lecturing for his job, and relaxed only to play with his two daughters.

Before embarking on the proof he spent 18 months familiarising himself with the latest mathematical developments, looking for ways to attack the proof. The idea he formulated was in two parts, the first of which he achieved within a few months. For years he tried a wide range of techniques to complete the second hurdle, relieved when a flaw undid a rival claimant's attempt at a proof, but growing despondent himself before eventually deciding to return to the conference circuit to learn about the latest new ideas. His attention caught by a technique from the field of modular forms, he returned rearmed to his attic and made rapid

progress with this new tool. A few steps still eluded him, however, and required vast development of the technique, known as Kolyvagin–Flach. Being less familiar with this field of mathematics, Wiles brought in a Princeton colleague, Nick Katz, in January 1993 to verify his work, swearing him to secrecy. The mathematics was so complex that they decided to set up an innocuously titled lecture course for Princeton students, during which Wiles could teach the new material to Katz. The level of difficulty quickly reduced the audience to just Katz, but the course continued and Katz could see no errors. So Wiles returned to his attic, completing the proof by May.

Wiles decided to announce the proof at a conference at the Isaac Newton Institute back in Cambridge in June. Meanwhile he checked and rechecked every line. Rumours began spreading about the content of his lectures at the conference, and on 23 June 1993, the day of his final lecture, the auditorium was packed and the atmosphere charged. After 50 minutes of complex scribbling on the blackboard, Wiles wrote up, "Hence Fermat's Last Theorem", and said, "I think I'll stop there".

Now Wiles's 200-page proof had to be scrutinised by referees and he spent an anxious summer clarifying the arguments for them. The chapter on Kolyvagin–Flach was sent to Katz who, by early September, had discovered a flaw unnoticed during the earlier lecture course at Princeton. Wiles desperately tried to repair it, but every attempt produced an error elsewhere. Working now under the intense pressure that he had always dreaded, he finally admitted publicly in an email in December 1993 that there was an error, but still refused to publish the other chapters, all containing new mind-bending mathematics, in case someone else managed to repair the hole and take the glory.

Wiles now sought assistance from another of the referees, a former student, Richard Taylor. Endlessly going over the work, and recovering from the shock of an April Fool claim that Fermat had been proven wrong by the discovery of three whole numbers satisfying the equation, Wiles had nevertheless reached the point of defeat by September 1994. Persuaded by Taylor to have one last attempt, he returned to the original proof to understand exactly why it had broken down. Then on 19 September a flash of inspiration came to him that the hole could be mended, and the argument simplified, using a theory that he had abandoned in 1991. Together Taylor and Wiles wrote a paper on the necessary link between these two methods, and on 25 October 1994 the whole proof, now totalling only 130 pages, was released to the world, together with this extra paper.

Hitting the headlines again, Wiles's eight-year struggle received enormous praise. Honours were heaped on him, including the US$50,000 Wolfskehl Prize, reserved for the solver of Fermat's Last Theorem. Now aged 41, he was too old to be awarded the Fields Medal, the "Nobel Prize for Mathematics", which he would undoubtedly have gained the previous year if the error in his proof had not been found. Instead he was awarded the International Mathematics Union Silver Plaque, and also the 1996 Common Wealth Award for science and invention. In 1997 he was elected to the US National Academy of Sciences.

Oprah **Winfrey**

Oprah Winfrey hosts a US television talk show which outstrips all others in both ratings and awards, and has also won plaudits as a film actress. The most powerful person in show business, she has reached this status and risen from poverty to become the country's wealthiest African–American, thanks to the public response to her appeal as "a normal person". Her defining characteristic is emotional openness about social, political and personal issues that affect her directly, in particular relating to sexual abuse (which she experienced herself in childhood), education and the empowerment of women and children. The Oprah Winfrey Show *has spawned both imitators and more blatantly sensationalist rivals, a trend she herself deplores.*

Oprah Gail Winfrey was born on 29 January 1954 in Kosciusko, a racially segregated small town in Mississippi, Ohio, USA. The name Oprah resulted from an accidental misspelling – she was meant to have the unusual biblical name Orpah, sister of Ruth. Her mother Vernita Lee, only 18 and not married to her soldier father Vernon Winfrey, left the child to be brought up by its grandmother on the farm, and moved north in search of work. Oprah's grandmother taught her to read at three and, nurturing her precocious talent for public speaking, encouraged her recitations at the local church. At six she was taken north with her mother and younger step-siblings. Living in Milwaukee, Wisconsin, she idolised her elementary school teacher, but at home began suffering abuse from family members; she was raped by her cousin at nine, abused and molested by an uncle, tried to run away, became pregnant and then lost the prematurely born baby at the age of 14. Her mother took her to a juvenile detention home, but she was rejected apparently because there were no beds free there, so finally she was sent to live with her father in Nashville, Tennessee. He insisted on a strict regime and pushed her to high achievement in school. She excelled at public speaking and was selected to represent her high school as the Outstanding Teenager of America.

The local radio station gave Oprah Winfrey her first break in the media, a news-reading job, after her impressive interview answers had helped win her a Miss Fire Prevention pageant at 17. She also won the titles of Miss Black Nashville and Miss Black Tennessee in 1972, and went to Tennessee State University (TSU) that autumn, on a full scholarship, majoring in speech and drama. A year later, however, she was offered a job on Nashville television, the first black person and first woman to anchor its news programme. Deciding to pursue this rather than continue at college (she eventually did obtain her degree from TSU in 1987), she worked there until 1976. Moving on to Baltimore, she failed to impress as a news presenter and was demoted to co-host the morning talk show *People Are Talking*. Finding herself ideally suited to a form of interviewing with such scope for empathy and personal involvement, she stayed in Baltimore until 1983 doing that show, then moved to Chicago to host the talk show *A.M. Chicago*. It was her impact here that really made her name. In 1985, the programme was renamed *The Oprah Winfrey Show* and the following year it was syndicated nationwide, since when it has topped the national talk show ratings year on year. The winner of many television industry awards, *The Oprah Winfrey Show* is seen by some 15 million US viewers daily and has been sold to 132 countries worldwide.

The show's success is based on Oprah Winfrey's capacity for airing social and economic problems in a way which directly engages the emotions of ordinary viewers. Her willingness to share her own intimate or traumatic personal experiences on air has won her the confidence of her viewers to the extent that her views, and causes she espouses, have become extraordinarily influential. As a passionate reader, for example, she has not only popularised the discussion of books on television, but also made a major best-seller of every title chosen for Oprah's Book Club since she started that feature in September 1996. Her openness about her abused childhood, and about the emotions she experienced in coming to terms with it, helped win public support for a national database of child abusers. Strongly identifying herself with the campaign for a National Child Protection Act, she testified before the Senate judiciary committee on the issue, and was present in December 1993 when President **Clinton** signed the legislation (dubbed the "Oprah Bill") into law. Her battle with her weight, which has seesawed between glamorous slimness and obesity, is another issue on which viewers identify with her as especially human, and has also been the launchpad for an enormously successful cookbook and the 1997 fitness and health video, *Oprah: Make the Connection*, while her unguarded reaction on the health threat from BSE in cattle, that it "just stopped me cold from eating another burger", caused such

consternation in the industry that she was sued (unsuccessfully) for damage caused by putting viewers off beef.

Contracted to continue her talk show until 2000, Oprah Winfrey has lately been putting a major effort into Oxygen, a project for a cable television network by and for women. Meanwhile, her career as a film actress, which began with great success when she appeared as Sofia in *The Color Purple* (1985) and won an Oscar nomination for best supporting actress, brought her more critical praise with the release in 1998 of *Beloved*. Based on the novel about slavery by Toni Morrison, which had impressed her so forcefully that she had bought an option on the film rights when the book first came out, *Beloved* was a box office failure. It was produced by Harpo Films, part of the company Harpo Productions which she set up in 1986, the company name being derived from spelling Oprah backwards. Harpo also owns and produces her talk show, and has produced other television programmes and films, notably *Women of Brewster Place* and the 1993 television special *Michael Jackson Talks ... to Oprah: 90 Prime-Time Minutes with the King of Pop*.

Oprah Winfrey, who has lived since 1986 with partner Stedman Graham, overtook **Steven Spielberg** in 1998 on *Entertainment Weekly*'s list of the most powerful people in show business. Estimates by *Forbes* magazine put her fortune at US$550 million and her 1998 earnings at US$125 million. She contributes, and uses her influence to mobilise public contributions, to numerous charitable causes concerned particularly with education and empowerment, and is spokesperson for A Better Chance, a scholarship programme for students from inner-city school districts, but has had to acknowledge the failure of the Families for a Better Life project which she launched in Chicago in 1994, supporting poor families and aimed at "destroying the welfare mentality".

James **Wolfensohn**

*An Australian who formally took US citizenship during a successful career as a Wall Street banker, James Wolfensohn became a key figure in the international development debate when in 1995 he took over the presidency of the World Bank, a post traditionally held by a North American. His high-flying career in international banking had earned him the reputation of being Australia's most successful businessman in New York after the media tycoon **Rupert Murdoch**. Despite his sometimes abrasive manner, he has successfully implemented structural and policy reforms at the World Bank, which have raised its international profile and effectiveness, and is a leading advocate of plans to cancel much of the debt owed by third world countries.*

James David Wolfensohn was born in Sydney, Australia, on 1 December 1933, the son of Hyman and Dora Wolfensohn. He studied law at the University of Sydney, gaining first a bachelor's degree and then a master's degree in 1957. He was also a successful sportsman, representing his country in the Australian Olympic fencing team in 1956, and an officer of the Royal Australian Air Force.

After working for the Australian law firm Allen, Allen & Hemsley he went to the USA and gained another master's degree from the Harvard Graduate School of Business. In 1961 he married Elaine Botwinick, an education specialist; they have three children, Sara, Naomi and Adam.

Moving from law to investment banking, Wolfensohn worked as a consultant in his native Sydney, then as a stockbroker there, before he and his wife decided to make their lives in the northern hemisphere. They moved to New York, where he obtained the post of president of the J. Henry Schroder Banking Corporation, responsible for building this company up as a North American arm of the UK-based merchant bankers Schroders. He then transferred to London, becoming executive deputy chairman and managing director of Schroders Ltd, but left in 1976 when he was passed over for the top post following the retirement of the chairman. Back in the USA once again, he soon became executive partner and head of the investment banking department of Salomon Brothers merchant bank in New York. In 1981, a year after he formally assumed US citizenship, Wolfensohn established his own firm, James D. Wolfensohn Inc., an international banking and corporate finance concern which was both successful, and renowned for its charitable contributions. He relinquished his position as president and chief executive officer in June 1995 when he took up the World Bank post, and later sold the company to Bankers Trust.

On 1 June 1995 Wolfensohn moved to take over the presidency of the World Bank (the International Bank for Reconstruction and Development – IBRD) from Lewis Preston. His nomination by US President

Bill Clinton, for a five-year term, was criticised at the time on the grounds that he lacked the necessary experience of international development issues. However, in office he has given the organisation a much higher profile than it had under his predecessor, working to improve the public perception of its development role. He has made the World Bank more political, with outspoken criticisms of governmental corruption. Also controversial is his active role in pressing for the cancellation of international debt where the burden of interest and repayments is crippling the economies of third world countries. His reforms have allowed the organisation to realise much greater potential and he has won praise for inaugurating such initiatives as the "micro credit programme", providing loans to small concerns in order to enhance their effectiveness.

By the time the UN's second summit meeting on the environment was held in New York in June 1997 Wolfensohn had been coming under increasing pressure over the Bank's record in supporting projects without sufficient concern for their environmental impact. The focus of this controversy was the Narmada Dam and associated huge-scale river irrigation project in India. At the meeting, Wolfensohn gave a public pledge that the Bank would henceforth take a country's forest protection record into account when allocating assistance. The Bank's stance on other controversial major dam-building schemes, some of which it continued to fund, became a litmus test of Wolfensohn's grasp of the global sustainability agenda, in which economic development is seen as inseparable from its environmental consequences and social and ethical contexts.

Wolfensohn has sought to enhance the World Bank's ability to combat world poverty and to adjust to the rapidly changing economic environment by adopting what he has called a "strategic compact". Under this compact the Bank is moving resources to "front-line" lending and operations services by decentralising its operations, with the aim of bringing the Bank closer to its customers.

Central to this task is Wolfensohn's modernising vision of the Bank as a "knowledge bank", which seeks to harness the benefits of the information revolution so that it can act as a clearing house for advice and expertise as well as funding on development issues. He set out this vision in the Bank's 1998 annual report, entitled *Knowledge for Development*, which argues that technical and medical knowledge can be as important in improving health and living standards as physical and human capital. The report proved controversial in development circles, attracting criticism from non-governmental organisations such as Christian Aid and Oxfam, both over its sometimes patronising tone and, more importantly, because of concern that the Bank's strategy overlooked the fact that the poor cannot afford to pay for knowledge.

Wolfensohn is an accomplished cellist and has worked on a voluntary basis for numerous cultural and arts organisations. He was chairman of the board of the Carnegie Hall Corporation from 1980 to 1991 and chaired the team which raised funds for the renovation of the hall. He also chaired the board of trustees of the John F. Kennedy Center for the Performing Arts (including the affiliated National Symphony Orchestra) from1990 until 1995, when he became chairman emeritus. He has in addition worked as president of the International Federation of Multiple Sclerosis Societies, as director of the World Business Council for Sustainable Development, and with the Rockefeller Foundation, the Population Council and Rockefeller University.

Boris **Yeltsin**

*Boris Yeltsin has been Russian president since the beginning of the 1990s, both before and after the break-up of the Soviet Union in 1991. A former communist party official and protégé of **Mikhail Gorbachev**, he proved to be an effective populist politician, whose finest hour came with the defiance of the August 1991 coup attempt in Moscow, rallying the crowds in front of the Russian parliament building in the name of the great reform experiment. Five years later, despite having tarnished his image badly by the use of force in a confrontation with parliament, and despite being blamed for an immensely costly offensive against secessionists in Chechnya, he recovered enough of the old magic to win re-election, as the best available pro-reform option to defeat the communist challenge. Thereafter, however, his confrontations with parliament, his erratic and often embarrassing public behaviour, and his relapses into illness linked to his major heart surgery at the end of 1996, kept the succession issue to the fore in an atmosphere of recurrent crisis.*

Boris Nikolayevich Yeltsin was born on 1 February 1931 in Butka in the Sverdlovsk region. His family had a peasant farming background, but his father became a construction worker and his mother a seamstress. In his youth, Boris blew off two fingers on his left hand while playing with a live grenade. Nevertheless, whilst he was a college student he played professional volleyball for Sverdlovsk, one of the leading Soviet teams at the time. Expected to pursue a career in industry, he completed his degree in construction engineering at Kirov Polytechnic School in Sverdlovsk (now Yekaterinberg) in 1955. He married a fellow engineering graduate, Naina Iosifovna Girina, and they have two daughters, the younger of whom, Tatyana, is his official image adviser. Becoming a grandfather later in life gave Yeltsin obvious pleasure, and he did not shrink from exploiting the photo opportunities it provided.

Yeltsin's first job as a Soviet industrial manager was in a heavy tubing manufacturing plant. Between 1957 and 1967 he was manager, then executive engineer, then director of the Yusgorstroy Construction Trust. It was during this period that he first began to be heavily involved in politics. Having joined the Communist Party of the Soviet Union (CPSU) in 1961, he became secretary (in 1969) and then chairman of the party regional committee in Sverdlovsk, and in 1980 became a member of the CPSU central committee.

The election of Mikhail Gorbachev as party general secretary in 1985 marked a turning point in Yeltsin's career. Moving to Moscow, he was made first secretary of the CPSU in the city, joined the central committee's powerful secretariat and became a candidate member of the politburo. Quickly identified as a radical, he grew increasingly popular with the people of Moscow for his informal manner and his willingness to criticise the Soviet system over such failures as poor housing and empty shops. Apparently disillusioned with the pace of *perestroika* (restructuring), however, he became involved in open confrontation with leading conservatives in the party at the end of 1987, and was dropped from the politburo, criticised by Gorbachev, and shunted from the Moscow leadership to a position with much lower visibility, as minister of construction.

Election by a huge majority in March 1989 to represent a Moscow constituency in the Soviet Union's newly restyled Congress of People's Deputies gave Yeltsin a fresh chance to demonstrate both his popularity and his political flair. A founder member of the oppositional Inter-Regional Group in the Soviet parliament, he dared to discuss multipartyism and called passionately for the transfer of more power from the centre to the republics. He became a member of the Russian Federation Congress of People's Deputies, elected in March 1990, and in May that body chose him as chairman of the Russian Federation Supreme Soviet – thus making him *de facto* Russian president. Deciding that this was incompatible with party membership, he threw his party card on the floor in front of Gorbachev at the party congress in July 1990, expressing disgust with the slow pace of reforms.

Within the Russian republic Yeltsin decided to go for more radical change with a 500-day "dash to the market economy" package and a declaration of sovereignty. He also managed a temporary reconciliation with Gorbachev to ward off a conservative backlash. Yeltsin strengthened his own hand, as Gorbachev did not, by getting a popular mandate for his leadership, winning the first-ever direct election for the Russian presidency with 57 per cent of the vote in June 1991.

Two months later, the hardline August coup in Moscow threatened not only to depose Gorbachev from the Soviet leadership but to reverse the growing autonomy of the republics and to halt the whole reform experiment. Yeltsin famously led the resistance from the Russian parliament (the White House), emulating a pose of Lenin when he addressed the crowds from the top of a tank, and retaining the political initiative when the coup collapsed.

The rapid dissolution of the Soviet Union within the remaining four months of 1991 left him in an apparently very strong position. He was a powerful and popular executive president of the Russian Federation, while the new Commonwealth of Independent States (CIS) offered him the prospect of maintaining links between the former Soviet republics in a manner which would reflect the role of Russia at its core. His courageous stand against the August coup had won him great prestige, but he faced an enormous task in terms of reconstructing the economy and reconciling conflicting political pressures.

In the course of 1992, however, Yeltsin became locked in a struggle with the conservative forces in the Russian parliament over the sometimes ill-conceived attempts of his liberal ministers to implement economic reforms. The constitutional court also opposed what it regarded as his attempt to assert excessive powers, successively over the creation of ministries, the banning of the communist party, the appointment of the prime minister, and his decision in 1993 that he would rule by decree. In parliament the conservatives fell narrowly short in a vote to impeach him in March 1993. The following month he won a vote of confidence in a popular referendum, but in September, when he issued a decree disbanding the parliament, conservative communist and right-wing nationalist forces combined to resist him by force. Proclaiming Gen. Rutskoi as president in Yeltsin's place, they attacked strategic points in Moscow, and held out in the parliament building when Yeltsin called in loyal troops.

The violent power struggle against the parliament exposed Yeltsin's authoritarian intolerance of opposition. The shelling of the White House on his orders sent out a powerful negative image, at the scene of his own stand for freedom three years previously, from which his liberal democratic credentials never recovered. Elections to a new parliament in December 1993 returned large numbers of communists and ultra-nationalists, although Yeltsin did get his way with the narrow endorsement of a new constitution which gave him strong presidential powers.

Yeltsin's popularity touched a low point in 1995 as Russian troops fought a long and bloody war in

Chechnya, where he had despatched them the previous December in a high-risk effort to end a separatist rebellion. Many of his erstwhile liberal allies condemned the war, while the economy languished in serious recession, organised crime undermined the authority of the government, and the president himself suffered two mild heart attacks. The communist party topped the poll in fresh parliamentary elections at the end of that year, and pro-reform factions remained divided in the run-up to the presidential elections scheduled for mid-1996. A populist campaign of unexpected vigour, however, saw Yeltsin top the first-round poll on 16 June, as the best available pro-reform option to ward off the communist challenge. He effectively disappeared from sight between the first and second rounds of voting and it was confirmed much later that he had had three heart attacks during the campaign. His support held up, however, in spite of the spate of fresh speculation about his ill health and frailty, and he defeated the communist leader Gennady Zyuganov in the run-off on 3 July, with almost 54 per cent of the vote.

Sworn in again on 9 August, Yeltsin suffered another collapse and needed quintuple coronary bypass surgery in November. Many believed that his career was over. To great surprise, he made a recovery, marking his comeback with a complete reshuffle of his government in March 1997. The issue of his health, however, once again in the forefront at the end of 1997, became a dominant factor as factions jockeyed for position in a post-Yeltsin era. Bouts of illness, which overtook him suddenly and several times, caused the last-moment cancellation or abrupt early ending of foreign visits, and a series of bafflingly incoherent remarks and other highly embarrassing incidents, reviving memories of an occasion when he had failed to leave his plane for an intended stopover meeting in Ireland on his way home in 1994. His medical problems were linked to other illnesses as well as his heart condition, including pneumonia, the stomach ulcers for which he had surgery in January 1999, the "high blood pressure and fatigue" which tended to predominate in official explanations, and persistent evidence that he was unable to bring a long-standing drink problem under control.

Domestic policy during Yeltsin's second term continued to oscillate between an apparent strengthening of commitment to economic reform, and changes of government personnel and periods of retreat in the face of unpopularity. In 1998 this reached extremes which brought his struggle with the communist-dominated parliament to a head. Attempting to assert himself and send out signals of vigorous action on the economy, he first sacked Prime Minister **Viktor Chernomyrdin**, then, after a few months, decided just as suddenly in August 1998 to reappoint him. The parliament, which had resisted the first change, blocked the second. Fresh urgency was given to moves to impeach the president. This process had been initiated in June, when parliament set up a commission to look at possible charges (notably his signature of the agreement to dissolve the Soviet Union in December 1991, which could be construed as treason, and, more seriously, his attack on parliament in 1993 and the launching of the Chechnya offensive in December 1994).

An eventual compromise, concluded as the economic crisis reached meltdown point and the rouble crashed, emphasised how fast Yeltsin's powers had ebbed away. While he refused to resign, insisting that he would continue until elections due in 2000 (but not seek a further term), he did accept the appointment as prime minister of Yevgeniy Primakov, a candidate acceptable to the communist bloc in parliament. He ceded to the prime minister the main role in choosing the cabinet, and agreed to the strengthening of parliament's role in such appointments and, to the consternation of liberal reformists, also accepted a package of economic proposals heavily influenced by the communist insistence on greater government intervention. Over the ensuing months, it became increasingly apparent that Primakov, not Yeltsin, was running the government, even to the extent of taking on (and apparently breaking the power of) the business and finance tycoon Boris Berezovsky, whose influence had owed much to his links with the Yeltsin family, and launching investigations into related corruption allegations.

In February 1999, Primakov proposed a deal to parliament, whereby Yeltsin's power to dismiss the government or dissolve parliament would be suspended – pending the completion of the current parliamentary term and the holding of elections in December 1999 – in return for the ending of impeachment proceedings against the president. President Yeltsin would be allowed to remain in office until his full term was completed in the year 2000, an objective clearly of great significance to him, and would also get the protection of a new law to guarantee the safety and welfare of retiring presidents. It was a proposal Primakov had clearly not discussed with Yeltsin, who, from hospital, categorically rejected it.

Extraordinarily, despite the relative successes of the Primakov government and his high popular approval ratings (as against opinion poll support for Yeltsin running at just 2 per cent), Yeltsin hit back against the man he now saw as his chief rival in power, and announced in mid-May 1999 that he was dismissing Primakov. Moreover, the president's position was strengthened both by the reassertion of Russia's international role (with its crucial involvement in ending the conflict between NATO and Yugoslavia over Kosovo), and by the defeat in the parliament on 15 May of the five impeachment charges. Although all five obtained majority support, only the charge that he had exceeded his powers in ordering the Chechnya offensive came close to the necessary two-thirds majority; it gained 283 votes out of 450, including those of the liberal *Yabloko* party as well as the communist-led bloc.

Yeltsin's nominee to succeed Primakov was the little-known interior minister Sergei Stepashin. This nomination was subsequently accepted by the parliament as it backed off from provoking a deadlock, preferring not to precipitate the calling of elections which were anyway due in six months. It was by now too late, however, for Yeltsin to recover any measure of the respect he had once commanded at home or abroad, and it was a matter of conjecture whether his health would hold out to allow him to complete his term of office.

Photo credits

Adams, Gerry	Associated Press AP
Ahern, Bertie	Department of Foreign Affairs, Dublin, and the Embassy of the Republic of Ireland to the UK
Annan, Koffi	Executive Office of the Secretary-General, United Nations
Aquino, Cory	Associated Press AP
Arafat, Yassir	Associated Press
Ashrawi, Hanan	Associated Press AP
Assad, Hafez al-	Associated Press
Aung San Suu Kyi	Associated Press AP
Berlusconi, Silvio	Associated Press AP
Bhutto, Benazir	Office of Benazir Bhutto, Pakistan People's Party
Blair, Tony	Office of the Prime Minister, UK
Boutros Ghali, Boutros	Associated Press AP
Branson, Richard	Associated Press
Brundtland, Gro Harlem	Office of Information, World Health Organization
Buffett, Warren	Associated Press AP
Bush, George	Office of George Bush
Camdessus, Michel	Public Affairs Division, International Monetary Fund
Campbell, Naomi	Associated Press AP
Cardoso, Fernando	Embassy of Brazil to the UK
Castro, Fidel	Associated Press AP
Chernomyrdin, Viktor	Associated Press AP
Chirac, Jacques	Embassy of France to the UK
Çiller, Tansu	Associated Press AP
Clinton, Bill	Associated Press AP
Clinton, Hillary	Associated Press
Collor, Fernando	Associated Press AP
Dalai Lama	Tibet Images, Brian Beresford
De Klerk, F.W.	Office of F.W. De Klerk
Delors, Jacques	Office of the President, Association Notre Europe
Deng Xiaoping	Associated Press AP
Diana, Princess of Wales	Associated Press AP
Duisenberg, Wim	De Nederlandsche Bank
Eisner, Michael	Walt Disney Company
Fahd, King	Embassy of Saudi Arabia to the UK
Farrakhan, Louis	Associated Press AP
Fujimori, Alberto	Embassy of Peru to the UK
Gandhi, Rajiv	Associated Press AP
Gates, Bill	Associated Press AP
Gingrich, Newt	Associated Press AP
González, Felipe	Partido Socialista Obrero Español (PSOE)
Gorbachev, Mikhail	Associated Press AP
Greenspan, Alan	Board of Governors of the Federal Reserve System

Havel, Vaclav	Office of the President, Czech Republic, and the Embassy of the Czech Republic to the UK
Hawke, Bob	Associated Press AP
Hawking, Stephen	Associated Press AP
Hussein, Saddam	Associated Press POOL INA
Iacocca, Lee	Associated Press AP
Jiang Zemin	Associated Press XINHUA
John Paul II, Pope	Apostolic Nunciature of the Vatican City to the UK
Jordan, Michael	Associated Press AP
Kabila, Laurent	Associated Press AP
Kadhafi, Moamer al-	Libyan Interests Section, Embassy of Saudi Arabia to the UK
Karadzic, Radovan	Associated Press AP
Keating, Paul	Associated Press AP
Khamenei, Ayatollah	Embassy of Iran to the UK
Kim Dae Jung	The Korea Foundation, Seoul
Kim Il Sung	Associated Press
Kohl, Helmut	Inter Nationes Bonn Press and the Embassy of Germany to the UK
Kumaratunga, Chandrika	High Commission of Sri Lanka to the UK
Lafontaine, Oskar	Embassy of the Federal Republic of Germany to the UK
Le Pen, Jean-Marie	Office of the President, Front National
Lebed, Aleksander	Associated Press
Li Peng	Associated Press XINHUA
Madonna	Associated Press EFE
Mahathir Mohamed	Ministry of Foreign Affairs, Malaysia
Mandela, Nelson	High Commission of South Africa to the UK
Mandela, Winnie	Associated Press POOL
Menem, Carlos	Office of the President, Argentina
Milosevic, Slobodan	Associated Press AP
Mitterrand, François	Associated Press AP
Mobutu Sese Seko	Associated Press AFP
Mubarak, Hosni	Embassy of Egypt to the UK
Murdoch, Rupert	Associated Press AP
Netanyahu, Benjamin	Embassy of Israel to the UK
Papandreou, Andreas	Associated Press AP
Peres, Shimon	Associated Press AP
Pérez de Cuéllar, Javier	Associated Press AP
Pinochet, Augusto	Associated Press AP
Pol Pot	Associated Press BANGKOK POST
Powell, Colin	Associated Press AP
Prodi, Romano	Embassy of Italy to the UK
Rabin, Yitzhak	Associated Press
Rafsanjani, Ali Akbar	Islamic Republican Party
Rawlings, Jerry	Embassy of Ghana
Robinson, Mary	Office of the UN High Commissioner for Human Rights and the Embassy of the Republic of Ireland to the UK
Rogers, Richard	Richard Rogers Partnership
Rushdie, Salman	Associated Press AP

Santer, Jacques	EU Commission
Schröder, Gerhard	Embassy of the Federal Republic of Germany to the UK
Shevardnadze, Eduard	Embassy of Georgia to the UK
Sihanouk, King	Office of H.R.H. King Sihanouk, Cambodia, and the Embassy of Cambodia to the USA
Simpson, O.J.	Associated Press AGENCE FRANCE PRESSE POOL
Soros, George	Associated Press AP
Spielberg, Steven	Associated Press LONG PHOTOGRAPHY
Suharto	Office of the President, Indonesia
Tarantino, Quentin	Associated Press AP
Teresa, Mother	Associated Press AP
Thatcher, Margaret	Office of the Rt. Hon. the Baroness Thatcher, House of Lords
Tietmeyer, Hans	Press and Public Relations Office, Deutsche Bundesbank
Trimble, David	Associated Press AP
Trump, Donald	Associated Press AP
Turner, Ted	Associated Press AP
Tutu, Desmond	Office of the Chairperson, Truth and Reconciliation Commission
Vajpayee, Atal Bihari	High Commission of India to the UK
Versace, Gianni	Associated Press AP
Waite, Terry	Terry Waite
Walesa, Lech	Associated Press AP
Wiles, Andrew	Associated Press AP
Winfrey, Oprah	Associated Press AP
Wolfensohn, James	Associated Press AP
Yeltsin, Boris	Associated Press ITAR TASS